Penguin Books
The Broken Years

Bill Gammage is a lecturer in Australian history at
Adelaide University. He grew up at Wagga Wagga,
New South Wales, and graduated from the Australian
National University, where he did most of the work for
this book. In 1970 he visited most of the First World
War battlefields where Australians fought.

BILL GAMMAGE

THE
BROKEN
YEARS

AUSTRALIAN SOLDIERS
IN THE GREAT WAR

Penguin Books

Penguin Books Australia Ltd,
487 Maroondah Highway, P.O. Box 257
Ringwood, Victoria, Australia
Penguin Books Ltd,
Harmondsworth, Middlesex, England
Penguin Books,
625 Madison Avenue, New York, N.Y. 10022, U.S.A.
Penguin Books Canada Ltd,
2801 John Street, Markham, Ontario, Canada,
Penguin Books (N.Z.) Ltd,
182–190 Wairau Road, Auckland 10, New Zealand

First published by the Australian National
University Press, Canberra, 1974

Published in Penguin Books 1975
Reprinted 1980, 1981 (twice)

Copyright © Bill Gammage, 1974

Made and printed in Australia
at The Dominion Press, Blackburn, Victoria
Set in Linotype Times
by Wilke and Company Limited, Clayton, Victoria

Gammage, William Leonard.
The broken years.

Index
Bibliography
ISBN 0 14 003383 1

1. Australia. Army. Australian Imperial Force.
2. European War, 1914–1918—Personal narratives,
Australian. I. Title.

940.4'81'94

Contents

Illustrations and Maps

Maps drawn in the Cartographic Office, Department of Human Geography, Australian National University.

All photographs are from the collection in the Australian War Memorial, and permission to reproduce them is gratefully acknowledged.

The front cover photograph is of Edwin McKenzie Gardiner, reproduced by permission of his family.

Abbreviations

Abbreviations used but not listed here are in the *Concise Oxford Dictionary*.

(a) Unit

AAMC	Australian Army Medical Corps
AIF	Australian Imperial Force
Amb	Ambulance
Anz	Anzac
Anzac	Australian and New Zealand Army Corps
Arty	Artillery
Bde	Brigade
Bn	Battalion
Bty	Battery
Coy	Company
Div	Division
Eng	Engineers
FAB	Field Artillery Brigade
Fld	Field
ICC	Imperial Camel Corps
LH	Light Horse
LR Op	Light Railway Operating
LTM	Light Trench Mortar
MG	Machine Gun
Mtd	Mounted
Regt	Regiment
Sig	Signal, Signalling
Squad	Squadron
Trp	Troop
Tunn	Tunnelling

(b) Rank

Dvr	Driver
Gnr	Gunner
RQMS	Regimental Quartermaster Sergeant

2/Lt	Second Lieutenant
Sgr	Signaller
Spr	Sapper
S/Sgt	Staff Sergeant
Tpr	Trooper

(c) Cause of termination of service

When only the year of birth is given (e.g. b. 1885), the soldier concerned returned to Australia or was discharged in England after the Armistice.

D	Died
DOD	Died of Disease
DOI	Died of Injury
DOW	Died of Wounds
KIA	Killed in Action
RTA	Repatriated to Australia

(d) Repositories

| AWM | Australian War Memorial |
| NLA | National Library of Australia |

(e) Other abbreviations

A.W.L.	Absent without leave
D	Diary
L	Letter
re-enl	re-enlisted
RSL	Returned Services League
S.I.W.	Self inflicted wound

Note to the Penguin Edition

Since the Australian National University Press edition of this book was published in 1974, several old soldiers or their relatives have sent me photos or letters or reminiscences of the Great War, or offered corrections or additional details to parts of my book. I thank them, and I hope any Penguin edition reader who might add to this story will similarly contact me. Also, I am sure the Australian War Memorial in Canberra would welcome donations of records from any of Australia's wars. These would be made accessible to the public according to the wishes of the donor.

Bill Gammage

Acknowledgments

I have more and greater debts than I can acknowledge. Two hundred and seventy-two Great War veterans wrote to help me with this book; many wrote often and at length, many sent wartime diaries and letters, or books, articles, and magazines, and several cheerfully tolerated my frequent conversation and interrogation. All consigned an eventful past to a doubtful future; I thank them, and I thank particularly Mr W. F. Anderson; Colonel E. Campbell, DSO; Mr H. W. Cavill; Mr P. Constantine; Mr F. H. Cox; Mr A. W. Edwards, MM; Mr J. Gooder; Mr T. Gordon; Mr W. A. Graham; Mr R. F. Hall; Mr S. V. Hicks; Mr H. V. Howe; Mr D. Jackson, MM; Senator E. W. Mattner, MC, DCM, MM; Mr J. H. Sturgiss; Mr W. E. Williams; and Mr A. G. Wordley. At least half these old soldiers have died since I completed my research, and I much regret their passing.

For three years I held an Australian National University scholarship to write the thesis on which this book is based, and then and since many people helped me. Mrs Rona Fraser, Peter Lowe, Sir Frank Meere, Brendan Moore, Phil Moors, and Scott Roberts lent me Great War diaries or letters; and my wife Jan, Mrs Paddy Maughan, Mrs Ann Newsome, Pat Romans and Mrs Bea Willcock typed a difficult and disordered manuscript. Don Baker, Arthur Bazley, Eric Fry, Bruce Kent, Ken Inglis, John Ritchie, and Barry Smith worked great changes upon a draft with which they persisted throughout its length, and Alec Hill and Barbara Penny applied special knowledge to particular chapters. In various ways others assisted, among them John Bell, Ross Cooper, Arch Cruttenden, my brother Chris, my grandfather Mr W. J. Gammage, Iain Gosnay, Ken Inglis, members of the staff of the Central Army Records Office in Melbourne and of several libraries, especially the Mitchell Library in Sydney, Graham Morey, Hank Nelson, my friends at the

ANU Press, John Ritchie, Peter Temple-Smith, and the Visual Aids Department at the Australian National University.

I owe several particular debts. Arthur Bazley was a good friend and knowledgeable guide throughout: he joined Dr Bean's staff in 1914, was at the landing, and thereafter worked with Bean until the Australian official history of the war was written. He edited or co-edited the two best RSL journals, *Reveille* (NSW) between 1930 and 1940, and *Stand-To* (ACT) from 1940 until 1968. In my time his knowledge of the Great War was unrivalled—indeed I have met no one with such detailed command of any subject as he had of the First AIF. He died on 31 July 1972, a loss irreplaceable to historians of Australia, and to any who benefited from his patience and generosity.

The Director and staff at the Australian War Memorial and especially the Library staff under Bruce Harding and Miss Vera Blackburn for five years accepted my presence among them, giving me free access to all the records, and helping my work with a thousand kindnesses. In 1970 the Memorial's Board of Trustees gave me an invaluable grant to assist research overseas. My thesis supervisor, Bruce Kent, had often to use his considerable patience and ability to encourage me along a sometimes difficult path while at the same time restraining my ill considered excursions from it. Alitalia airlines, through their Sydney office, very generously enabled me to visit almost all the battlefields which concerned the First AIF, and to consult libraries and individuals in both Europe and the Middle East.

My wife Jan worked at least as hard as I did on the manuscript, typing and retyping, and her work was less rewarding, her patience greater, her cheerfulness and encouragement a constant comfort. I owe much to her, and to the friendship and assistance of everyone mentioned, and I hope none will consider their efforts too poorly rewarded by the quality of the work they have improved.

My last debt is to a man I never met, to Dr C. E. W. Bean, the able and gentle scholar who officially described Australia's part in the Great War. That work is a milestone in the writing of military history, and among the greatest contributions yet made to the history of Australia. Dr Bean overlooked nothing mentioned here, and his was the more compassionate writing, for clearly it pained him to write ill of any man. If occasionally this tended to be a fault in the historian, it was consistently a virtue in the man: he never lost his love or respect for humanity, and he kept faith in its progress despite all the dark circumstances which confronted his time. To him, and to Arthur Bazley, and to the thousands of great hearted men who were their comrades during the war, I dedicate these pages.

Sources and Conventions

This is *not* a military history of the First AIF. It is a study based on the diaries and letters of roughly 1000 Australians who fought as front line AIF soldiers in the Great War, and it attempts to show with what assumptions and expectations they volunteered to fight, in what ways their outlook was amended by their war service, and what new attitudes they evolved and brought back to their country after the war. Perhaps also, what happened to these soldiers throws light on how Australians passed from the nineteenth to the twentieth century, on how the days of Empire gave way to the tradition of Anzac, and on how men came to be as they are in Australia.

The soldiers described wrote for varying purposes. Some were writing home, others deliberately recording the climax of their lives. Some hardly mentioned the war, others rarely ignored it. Some minimised their discomforts, a few exaggerated them. Many, when it came to the point, described just what they saw and felt, because the tumult of the hour denied them an alternative, because they wanted an exact account for themselves if they lived or for their relatives if they died, or sometimes because they realised that the thoughts they wrote down might be their last on earth.

None was obliged to be accurate, and these pages report statements no doubt genuinely believed when written, but not true, and hearsay evidence and tall stories cloaked as truth by soldiers. I hope I have identified most such statements, and also omitted errors apparently peculiar to individuals. But since this book attempts to show what some Australian soldiers thought and felt during the war, it must include instances in which they erred. For the same reason my comments often describe what soldiers thought rather than what I think: for example, I use words like 'patriot', 'Hun', and 'native' with their contemporary colourings, not with my own. Readers should not assume the literal accuracy of statements made or quoted here, nor believe that these necessarily represent my own opinion.

The possibility of bias in the sources must spring readily to mind. Most of the manuscripts were collected following various appeals by libraries or individuals to the public, or by requests the Australian War Memorial made in the 1920s and 1930s to specific veterans or their relatives. Unless some sections of the community responded more willingly to these requests than others (which may be), there was no bias in the collection of the sources; but I have appended statistics about their writers which attempt to indicate grounds for possible bias in what they recorded, and the figures show some apparent discrepancies (see Appendix I). I cannot be precise about what imbalance, if any, these discrepancies may have introduced, but possibly they may have led me to exaggerate 'positive' factors in the early chapters: for example, the importance of Empire or nationalist sentiment, rather than the desire to be 'in it' or to act in concert with mates, as causes for enlistment. In the sources used to describe the fighting and its consequences, differences in attitude seem to cut across civilian backgrounds, so that no unevenness is apparent there; but there were some Australians who wrote little about the war, and it may be that they differed from their more expressive comrades in their reactions to the struggle. If so, their testimony would qualify this record, whereas of necessity they have only passingly influenced it. Since censors concerned themselves mostly with place names and troop movements, I believe no other significant bias exists in the records.

But, as though to mock the attachments of gentler times, there are three particular omissions: religion, politics, and sex, and of these perhaps the most surprising is religion. These pages instance men who enlisted to defend their God, who remained devout Christians through every travail, and who, if they became fatalists, became so by trusting God entirely. Yet the average Australian soldier was not religious. He was not a keen churchman: he avoided church parades, or if he could not avoid them he tended to show sudden enthusiasm for whichever denomination worshipped within easiest marching distance. He distrusted chaplains, and sometimes detested them, because he was an Australian, and because they were officers, enjoying the privileges of leaders but not the concomitant risks and responsibilities of battle. Of course there were exceptional chaplains, men who ignored minor blasphemies to confront major evils, who showed themselves brave under fire, and who ranked the needs and welfare of soldiers above the patriot religion of the wartime pulpit. These men taught by practice and example, and were among the most respected in the AIF. But, though it was not their intent, they tended to demonstrate that the rewards of virtue were on earth rather than in Heaven, and to be admired as men rather than as chaplains. Probably they advanced the piety of their flock only incidentally.

Most Australians found little in war to prompt consideration of a higher divinity. Some turned to God in moments of stress, but the majority kept their minds squarely upon the world around them, displaying a practical concern for the exigencies of battle, and a preoccupation with questions of food and rest, dead mates, leave, and the next fight. Not often during that blind struggle did they consider the Almighty Being who supposedly directed their existence.

Politics interested them even less. Some debated conscription, and a few reviled strikers in Australia, but these were issues of war, not politics. 'Discussion on Politics Is Not In the Fashion Here', a soldier in France told his brother, a Sydney MLA, 'we Have a lot more Serious Subjects to Juggle with Its mostly old Fritz & so on.'[1] Faction and preference, socialism and capitalism, were civilian luxuries, far too remote to move men embroiled in the deadly business of war.

Although one or two soldiers discussed their love affairs, most never wrote about sex, so that consideration of the subject is not possible here. To judge from venereal disease statistics, some applied taboos about sex to words but not to actions, and I am told that many men took advantage of whatever 'horizontal refreshment' chanced to offer. Yet apparently sex did not loom large among them. In talk they discussed and joked about it, but less frequently than about the incidents of war. In practice the manner of their lives rarely made sex possible, and when it did, probably, most honoured the honourable, and availed themselves of the available.

In these and all other respects I make no claims about the uniqueness of the Australians I describe, or of any Australian soldier: I believe that much of what is written here might apply to New Zealanders or Canadians, and that some of it would be true of

1. Sgr G. H. Molesworth, 35 Bn, Fruiterer, of Hurlstone Park, NSW. b. 1885. L 7/3/18.

soldiers in every army. Yet, because such comparisons fell neither within the scope of my research nor within the subject of this book, even when they seemed temptingly obvious I have refrained from them.

There are several simplifying conventions, used chiefly in footnotes.

The fullest information about any soldier is contained in a footnote on the page which first refers to him, and this page is the first listed after the soldier's name in the name index. Subsequent footnotes acknowledging the same soldier cite his surname or his surname plus initials where necessary, so that reference back to the original footnote can be made via the name index.

Ranks, decorations, and units are those with which a writer terminated his AIF service from any cause: where a footnote gives a year of birth in place of a cause for termination of service, the writer returned safely to Australia after the war or on '1914 leave' in October 1918.

The text is liberally interspersed with imprecise indications of number—'most', 'many', 'some', 'a few', etc. Though it is unlikely that I have always succeeded, I have attempted to give these indications some validity, and in doing so have been guided by the weight of internal evidence, by Dr Bean's work, by discussion with returned men, and by what seemed to me probable. Because none of these produces certain results, and particularly because each assumes that what soldiers said or wrote is what they thought, readers should take these words to indicate rough approximations only.

To avoid frequent interruptions to the narrative, I have not used *sic* to indicate punctuation or spelling errors in quotations, and I hope all errors shown occur in the original.

Finally, this book is based on a thesis now in both the Menzies Library at the Australian National University, and the Australian War Memorial Library, in Canberra. Economy and readability required that much of the evidence included in the thesis should be omitted here, and readers wanting such evidence, or doubting the grounds for what might here appear as mere assertion, are asked to consult the original.

Author's Note

There never was a greater tragedy than World War I. It engulfed an age, and conditioned the times that followed. It contaminated every ideal for which it was waged, it threw up waste and horror worse than all the evils it sought to avert, and it left legacies of staunchness and savagery equal to any which have bewildered men about their purpose on earth.

Among those who fought in the war were 330,000 Australians. They were men who enlisted into the Australian Imperial Force, civilians who sailed to defend King and country, or for the novelty of it. Overseas a maelstrom caught them, and in four years swept most of their assumptions away. Although their spirits were rarely broken, they amended their outlooks to absorb the unexpected challenges they met, and returned to Australia bearing the remnants of old ways, but also the seeds of a new world and a new century.

One thousand of these soldiers left the documents which inspired what follows, and generally the book considers only them. Yet wider speculations readily assert themselves, and not merely about the AIF at large, or about kindred soldiers from New Zealand or Canada or Scotland, or about men at war. It may not be possible to discern the nature of man, because each guesses at that from his own standpoint, and in describing others makes a puppet of himself, and dances to his own invention. Yet if these men do not answer great questions, they might be seen to raise them, for they too had to ask whether their actions benefited mankind or corrupted it, and whether mankind itself is great or depraved, and whether men serve events or master them.

I commend their original records to the reader. They possess a tragic nobility beyond the ability of the following extracts to convey, and the spirit of an age moves through their pages more perfectly than through mine.

Adieu, the years are a broken song,
And the right grows weak in the strife with wrong,
The lilies of love have a crimson stain,
And the old days never will come again.

From the diary of an Australian soldier, September 1917

Prologue: Australia before 1914

> Australia has so far achieved nothing great from the national standpoint. It cannot be said to have failed, because it has not yet been called upon . . . The Australian must be prepared, in the event of great emergency, to die for something or for somebody.
>
> A. Buchanan, *The Real Australia*, 1907, pp. 20–2

Before 1914 most Australians wanted a paradise for the majority in Australia. Being relatively secure economically and reasonably untrammelled politically, their chief aim was to improve social conditions: to rid their society of old world evils, and to make it more egalitarian, and more democratic. They hoped to convert to this aim those who obstructed it, the boss, the wowser, the new chum, and the blackleg, and they expected in the end to create a new world, in which all should be happy and none should starve.

Yet they did not want a brotherhood of man in Australia—they refused to embrace those who were not of their race. 'Race' was a term Australians used variously: they spoke of an 'Australian' race to distinguish themselves from Englishmen, or of a 'British' or 'Anglo-Saxon' race to differ from Boers or Germans or Frenchmen, but essentially, when they referred to race, they meant a union of colour, and their most determined attachment was to a white Australia.

It was, they knew, a white Australia in an Asiatic world, and they feared for its safety. They imagined millions of yellow men, teeming from the north and overrunning the continent they held so sparsely. They watched with particular unease the rising power of Japan, her army victorious over Russia in 1904–5, her navy and ambitions apparently daily increasing. Their inability to counter this yellow peril thoroughly alarmed them, and for protection they looked to the great British Empire from which their race had sprung.

The chief instrument of Imperial power was the Royal Navy. The

1

fleet underwrote Australia's security: it was a wall stemming the yellow tide. But it also defended another island twelve thousand miles away, and after 1900 Australians became increasingly concerned about how the fleet was being used. In 1902 Britain allied herself with Japan, and by 1907 she had withdrawn most of her Pacific ships to European waters, in effect transferring her naval responsibilities in the Pacific to her new partner.

A policy so trusting of Asiatic integrity dismayed Australians, and also placed them in a dilemma. They would never yield up their white Australia, yet alone they could not defend it. The Empire had power to shield them, but neither British protection nor British commitment to a white Australia seemed certain. Nothing secured them entirely.

In this predicament most Australians compromised, by adjusting their aspirations to Imperial imperatives. Specifically they supported the development of Australian naval and military forces within the Imperial framework, and by 1914 their country possessed the most powerful of the 'colonial' navies, and had embarked upon an extensive programme of universal military service. More generally they sought to express Australia's individuality while elevating her Imperial status, and by 1914 they wished for neither dependence nor independence, but for tangible partnership in a great association of race and civilisation and affection.

These ambiguous emotions engulfed young boys growing up in Australia before 1914. Upon them would devolve the defence of their race and country, and they were taught ceaselessly how they must react when the inevitable call came. The most popular Australian writer of the day, W. H. Fitchett, wrote books such as *Deeds that Won the Empire* (1897) and *The New World of the South* (1913), deliberately to teach young Australians the virtues of patriotism and the glories of race and Empire. In New South Wales state and Catholic schools every educational influence—policy, the syllabus, text books, the school magazine, school ceremonies, and recreation—was designed to awaken in children a patriotic affection for both nation and Empire. A martial spirit was encouraged and channelled practically: from 1908 boys in New South Wales could go twice a year to camps conducted by the Education Department, and run on military lines, with Reveille at 5 a.m., parades to honour King and flag, and the Last Post at 8.30 p.m. Schools in other States nurtured similar emotions; and in 1909 and 1910 Defence

Acts rendered liable for compulsory service all British males aged between twelve and twenty-six years, and of six months residence in Australia.

Some Australians were unhappy with all this. Between 1 January 1912 and 30 June 1914, 28,000 boys or their parents were prosecuted for avoiding the call-up, and on the fringes of cultural instruction—in the far bush or among the city larrikins—there were boys unmoved by any martial or Imperial enthusiasm. But they were a minority. By 1914 most young Australians had thoroughly learnt an adherence to war, race, and glory, and to two nations separated by the world. They vaunted their sunlit land, and drew snowmen on Christmas cards. They proclaimed their achievements in sport, and feared whether the British race degenerated in the antipodes. They heralded a new society, and venerated the English King. They were 'independent Australian Britons', defenders of the white race in the Pacific, volunteers to die in the defence of the ideals they had chosen.

Their eagerness anticipated an Imperial defence of Australia, but when the expected day came, on 4 August 1914, they were called to defend England. What had begun chiefly as a concern for their own security was to take them to the uttermost ends of the earth, to die in tens of thousands in a war in no way of their making.

1 Australia during the War

Civilization is at stake. Free government is at stake . . .
Everything is at stake—spiritual, moral, and material—
for which we as a people stand.

W. M. Hughes, *The Day—And the Day After*, 1916, pp. 78–9

Australians hailed England's declaration of war on Germany with the most complete and enthusiastic harmony in their history. 'It is our baptism of fire', exulted the *Sydney Morning Herald* on 6 August, 'Australia knows something of the flames of war, but its realities have never been brought so close as they will be in the near future.' Crowds gathered to celebrate, laughing, cheering, and singing, surging with strength and joy and confidence. At Labor Party headquarters, at Melbourne University, and on a Queensland cattle station men sang 'Rule Britannia' and the National Anthem after work. Children sold pets, school prizes, and the treasures of a lifetime to help patriotic causes. Strangers embraced as brothers, cheers were given on the slightest pretext, flags waved frantically, tumult and merriment ruled everywhere. The land was full of visions of glory, and the historic importance of the occasion.

Through the commotion ran the affections of nation and Empire. Australia had not resolved her status within the Empire, because she had never weightily contributed to Empire defence. Now she could realise her hopes for partnership, and blend her history into England's magnificent traditions. Every particle of antipodean emotion ranged beside Australia's oldest friend, and endlessly and untiringly repeated the phrases of loyalty: 'if Britain goes to her Armageddon so do we', 'who lives if England dies', and 'the last man and the last shilling'.

England's trial was cause enough, but, the Empire's destinies being indivisible, Australians feared also for their own safety. 'The

4

moment the British fleet is defeated . . .', wrote the Wagga *Daily Advertiser* on 4 August, 'Australia will have to fight for her position in the world', and in its first war issue the Melbourne *Punch* stated, 'The British fleet is our all in all. Its destruction means Australia's destruction, the ruin of our trade and institutions, and the surrender of our liberties. The British Empire is our family circle, and we cannot live outside it.'

Very quickly these emotions launched themselves into a violent crusade against Germany and the Germans. Initially this more or less confined itself to the Kaiser, but after real and concocted reports of German atrocities reached Australia all Germans began to be considered evil and barbarous, bent upon hounding liberty and humanity to extinction. 'The german is a "COW"', a contributor to the Sydney *Bulletin*'s Red Page declared, 'A dirty "COW". A dirty - - - - "COW". The dirtiest of all - - - - "COWS"', and the *Daily Advertiser* clamoured, 'when you are fighting a mad dog you cannot afford to consider the humanity, or the christianity, of the matter. The vital thing is to kill him lest he kill you.'[1] By early 1915 Australians had charged every conceivable bestiality against the Central Powers, and as the war progressed they sought the destruction of their enemies with ever deepening hate and conviction.

By October 1914 most German nationals in Australia were interned, and most citizens of German origin or extraction were subject to social, economic and legal bars. Some patriotic Australians demanded more:

No doubt many . . . [aliens] pass in society as loyal British subjects when all the time they are hating the flag which shelters them, and are animated by a secret desire to see the British nation crushed under the brutal heel of the dictators in Prussia . . . To permit this kind of folly to go on is to continue the very conditions which in recent years have enabled the German nation to acquire immense sums of money from Australia and England while at the same time treacherously preparing . . . to bring about the overthrow of the Empire . . . There is a limit to even the patience and tolerance of the easy going Australian: and if sympathisers with the Prussians overlook this fact and persist in looking for trouble they may find it in rather full measure before this war is done with.[2]

1. *Bulletin*, 8 April 1915; *Daily Advertiser*, 5 May 1915.
2. *Daily Advertiser*, 23 October 1914.

Australian Germans were beaten up, spat on, dismissed from jobs, expelled from clubs and associations, abused for attendance at church, and refused service at stores and theatres. Their homes were stoned, their property destroyed, their children forced to leave school. The law, the courts, the trade unions, and the universities discriminated against them, and they had to drink the loyal toast or sing the anthem or salute the flag at the beck of any malevolent patriot. They changed their names, left districts which had sheltered them for years, attempted by generous donations to purchase acceptance. Every action provoked greater mistrust, and harder penalties. Worse was to come for citizens of German blood in Australia.

Race, nation and Empire swayed those most directly affected by the news of war. Although men could offer their names earlier, recruiting for the Australian 'Expeditionary Force' did not commence until 11 August. In Sydney on that day an orderless mass jostled and fought before the recruiting tables, and by nightfall enlisting officers had selected 3600 of them. Men of thirteen and seventy-one tried to enlist, and for weeks volunteers rushed the recruiting centres in seemingly limitless numbers. One wrote,

Left home early in the morning and went to Victoria Barracks had to wait outside the gates with about 1,000 or more other recruits for about an hour. When the gates opened there was a big rush of men to get in. We were then drafted into two batches one body composed of those who had done soldiering before and those that had not[3]

and most of those that had not were rejected. By 20 August over 10,000 men had enlisted in Sydney.

After a week the back country men began to come in. They had to enlist in a capital city, and some made great sacrifices to do so. At least one walked off his farm, and others abandoned jobs and homes or sold their properties on the chance of being accepted into the army. An heir to the titles of the victor of Trafalgar deserted Australia's Permanent Forces to join the AIF, and his brother left an outback station to heed his famous ancestor's behest to do his duty.[4] A Queensland drover set off to ride 350 miles to Brisbane,

3. Pte C. Lee, 1 Bn, Horse driver, of Newtown, NSW. KIA 5/6/15, aged 22. D 17/8/14.
4. Pte A. H. Nelson, 13 Bn, Station overseer, of Rosehill, NSW (b. England). b. 1890. Pte C. S. Nelson (served as J. Cooke), 20 Bn, Labourer [sic!], of Rosehill ?, NSW (b. England). Discharged in England 20/10/16, aged 20. A third brother served with the expeditionary force in New Guinea.

but when the hot summer wearied his horse he pressed on, walking to the city in less than a month, on a small ration of flour and water, with waterholes up to thirty miles apart along the drought-stricken track. Another rode 460 miles to a railhead in central Australia and thence went by rail to Adelaide; rejected there, he sailed to Hobart, was rejected, and finally enlisted in Sydney. Two thousand mile rides to the recruiting barracks were known, and 150 and 200 mile walks were frequent. Bushmen and clerks, clergymen and swagmen, fathers and sons, work mates and team mates, teachers and pupils presented themselves together. By the close of 1914, 52,561 men (from roughly 820,000 eligible by age) had enlisted. It was to be a great war.

Many volunteers were disappointed. The army wanted men 5 ft 6 inches and over, at least 34 inches about the chest, and between nineteen and thirty-eight years, but so many volunteered that these minimums or any defect—lack of military experience, unfilled teeth, flat feet, corns or bunions—often meant rejection. Doctors set deliberately artificial standards, so high that even in 1918 the survivors of the '1914 men' stood out clearly from other soldiers. One man with flat feet walked to Sydney from Bourke (about 500 miles) to enlist, but was rejected several times, until finally he despaired and walked back to Bourke. Another was told that his eyesight was defective and was twice turned away before a £2 tip facilitated his passage into the AIF. Rejected men stumbled in tears from the tables, unable to answer sons or mates left to the fortunes of war. They formed an Association, and wore a large badge to cover their civilian shame. Those who sailed against Turkey were the fittest, strongest, and most ardent in the land.

Most of that early avalanche of volunteers was roused by a sense of adventure. Great wars were rare, and short, and many eagerly seized a fleeting opportunity. They were the first Australians enabled to unsling the drums of the Empire's glory, they would engage in the splendour of the charge, and in some glorious moment of cut and thrust balance the chance to kill with the risk of death. And they would do this overseas, on horizons hitherto only the wisps of boyhood dreams. '[T]hose idealistic views of youth', recalled a soldier in 1919,

were built chiefly upon the spirit of chivalry and romance that permeated my history books and such poems as Macaulay's

'Lays of Ancient Rome' and his ballad of 'How well Horatio kept the bridge in the brave days of old.' War presented itself chiefly under the mantle of brilliant uniforms, marching soldiers, music, drums and glory[5]

and before war began an eighteen year old Englishman in Melbourne informed his parents,

if we go to war and they call for men here I will make one quick and lively. I think I know what it is to rough it now and if it is my lot well here goes I am iching to get a dig at a few Germans . . . we have all got the war fever . . . I am too excited to give my mind to writing tonight I shall have to be off to get another Herald to see how things go[6]

Some volunteers felt obliged to enlist. They had learnt before the war that readiness to die for one's country equated with sexual maturity, and now their manhood took up the gauntlet. '[I]f I had stayed at home,' a Victorian mint official wrote, 'I would never have been able to hold my head up & look any decent girl in the face',[7] and an Irishman told his parents,

I have [enlisted] . . . and I don't regret it in the very least. I believe it is every young fellow's duty. There are far better men than any of us have already gone . . . besides every paper one lifts it has something to say about young fellows being so slow in coming forward . . . we are the sort of men who should go.[8]

Other volunteers explained similar impulses in more general terms: they offered to do 'their bit', or 'their duty', or to 'answer the call'.

Those who first offered themselves expressed their feelings of duty or adventure in the language of contemporary patriotism. A powerful inducement to enlist in the early days was love of Empire. Many volunteers had been born in the British Isles, but for numbers

---

5. Lt A .W. Edwards, MM, 1 Bn, Public servant, of Balgownie, NSW b. 1890. *Narrative*, p. 2.
6. Cpl R. E. Antill, 14 Bn, Cabinet maker, of Windsor, Vic (b. England). KIA 5/7/17, aged 21. *L* 3/8/14. Generally, a soldier's age has been calculated from that given on enlistment. No doubt some very young and some very old men were concerned more with enlistment requirements than with accuracy—there were fifteen year olds on Gallipoli, for example.
7. Bty SM N. G. Ellsworth, 102 Howitzer Bty, Mint official, of South Yarra, Vic. DOW 31/7/17, aged 31. *L* 16/3/15.
8. Pte A. J. McSparrow, 18 Bn, Railway employee, of Parramatta, NSW (b. Ireland). DOW 5/8/16, aged 26. *L* 18/3/15.

of Australians the Empire's 'need' was by itself sufficient cause to fight. 'Surely everyone must realize that the Empire is going thro a Crisis it has never gone thro' before,' the mint official exclaimed, 'and that every one is expected to do his duty *now*.'[9]

Fears for Australia propped the banners of England. 'I have enrolled as a volunteer . . .', a young Australian reported,

one [son] can be spared for the defence of Australia and Australia's fate is going to be decided on the continent and not out here . . . being suited in physique and occupation and being prompted by a sense of duty and spirit of adventure I can hardly do anything else but volunteer.[10]

Other men enlisted from hatred of Germany. A South Australian declared that he was

very keen to get to grips with those inhuman brutes . . . to do something to help wipe out such an infamous nation. The Parson this morning preached on this text—'What shall a man give in exchange for his soul?' But he altered 'man' to 'nation'. I am sure that God will take a strong hand in the war and thoroughly punish Germany[11]

As the war progressed and the trials of the Allies multiplied, hatred of the Hun attracted an increasing proportion of recruits to the colours. Many of these were men who from conviction or circumstance had not rushed to the fray, but came into it thoughtfully and determinedly. One wrote,

the outlook of the War is getting worse . . . it is just 12 weeks, 12 long weeks of awful bloodshed, property smashing, killing and crippling of men to, today and may it all soon be over, but I am afraid its not to be and we people of the British Empire will all feel the strain of it . . . before that so called civilized and cultured nation of Germany is crushed underfoot.[12]

He enlisted the following month. Another, more bloodthirsty, recalled,

9. Ellsworth, *L* 16/3/15.
10. L/Cpl F. C. Mulvey, 2 LH Regt, Hydrographic surveyor, of Newcastle, NSW. KIA 14/5/15, aged 21. *L* 23/8/14.
11. Lt E. H. Chinner, 32 Bn, Bank clerk, of Peterborough, SA. D while POW 20/7/16, aged 22. *L* –/5/15.
12. Gnr R. W. Betts, 102 Howitzer Bty, Orchardist, of Mildura, Vic (b. England). DOW 20/4/17, aged 30. *L* 10/11/14.

I thought that [the war] . . . was too colossal to last long and that Christmas 1914 would see it all over. But . . . I then realised that it was going to be a long struggle, and that it was time I got a wriggle on . . . [By January] I felt very fit for a big fat greasy German[13]

There were in addition a thousand particular and personal reasons for enlistment. Loneliness, family trouble, public opinion, and unemployment each contributed a measure. The 1914 drought, for example, reduced the wheat crop by two-thirds, and created widespread unemployment. The army paid well, and a young Englishman told his parents,

I tell you what I have joined the Australian army . . . its not bad money here 5/- a day and clothes and food thats nearly as good as good Cabinet Making and not half as hard. You may thint it funny mee turning up such a good job but it was like this Philpott had only about 3 days work left for us and things are so bad out here for there is a drought on we haven't had any rain for months so I thorrt I would join the army

and two days before he landed at the Dardanelles he repeated,

things were so bad in Melbourne . . . and they are a jolly site worse now for I saw a Melbourne paper a few days ago . . . so wear would I have been, not too well off, eh . . . every day that passes 4/- goes down to me and this war is bound to last a good while yet, so I will have a few £ for you, if this war lasts 12 months they will owe me £60 but I think it will last a little longer than that don't you, but of corse if I am killed you will get what is due to me just the same, as it goes to the next of kin.[14]

He professed no sense of right, no statement of belief: he was a 'six bob a day tourist', and even in that age of conviction he was not alone. Other men came forward because they had had peacetime military experience, or because they were in the public eye and

13. 2/Lt A. C. Youdale, MC & 2 bars, 7 LH Regt, Commercial traveller, of Ashfield, NSW. KIA 23/12/17, aged 28. D 8/1/15.
14. Antill, L 17/11/14 and 23/4/15. An AIF private was paid 5 shillings a day on enlistment; and 6 shillings a day on embarkation, of which 1 shilling was deferred until his termination of service, and an amount he nominated, usually 2 or 3 shillings, paid to his next of kin. A private in the British Army received 1 shilling a day at this time.

were expected to volunteer. A forty-nine year old militia officer
told his wife,

*I don't think they will take married officers of my age, but after
thinking for hours over it I feel I must offer my services. I know
that you would not have it said . . . that although I talked a lot
about loyalty and defence of the Empire &c, that I didn't offer
to go myself. I am worried to death about it. I would do almost
anything in the World to avoid leaving you . . . , but I feel I
couldn't look men in the face again . . . I must offer.*[15]

Another volunteer had been sacked after punching his boss; Bill
Harney volunteered from the Queensland Gulf country partly
because his horses were poor;[16] one or two men, their enthusiasm
no doubt quickened by alternative offers of a prison sentence,
accepted magistrates' suggestions to enlist. Men offered because
they had friends in Europe, or mates enlisted, or because everyone
else in the district had gone and they could not bear the abuse of
elderly women. The list was almost infinite.

Whatever their incentive, the early volunteers went readily to
fight. Even the most sober recruit was willing to accept discomfort
and death for the cause. This they had in common, and it set them
apart, for as the war progressed their like appeared less and less
before the recruiting tables.

On 29 April 1915 the Prime Minister, Andrew Fisher, told the
nation that Australian troops were in action at the Dardanelles. The
news thrilled the country. 'Advance Australia!', headlined the Melbourne *Herald* that day, and Australian hearts and heads swelled
when England praised the 'magnificent achievement' of the Anzacs.
After the Englishman Ellis Ashmead-Bartlett's glowing account of
the landing was published in Australia (8 May), the *Sydney Morning
Herald* headed its editorial 'The Glory of It', and a Ballarat school-
teacher wrote[17] to a wounded Australian hero, 'Every Australian
woman's heart this week is thrilling with pride, with exultation, and
while her eyes fill with tears she springs up as I did when the story
in Saturday's *Argus* was finished and says, "Thank God, I am an

15. Maj Gen Sir G. de L. Ryrie, KCMG, CB, VD, 2 LH Bde, Grazier, of
Michelago, NSW. b. 1865. *L* 7/8/14.
16. W. Harney, 'Harney's War', p. 3. (Pte, 9 Bn, Bushman, of Charters
Towers, Qld. b. 1895.)
17. On 12 May. The full text of the letter is in E. C. Buley, *Glorious Deeds
of the Australasians in the Great War*, pp. 151-2.

Australian." Boys, you have honoured our land'. Her letter touched
the temper of the nation, and was widely publicised. For years it
had required only one great Imperial deed to consummate the
highest hopes and expectations of the Australians; now, in the
fullest and most glorious measure, it had come. By the grace of
fortune they were a nation, by the valour of their soldiers, partners
to Imperial destiny.

Flushed with their new found status, the patriots—those who
were keenest to maintain an unreserved Australian commitment to
the war—doubled their efforts for victory. A little boy enclosed a
note in a soldier's hamper: 'to the Solder who has no little boy to
pray for him. I ask God in my Prays at night to ease you pain I only
wish I was a man and by Jingoes I would give it to the Turk that
made you Suffer I am 7 years of age'.[18] Older patriots, who wished
they were men or younger or fitter, were equally ardent. On 15 May
the first appeal day organised on a State basis, for the Belgians,
collected £100,000 in New South Wales and proportional amounts
elsewhere, while on Australia Day (30 July), New South Wales gave
about £839,000 for wounded Australians, and Victoria about
£312,000. Newspaper advertisements lauded the soldier, then
quoted his testimony to support their products ('Zam Buk keeps
V.C. winner fit', 'Lux Won't shrink from Khaki', 'eighty returned
soldiers testify to . . .', 'soldiers at the Front request . . .'), and
patriots were exhorted to meet the 'demands' of men at the front by
sending watches, cold cures, liver pills, chewing gum, nerve
emulsion, and tobacco. Only British goods were acceptable for
home use, and abuse of the Kaiser accompanied advertisements for
lime juice, traditionally British, candles, because by-products helped
the war effort, starch, for a White Australia, clothes, tyres, oint-
ments, shoe polish, and many other goods. Australians responded
enthusiastically to every variety of patriotic exhortation, knitting
socks and other comforts for soldiers, collecting money for martial
causes, and organising farewells and presentations for new recruits.
Exertions of this sort consoled many unable to take a more direct
part in the war.

But the landing at Anzac, which brought this tumult to a head,
also began to work its destruction. On 2 May the first Australian
casualty list appeared in some papers, naming twenty-two wounded

18. Pte E. C. N. Devlin, 18 Bn, Clerk, of Manly, NSW. KIA 30/5/16, aged
25. *L* in his records, 1915.

of the Third Brigade, all officers, and on the following day the names of the first dead were published. The press celebrated the casualties with much pomp, a photograph and a short biography of every hero, but losses so severe shocked Australians, and as the weeks went by and the lists heaped up the dead and wounded in ever more monstrous numbers, the first flickers of doubt appeared. By 7 May, 238 casualties had been announced; by 8 May, the day of Ashmead-Bartlett's despatch, 473; by 25 June, almost 10,000. The dead came not from a Crimean charge or an embattled square of British red in Afghanistan or Zululand, but from Australian homes. Cruel realities rose up to question the certainties of the early months, and Australians never afterwards shook them away.

Time had already begun to slacken the flow of volunteers. 10,225 men had enlisted in January 1915, but numbers fell progressively to 6250 in April, for by then the keenest men were almost all in the ranks. News of the landing struck fresh sparks from eligibles, and 10,526 volunteers, many carrying Ashmead-Bartlett's despatch, offered themselves in May, and 12,505 in June. Some came forward because they realised for the first time that Australian soldiers would actually fight in the war, but most were moved by a sense of tragic necessity, and offered themselves to fill gaps daily created in the ranks, or to avenge killed mates, or because the war would clearly demand greater efforts, or because a real man could not now hold back:

I am going to have a try for the war . . . I think I ought to go, they want all they can get and . . . I think it is the greatest opportunity for a chap to make a man of himself, those that come back from this war will be men of the right sort that anybody would be proud of[19]

When the news of the Anzac Landing came through to Sydney, and the huge A.I.F. casualty list which soon followed, my Dad at last unwillingly gave his permission for me to enlist[20]

Things are now looking so serious, and the Russians and Allies are getting so many knock backs, that after a long talk with the

19. Lt D. G. Armstrong, 21 Bn, Bank clerk, of Kyneton, Vic. KIA 9/10/17, aged 24. *L* 18/5/15.
20. Lt B. W. Champion, 1 Bn, Dental apprentice, of North Sydney, NSW. RTA 30/6/18, aged 21. *D* re 11/5/15.

manager I have decided to [enlist] . . . the time has come for every able bodied man without ties to go and help.[21]

The spirit of adventure was dying away, and the war had erected its own incentives, which gnawed at the consciences of eligible Australians.

Even so the numbers of men enlisting were inadequate, for the Australian leaders had compounded the Gallipoli losses by offering more troops to the Empire. The first serious appeals for volunteers appeared towards the end of June, when moderate advertisements in the press or on billboards asked for fit recruits and outlined the conditions of enlistment, or called war meetings to discuss recruiting, or at most urged that the war would be more arduous and the need for men more pressing than many Australians imagined. At about the same time soapbox recruiters appeared on street corners, the Minister for Defence gave support to films calculated to attract volunteers, and newspapers began to publish soldiers' letters asking for aid at the front. More ominously, an Anglican bishop declared unenlisted eligibles pro-German,[22] and by July 1915 the minimum height for recruits had been lowered to 5 ft 2 inches.

Initial results were impressive. In Victoria, where the campaign first got under way, enlistments rose from 1735 in May to 21,698 in July. The Commonwealth accepted 36,575 men in July, three times the June total. The campaign appealed to men who, until they were asked, had not thought they would be needed, and to men hitherto barred from service by the high physical requirements:

I enlisted on last Sunday week . . . but whether I shall see any fighting or not I don't know, I sincerely hope not, as I would not like to see this war go on into another winter; but in case it may, and in view of its present status, I think the time has undoubtedly arrived when everything else . . . should be laid aside until this truly awful bugbear has been gotten rid of. Up to a few weeks ago the Government here seemed to be getting as many volunteers as they could or wished to handle, and as fighting is entirely out of 'my line', I did not feel called on to offer myself. However, they now are prepared to enrol as many

---

21. L/Cpl F. J. Gibbons, 26 Bn, Store manager, of Launceston, Tas (b. England). KIA 29/7/16, aged 38. *L* 30/6/15.
22. *Sydney Morning Herald*, 6 July 1915.

as will come forward, and . . . I must not hold back any longer.[23]

The reduction of the standard has enabled me to get through . . . I was . . . [never] a great man for heroics but . . . there are some things worth more than life. I curse the systems of government . . . which permits this dreadful welter of blood and suffering to have enveloped the world . . . I go . . . believing that the only hope for the salvation of the world is a speedy victory for the Allies[24]

The echo of these July volunteers sounded throughout 1915. 'I . . . [could not] stand the criticism of all the papers and all the people unable to go',[25] explained one recruit, and another,

I hear that clear, insistent call for more and more men. Our check at Sari Bair was due to lack of reinforcements . . . thousands should go before me—men who are more physically fit and men who have made no sacrifice . . . But . . . in this struggle which will determine whether spiritual principles or a military despotism will control this world of ours, I feel . . . 'twere better to die in fighting for such a cause than to live in life long self-abasement for having failed to respond to 'the Call'. Should we be defeated life would be intolerable.[26]

Yet shortly the numbers of these men also dwindled. July's recruiting total was the highest of the war; it fell to 16,571 by September, and to 9119 by December. Most willing volunteers, if they were eligible, had already enlisted, and the war was now asking much of men in uniform, promising little glory, doubtful reward, long months of toil, and almost certainly death or wounds. Unless a particular crisis provoked it or a particular pressure forced it, after 1915 not many men were prepared to enlist, and pacifists and radicals, thriving in the changing atmosphere, began to speak safely in public, and even to attract one or two to listen.

About one matter there was no division. After the landing no

23. Lt C. H. Alexander, 9 LTM Bty, Tutor, of Armidale, NSW (b. Ireland). KIA 8/6/17, aged 33. *L* 26/7/15.
24. Lt J. A. Raws, 23 Bn, Journalist, of Melbourne, Vic (b. England). KIA 23/8/16, aged 33. *L* 12/7/15.
25. Lt R. C. Hunter, 2 Bn, Solicitor, of Forbes, NSW. KIA 13/6/16, aged 24. *L* 15/9/15.
26. Capt R. D. Mulvey, MC, 30 Bn, School teacher, of Gosford, NSW. RTA 10/1/18, aged 28. *L* 19/9/15.

patriot in the unions, in Government employ, in business, or in the universities would work with enemy aliens, and they forced many of German origin, among them South Australia's Attorney-General, to resign their posts. They refused 'lager' beer and 'frankfurter' sausages, slandered businesses and individuals with Teutonic names, and objected to public recitals of Beethoven, or Wagner, or Schubert, or Brahms, or any other Hun, as unpatriotic. At Liverpool Camp in July 1915 a Royal Commission examined a Macquarie Street doctor, for seven years a captain in the Citizen Forces Medical Corps. He had been born in Victoria in 1883, but his parents had emigrated from Germany in 1865, and the volunteers he was examining suspected him. The Commission asked him, 'Do you know any relative of yours capable of fighting for Germany?', 'Do you speak German?', and questions of like quality. Then the prosecuting counsel declared that the 'charge' was not whether the doctor *was* guilty of being pro-German, but whether some people 'erroneously or otherwise' *thought* him so guilty. The man stood before his judges only on that belief and, although some Australians were prepared to defend him, the Commission accepted a recommendation for his dismissal.

The energies so thoroughly employed against Germans and naturalised aliens in Australia turned as well after about mid-1915 upon any sign of Australian disaffection. Regulations under the War Precautions Act (1915) punished eighty-one major offences, from interfering with sentries or exhibiting the red flag to showing disloyalty or hostility to the British Empire or spreading reports likely to cause alarm. 3474 prosecutions were made under the Act, and 'singularly few' produced acquittals. At Tumbarumba, New South Wales, a drunk was heard to state in the Royal Hotel that it was a capitalists' war, and should be fought by them. The indiscretion cost him £100, and he avoided a six months' prison term as well only because his son was then in the trenches at the Dardanelles. He had been charged with making statements prejudicial to recruiting, an offence for which 150 Australians were fined or imprisoned during the war. The patriots approved such stern concepts of duty; further, they demanded the dismissal of all eligibles from Government employ, barred eligibles from some clubs and associations, and shunned or abused them in the streets.

This tyrannical atmosphere facilitated the efforts of recruiters. In November 1915 the Federal Parliamentary War Committee asked every eligible, '1. Are you prepared to enlist now? . . . 2. . . . at a later date? If so, name the date. 3. If you are not prepared to enlist, state the reasons why'. The Federal Government established State War Councils to prosecute the war effort, and divided the country into thirty-six recruiting areas, each with a quota, each with a network of increasingly active recruiting committees. Bands became essential to arouse patriotic fervour at recruiting meetings, pretty girls offered a kiss to eligibles who would enlist, women were urged to send their men to fight, and a valiant 'shrieking sisterhood' inflated their traffic in white feathers. Everywhere the voice of the recruiter grew more strident.

In late 1915 New South Wales patriots began to organise recruiting marches. The first, of men called the Coo-ees, left Gilgandra in late October thirty strong, and walked 320 miles to the Sydney recruiting tables. At least a dozen similar marches were organised, the longest being from Wagga to Sydney (350 miles) in December 1915. Loyal citizens along the route welcomed and refreshed the marchers, and the men on the road appealed for comrades and cash. They met with miserable success. The nine best known marches covered 2140 miles and attracted only 1115 recruits en route. The Kangaroos, halted for lunch near Bowning, appealed to several hundred railwaymen by arguing that the men in the trenches were unionists fighting for the Empire, while those at home were blacklegs. They extracted nine shillings and nine men; and in January 1916 the marches were abandoned. The gap between patriot ineligible and unenlisted eligible was widening.

At this point the Australians were struck by a fresh blow. In December 1915 Anzac was evacuated. Those acres of Turkey had become sacred soil to Australians, the ground of their nationhood, the origin and proof of their Imperial partnership. Now their soldiers, who almost daily during the past months had enhanced their glory, were retreating. It was hard fortune, solaced only because no Australian could be held responsible for it. The English press blamed their generals or the British troops at Suvla Bay, considered the Anzacs 'in no way to blame', and hailed their first landing as the 'supreme exploit of the British infantry in the whole of its history'. The Australian papers eagerly reported this, because it preserved the nation's heritage and was great comfort. '[T]he name of Gallipoli will never spell failure in Australian ears', the *Argus* announced on 22 December,

It was there that our young and untried troops . . . given as their baptism of blood a task before which veteran soldiers might well have blenched, quitted themselves as men, and gained the plaudits of the world. They might have done equally valiant work, almost unnoticed, amidst the vast armies in Belgium or France; but Gallipoli provided a conspicuous theatre for their achievement, and focussed [on them] the attention of the world.

The evacuation of Anzac, although it chastened the spirit of Empire a little, guaranteed Gallipoli a place in the heart of Australian sentiment.

Nevertheless the evacuation darkened the future of the Allies, and was one of many reverses they had to endure. 1915 had seen not victory, but the forces of light on every front discomfited. By 1916 not merely the threat to their Empire, not merely the peril of their country, but a fate inconceivably dreadful hung over Australian patriots: the upset of centuries of tradition, and the vanishing away of normal existence. As the length of the war manifested Germany's capacity, the Hun became a hideous monster, bereft of humanity, purveying an unearthly Kultur, shunned by the Devil, and damned by future generations of men. The patriots wanted no negotiations with him, but total and lasting victory, and the complete destruction of Germany's political system in order to secure eternal peace. By 1916, in other words, they were fighting a war to end all wars.

Germans and aliens in Australia did not escape the malice and misanthropy hurled against the foes of democracy. The official historian Ernest Scott was to claim that by 1916 the strain of the struggle had 'slightly unbalanced' large numbers of worthy citizens, to whom anything German was toxic. Existing iniquities were aggravated, and fresh injustices concocted. Public bodies demanded the disfranchisement of persons of enemy origin *or descent*, in 1917 a law disfranchised naturalised aliens of enemy origin, men of German descent were discharged from the AIF in Australia, the honours of German citizens were wiped away, and by 1918 the names of ninety-one Australian towns had been altered to remove the Teuton stain.

These diversions did not resolve the difficulties the patriots confronted. There were still eligibles being persuaded that their duty was to fight, but their numbers continued to fall, from a high 22,101 in January 1916 (the month after the evacuation of Anzac) to 6170 in August. It did not serve the cause well enough, and the patriots, convinced of their rightness and fearful for their country, reacted strongly. They made disaffection treason, doubt disloyalty, hesitancy cowardice, pacifism stupidity, opposition a crime, and they welcomed the news of a conscription referendum which in August 1916 the Prime Minister, W. M. Hughes, at last announced. Conscription, they felt, would close the Australian ranks, and supply the fuel the flames of war required.

After Hughes's announcement enlistments rose, for the threat of conscription created a new inducement to volunteer. In Melbourne the governor's footman announced, 'I am a Soldier in the Australian Imperial Forces . . . every young man has been called up and if the Referendum passes, he will be a conscript . . . so I went before the Medical Board again, and I've been passed',[27] and in New South Wales a grazier declared, 'I had no intention of allowing the Military crowd to ask me why I did not go to the War. I hate making excuses no matter how good the reasons so . . . volunteered'.[28]

But opposition to conscription had been gathering for over a year, and in September 1916 Hughes was expelled from the Labor Party in New South Wales. The bulk of that party, the pacifists, some Irish and some Roman Catholics, some still the servants of a free conscience, and no doubt many of the eligibles and their friends, opposed this and the 1917 referendum. Against them the forces of order and propriety drew up their massive resources, and their triumph seemed sure, but the severity of the war and its distance from Australia worked against them.

The two conscription referenda were fought to the full with that sense of absolute right which had exploded so swiftly into the open in 1914. They were the most savage disputes in Australia's history, racked with execration and perfidy, manifesting the fears, doubts and imbalances of Australian thought in the middle war years, and plunging to ruin those strong ideals which in 1914 had seemed so immutable.

The proposals were lost. They confirmed the doubters in their course, they converted many to oppose the war. Far from uniting the Australian ranks, as the patriots expected, they split them; and

27. Pte H. I. Bridge, 2 MG Bn, Footman, of Melbourne, Vic (b. England). KIA 8/7/18, aged 27. *L* 16/10/16.
28. Pte W. H. Morrice, 6 LH Regt, Grazier, of Moss Vale, NSW. b. 1887. *L* 3/11?/16.

defeat faced the patriots with a melancholy future. The tide of war apparently flowed against them, yet volunteers to dam the flood decreased. They were caught, by their own convictions, between the Devil and the Deep Sea, and they could only rail, and lash those who brought them anguish. 'We can now divide the Commonwealth into two parties,' wrote 'Father of Three Soldiers' to the *Argus* on 4 October 1917,

(1) The soldiers and their relatives, and all who are making sacrifices for the Empire; (2) men who are making no sacrifice, but are drawing large salaries—shirkers, and traitors. The sooner the people get hold of this division the sooner shall we put an end to the present tomfoolery.

His letter was acclaimed the following day.

Patriots such as these neglected no recruiting method that ingenuity or earnestness could suggest. Women swore to die old maids rather than flirt with unenlisted eligibles, sportsmen, returned soldiers, miners and public figures tried to recruit their 'Thousand' to go to the front with them, Australians produced such recruiting films as *A Cooee from Home* (1917) and *Australia's Peril* (1917), 6 ft by 4 ft recruiting posters in full colour were displayed everywhere, and refractory eligibles were almost daily inundated by post with propaganda. 'You boast of Your Freedom. Come and fight for it', pamphlets urged, and 'Whose Son are you? Enlist today', and 'Are you a Man?', and 'Defend your Homes your Women and Children', with illustrations depicting the rampage of the bestial Hun through Australian hearths. Every emotion was plucked at, but by about late 1916 shame, not love of Empire, had become the major inducement.

The authors of this literature accepted much dishonour to discredit their foes. One pamphlet, for example, quoted from Jakob Burckhardt's *Weltgeschichtliche Betrachtungen*, supposedly written after two visits to Australia, the last in 1914:

the younger generation [of Australians] . . . have proved themselves . . . the most arrant cowards. The young males are spineless jellyfish. The only people they bully are their aged parents . . . they go to church . . . [to waylay] the young maidens . . . We will put them in gangs on the roads, and making fortifications, locking them in stockades at night . . . After a time we will allow the womenfolk freedom . . . They will soon . . . embrace us

The great scholar did write the book here claimed for him. It was published in 1905. It was a book of lectures, and one of these does refer to war, it laments the war of 1870, which raged as it was being written. It contains no passage similar to that quoted. Burckhardt apparently never visited Australia, and died in his native Switzerland in 1897.

The patriots gained little for the trade of their souls. Recruits fell from 11,520 in October 1916 to 2617 that December, and thereafter an average of only 3180 men per month offered themselves. Although eligibles who refused to volunteer were threatened with dismissal and other forms of economic discrimination, local and personal factors usually provided the chief, almost the only, incentives for enlistment during the latter part of the war. Men enlisted,

because public opinion told them to, or if they didn't want to be out of an entertainment all the boys were in: or if they felt they ought to: or if they wanted occupation or excitement or a world tour . . . While they are in the army they are free from feelings of discontent or shame: they may feel they are seeing life: they may, if they're Imperially minded, feel they're saving their country: they may at least feel they're helping their country to carry out a job it has begun, for good or ill: they may feel they are 'helping civilisation': they may feel among the boys.[29]

But not enough men came forward for any reason. Some Australian battalions, theoretically comprising 1000 men, were broken up in France for lack of reinforcements, others went into battle a mere eighty strong sometimes, and late in 1918 the disbandment of at least one Australian division seemed certain, but for the end of the war.

As well, war weariness was spreading through the public. War films such as the documentary *Sons of the Empire* could no longer recover their expenses, and in November 1917 recruiting officials by and large abandoned their use, while Australian film makers turned to more 'light hearted and local' themes. The political and industrial

29. Gnr E. M. Higgins, 6 FAB, Student, of Maryborough, Vic. b. 1898. L 24/7/18.

left wing, although in the main not outrightly opposed to the war, advanced from being anti-conscriptionist to inquire more closely into the conduct of the struggle and Australia's part in it. From December 1916 large sections of the left began to consider a negotiated peace, and by mid-1917 many were converted to that course. During a 1918 by-election the Labor Party stated that it was

not for peace-at-any-price . . . [but] the security of the British Empire is now beyond doubt, and . . . [the party] believes that so far from preventing future wars, the humiliation of a nation creates in its people a spirit of revenge . . . We favour the immediate cessation of the war[30]

This was the despair of the patriots, and an attitude they could never understand. Yet they could not silence it, and there was little more they could do for the war. Through the final wearing, waiting months, as hope and melancholy juggled to the fortunes of war, they plodded through a crippled world, enduring until light at last should shine through the blackness. In 1917 a Launceston editor lamented,

Europe was equipped with resources in knowledge, money and experience and latent goodwill sufficient to transform the face of the world, to fulfil the hopes and dreams of patriots and reformers, to give a new direction to civilisation, to enlarge the boundaries of human brotherhood . . . The divine event to which all creation moves would have been so much the nearer. Instead . . . all the dreams . . . [are] subordinated to the bitterness and rancour of war . . . Dynasties, personal ambitions, pride of race, intolerance, despotism, discipline [have] run mad[31]

It was a sad farewell to a vanished age, to those same ideals which men three years before had placed so high.

For a brief time a great crisis partially reconciled the factions. In March 1918 the German Army's offensives on the Western Front brought it close to victory, and the Allies closer than ever before to defeat. As German shells fell on Paris, the patriots and some disaffected came to a temporary compromise. The left conceded most: many Labor leaders, although by no means all, attended a recruiting conference called by the Governor-General in April 1918, and

30. I. Turner, *Industrial Labour and Politics*, p. 174.
31. *Daily Telegraph*, 27 August 1917.

there agreed, without binding other Laborites, to support recruiting efforts. T. J. Ryan, the Labor Premier of Queensland, first in influence and ability among left wing Australian nationalists, signed a recruiting appeal pronouncing that an Allied defeat would gravely endanger Australia, and the left did not object to the lowering of recruiting standards on 6 May 1918, although these were already low, and dangerously interpreted.[32] Some Labor leaders re-appeared on the recruiting platforms, and the left suffered the revival of recruiting marches—the marches to freedom—by the patriots, the first of which dragged an 18-pounder gun, a searchlight, and two medical officers in its weary train. In May 1918, 4888 men volunteered, many of them boys between eighteen and twenty-one hitherto barred from offering without parental consent: this was the highest monthly total in the last two years of the war, and over 1000 above any monthly tally during the same period.

It was a false summer, fading with the crisis. At the April con-ference, J. H. Scullin (Labor) had described Fisher's 'last man and last shilling' as a rhetorical phrase of the type commonly made at election times, and Hughes, now leading the Nationalist Govern-ment, had flung in the faces of his former comrades his disappoint-ment at their equivocal support for recruiting. Divisions so lightly bridged could not be healed, and in June 1918 Labor's triennial Interstate Conference in Perth resolved not to support recruiting until the Allies sought a negotiated peace, without annexations and indemnities. Recruits fell to 2540 that month, as the German drive was halted, and thereafter there was no ground between patriot and eligible, between left winger and imperialist. Only peace would prevent further division, and only victory baulked the emergence of an anti-war party.

Early in November 1918, a series of rumours reported peace signed and victory won. These kept the Australian people in constant turbulence, but did not diminish their active enthusiasm

---

32. Minimum requirements then became: height 5 feet (machine gunners, drivers, and other listed specialists could be shorter), chest 33 inches. Youths between eighteen and twenty-one could enlist without parental consent. A battalion diary noted that only 60 per cent of a new draft arriving in France in January 1918 were up to the standard of the 1916 men. At least 14 per cent were unfit for field service: one man was aged fifty-two, another forty-nine, another forty-six. (C. E. W. Bean, *Official History of Australia in the War of 1914-18*, V, p. 1n.) Even before the standards were lowered, recruits of 1914 quality were almost non-existent. See A. G. Butler, *Official History of the Australian Army Medical Services*, II, pp. 902, 903.

when on the evening of 11 November the true tidings at last reached them. Joy and relief fired the country. The streets crowded with faces, laughing, singing hymns and patriotic songs, cheering, weeping, exulting in victory and at the shackles cast from their minds. Order was impossible, and police in Sydney did not attempt to restore it until 15 November. The Kaiser was hung, executed, or burnt in effigy in many towns, church bells pealed all day, flags flew from almost every building, processions formed, and work halted as each man congratulated his neighbour on the victory of their arms. The years of trial and tragedy faded as peace lifted from them the weariest and heaviest burden Australians had ever endured.

A simple sense of their own rightness had never deserted most of them. They rejoiced at the Armistice, for they had repulsed a barbarian horde, and defeated the greatest threat progress had yet encountered. In doing so they had lost some of their innocence, but they had gained their strongest traditions. Their country had become a partner to Empire, and almost at once a nation, standing in outlook in a fair measure of independence beside the Allies. The strength of their pre-1914 values was proven, and they saw ahead a brave new era, of eternal peace and light.

Yet a world had changed in the time since 1914. The *Sydney Morning Herald*, which had proclaimed so vauntingly at the outbreak,[33] wrote at the peace,

The flower of this generation has perished. The men who promised great things in statesmanship, in science and the arts have gone, because their sense of duty was clearer than that of their contemporaries. Their loss is irreplaceable, but their sacrifice makes an unanswerable appeal for the democracy they have honoured and preserved.[34]

And the sure and almost unanimous mood of the years before the Great War had vanished into faction and strife. Australians then had talked of Empire and glory, and splendid assumptions had supported their talk. By 1918 these things had gone out from their homes, and lay scattered over the hills and plains of a score of foreign lands. They could never be brought back. Could they have seen the years ahead, Australians might well have been less jubilant in August 1914, for their country paid dearly for its maturity.

33. See p. 4.
34. 12 November 1918.

2 From the New World

Rally round the banner of your country,
Take the field with brothers o'er the foam;
On land or sea, wherever you be,
Keep your eye on Germany.
But England home and Beauty, have no cause to fear,
Should auld acquaintance be forgot?
No! No! No! No! No! Australia will be there,
Australia will be there.

W. W. Francis, August, 1914—'Australia Will be There'
(Allans Music Australia Ltd.)

Here's to the Kaiser, the son of a bitch,
May his balls drop off with the seven year itch,
May his arse be pounded with a lump of leather,
Till his arsehole can whistle 'Britannia forever.'

From the notebook of an Australian private, 1916

Recruiting officers deliberately introduced a bias into the First Australian Division.[1] Over 96 per cent of its officers and slightly fewer than three in five of its men had previous military experience; of these, more than a tenth had been British or Australian regulars, and over a quarter had been militiamen. This wealth of experience, the recruiters hoped, would make the Australian Imperial Force a competent and disciplined army, a credit to Australia, and a danger to the foes of the Empire.

But the war easily outlasted Australia's reserve of trained soldiers, and in any case peace time training had preferred field exercises—riding, shooting and skirmishing—to parade ground drill, the type of training which made English soldiers creditable and dangerous. In 1910 Kitchener and in 1914 Sir Ian Hamilton, both English generals on tours of inspection, had criticised Australian training as moving too fast, neglecting essential preliminaries (presumably on the parade ground) for more advanced studies (in the field). To British traditionalists, the old soldier in 1914 grasped basic military skills little better than the novice.

1. An Australian infantry division contained three brigades, usually of four battalions of about 1000 men each, plus attached specialist units. For most of the war most units were regionally based: the four battalions of the First Brigade, for example, were obtained by dividing NSW into four separate areas. The effect on an area when its unit lost heavily in battle can be imagined.

The AIF's initial training often encouraged the ignorance of both. The earliest volunteers were dumped in animal pavilions at city showgrounds, or in open fields called camps, such as Frasers Paddock, Broadmeadows, Enoggera, or Blackboy Hill. '[T]hings were topsy-turvy,' recalled a Victorian recruit of one camp, 'And of uniforms, some men possessed military hats only, others . . . military shirts, others military breeches . . . the majority wore their civilian clothes. Busy men were to be seen; but just as many loafed round.'[2] The first soldiers left Australia less than three months after war was declared, untrained in unit manoeuvres, and unaware of many aspects of military technique. But they fared better than some later recruits, who left without having fired or even handled an army rifle, or who fired it once before they sailed, or who embarked without rifles and other equipment after only a week in camp. They were trained further in camps overseas, but by then many had accepted standards in training and discipline which their superiors later found difficult to extinguish.

Many resented the restrictions the army imposed on them. A few wanted to bypass training and get to the front before the fighting ended, most saw the need for some training but objected to that given them, almost all dismayed those who expected them to emulate the demeanour of a British regiment. They remained incorrigibly civilian, for they were not and did not wish to become regular soldiers. They were young men answering their country's call; they would fight willingly, but they saw no point in the rigours and inanities of parade ground discipline, and until they reached the front they considered the army a job which should be regulated by the conventions attached to any employer-employee relationship. Out of working hours their time was their own, and men cheerfully left their training camps after work to go home or to town, reporting for work next day as a matter of course. Many treated officers as managers rather than as employers, tending to greet them with an easy familiarity, and viewing rebuffs as proofs of malice or want of intellect in their seniors. They drilled or went through an exercise only if they thought the job demanded it, and they were quick to argue with wayward NCO's, to chastise authoritarian excesses, and to strike for better food or conditions from the management. They always retained the right to be ruled by their own judgment.

2. 'S. de Loghe' [F. S. Loch], *The Straits Impregnable*, p. 10. (Bdr, 2 FAB, Grazier, of Gippsland, Vic (b. England). RTA 24/8/16, aged 27.)

Many very soon learnt to blend prerogative with discretion. When they went home because camp life did not suit them, for example, they were dragged back as though they were criminals. When they talked on parade they were arrested, when they indignantly objected they were docked pay. So they came to perceive distinctions between army life and an ordinary job, although generally the perception made them more cautious, not more submissive, and most continued to judge the army by civilian standards.

A sense of the nation's debt to its soldiers compounded their attitude. Why, some men felt, should they not leave camp after work, if they had volunteered to risk death? Why should they dither with precision and polish, which could have no effect on the enemy? Few proposed tamely to suffer unnecessary disabilities because they were patriotic, and some felt entitled to extra privileges—by late 1915, for example, to be allowed free public transport. Shortly after he had been commissioned, Charles Alexander, an Irishman who had taught at the Armidale School since 1909, wrote to his parents about this and other aspects of Australian discipline,

You may remember that, in my remarks on the character of the Australian school-boy, I dwelt on his independence and his lack of appreciation of what Discipline means, or even what is meant by respect to elders and seniors. Well, exactly the same spirit is shown in the boys of a larger growth . . . they would possibly be considered 'impossible' by a home soldier. Things have come to such a pass that at present the men seem to do just as they please, in defiance of all orders!—and sometimes they please to do very dastardly things, in the way of rioting and smashing up shops where, perhaps, they have been asked to pay for something that they didn't feel inclined to pay for! because they didn't consider things were being run as they thought fit. They 'break camp' when they list, brushing aside any resistance in the shape of, say, special guards with fixed bayonets, etc.; and for some time now they have decided that the Government has no right to charge them fares on the railway up to Sydney—so they simply don't buy tickets; they laugh at the ticket-collectors and sometimes bundle them off the trains if the trains slow up passing a station! Special picquets posted on the terminus platform are taken no notice of, and anyone who dares cross their path may get very roughly handled. It seems pretty obvious they can't be coerced, perhaps they might respond to good leaders[3]

In battle Australians did respond to good leaders, but in Australia few saw the need for any leaders, because their job had not begun.

At the time Lieutenant Alexander was writing, some maladministration reinforced this proclivity. Towards the end of 1915 severer leave restrictions, longer training hours, and heavier penalties for misdemeanours were introduced into the military camps around Sydney. This offended the men, who claimed that the system which had trained the heroes then on Gallipoli should train them, for they, like their predecessors, had come to fight, not drill.

They were ignored, and early in 1916 several hundred recruits marched from Casula camp to Liverpool camp, in orderly array, and under the control of leaders they had appointed. Their numbers increased at Liverpool, until about 2000 men faced the military authorities to put their case. They were listened to, and afterwards Casula camp was closed and several improvements made at Liverpool.[4] The marchers had laid themselves open to charges of mutiny and desertion; their actions were those of strikers stating legitimate grievances and expecting redress, and apparently the authorities did not think this unnatural. The habit of free men was heavily etched into the Australian community.

Volunteers in Australian camps were much concerned with food, leave, and their separation from home. 'Here is the routine of the day', wrote a new arrival at Seymour camp,

up 6 am roll call 6.5 am and on parade at 6.45 till 7.30. Then we have black coffee with no sugar or milk dry bread & bully beef. that is our morning fare which is substantial but not very tempting then on parade again at 9 am till 12 then more dry bread and stew with black Tea then on parade at 2 till 4.30 then more black Tea with bread and Jam which is the whole menu of our tea. then all lights out at 10.15 pm.[5]

3. Alexander, L 10/1/16.
4. On the return march to Casula some troops rioted and looted shops in Liverpool township; a few ringleaders were discharged from the AIF for this. Other soldiers, many of them drunk on looted beer, caught the train into Sydney, where pickets on Central Station fired into a group of them, killing one and wounding nine.
5. L/Cpl J. C. Stephen, 3 LH Bde Sig Trp, Telegraphist, of Rochester, Vic. b. 1892. L 9/7/15.

Often rations were better than this, and by the standards of other armies Australian soldiers were well fed, but army fare was less than most were used to, and canteens selling milk, fruit, jam, pies, and chocolate were popular. Beer was restricted but usually obtainable, although some soldiers had already given up drinking, at least temporarily, lest it impair their fighting efficiency. If they could not go home, men spent free nights in town, or watching concerts or boxing tournaments in camp, or writing letters.

Most recruits considered that active service began on the day they left Australia.[6] They embarked with the stamp of the soldier noticeably upon them, but they were still largely civilians. The Governor-General noted that the men of the first contingent were better educated and had more initiative than an ordinary British recruit,[7] but some other observers doubted that they would reach the front line. Many photographs of troops marching to their ships show slightly uneven lines of men, wearing assorted headgear, out of step, walking rather than marching, and smiling at the camera or the crowd. Despite their military trappings many look as though bound for a picnic.

Some felt exactly that. 'At 10.15 we moved off,' a man in the first convoy wrote, '. . . the men cheering and singing alternately . . . At last we could say we were "On Service" Hurray'.[8] He had no qualms about the future, and his enthusiasm typified many in the AIF during the early war years. A soldier on the second convoy noted, 'We are at last started out on the job for which we volunteered and all the boys are in excellent spirits. Hopes are that we shall see some active service, and return to our own dear land covered with honour.'[9] Even in 1916, the year of the Somme battles, a young Victorian reported, 'sailing [soon] —. The boys are dead excited . . . all rushing round and singing "I'm going to leave the old home" "Goodbye girlee"',[10] and a Queensland farmer told his parents, 'We are leaving for Sydney tomorrow morning, to embark, the boy's are all cheerfull, and mad for gore.'[11] These were confident, carefree

6. Many soldiers' diaries and letters began on the day of embarkation.
7. Letter to Lord Roberts, 14 October 1914. Novar Papers, 3671, NLA.
8. Maj H. J. F. Coe, 12 FAB, Mechanical draughtsman, of Malvern, Vic. b. 1894. *D* 20/10/14.
9. CQMS A. L. Guppy, 14 Bn, Farmer, of Benalla, Vic. DOW 11/4/17, aged 30. *D* 23/12/14.
10. Pte J. S. Bambrick, 37 Bn, Bank clerk, of Swan Hill, Vic. KIA 10/2/18, aged 20. *L* 30/6/16.
11. Pte J. E. Allen, 49 Bn, Farmer, of Gin Gin, Qld, KIA 7/6/17, aged 31. *L* 5/10/16.

men, sailing joyously to the challenge and excitement of a great adventure.

Many who wrote thus had already farewelled their friends and relatives in the distant places they came from. Particularly after the casualty lists began to come in, most men felt little joy in leaving their friends and country. They knew that embarkation also meant separation, and on the wharves the sadness of their goodbyes generally overcame every other emotion. '[S]aid goodbye,' wrote a Queenslander whose family had come to Sydney to see him sail, '. . . and with a lump in the throat the job was started and the journey commenced',[12] and a New South Wales gunner recorded, 'On arrival at the wharf we were allowed a few minutes to say farewell, for some it was au-revoir, for others goodbye.'[13] One or two men, shrinking from an onerous duty and an uncertain future, deserted at the last, but the majority were convinced of the necessity of their task, and that consoled their unhappiness. 'I'll try to conduct myself so that none of you will be ashamed of me, whether I come through or not,' a soldier told his family, 'Some on this boat won't come back, but many will and I can only trust that I'll be one of them.'[14] An officer consoled his wife and parents, 'it hurt me very much waving goodbye to you yesterday . . . but still no matter how much we may feel it, we must realise that it is a matter of duty and if, with me, you will look at it in that light it will help us all a great deal',[15] and a private wrote,

I don't mean I felt glad to say 'Goodbye' to Australia, home and loved ones, oh no. I mean I felt glad because I was now going to do my bit . . . It seemed to come to us of a sudden the fact what we were there for, what we were expected to do, but the one thing stood most to be answered was, How long before we shall see that wharf, those faces again, or who shall not see them again?[16]

---

12. Lt J. S. F. Bartlett, 3 Bn, Chemist, of Morningside, Qld. KIA 25/7/16, aged 32. *D* 31/3/16.
13. Gnr F. G. Anderson, 104 Howitzer Bty, Bank clerk, of Bondi, NSW. b. 1896. *D* 15/12/15.
14. Pte R. E. Avery, 59 Bn, Drover, of Charleville, Qld. KIA 4/4/18, aged 38. *L* 6/5/16.
15. Lt F. R. Fischer, 6 Bn, Accountant, of Melbourne, Vic. KIA 10/8/18, aged 32. *L* 5/8/17.
16. L/Cpl L. Allchurch, Wireless Corps, Clerk, of Adelaide, SA. b. 1898. *L* –/5/18.

Once or twice the army embarked troops without warning, and at times the lengthening list of killed Australians mocked the brave cheers and the flags and the bunting which bid most convoys Godspeed. A man described a departure from Sydney in August 1916, when lists of the Somme casualties were daily dominating the press:

Women and children who had waited all night in the cold were scurrying here and there inquiring for their husbands . . . every now and then a cry of joy showed that some sweetheart or wife had located her man. They forced themselves into the lines and marched with the column, some of the wives taking their soldier husbands white kit bag the husband taking the child . . . We embarked alright and the crowd were let onto the wharf about 8 am., just as we commenced to draw out from the wharf. Streamers were thrown and the same sad hopeless scene commenced all over again. I never want to see so many hopeless despairing womens faces again . . . the men going now have a harder task to face than those who hurried away before our big casualty lists started[17]

Whatever their private feelings, in public most Australians endeavoured with varying success to overcome the melancholy of departure. They thought that war was glorious, an opportunity to play out the highest roles open to man, and so they believed that embarkation was rightly an occasion for joy and festivity. A printer reported,

relatives and friends of the boys were allowed on the pier; guess there was about 2000, then began the fun, the boy's on the boat catching sight of a friend would call out, then a streamer would shoot by your head, everywhere was excitement, the chaps struggling for positions, and getting mixed in the streamers . . . as the boat moved out the streamers crossed and uncrossed looking not unlike a silkworm cocoon . . . when we had steamed out of sight, we settled down to a good dinner[18]

and an Australian Army regular claimed,

There is far more laughter than tears in this drama . . . the buoyancy of spirited youth is not subdued by the thoughts of

17. Pte D. B. Fry, 3 Bn, University tutor, of Lindfield, NSW. KIA 10/4/17, aged 22. *D* 22/8/16.
18. Lt J. W. Gration, 39 Bn, Printer, of North Fitzroy, Vic. b. 1892. *L* 22/7/16.

tragedies to come, for are not all these strong men eager to shew, by non-chalant behaviour, that for them Death has no sting and the grave no victory . . . [they are about to achieve] one of the great thrills of life—departure on active service[19]

But he implied that at least some men forced their laughter, and at best considered the act of departure bittersweet. A Victorian commented,

There were very few on Board without some friend to see them off . . . It was a pretty yet sad sight and a grand send-off . . . Here are a couple of remarks I heard 'It is hard work to be cheerful and then you cannot cheer them up' 'They allowed just enough time, for I would have been in tears myself if we had stayed longer.' 'My people were very kind and saw me off with smiling faces while I found it very difficult to smile.'[20]

His words suggest the range of emotions contending within his comrades. They felt the sorrows of leaving those they loved, perhaps forever, but their duty and their task comforted them. Not long after their ships had drawn away, most soldiers put the emotions of embarkation behind them, and turned to consider the novelty and adventure of the future. A day after the Australian coastline had disappeared below the horizon a New South Welshman remarked, 'This is the start of perhaps the most adventurous period of my life, and it is even very likely the last period . . . for the first time we . . . have really began the game in deadly earnest',[21] and this was probably the sense of most of those who sailed from Australia to battle against the foes of the Empire.

Complaints about food, beer restrictions, canteen facilities, and the distribution of mail were fairly frequent on board the transports, but there were only two real discomforts: seasickness, or 'practising singing', and boredom. With a spirit that was to support them well in harder times, men tried to laugh seasickness away ('If I was Christ, I would get out and walk home'[22]), and they had a ready counter to boredom:

19. Capt S. C. Calderwood, MC, 20 Bn, Soldier, of Eglinton, NSW. RTA 24/1/18, aged 26. *Narrative*, 23/12/15.
20. Cpl A. S. K. Rusden, 59 Bn, Clerk, of Ballarat, Vic. KIA 4/7/18, aged 21. *D* 1/4/16.
21. CQMS C. F. Laseron, 13 Bn, Taxidermist, of Mosman, NSW. RTA 24/6/16, aged 29. *D* 23/12/14.
22. CSM A. A. Brunton, 3 Anz LR Op Coy, Engineer, of East Melbourne, Vic (b. England). RTA 28/9/18, aged 35. *D* 13/4/16.

Gambling is a favourite pastime on board. I suppose 60% of the troops indulge in these games, more or less. There are the crown and anchor, house, cards, and two up. Any time of the day and up to 9 p.m. one will find crowds congregated together at different parts of the ship, playing one or other of these games . . . the first thing that met my eyes on coming up from below this morning was the coins being tossed . . . at the stern . . . the crowd . . . started their gambling and kept it up all through the [church] service . . . I don't think it possible for them to lift their minds off the two coins in the air.[23]

Australians necessarily tolerated their confinement at sea, but they resented being kept on board a ship in port. Authorities invariably attempted to restrict shore leave, and large numbers of men invariably ignored such attempts. General Bridges[24] wrote that discipline on the first two convoys was good, the chief difficulty being in off-loading civilian stowaways at Albany. In fact men from these convoys regularly went absent without leave, often only a small proportion of those given leave returned when it expired, and troops kept under special guard on board serenaded their officers with such songs as 'Britons never shall be slaves' and 'Every dog has his day'.

Later in the war, particularly at ports overseas, more serious trouble erupted. An English born private stated that at Fremantle,

the Major in charge positively asserted that we could get no leave whatever. He then . . . saw . . . soldiers were climbing over the side . . . [and] The men refused to allow the coalers to go on with their work until leave was granted. The Major realised that the men were in earnest and consented to their demands. This will just serve to show you the independence of the Australian. If the same thing had been done in the British Army a Court Martial would have followed . . . The next day some of the men took to pelting a few officers with orange peel and apple cores.[25]

23. Bdr W. E. Baker, 2 FAB, Telephone mechanic, of Northcote, Vic. KIA 21/3/18, aged 27. D 29/10/16.
24. Maj Gen Sir W. T. Bridges, KCB, CMG. Commanded 1 Div and AIF 1914-15. DOW 18/5/15, aged 54.
25. Pte F. B. H. Lesnie (served as F. Bernard), 17 Bn, Electrician, of Darlinghurst, NSW (b. England). KIA 2/3/17, aged 20. L 17/7/15.

At Cape Town an officer noted, 'men . . . not allowed ashore because their officers did not trust them. About 120 men got off the ship in two rushes, 3 men being bayoneted.'[26] Similar violence broke out several times at Colombo. A Victorian wrote,

I happened to be on duty at the gangway . . . and before I knew where I was I saw a mob rushing towards me, one sentry who tried to stop them was knocked down and had his rifle taken away from him, three other sentries not far away . . . and [I] decided to try and stop them . . . We . . . put our bayonets out to the mob, at first they didn't like the look of them but they soon took courage and started jostling and pushing us; then an officer . . . ordered me to fire on the row-boats that were waiting to take the men ashore—I fired two shots over their heads and they got away pretty quick, after half an hour, in which I got a black eye and another chap his nose broken the mob went away leaving two men who we had knocked out with our rifle butts. I knocked the one who had given me the black eye.[27]

Neither bullet nor bayonet could persuade some men to submit to what they considered injustice. They were impatient at the perpetual monotony of the troopship, and they held firm opinions about their rights. In mid-1915 soldiers on a troopship at Colombo were refused leave, and were fined when they took it. They were not allowed to buy beer or fruit from the natives, but after the ship left port the canteen sold Colombo fruit at rates 200 per cent above Colombo prices. 'The Australian spirit' having been roused by these injustices, the troops rioted. They pushed officers about, assaulted the military police, broke open the canteen and the detention cells, and threw furniture overboard. When their commanding officer attempted to address them, he was hooted, hissed, and threatened with ejection over the side, until at last he withdrew. The men finally dispersed when more leave and cheaper fruit had been promised them, but by then in any case they had exhausted their opportunities and energies for riot and revelry.

The man who described these events, a Victorian private, defended them by pointing to the injustices done at Colombo, and

26. Lt E. M. Brissenden, 3 Div HQ, Barrister, of Sydney, NSW. b. 1862. D 20/6/16.
27. Pte H. T. C. Alcock, 23 Bn, Agricultural student, of Toorak, Vic. DOD 14/2/16, aged 19. L 14/6/15.

by listing other iniquities: the men had been kept below deck when they left Australia and so had missed the last goodbyes; the voyage had been insufferably monotonous; there had been no fruit on board until Colombo and seasick men craved fruit; the commanding officer had broken promises about leave and refreshments; the detention cell was hot and dirty, so that men were carried to hospital from it.

Certainly the men on that ship considered themselves unfairly treated. They rioted again at Alexandria, because officers and NCO's were given leave, but

the men were told to remain on board . . . immediately ropes were thrown from the decks to the pier and down slid the men, like sheep one starts and away go the rest. Soon the side of the boat was covered with ropes . . . the officers tried to prevent this but had to give it up. Armed guards were placed on the piers, but they were useless. We had been boxed up for over a month and who could expect that the Australian boys would stand alongside a pathway to an evenings enjoyment and not place a foot on it. I confess I was not far from the lead in going over the side.[28]

That night only 60 of the 2000 odd troops on the ship remained aboard. It seemed unlikely that such men would ever accept the discipline conventional to British units.

To the dismay of most Australians, who had expected to sail to the Motherland and then to fight the Hun, the AIF was landed in Egypt. The soldiers of the first convoy began disembarking at Alexandria on 3 December 1914, five weeks after they left Albany, and soon they were camped near the Pyramids, on the sandy flats that were to become Mena Camp.[29] Egypt was a singularly unfortunate environment in which to deposit Australian troops. Its attractions were in the dead past, there was nothing to do. Men visited the pyramids and scarred their peaks with Australian names, inspected the museums and palaces, toured the zoo (because it was

28. For this and the two preceding paragraphs, Lt H. S. Trangmar, 57 Bn, Book keeper, of Coleraine, Vic. b. 1888. *D* 29/5 and 13/6/15.
29. The Light Horse camped at Ma'adi, south of Cairo. Mena was abandoned in April 1915, but by early 1916 Australian camps or posts were at Heliopolis, Helouan, Tel el Kebir, Zag-a-Zig, Zeitoun, and along the Suez Canal at Ferry Post, Ismailia, Kantara, Moascar and Serapeum.

near Mena), and wandered through the gardens and the mosques. This was the work of a few days, and in a short time those restless thousands faced an unrelievedly monotonous future.

They had come across half a world to fight for one of the noblest causes that uplifted men. They were sustained by notions of splendour and battle and glory. They were the first and finest of their country. And they had been dumped on bare sand among hordes of natives so persistent that a man had to buy a stick to beat them off, they were obliged to drink 'poisonous' beer or none at all, they were expected to endure heat, sand, dust, flies, and monotony without hope of alleviation, and in and out of training hours they had, as they put it, to march, drill and meander uselessly about the desert 'like a pack of bloody dills'. It was not for this that they had come. They dubbed Egypt land of sin, sand, shit and syphilis, and set about devising their own entertainment.

Australians with and without leave crowded into Cairo, first to a good meal at a 'posh' hotel, then, often, to the drinking and vice dens about the Haret el Wasser. They hired donkeys from the natives and ran wild, laughing races down the streets and along the footpaths and through the hotels. They upset fruit and lolly trays, they gambled, fought, and played pranks, they brawled and rioted, they assaulted military police. When they were ready to return to camp, they would crowd onto a tram, toss off the driver, and career wildly at full speed through the darkened streets, some of them clinging boisterously to the sides and roof of the vehicle until at last it halted outside the camp. Or they commandeered gharries or bikes or donkeys to make the return journey; and on Christmas Eve 1914 General Birdwood's[30] car was mysteriously transferred from outside his headquarters to the sands beside Mena, an occurrence the general stoically accepted.

Military offences multiplied: during December 1914 absence without leave, desertion, insubordination, drunkenness, assaults on natives and military police, robbery, and venereal disease all increased markedly. Men broke bounds at will, and over 300 in the First Division were posted absent without leave by early January 1915, despite stricter penalties and closer supervision. On one day two-fifths of one 10th Battalion company were absent without leave

30. Field Marshal Lord Birdwood, GCB, GCSI, GCMG, GCVO, CIE, DSO. Commanded A & NZ Corps (later Aust Corps) 1914-18, Fifth Army 1918-19, and AIF 1915-20. b. 1865.

at roll call, and half of them were still absent a day later. On Boxing Day 1914 the 2nd Battalion was obliged to cancel a parade because it could not muster enough men to hold it, even after it had included sixty 2nd Battalion men then in the unit prison. Far from making civilians soldiers, the authorities feared, training in Egypt was reducing recruits to rabble, and by the close of 1914 'matters were swiftly coming to a point when discipline in the A.I.F. must either be upheld or abandoned'.[31]

In January 1915 training hours were extended, long desert marches were introduced, a strong standing picket was placed across the Cairo-Mena road, and some Australian units were sent to garrisons along the Suez Canal. On 3 February 131 disciplinary cases and twenty-four men with venereal disease were returned to Australia in disgrace, while a despatch to the Australian public explained that these men had stained their country's reputation.

These measures were partly effective. Exhaustion and shame limited Australian excesses, and by 1 February the bearing of the men had so improved that they were allowed a day off every week, besides Sundays, and trained for only eight hours a day on week days. Yet probably prudence, not conviction, inspired the improvement, for many Australians were prepared to justify what the authorities chose to consider transgressions. Even during the last week of 1914, the period of worst disorder, at least one man judged that,

Taken all through, the discipline in all ranks has been good . . . we are freeborn men, used to living a free life, with very few restraints of any kind, recognising no one as Master . . . [considering this,] the discipline is good. Certainly there are some undesirables, but they are very far in the minority[32]

Throughout 1915 the AIF retained its reputation for indiscipline and for opposition to seemingly pointless or unfair restrictions. Australians would not accept that an army was regulated by norms and rules not civilian, and the military way remained entirely outside their conventions. Without many Australians noting much amiss, a guard could leave its post to get dinner, a man could fall out from a march to light his pipe or to speak with a nurse, soldiers could

---

31. Bean, *Official History*, I, p. 128.
32. Sgt E. Murray, MM & bar, 14 Fld Coy, Engineer's mechanic, of Duntroon, ACT. b. 1881. *D* 31/12/14.

wander about Cairo in singlet and shorts, men could approach an officer and casually ask for a loan, and NCO's who seriously administered 'no leave' orders could be considered wanting in propriety.

None but their own officers could hope to sway such men. An Australian corporal was swimming with his working party in an out of bounds area of the beach at Alexandria when,

a choleric Colonel of the British Army swept down on me and called for the man in charge. I came out and he roared at me to 'stand to attention', which I did. After asking me my name, he roared at me, 'Answer me properly, call me Sir!' and after I'd given him my name, address etc. he roared again 'Show me your metal disc' (meaning my identification disc) then saying I was under arrest he told us to go, we swam the horses and bathed ourselves to our satisfaction.[33]

Some would have held that colonel gently treated. Until they had indicated their calibre even AIF officers had little real influence upon their men, particularly if they came from another unit or were outside the camp. Most officers were only grudgingly saluted: a Fifth Brigade circular, one of many issued by commanding officers, complained that not one man in a hundred saluted, and that officers and NCO's, from fear of 'putting on side', rarely demanded it. 'Right from the start I objected to saluting officers', wrote an old soldier in 1967, 'It is a survival of an ancient time and at no time in the war did I see where it did any good.'[34] To almost all Australians a salute signified respect for the recipient, not for the system, and they accorded respect willingly only to very exceptional men.

They conceded nothing to unpopular or inefficient officers, who were 'counted out', anonymously enlightened about their origin, entertained with rude songs when they escorted ladies, and, at least once or twice, beaten up. From inclination and policy good AIF officers tolerated what might have been punished in the British Army, and, if they were efficient and just, this was as much as they could do to establish their authority until they had undergone the test of battle. The officer commanding the 7th Battalion, for example, ordered his men to wear their Australian hats on parade,

33. Lt R. W. McHenry, MC, 2 FAB, Customs officer, of Ivanhoe, Vic. b. 1893. *D* 29/5/15.
34. Statement by Mr D. Jackson, MM (formerly Pte, 20 Bn, Farm labourer of Sydney, NSW. b. 1895), 4 July 1967.

not the British-style cap. Soon afterwards a man appeared on parade wearing the wrong headpiece, and when he explained that he had lost his Australian hat, his CO told him in blunt terms that any real soldier would have acquired another. On the next parade the man appeared correctly attired. His CO, upright in adversity, wore a British cap. One night a 2nd Battalion captain accompanying a brigadier on inspection noticed a guard on duty eating a pie. Hotly he ordered the soldier to present arms, at which the man asked the brigadier to hold his pie while he performed the required ritual. Neither soldier necessarily intended disrespect: both were behaving as they had since birth, and neither had seen cause to change.

Occasionally men in the AIF committed more serious offences. On the night of Good Friday, 1915, after some units had received orders to pack for the front, Australian and New Zealand soldiers rioted in the Wasser, the brothel district of Cairo. There were long standing grievances against the bad drink and diseased women sold in the area, and when the story spread that some soldiers had been stabbed in a brothel, a crowd of men gathered, threw prostitutes and standover men from several houses into an alley, piled beds, mattresses, cupboards and everything else portable or detachable into the street, and set fire to them. At least one building was incinerated, and the mud walls or the balconies of several others were pulled down. The native fire brigade had its hoses cut while struggling gallantly through the mob to attack the fire, and some firemen were assaulted. British military police arrived on horseback and attempted to disperse the rioters by firing revolvers at them. They wounded several soldiers, but in return were bombarded with rocks, beer bottles, lengths of fire hose, and abuse, and wisely withdrew. A few men then took to looting nearby shops, and there was more burning: one Australian claimed that a car outside Birdwood's headquarters (at Shepheard's Hotel, near the Wasser) was upended and burnt. The mob was by now in dangerous disorder, and the Lancashire Territorials, whom most Australians liked, were drawn up with fixed bayonets across the roadway. Some rioters were tempted to breach even this barrier, but most slowly dispersed, and by early morning the excitement had died away.

The affair was 'not heroic',[35] nor was the second Wasser riot, a

35. Bean, *Official History*, I, p.130n. C. Malthus, *Anzac—A Retrospect*, p. 113, states that a car load of Australians ran down an Arab boy during the first Wasser riot.

similar outbreak, in July 1915. Both betrayed some of the worst
aspects of Australian character. Some Australians so viewed them,
but others welcomed the diversions ('The greatest bit of fun since
we have been in Egypt',[36] one man called the first riot) and several
defended the destruction as eradicating menaces to public health
and the Egyptian authorities.

Both 'battles' followed real or imagined grievances. Particularly
before the first riot, men felt their sense of right offended, and the
sight of mounted MP's firing revolvers at them was certain to
provoke, rather than subdue, their hostility. 'What I have found of
the Australians,' wrote an English immigrant in the AIF after
watching the second riot, 'is that they are men who will stick out for
their rights and are not satisfied till they get them. They have been
taught this system by their form of Government at home'.[37]
Probably these Australians were over-ready to convert their own
impulses into a system of justice, and to consider opposing attitudes
malign, yet it remains clear that, on the eve of action, the men of
the AIF still clung to an uncompromising independence.

At least one Australian justified the events of Good Friday by
protesting that there was still nothing in Egypt for soldiers to do.[38]
That was true, and from sheer boredom a few men schemed to be
sent to gaol. But, the man who described their schemes continued,
'this would vanish if we "could get at them" which is what we came
for',[39] and man after man repeated that belief. No matter what their
purpose in originally enlisting, the Australians with very few exceptions came to wish above all else for the firing line, and men of
every outlook expressed disgust with Egypt. In January a twenty
year old Queensland cane cutter complained, 'I haven't had any
sport Turkey roasting yet . . . this inaction here in Egypt is enough
to get on anybodys nerves and I hope it won't be long before we get
a move on as I'm sick of it.'[40] In February a Victorian soldier
repeated,

I have . . . become fed up generally with our stay for such a

36. L/Cpl E. H. Ward, 1 Bn, Tailor's cutter, of Bathurst, NSW. RTA
10/7/16, aged 26. D 2/4/15.
37. Trangmar, D 31/7/15.
38. Sgt D. V. Walford, 45 Bn, Draughtsman, of Woollahra, NSW. RTA
13/2/17, aged 24. D –/4?/15.
39. Pte L. R. Donkin, 1 Bn, Labourer, of Maitland, NSW. KIA 15/8/15,
aged 23. D 23/3/15.
40. Sgt T. M. Scott, 49 Bn, Sugar cane cutter, of Gin Gin, Qld (b. England).
KIA 5/4/17, aged 25. L 16/1/15.

*long period here. We have been on the job for about six months
and haven't had so much as a shot fired . . . tell [all at home]
I'm quite safe—too safe for my liking worse luck!*[41]

and in April a cabinet maker stated,

*the sand and hot weather is killing [us] . . . whole sale . . . the
sooner out of this place and in the firing line the better I don't
want to die in the attempt I want to do some thing first what do
you say if its only 1 German . . . soon we shall round the Dar-
denals or in the south of France and then the fun will start*[42]

Australians in Egypt after the Gallipoli landing, when men might
have been less eager to fight, and when in any case most spent less
time in training, were equally impatient. After nine days in Egypt a
reinforcement wrote, 'Getting fed up with Egypt the Gyppos etc.
Have had all the Cairo I want and most of us are anxious to get
away from this everlasting drill.'[43]

Before the landing the Australians had to endure their frustration
until called upon, but after April men often tried to transfer or
desert to units marked for the front. A few stowaways succeeded
in reaching Anzac, and at least two were killed there.[44] A man of
the 2nd Battalion, ordered to remain when his unit sailed, hid for
twenty-four hours in a hold, until his ship was well out to sea and
he deemed it safe to come on deck. His sergeant and then his officer
abused him, but he was put onto the strength of his unit, and he was
among those who stormed the Turkish hillsides on that last Sunday
in April.[45] In August 1915 four artillerymen stowed away, but
were discovered at sea and passed several days in the brig with
eight others similarly detected. They were released between Lemnos
and Anzac, and filed to the beach under the apparently vacant eyes

41. Sgt W. W. B. Allen, 9 Bn, Soldier, of Heywood, Vic. D while POW
25/4/15, aged 28. *L* 14/2/15.
42. Antill, *L* 1/4/15.
43. Cpl F. V. Addy, 4 Bn, Iron turner, of Moore Park, NSW. b. 1889. *D*
19/9/15.
44. A KIA card in the Australian War Memorial reads, 'Young, C. E. This
man unofficially attached himself to 16th Bn. in trenches at Gallipoli: No
trace can be found of any enlistment or any N.O.K. Was K.I.A. 14/11/15
. . . It is suspected that he was a member of another unit on duty in Egypt
and proceeded to Gallipoli without authority.' The other known man was
Pte J. Gurry, 10 Bn, Labourer, of Petersburg, SA. KIA 19/5/15, aged 26.
45. Cpl H. E. Wyatt, 2 Bn, Boundary rider, of Surry Hills, NSW. DOW
11/4/17, aged 22. *D* 4, 5, and 6/4/15.

of the ship's officers. Ashore they applied to join the 5th Battalion, and then the 1st Battalion in the Lone Pine trenches, but, though no officer arrested them as deserters, none did more than feed them and pass them on. After two days touring the Anzac defences, the four travellers reported to Divisional Artillery headquarters. They were arrested, returned to Egypt, and fined twenty-four days' pay. One at least considered his outing cheap at the price.[46]

Probably only the unlikelihood of success prevented more Australians attempting such enterprises. Most had to wait, which sharpened the ardour of some formerly unhappy at the prospect of combat, and led those already eager to fear that the war would finish before they could get to it. 'If they don't hurry up and get us away', a private exclaimed, 'I am afraid we will miss the boat altogether and will go back to Australia without having a shot',[47] and an officer yet to reach Egypt thought, 'Perhaps the war will be over by [the time we get there] . . . We anxiously await the daily news in the fear that it may be'.[48]

Inactivity also added conviction to the chief impulses which had initially persuaded Australians to volunteer. Whatever those impulses, a man's presence in the army and in a community of like minded men tended to convince him that every objective and principle proclaimed by the Allies was his cause, and that his cause, because he was committed to it, was just: what were passionate assumptions in the civilian became motives for existence in the soldier. At this time men usually expressed their commitment in terms of Imperial ardour and the sanctity of the Empire's martial prestige. An ex-militia officer wrote, 'My fighting blood has been awakened now at seeing what Britain is doing and I will do my utmost to keep the flag flying'.[49] This was the language and sentiment of many of his comrades, and to such men the news of casualties or the sight of wounded opened glorious possibilities. Idealising death, and considering pain the welcome price of duty and a good proof of manhood, they were impelled forward by losses and reverses at the front. 'The wounded are rolling in here every day', a Queens-

46. Dvr H. E. Lucas, 103 Howitzer Bty, Farm hand, of Marrickville, NSW. b. 1885. *D* –/8/15, pp. 57-66.
47. Lt J. D. Campbell, 6 MG Coy, Station manager, of Geraldton, WA. KIA 9/10/17, aged 39. *L* 6/8/15.
48. Maj G. I. Adcock, 2 Aust Tunn Coy, Mining engineer, of Rutherglen, Vic. b. 1895. *L* 8/7/15.
49. Capt C. H. Linklater, MC, 33 Bn, Wool buyer, of Wollstonecraft, NSW. DOW 11/6/17, aged 34. *L* 10/3/15.

land private in Egypt reported during the August offensive on Anzac, 'every available place is full and they are erecting wooden sheds every day for more. We realise now what a serious thing for England war is', and a fortnight later he noted, 'I have never regretted joining and even less so now that I will be able to relieve 1 of these chaps and let him have a spell.'[50]

News of casualties prompted in some men a longing not merely to replace their stricken comrades, but to take part at once in the great adventure now surely not far before them. '[I see] my duty to my country', one man stated,

and now seek revenge on the enemy who have done so much to destroy the fine sturdy lads of our own Australia and who have helped to hold back the progress of the world for years to come. I feel with each days training that I could take my part as a true Australian and help hold up the glorious reputation our lads have given us to hold, and I hold my life equal to 3 of our enemy if such be my lot I am satisfied, but in the Machine Gun Section I hope for more than my value[51]

and a Tasmanian private wrote,

I feel calm and fit and just a little eager to get out and into the line of fire—avenge some of the wrongs committed on defence-less women. I shall hate to take life but I feel justified in wreaking vengeance on these allies of the Unspeakable though 'cultured' Huns . . . We see thousands of wounded in the hospitals here and the hundreds coming in daily . . . could the Theatre Johnies in Aust. see and know these disfigured and broken down heroes, and then see the blood soaked Peninsular of Gallipoli they would hesitate no longer[52]

The pain of their comrades could not warn such men. The Imperial vision held them firmly, and they would go into their first battle attuned not to the bloody realities around them, but to the romances of a tradition brought from a distant homeland and an ancient past.

50. Lt W. A. Mann, 25 Bn, Letter carrier, of Charters Towers, Qld. b. 1896. *L* 19 and 31/8/15.
51. Trangmar, *D* 13/6/15.
52. Lt W. E. K. Grubb, 40 Bn, Commercial traveller, of Launceston, Tas. KIA 28/3/18, aged 28. *D* 1/9/15. The two men last quoted thought their foe to be not Turkey, though Turks had inflicted the wounds, but Germany, the architect of world misery. There was a general conviction that Germany was the only real opponent.

Every influence men felt between their enlistment and their first entry into the firing line, then, urged them to battle. Summarising the period, a West Australian wrote,

at Blackboy Hill I had to drill and generally make a fool of myself . . . When the instructor said left turn one would turn right sure as eggs, then he would condescend to tell you all about your relations, etc . . . when [he] . . . had taught us which end of the rifle the bullet come out . . . we were sent to Osbourne Rifle Range . . . Our section done some real good shooting so we only done the one course, worse luck—the shooting was the best part of it. However it come to a finish like everything else, and we marched back to camp about 32 miles . . . then we embarked . . . and of course we were put in Egypt. Days we hung about thinking we would have a scrap in the Suez, but it never came off. They dumped us off at . . . Mena Camp . . . it was rotten . . . sand, sand, sand in your tucker, in your ears, eyes, nose, everywhere, and anywhere, it was real crook we done marching, skirmishing and digging for weeks and weeks . . . I was heartily sick of it . . . we left . . . about 25th February . . . [and] stopped [on Lemnos] . . . eight weeks, going on shore; long marches and climbing hills, etc., getting fit; at last the word came—we were going to have a fly at the Turks. Well you can bet it was like putting a bit of roast meat to a starving man—we sprung to it[53]

When orders to pack for the front at last reached the men of the AIF, they did spring to it, almost to a man. '[W]e . . . are about to leave for the Front and nothing could give me more infinite joy than to tell you this glorious news,' exulted an artilleryman, '. . . as we have been told that we will probably land under fire, we are full of joyous expectancy . . . I am at present about to enter in the joy of my life, & one of my highest wishes have been gratified.'[54] 'We are leaving here to night,' echoed a young Englishman in the original[55] 14th Battalion, and he welcomed the blood and the toil to come:

53. CSM G. S. Feist, 52 Bn, Wheat agent, of Mount Kokeby, WA (b. England). KIA 3-4/9/16, aged 28. *L* −/5/15.
54. Ellsworth, *L* 4/4/15.
55. At first conferred upon units and men who had been at the landing, an 'original' unit came to mean one before it first went into battle, and an 'original' usually a man who had belonged to such a unit since its formation.

and our next landing place will be under fire and pretty hot at that too and I am now in the Machine Gun Section which is genarly the first to be wiped out, so I don't fancy my chance much. Well we are all in the best of spirits all egar to get at it . . . and only too glad to leave that sandy piece of land they call Egypt.[56]

A 6th Battalion reinforcement recorded, 'Left . . . on a journey that we were waiting for for 6 months and glad to get away. We were a happy lot anybody would have thought that we were going to a sports meeting on New Years Day.'[57] 'We have got our marching orders at last . . . Everyone is hugely excited', reported a nineteen year old infantry sergeant,

If I am killed Ross and Ray will write to you & let you know all about it . . . I think God will pardon my many sins and we shall all meet together again in Heaven. Good bye Mum & may God watch over you & me while we are apart[58]

and a young private about to reinforce the 7th Battalion exclaimed,

I am sick and tired of wasting leather on the gritty paving stones of Cairo . . . Egypt is all right for a week . . . but . . . soon everything becomes a drag, so now I am going to a place where monotony is unknown, and a year seems like one crowded hour of glorious life . . . I [am] on the eve of entering the firing line, and rejoicing[59]

The confidence and splendour of an Empire marched with these men down to their ships, and they sailed from the desert to the roar of bands and the cheers of less happy comrades left behind. They were strong and fit men, free from the restraints that had sobered their departure from Australia, and they went rejoicing to a momentous future.

Some among them gave serious consideration to the grim possibilities ahead. One of the AIF's best known soldiers wrote to his wife before he landed on Gallipoli with the 10th Battalion,

---

56. Antill, *L* 11/4/15.
57. Pte D. R. Argyle, 6 Bn, Pastoralist, of Gunbower, Vic. KIA 20/10/17, aged 24. *D* 11/8/15.
58. Capt F. W. Moulsdale, 7 MG Coy, Draughtsman, of Marrickville, NSW. DOW 12/4/18, aged 22. *L* 15/8/15.
59. Capt W. M. F. Gamble, MC, 15 LTM Bty, Student, of Macleod, Vic (b. Scotland). b. 1896. *L* 18/9/15.

Transport A·31
Serangdoon
April 24/15.

Dearest Wife

We have received our sailing orders, and inside of a few hours shall be in the thick of the greatest combined naval & military operation in history, with Australia in the pride of place. — That we shall succeed I do not entertain any doubt, but that I shall come through unscathed and alive is not so certain. — As this may be the last opportunity I have of talking to you, I want to say briefly that, in the event of my going out, you are to believe that I do so with only one regret, which is, the grief that this will bring to you and Bert. and Mat. — For myself, I am prepared to take my chance. — While, on the one hand, to win through safely would mean honour and achievement, on the other hand to fall would mean an honorable end — At best I have only a few years of vigour left, and then would come decay and the chill of old age, & perhaps lingering illness. — So, with the full and active life I have had, I need not regard the prospect of a sudden end with dismay. — I am greatly comforted to know that you will be well provided for, and will be surrounded by many friends, who, for my sake, will help you to win through all difficulties that may beset you in the future. — I am sure you know how deeply I have always loved you, and how in all things I have tried to act in your best interests. — I know also that you have loved me dearly, and will honor my memory.

Your husband John Monash.

Colonel John Monash's letter to his wife, written on the eve of the landing at Anzac

I trust that I will come through alright, but it is impossible to say, and I must do my duty whatever it is. But if I am to die, know that I died loving you . . . if in some future time you should think of remarrying, always know that I would wish you to do whatever is for your own happiness. But think well, dear, and make sure what manner of man you take[60]

'Dear Gladys there is a little matter', a Boer War veteran told his wife as he lay off the Anzac coast three weeks after the landing,

We are about to take part in some very severe fighting and there is no doubt that those who come through it alive will be very lucky. If I should go under there is no need for me to say of whom my last thoughts will be . . . I hope you will always remain on the best of terms with my mother and the others and if in the years to come you require genuine friends you can rely on finding them among my family . . . mere written words could not convey my feelings regarding you dearest, I know that you know, and that is sufficient.[61]

Other Australians expressed more public sentiments. '[I]f we go down you can rely that we've done our best for King and Country',[62] a South Australian teacher commented, and as he sailed towards the Dardanelles after the bloody August fighting there a Victorian student stated,

the decision [to serve my King and Country] . . . was not only the right *one but absolutely the* only *one consistent with honour. With this elevating ideal of duty clear before me it is quite easy to enter the struggle light hearted and hoping for the best . . . Above all do not worry about me . . . it rests in the hands of God.*[63]

Three days before the landing the 1st Battalion's adjutant, an old regular who had seen service in India, wrote farewell to his wife:

60. Maj B. B. Leane, 48 Bn, Warehouseman, of Prospect, SA. KIA 10/4/17, aged 27. *D* 23/4/15.
61. Sgt M. J. Ranford, 1 LH Regt, Ganger, of Semaphore, SA. KIA 5/8/16, aged 35. *D* 11/5/15.
62. Capt H. E. S. Armitage, 50 Bn, School teacher, of Norwood, SA. KIA 3/4/17, aged 22. *D* 27/5/15.
63. Lt F. G. Kellaway, MC, 22 Bn, Law student, of Northcote, Vic. KIA 4/10/17, aged 23. *L* 4/9/15.

*I trust . . . that soon oh soon we may be together again . . . at
the same time I would not be out of this for worlds. When we
think of what might be should Germany won! Our days are fast
coming to a close, come what may, and if it should be, let one
name go down in history unsullied though deeply mourned . . .
'better die a hero's death than be branded a coward', for, how
can man die better; than fighting fearful odds, for the ashes of
his fathers, & the temples of his Gods. Always rember that
there is a home from which there is no parting, and at the best,
our days here are short, and if our efforts here can make this
world a better one, let us do it. for the sake of those we leave
behind.*[64]

At peace with their Maker, and professing an unshakeable faith in
the rightness of their country, these men went forward willingly to
triumph or oblivion in the great ordeal of war.

There were several other reactions to the news of approaching
battle. Some wondered whether they would pass the test:

*We are getting very near to our destination, some of us never
to return, I expect. It makes one's blood run fast to think that
in a few hours we will be taking active part in the greatest war
of time, many of us untried all fighting our maiden battle. The
one thought uppermost in my mind as I sit here is that I shall
not be found wanting, shall not find myself a coward.*[65]

Long inactivity engendered a sense of anticlimax in a few, but
others, including several initially not keen to fight, accepted the
inevitable and welcomed the coming storm:

*Well Ma, I shall soon be seeing the real thing and believe me,
I am looking forward to it. When I was at Broadmeadows I
used to think it was silly when I heard others talking like that
but now that I am right up against it, I want to be there.*[66]

The great majority felt as they had when leaving Egypt. Two
hours before his regiment went ashore a light horseman remarked,

---

64. Maj W. Davidson, 1 Bn, Soldier, of Oatley, NSW (b. Scotland). KIA
19/8/15, aged 49. *L* 22/4/15.
65. Bdr C. B. Giffin, 14 FAB, Farmer, of Manildra, NSW. b. 1880. *D*
18/5/15.
66. Pte N. B. McWhinney, 23 Bn, Clerk, of Hawthorn, Vic. KIA 28/7/16,
aged 20. *L* 18/11/15. Particularly later in the war, I believe this feeling was
stronger than the records literally indicate.

The boys are talking like a lot of school kids, to see them one would think it was a picnic they were getting ready for, but they have got their rifles clean & their bayonets have been sharpened in a very business manner.[67]

A New South Wales trooper asserted,

We are all looking forward to showing the world what we are made of and I, for one, have not the slightest fear of what there probably is in store for me (loss of limbs, a mortal wound, loss of memory, deafness etc) but I have impressed upon my mind our return to Australia, covered with glory and this vision I can't get away from.[68]

He never returned to Australia, nor did a young Victorian corporal who offered himself at the altar of his Empire:

Today I am eighteen . . . and I received the best news I think I ever got . . . In forty eight hours, we proceed to the place Australia had made famous!! . . . I don't think I was ever so happy in my life . . . should . . . you have to make the supreme and grand sacrifice, it will be easier to bear when I say that since I left home I have acted absolutely square to my mother's teachings and always as an Englishman should. Have no fear for me; I have make peace 'twixt God and man. and am prepared to join the glorious list.[69]

Perhaps truly for such men death had no sting and the grave no victory. The gay Cavalier had touched their spirits; they thought themselves equal to twenty Turks, they bowed to no man, and with the eagerness of children they restlessly awaited their glory.

On 24 April 1915, the first Australians who would fight in the old world were assembled on Lemnos Island, a night from the Turkish defences along the Dardanelles. Towards dusk the leading ships, carrying the Third Brigade, cleared harbour and rounded east towards their destination. During the night a British convoy of battleships, destroyers, and transports followed them, bearing

67. Sgt J. G. Burgess, 6 LH Regt, Tram conductor, of Redfern, NSW. b. 1887. *D* 20/5/15.
68. Capt D. V. Mulholland, 1 MG Bn, Bank official, of Ashfield, NSW. DOW 31/5/18, aged 27. *L* 8/8/15.
69. Lt E. S. Worrall, 24 Bn, Medical student, of Prahran, Vic. KIA 4/10/17, aged 20. *L* 1/10/15.

soldiers from France and from several parts of the Empire. In the morning these men would undertake the largest amphibious landing in the history of war, and, some in the AIF believed, the first major assault against a defended coast in 850 years of British history.

The Australians were conscious of the importance of their task, but they were moved also by a particular consideration, which, however their fortunes went, would distinguish them forever from other Australians. They were virtually the first soldiers of an untested nation, and the world would judge their country by their achievements on the morrow. Their Empire had assigned them a fair field for the judgment—a dramatic and hazardous enterprise, in an arena predominantly their own. Gladly they weighed the glory and the burden of their fortune. 'Today most momentous in Australian history—Australian force moves forward to attack Turkey from sea,'[70] noted a young Sydney clerk. 'Now the world can watch the success of "Australian Arms". The officers and men are very keen. Sir Ian Hamilton expects a lot from us',[71] a Victorian salesman echoed, and another Victorian predicted, 'It is going to be Australia's chance and she makes a tradition out of this that she must always look back on. God grant it will be a great one. The importance of this alone seems stupendous to Australia'.[72] A legend was awaiting birth, and almost before they had begun the original Anzacs were marked out from their fellows.

As they filed into their landing boats, their thoughts turned to the test of the coming dawn. They were fit, confident, and well trained. They were taller and bigger than other soldiers, physically the finest their country could offer. They had no knowledge of war, but they were masters of everything they had encountered, and they never doubted their ability to accomplish their task. Although the First Division had never exercised as a unit, a better division had not often gone to battle, and soon its men would be called to show their mettle. They were ready. 'All the boys tonight are singing and are in great spirits, bayonets are sharpened and everything made ready for tomorrow',[73] noted a sergeant in the 4th Battalion. '[M]ight get

70. L/Cpl H. J. S. Smith, 3 Bn, Civil servant, of Naremburn, NSW. KIA 23/6/15, aged 20. *D* 24/4/15.
71. Lt H. T. Elder, 5 Bn, Salesman, of Newtown, NSW. DOW 9/5/15, aged 23. *D* 24/4/15.
72. Lt A. D. Henderson, 7 Bn, Accountant, of Hawthorn, Vic. DOW 25/4/15, aged 20. *L* 24/4/15.
73. Sgt A. L. de Vine, 4 Bn, Electrical engineer, of Maroubra, NSW (b. England). b. 1884. *D* 24/4/15.

killed —', another man observed, 'somehow feel as if I will be—anxious to be there all the same.'[74] The possibility of dying and the enterprise they faced drew many men together. Ellis Silas, an artist in the 16th Battalion, was a gentle man who detested war. By early 1915 his delicate sensibilities had made him a Philistine among his fellows,[75] yet in the last minutes before landing he could feel at one with those who had cast him out:

we have been told of the impossible task before us, of probable annihilation; yet we are eager to get to it; we joke with each other about getting cold feet, but deep down in our hearts we know when we get to it we will not be found wanting . . . for the last time in this world many of us stand shoulder to shoulder. As I look down the ranks of my comrades I wonder which of us are marked for the land beyond.[76]

Many were marked, but that troubled few; at least, few would confess it. As they waited excitedly before the gates of history, most Australians pretended a light hearted indifference to their comrades and the world. 'Here goes for death or glory. So Long All',[77] remarked a lance corporal in the 10th Battalion. He was George Mitchell, a man afterwards commended for bravery and fined or imprisoned for indiscipline with almost equal regularity, a vain man, but a good soldier, whose outlook was often during the war to typify the irreverence and valour of the AIF. Mitchell tried to analyse his feelings as he sat in his tow during the silent minutes before dawn on that first 25 April, but could not. 'I think that every emotion was mixed—exultation predominating', he confessed, 'We had come from the New World for the conquest of the Old.'[78] It was a phrase Fitchett had used in 1913.

74. Sgt J. L. B. Coulter, 8 Bn, Farmer, of Ballarat, Vic. DOW 10/8/15, aged 37. *D* 24/4/15.
75. Sgr E. Silas, 16 Bn, Artist, of Perth, WA (b. England). Discharged in England 17/8/16, aged 32. *D* 3 and 9/1, and 16/3/15.
76. Silas, *D* 25/4/15.
77. Capt G. D. Mitchell, MC, DCM, 48 Bn, Clerk, of Thebarton, SA. b. 1894. *D* 24/4/15.
78. Mitchell, *D* 25/4/15.

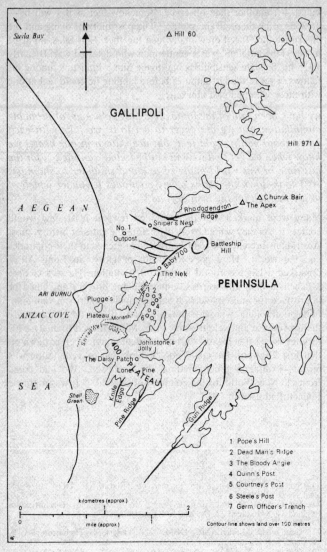

Suvla Bay

N

△ Hill 60

GALLIPOLI

Hill 971 △

A E G E A N

△ Chunuk Bair
△ The Apex

Rhododendron
Ridge

Sniper's Nest

No. 1
Outpost

Battleship
Hill

Baby 700

The Nek

PENINSULA

Valley

ARI BURNU

Plugge's
Plateau

1
2
3
4
5
6

Monash

ANZAC COVE

Sniper's Gully

7

400
PLATEAU

Johnstone & Jolly

The Daisy Patch

Lone Pine

S E A

Shell
Green

Knife Edge

Pine Ridge

Gun Ridge

1 Pope's Hill
2 Dead Man's Ridge
3 The Bloody Angle
4 Quinn's Post
5 Courtney's Post
6 Steele's Post
7 Germ Officer's Trench

kilometres (approx)

0   2

mile (approx)

0   1

Contour line shows land over 150 metres

Anzac

ANZAC

3 Trial by Ordeal

There's a torn and silent valley;
There's a tiny rivulet
With some blood upon the stones beside its mouth.
There are lines of buried bones:
There's an unpaid waiting debt:
There's a sound of gentle sobbing in the South.

Sergeant Leon Gellert, 10th Battalion, January 1916
—*Songs of a Campaign* (Angus & Robertson)

The ships arrived off the appointed coast at about half past two in the morning. The moon had set, so darkening the night that none could pick out the land ahead. A swift tide ran, but the sea was smooth, and the stars shone brilliantly, foretelling a clear day. The Third Brigade, the covering force, would land first; it was already in its tows, thirty to forty men per boat, each man carrying over 90 pounds of equipment, with magazines empty, and bayonets fixed. Eyes patrolled the night for sign of discovery, but there was nothing. Silence shrouded them all.

At three thirty the steamboats cast off from the battleships, towing half the strength of the 9th, 10th and 11th Battalions. Half an hour later the destroyers followed, pulling the remainder of these battalions and the 12th Battalion, the reserve. The sky lightened before the coming dawn as the boats moved shoreward, but no sign of life came from the land. Nearer and nearer the boats crept, the quiet pressing every man. To the south, when the closest boats had 40 or 50 yards to row, a light showed for half a minute, then went out. Nothing happened. The first boat touched land. Australians sprang out, and began to throw off their packs. They were Queenslanders, of the 9th Battalion. It was four twenty nine a.m. Still no sound came from the cliffs above.

Three hundred yards out to sea, the engineers attached to the covering force sat tensely in their tows:

Shall we be seen, or not? That's our anxious question.
  'Why don't the — fire at us?'
  'Look, there's a light!'
  'No, it's only a bright star creeping up behind the hill.'
*. . . no challenge rings out. How we wish they would fire—or
that we could land . . .! The suspense is nerve-racking. All we
can do is follow the pinnace towing us about. The thought
comes to me that perhaps we are the unfortunate ones to be
sacrificed in drawing the enemy's fire, Such a cheerful thought!
. . . Oh, why the dickens don't they fire at us! There are a
couple of lights flashing about—they must have seen us . . .
Crack! Swish! Ping! At last we breathe a sigh of relief, the
suspense is over! . . . some get ashore safely, some are hit
slightly, others are drowned in only a couple of feet of water
because in the excitement no one notices their plight . . . [One]
fellow remains in the boat after all the others have disembarked
. . . he . . . looks at us dazedly, leaning forward on his rifle. A
sailor . . . touches him on the arm, and the soldier falls forward
in to the bottom of the boat, dead.*[1]

Another engineer recalled those first Australian moments in the old
world: about 40 yards from the beach, 'one single shot rang out
followed by a dead silence . . . by now we were hoping, for all hell to
be let loose every second, machine guns, shrapnel, anything but this
nerve-racking silence.'[2] He had not long to wait. Soon after those
first Queenslanders touched the shore, the bullets came.

On the left flank, the tows of the 11th Battalion carried them
north of Ari Burnu Point, and they were obliged to cross 200 yards
of sea after being discovered. During that whole fearful journey
bullets thudded into the crowded boats, striking down the helpless
men as they rowed desperately for land. 'Some were shot and others
at once took their place', a survivor wrote later, 'and not a word was
uttered. Presently we grounded and in an instant we were in the
water up to our waist and wading ashore with bullets pinging all
round us.'[3] Then they charged up the hill.

1. Sgt W. E. Turnley, 1 Fld Coy, Telephone mechanic, of Sydney, NSW
(b. England). RTA 10/6/16, aged 25. *D* re 25/4/15.
2. L/Cpl W. Francis, 1 Fld Coy, Surveyor, of Hull, England. RTA 29/1/16,
aged 31. *L* 25/4/15.
3. Maj A. H. Darnell, DSO, 11 Bn, Civil servant, of Perth, WA (b. Ireland).
DOW 24/9/18, aged 32. *L* 27/5/15.

The 12th Battalion was also well out to sea when the firing began. 'I was in the second tow,' one man remembered,

and we got it, shrapnel and rifle fire bad. We lost three on the destroyer and four in the boat getting to land. The Turks were close on the beach when we got there. We had to fix bayonets and charge. We jumped into the water up to our waists and some of them their armpits . . . we had to trust to the penknife at the end of our rifles. When I got there it was not long, but . . . I tell you, one does not forget these things . . . all we thought of was to get at them. One would hear someone say 'They've got me' and you register another notch when you get to them, that's all.[4]

Lance Corporal Mitchell, in the 10th Battalion, was a hundred yards from the beach south of Ari Burnu when the first bullets shattered the stillness.

'Good!' I remember saying 'the —s will give us a go after all.' 'Klock-klock-klock. Wee-wee-wee' came the little messengers of death. Then it opened out into a terrific chorus . . . The key was being turned in the lock of the lid of hell. Some men crouched in the crowded boat, some sat up nonchalently, some laughed and joked, while others cursed with ferocious delight . . . Fear was not at home[5]

The men threw their packs on to the beach, and turned to the enemy. All was confusion before them. Instead of the open plain they expected, the scrub-covered hills rose steeply away. The bushes winked with Turkish rifle and machine gun fire, and bullets enfiladed many parts of the beach. The Australians were on a strange shore, being shot down by an unseen foe. Someone had blundered.

The covering force did not hesitate. Concerted movement was impossible, but groups of men plunged immediately into the waist high scrub and rushed upon the steep slopes before them. While morning cast its first pale shadows from the ridges they clambered swiftly upwards, overrunning a trench with the bayonet, sinking to hands and knees to scale vertical cliffs, chasing back the Turks.

4. Feist, *L* –/5/15.
5. Mitchell, *D* 25/4/15.

Within ten minutes the fastest of them had crested the heights, and stood triumphantly 300 feet and more above the coast.

As the men directly above the beach broke the skyline, some were struck down by the bullets of their comrades firing below, others by enemy riflemen lurking in front. But soon the Turks vanished into the dark tangle of gullies behind them, and their shooting died away. Realising this, many Australians paused, breathless and elated, thinking victory won. Only the keenest pushed on, thrusting inland after the retreating enemy, striving urgently to make good the prize they had gained. During the day individuals and small parties penetrated more than one and a half miles from the sea, but then they were halted, and pushed back, and until 1918 no Allied soldier was to pass the points they reached.

The enemy's defences had reacted swiftly. Fortunately for the Australians, only a company or so of the enemy had opposed their landing, but by a quarter to five that morning Turkish shrapnel had begun to burst among the troops along the ridges, and shortly after nine the men furthest out saw lines of Turks advancing. The counter-attack moved up the valleys, outflanking the scattered Australian outposts, shooting men in positions shortly before thought impregnable, and driving back the Anzac line.

Towards the southern flank, the 10th Battalion advanced directly inland from the beach in reasonably compact order to 400 Plateau, near the second ridge. They arrived there between six and seven a.m., and began digging in while the battalion scouts and a few others advanced to the third (later Gun) ridge. The enemy's fire was negligible at first, but it increased as the advanced parties were pushed in by the Turkish counter-attack, and soon men in the main body were under heavy enfilading fire. Many were shot, and the survivors were forced to lie and endure a merciless fusillade. Lance Corporal Mitchell was one of these: pinned by machine gun fire, he lay for most of the day unable to lift his head in safety, unable to dig further into the stony ground beneath him, unable even to shout for aid for the comrades who lay dying around him. Late in the afternoon he began to find the strain intolerable, and to seek the release of death:

'Fix bayonets and prepare to charge,' came an order . . . I think about one man in six in that line was capable of advancing, the others were all dead or wounded. We rejoiced as we gripped

our rifles. The long waiting should be terminated in one last glorious dash, for our last we knew it would be, for no man could live erect in that tornado for many seconds[6]

The charge was not ordered, but many men on this flank attempted to advance as their original orders had laid down. Their attacks swung back and forth across 400 Plateau, but were useless, and some of the finest in the First Division died making them. Men chiefly of the 6th Battalion attacked Pine Ridge (between 400 Plateau and the third ridge), but most were shot,[7] and the rest were driven back. Their gallantry was not rewarded, and the Australian line sullenly retired its advanced posts, and settled along the seaward edge of 400 Plateau.

To the north, a tall hill overlooked the invaders. This was Hill 971, and it quickly became clear that it and the ridges approaching it were critical objectives. After they landed, men of the 11th and 12th Battalions scaled the nearest heights on this flank, Baby 700 and Battleship Hill:

A brief pause on the beach to fix Bayonets and singing 'This bit of the world belongs to us' much swearing and cheering we charged up a hill so steep in places we could only just scramble up. No firing all bayonet work. Clean over a machine gun we went, men dropped all round me, it was mad, wild, thrilling . . . Not till I was near the top of the hill did I realise that in the excitement I hadn't even drawn my revolver[8]

Opposite these Australians stood Mustapha Kemal, commanding the only Turkish reserves on the peninsula, the Nineteenth Division. Kemal looked anxiously at the undefended approaches to 971, and moved two thirds of his division to oppose its assailants.[9] The Turks met their enemy advancing in scattered groups, outflanked or overran them, and forced them back. The Australians rallied and returned, and during the day, as reserves arrived for one side or the other, a vicious battle ebbed and flowed across the open ridge of

6. Mitchell, *D* 25/4/15.
7. Their bones were there still in 1919, scattered as they fell, in groups of three or four along the ridge.
8. Darnell, *L* 27/5/15.
9. His remaining regiment counter-attacked the Australians further south. One and a third Turkish divisions were thus committed to the defence of the general Anzac area, leaving two regiments (two-thirds of a division) to counter the British landing at Cape Helles, 13 miles to the south.

Baby 700. At last towards dusk the Turks, fighting with great bravery, won the vital ridges, and the Australians and New Zealanders formed a line of posts along the lower spurs.

Strategically, the landing had failed. Almost everywhere the Turk commanded the key positions, and that night the Australian leaders, Birdwood and Bridges, requested permission to withdraw. Snipers shot at the men from every direction, shrapnel showered upon them, thirst and exhaustion wore them down. But the soldiers were content, for they thought they had triumphed, and they never considered retreat. They made ready to stay, and they stayed.

In most respects they had won a great victory. They were landed on an unexpected coast, which unhinged their orders, and they found themselves amid a tangle of steep hills and scrubby gullies, country difficult to cross in peace time, and now shielding an unknown number of enemy. Many were in doubt, many were leaderless, but most remembered what they had learnt in training—to advance always, to find and follow an officer, to inform the rear of the trend of battle. With excellent discipline, they obeyed. They went forward; when the scrub divided them, they went forward still; when most had been shot, the rest went on, or clung grimly to the ground they held. They were not experienced soldiers, they were too precipitate and they made too many errors to be that. They were ardent, eager, brave men, naive about military strategy, but proud of their heritage and confident of their supremacy. Despite their mistakes, they did what few could have done.

They paid dearly for their glory. For a week after the landing exhausted men (many were given no real chance to sleep until 29 or 30 April) fought a hundred fights: attack and counter-attack followed in unwearying succession, and at the Daisy Patch, on Johnstone's Jolly, at Steele's Post, at Courtney's, and Quinn's, at the Bloody Angle, at Pope's Hill, and at The Nek the dead spread thickly over the ground. The rage of battle subsided early in May; by then most of the officers and about half of each battalion, on an average, had been swept away, and some sections and platoons had entirely disappeared.[10]

In the short term the sacrifice made outweighed the glory won. Instead of a heady charge to a great victory, 'The first day we

10. There are no exact figures for casualties at the landing. Between 25 April and 3 May Australian and New Zealand casualties were about 8100, including 2300 killed. (Bean, *Official History*, I, pp. xxiii, 605).

landed we ran into a real live Hell, schrapnel, bullets, machine guns all over the place. I do not know how on earth I ever got out of it alive.'[11] As Lance Corporal Mitchell lay open to the Turk rifles on 400 Plateau, he saw death not as the welcome risk of glory, but, perhaps for the first time, 'as a painful shutting out of all life's promise'. Illusions faded during the days that followed, and he wondered about the romance of battle, and wanted to see the war won and to go home intact. By early June he had abandoned even the hope of returning,[12] for he found himself not in a short Imperial campaign, but in a bitter, savage, bloody conflict. Hard truths had shaken the dreams of his past.

Private Antill, the young Englishman so keen to volunteer before the war broke out, was similarly disillusioned:

I am still alive but I can't tell you hardly how it is, for I have had some of the most marvellous escapes a fellow could have . . . amongst this slaughter and strife . . . I must honestly say I will be highly delighted when this war is over for it is simply terrible, for to see your pals shot down beside you and the roar of the big 15" naval guns the shrieks of our own artillery and the clatter of the rifle fire is enough to drive a fellow mad. For the last 19 days we have not been safe any where, and I am not even safe writing this letter here . . . but . . . I am born lucky to be here at all. The first night . . . I tried to get a couple of hours rest, and where I was I could not shift my position so I had to use a dead mans legs for a pillow[13]

'I know its right and proper that a man should go back and fight again,' confessed Private L. R. Donkin after being wounded at the landing, 'but Sunday's battle and the horrors of the trenches Sunday night . . . have unnerved me completely.' Later he wrote,

[We sailed] . . . off to death and 'Glory'. What fools we are, men mad. The Turk he comes at one, with the blood lust in his eyes, shouts Allah! Australian like, we swear Kill or be killed . . . Where are the rest of my 13 mates? . . . myself I consider lucky getting away from the acres of dead men . . . And now I go back there . . . God only knows what is in store for me[14]

11. Pte D. J. C. Anderson, 2 Bn, Meter inspector, of Zeehan, Tas. KIA 17/8/16, aged 23. *L* 12/5/15.
12. Mitchell, *D* 25/4, 12, 13, and 19/5, and 4/6/15.
13. Antill, *L* 14/5/15.
14. Donkin, *D* 27/4 and 16/5/15.

None of these men could ever hope to return to their old world, yet the past was too strong for them to abandon it completely. They knew what victory would cost them, but they still wanted very much to win, and soon. In time they put the bloody images of April from their minds, and propped their days with hope and illusion. 'Now that things are peaceful I am longing to scrap again', Corporal Mitchell declared in mid-June,

After the sternest days of fighting I had a keen desire to return
home in safety, but now I do not give it a thought. I shall hop
in for my [cut?] with the vanguard of the charge . . . life and
death has not the same significance it once had.[15]

'[S]o you can just see things were pretty bad then,' Private Antill continued, 'but still they have calmed off a lot now', and later, 'I think the worst of it is over well at least I hope so for I can tell you none of us want a lot like the last lot'.[16] 'I suppose a rest with quietness at Alexandria will put me right, and I hope to make a few suffer for me then,' Private Donkin wrote from hospital, and before he returned to Anzac three weeks later he consoled himself by reflecting, 'if I die . . . I have given my life for Australia and home.'[17]

Most men similarly reconciled their experiences and their beliefs. They saw 'things in a different light now, one does when he shakes hands with the shadows',[18] but they found ways to ease their disquiet and go on. At first many substituted stern necessity for gay adventure, so that they could remain true to King, country, and their own ideals of manhood. Chastened, but not less determined, they continued the fight. Then, after the tumult of the first days had quietened, old convictions reasserted themselves, and men again eagerly took up the business of war. 'A new spirit of jocularity is arising amongst the men', an officer on the First Division's staff noticed in mid-May, 'This is different to the first ten days when one didn't see a smile all day round the trenches'.[19]

Almost all the men evacuated with wounds during the early days were impatient to return. A Sydney carpenter wounded on the first

15. Mitchell, *D* 11/6/15.
16. Antill, *L* 14/5 and 23/6/15.
17. Donkin, *D* 27/4 and 16/5/15.
18. Feist, *D* –/5/15.
19. Maj R. G. Casey, DSO, MC, 1 Div HQ, Engineer, of Melbourne, Vic. b. 1890. *D* 14/5/15.

day assumed that the worst fighting on Anzac was over, and wrote from Alexandria,

I am slightly wounded . . . but am leaving tomorrow for the front again and very pleased I will be I want to get my own back I got it in the head and right arm. last Sunday it happened it has not healed up yet but I am quite fit to go back again.[20]

He died of his wounds three weeks later. A soldier who lost an eye during the early fighting was marked for repatriation to Australia, but late in August stowed away and returned to the front with a glass eye. It was blown out on his first day back.[21] Other wounded noted, 'it is a great disappointment . . . I hope soon to get back again',[22] and 'It is really vile luck . . . but I hope soon . . . to get back to the Front'.[23] 'I've seen scores of the wounded', reported a soldier in Egypt,

and they are very cheerful and anxious to get back to the front . . . all the doctors and nurses report . . . the amazing fortitude and cheerfulness of the Australian wounded. They say they never saw anything like it in the world. They are laughing and joking all day chatting about the dirty Turks and itching to be back again. I used to think the desire to be in the thick of things was a pose, or make believe, but I know differently now. They are actually angry when told they must remain in hospital for a few weeks.[24]

Often they had cause for anger: fit men were returned to the front very slowly, which made many impatient, and led some to stow away or to petition officers for their return.

Australians at the front fought the battles of May and June with aggressive enthusiasm,[25] notably at Krithia on Cape Helles (8–9 May), against the Knife Edge and German Officer's Trench (June

20. Pte A. T. Elwood, 2 Bn, Carpenter, of Glebe, NSW (b. NZ). DOW 17/5/15, aged 25. *L* 30/4/15.
21. Hunter, *L* 1/9/15.
22. Maj R. P. Flockart, 5 Bn, Clerk, of Camberwell, Vic. DOW 15/7/15, aged 29. *L* 28/4/15.
23. Lt D. G. Campbell, 51 Bn, Pastoralist, of Walgett, NSW. KIA 3/9/16, aged 31. *L* 6/5/15.
24. Maj O. Hogue, 14 LH Regt, Journalist, of Sydney, NSW. DOD 3/3/19, aged 38. *L* 7/5/15. I found only one man who did not want to return to the front during this period.
25. Some men were still searching for spies in mid-June, and possibly Australians were shot for this. This 'spy mania' suggests the difficulty Australians on Anzac had in separating the realities of their situation from the notions they had got during their past.

and July), and during the Turkish general attack at Anzac on 19 May.[26] The bloodiest and most incessant fighting was at Quinn's Post, a small ridge of land near the head of Monash Valley which overlooked almost the entire Anzac position. Possession of Quinn's determined who held the beachhead, so Anzac and Turk crowded into the narrow space. Their opposing trenches lay between twenty yards and two feet apart, and the land between became the most disputed on Gallipoli, but almost always the men who attacked across it were blown to failure and oblivion by the mass of fire that enfiladed them from every vantage point on the surrounding ridges. Bodies covered the ground and thickened the air, unreachable, while the living stayed silently in their trenches, periodically relieving their boredom by provoking bomb or bayonet fights which frequently all but annihilated both garrisons. Fresh garrisons took their places, and remained cautiously below the skyline until some new incident sparked them once more to slaughter. In quieter times men worked ceaselessly for an advantage over their invisible neighbours, converting a barricade, a sniper, or three or four riflemen into major objectives. In June for example, the 1st Battalion raided German Officer's Trench to destroy a single machine gun enfilading No Man's Land at Quinn's:

about 60 in all . . . in silence lined up along the parapet. Suddenly a whistle blast sounded & we were over the parapet & towards the enemy's trench. We fixed bayonets as we ran tripping over our own barbed wire & other obstacles. At first not a shot was fired by the enemy but just as the first of our men reached the trench the alarm was given and a murderous fire from rifles and machine guns broke out. We found the trench very strong with a firm sandbagged parapet studded with loopholes . . . [and] a strong overhead cover . . . with bayonets projecting . . . which we could not shift. In addition the Turks threw a number of bombs with good effect . . . we were forced to retire amid a heavy fire having however put the machine gun out of action . . . the whole affair occupied only some 10 minutes but nearly every second man was injured the total Casualties 27 wound 5 killed.[27]

26. See pp. 91-2.
27. Pte F. W. Muir, 1 Bn, Articled clerk, of Unanderra, NSW. DOW 18/11/15, aged 22. L 12/6/15. An account of this raid is in Bean, *Official History*, II, pp. 242-4.

If that machine gun was destroyed it could have been replaced, yet neither side abandoned such efforts. Miners and sappers at Quinn's were never inactive, and frequent bombing duels made it 'Deuced awkward not knowing when one is going to land on you . . . and having very little room to get away'.[28] Many times in the valley below, men turned anxious eyes towards the smoke and bomb bursts on Quinn's, for across those few yards their fate was continually being contested. Although their persistent activity and the invention of the periscope rifle[29] enabled the Anzacs to hold the post, for months at Quinn's both sides displayed a degree of endurance and tenacity not often paralleled in war.

This was trench fighting at its bloodiest. Usually it was less severe, consisting of digging, patrolling, and sniping, with sporadic raids and attacks. Between May and July the Australians engaged keenly in these activities, and became highly proficient at them. 'I had a narrow shave', reported a soldier after a raid, 'was enfiladed in a trench but managed to get out of the road as a bullet caught me across the back, only made a flesh wound, we gave the Turk a hot time . . . I enjoy the life and like all the men am well and happy'.[30] Most Australians shared his outlook, but after 7 June raids were largely abandoned by the staff—they lost much and gained little— and both sides continued the war underground, by mining under enemy held trenches or tunnels and blowing them up. An Australian engineer NCO described one explosion:

Enemy blew up two of our tunnels about 6 p.m. Sorry to say one of our men was buried alive . . . Our chaps worked hard (also the Inf) [to clear the earth] & a lot of them was overcome with the Gas & had to be carried out. I was very shaky but I was determined to stick to it until we found our comrade, as he belonged to my Section. On digging in about [28] ft we struck something like a sandbag, & . . . we then tore away a piece of brace[r] so we knew it was our lad. This was a very sad & nervous job, all the time the earth was falling in & I can tell you we used to jump back a good few yards, it gave us a great shock as we expected every minute to fall down into the

28. Pte F. T. Makinson, 13 Bn, Clerk, of Neutral Bay, NSW. KIA 29/8/16, aged 37. *D* 21/5/15.
29. By Sgt (then L/Cpl) W. C. B. Beech, 2 Bn, Builder's foreman, of Sydney, NSW. b. 1878.
30. Lt T. D. McLeod, 3 Bn, Watchmaker, of Cootamundra, NSW. KIA 6/8/15, aged 23. *L* 15/5/15.

*Enemy's trench . . . we got a rope & fixed it around & under-
neath his arm & then we began to pull, but I did not like the
job as I could hear his bones cracking, so we shovelled more
earth away & then had another pull, this time being successful
. . . we dragged him along the tunnel but I got that weak I had
to leave go & rush out into the open air . . . It was sad for our
lad as I suppose he is dead by this time.*[31]

There came a time, perhaps towards the end of June, perhaps
earlier, when it seemed to the troops that the fighting would be
unending. Local attacks gained nothing, trench warfare was inde-
cisive. The pointlessness of some actions shook the confidence of
the men in their generals, and the monotony of their daily existence
began to wear them down. Two up was dangerous, cards mundane.
Souvenir hunting, the great pastime of the early days, had by June
generally lost its attraction, and men took to pencilling their home
towns on their hats and wandering aimlessly through the trenches
searching for a chance to talk of home. Papers, especially the
Bulletin, and letters from Australia became their chief interest, and
the war dropped from their conversation. Disillusion and lethargy
began to taint their responses.

At the same time sickness began to spread through the army.
Every circumstance helped its progress. Soldiers on Anzac were
expected to carry their own supplies and water—every day at least
one man in eight had to carry water up the steep slopes—to
manufacture bombs, and to provide burial parties, as well as to fight
and dig. Most of these fatigues were not usually part of a front line
soldier's lot, and they kept the Anzacs perpetually exhausted, particularly as they had no relief, no back areas, no diversions. In
return they received a third of a gallon of water per day, for all
purposes, and a frugal diet, almost always of iron rations, which
taxed the strength of men already overworked.

Worse, despite their Egyptian experience, neither officers nor
men properly realised the need for sanitation, and by June flies,
hardly seen in April, were a plague, and men could not avoid
swallowing them with their meals. Flies caused most of the sickness
on Anzac: dysentery and other intestinal maladies began to infect
large numbers of men in June, and by July these diseases were 'quite

---

31. Capt R. A. Titford, MC, MM, 2 Fld Coy, Soldier, of St Kilda, Vic.
b. 1888. *D* 29/6/15. For this incident, see Bean, *Official History*, II, p. 278.

out of control' and 'almost universal'. 1.3 per cent of the Anzac
Corps was evacuated with disease in the first week of May, 3.5 per
cent during the last full week in June, and 5.3 per cent in the last
week of July. The sick rate was far greater than the wound rate, and
threatened to incapacitate the entire Corps. Yet many soldiers
stayed in the trenches rather than suffer the long delays in returning
fit men to the front, so that by early August probably half the force
was sick, and none of it was equal to the strain of a prolonged battle.

A few men surrendered to these afflictions, by malingering or by
self inflicting wounds, and although most doggedly carried on a
general malaise settled upon the army. An officer pleaded, 'Please
God this trying time will be soon be over I am beginning to feel the
continuous strain, as regards nerves . . . I try to keep a hold on
myself but often my frayed nerves give vent to anger.'[32] A former
rugby international, Tom Richards, wrote:

*It seems to me that war such as we read about and glory in,
such as honest open hand-to-hand or man-to-man conflicts
where the bravest man gets the upper hand, where the strongest
arm and the noble heart wins the honour and gratification of
the country is old-fashioned and out of date, like the flint-lock
rifle and the broad sword.*[33]

On Empire Day a Boer War veteran reflected,

*The old Queen's birthday: how as a young boy I remember
going to Montiforte Hill to see the review of our old red coats,
etc., how that handful of men with their rifles and bayonets
used to seem so wonderful and grand to me; to-day we have
been witnessing some of the real dark side of the business . . .
the dead . . . close around our section of the trenches . . . were
thick enough to satisfy the most martial, but further along on
our right they were in thousands acres and acres simply covered
with them, of course these were mostly Turks when they
charged so bravely, but were simply mowed down like hay
before the mower.*[34]

These men had never anticipated their dirty, fly-ridden existence,

32. Maj G. G. McCrae, 60 Bn, Architect's apprentice, of Hawthorn, Vic. KIA 19/7/16, aged 26. *L* 2/7/15.
33. Lt T. J. Richards, MC, 1 Fld Amb, Commercial traveller and miner, of Charters Towers, Qld. RTA 6/8/18, aged 36. *D* 11/6/15.
34. Ranford, *D* 24/5/15. Almost certainly the reference is to Montefiore Hill, in Adelaide.

nor the lice, nor the dead, nor the monotony, nor their weariness and depression. A young West Australian stated, 'I won't be sorry when the war is over & I can come home again,'[35] and many shared his feelings.

Yet before they went home they wished to win the war. They were still soldiers of their King, accepting discomfort, expecting victory. 'Of course I take a risk of getting daylight drilled through me', admitted an infantryman, 'but I hope they don't hit too hard . . . Well, let them all come we will show what sunny N.S. Wilshmen can do. They'll soon get sick of it.'[36] Other soldiers consoled themselves and maintained their determination by affirming the ideals of manhood and duty they had learnt before the war. A trooper declared, 'There is no doubt war is hell, and the men who are responsible ought to frizzle there for all eternity; but mind you I am just as keen on serving my country as ever, and would not miss seeing it out (or until I go out) for any consideration.'[37] An infantry private noted, 'the horrors of war [are] . . . a hundred time more awful than all the papers say. I'm only too thankful to have my share in it though',[38] and an engineer was prepared to risk any fortune to crush Germany.[39]

The resolution of these men contrasted with the excited expectancy of those who landed after April. At first the new arrivals were 'a bit nervous . . . shots flying over our heads . . . [and] did not sleep verry Comfortable',[40] but most acclimatised quickly, and, being comparatively safe, revelled in the glamour of the new experience. 'God grant that men will realize the greatness of this project and whatever the sacrifice, make it, in order that our Grand Old Flag may still wave over a United Empire',[41] a light horseman exclaimed, and an artillery reinforcement noted, 'We are now UNDER FIRE . . . one feels no fear only an excessive excitement'.[42] But as they

35. Pte W. R. Guest, 11 Bn, Clerk, of Perth, WA. b. 1895. *L* 28/5/15.
36. Capt M. J. B. Cotton, 2 Bn, Clerk, of Maitland, NSW. KIA 24/7/16, aged 21. *L* 30/5/15.
37. Ranford, *D* 23/5/15.
38. Capt C. R. Duke, MC, 5 Pioneer Bn, Architect, of Orange, NSW (b. NZ). b. 1888. *L* 29/5/15.
39. Lt G. F. S. Donaldson, MC, 4 Div Eng, Shipwright, of Elsternwick, Vic. b. 1884. *L* 16/7/15.
40. Pte E. Rider, 4 Bn, Steel engraver, of Waterloo, NSW. RTA 19/1/16, aged 21. *D* 18/6/15.
41. 2/Lt W. M. Cameron, 9 LH Regt, Farmer and agent, of Rushworth, Vic. KIA 4/9/15, aged 28. *D* 18/5/15.
42. Lt J. E. Adlard, 1 FAB, Labourer, of Rossdale, Vic (b. England). RTA 1/2/18, aged 21. *D* 18/6/15.

observed their older comrades, tired and dirty, and as trench life daily seemed more monotonous, the new arrivals came to look restlessly for that great eruption which the veterans had resigned themselves to expect. Before he reached Anzac in mid-May, Private Giffin stated that only the thrill of a real battle would satisfy him; two days after the landing he remarked, ''tis not very exciting I must say. I have not seen a Turk to have a shot at', and when there were rumours of a Turk attack in mid-June he was 'in a quiver of excitement waiting and hoping for them to come on, reckoning on giving them a pretty hot time, but . . . [was] doomed to disappointment for devil of a Turk came in sight'.[43] 'We are constantly under fire night and day', a reinforcement officer reported a day or so after his arrival, 'but are so well dug in that we suffer little loss . . . we are cheerful and await the orders to "advance".'[44] An artilleryman complained that he was not really at war, because all he saw of it was a few dead and wounded, and a few bullets whizzing overhead from some distant Turkish trench.[45] These men had grown to manhood on visions of martial glory, they resented the unkind fetters of the trenches, and they longed for the charge they believed would bring them to triumph.

Their time was coming. Late in July the Australian battalions learnt that they were to undertake another general assault. Old soldiers accepted the news philosophically, and also submitted to a cruel inevitability, realising that their lot was not to fight a brief and glorious campaign, but

battle after battle, in which, in the long run, there must almost certainly be one of two endings. They felt themselves penned between two long blank walls reaching perpetually ahead of them, from which there was no turning and no escape, save that of death or of such wounds as would render them useless for further service.[46]

They saw little adventure in fighting now, and only duty, a merciless and capricious taskmaster, and their own pride kept them to the job. They never doubted their course, but they truly resigned their lives and hopes to the fortunes of war, and became 'men devoted to die'.[47]

43. Giffin, *D* 18 and 24/5, and 8/6/15.
44. Armitage, *D* 2/6/15.
45. Coe, *D* 4/5/15.
46. Bean, *Official History*, II, p. 427.
47. Ibid., p. 429.

Their spirits rallied as the inevitable hour approached. If they must fight, they would do it well, and win. The new arrivals bolstered their optimism, by hailing the days ahead as a great opportunity. 'The whole front is in a state of suppressed excitement waiting for the order to advance',[48] wrote Private Giffin. 'I have been here now 2 months & 2 weeks', observed another soldier, 'and . . . we are just preparing for a big attack on the Turkish lines . . . we expect to succeed alright as everything is well prepared and the boys all eager for the fray'.[49] Many veterans became similarly confident, although most added sober qualifications. One was

going to make a big attack tonight So you will here before this reaches you if anything happens to me. One does not think of any danger now I feel quite as if [I] were going on some exciting chase or something. Everything is in great business and we are sure to win.[50]

A stretcher bearer hoped that the battle would at last finish the campaign on Gallipoli,[51] and the prospect of achieving a definite result probably encouraged most veterans. The remainder stood grimly to their duty, scarcely affected by the eager majority, still devoted to die. A light horse officer killed during the fighting typified their mood. '[E]re another entry is made in this book we will have passed through a very trying ordeal', he wrote,

We are leaving almost everything behind; whether we see it again or not will be a matter of luck. And now we go forward in the full consciousness of a 'duty clear before us,' and . . . we can only say 'Thy will be done.' God grant comfort to those in anxiety and sorrow and give our leaders wisdom.[52]

Although the Australians took them to be major enterprises, all but one[53] of their battles during August were feints, designed to decoy Turkish reserves from the landing and assault to be made by 25,000 British New Army troops at Suvla Bay, a mile north of Anzac. This was timed for the early morning of 7 August, and the

48. Giffin, *D* 6/8/15.
49. Pte B. A. Kelaher, 2 Bn re-enl 14 MG Coy, Clerk, of Orange, NSW. DOI 26/9/16, aged 26. *L* 6/8/15.
50. Cotton, *L* 6/8/15.
51. Pte H. C. Cicognani, 13 Fld Amb, Salesman, of Glebe, NSW. POW 1916, aged 28. *D* 5/8/15.
52. Cameron, *D* 5/8/15.
53. The night attack of 6 August, described after this account of Lone Pine.

first Australian feint was planned for half past five on the evening before, against the Turkish trenches at Lone Pine.

The attacking troops, of the First Brigade, had stacked their packs behind the lines that day, and sewn white calico distinguishing patches on their backs and sleeves. At two thirty they filed into the trenches opposite the Pine, one company from each attacking battalion (2nd, 3rd, and 4th) into a secret underground line 40 to 60 yards from the Turks, two companies from each attacking battalion into the main line 30 yards in rear, and the 1st Battalion into reserve. By five they were ready, waiting for the whistles. 'Our Artillery started to bombard their trenches at 4 & will continue till . . . we make the rush', a 2nd Battalion man, Private McAnulty, recorded during the wait,

There artillery are replying now & shells are beginning to rain on us. They are getting the range now, shelling the support trenches. Men are beginning to drop. Howitzer shells are dropping about 30 yards from us digging great holes where they land. the fumes are suffocating, the shrapnel is pouring all round us getting chaps everywhere. This is hell waiting here . . . Word given to get ready to charge must finish, hope to get through alright.[54]

At five thirty the whistles blew, and, with 'no fear at all . . . but . . . a little tremor of excitement and nervousness . . . as . . . before . . . a speech or song'[55] or a game, the Australians plunged over the parapet, and into the open.

Fire burst upon them almost immediately.

Talk about shrapnel, it sounded for all the world like blanky hail . . . the bush . . . [around] the daisy patch ([in] no mans land) caught alight and showed us up beautifully to the Turkish machine gunners . . . The fire was simply hellish, shell rifle and machine gun fire and i'm hanged if I know how we got across the daisy patch. Every bush seemed to be literally ripped with bullets . . . our luck was right in.[56]

54. Pte C. A. McAnulty, 2 Bn, Clerk, of Melbourne, Vic. KIA 7-12/8/15, aged 26. *D* 6/8/15.
55. Lt F. H. Semple, 18 Bn, Company secretary, of Mosman, NSW. KIA 19/5/18, aged 29. *L* 12/8/15.
56. Pte W. E. Bendrey, 2 Bn, Telegraphist, of Uralla, NSW. RTA 8/18/16, aged 24. *D* 6/8/15.

the next thing was charge. (oh mummer.) The Turks poured machine gun fire, Artillery, shrapnell shells, and Bombs, rifle fire, Lydite, and the Lord only knows what into us. We had to get over 80 yards of Flat grounds covered in barbed wire.[57]

After crossing No Man's Land the southern half of the line met an unexpected check at the enemy's front trench: it was covered by sand and heavy pine logs. The men halted for a moment, baffled. Soon some raced on into the heart of the Turkish trench system, while others stood for nearly 15 minutes in the open and tore at the cover as the Turks below shot them. Then, one by one, they jumped down into the sudden darkness, and the waiting circles of the enemy.

Many Turks in the front trench had hidden in tunnels to escape the artillery bombardment, and the Australians, trapping them there, took the first line fairly easily. The heaviest fighting went on in the rear trenches. The attackers spread over this area looking for suitable points of entry, and some sharp hand to hand fighting took place, but within half an hour the attack was won. Seven or eight posts were established along the captured perimeter, the flanks were secured, a new front was presented to the enemy, and by eight that night the reserve battalion had been dribbled into the captured position. At some time during those hectic hours, or perhaps during the following day or so, Private McAnulty snatched a few moments to confide,

I've pulled through alright so far, just got a few minutes to spare now. I'm all out, can hardly stand up. On Friday when we got the word to charge Frank & I were on the extreme left of the charging party. There was a clear space of 100 yards to cross without a patch of cover. I can't realise how I got across it, I seemed to be in a sort of a trance. The rifle & machine gun fire was hellish. I remember dropping down when we reached their trenches, looked round & saw Frank & 3 other men alongside me. There was a big gap between us & the rest of our men . . . [who] were behind the shelter of the Turkish parapet . . . We were right out in the open . . . I yelled out to the other 4 chaps, 'This is suicide boys. I'm going to make a jump for it'.

57. Cpl R. P. Brett, 2 Bn, Labourer, of Sydney, NSW. KIA 8/1/18, aged 26. L c.12/9/15.

I thought they said alright we'll follow. I sprang to my feet in one jump[58]

At that moment he was killed, as he was writing.

He was one of thousands who died at Lone Pine, for the battle was only begun with the taking of the trenches. Unless they provoked counter-attacks which absorbed Turkish reserves, the Australians had done nothing worthwhile. The generals had hoped to embroil two Turkish reserve regiments in the Pine area; in time the soldiers attracted not only these, but an additional enemy division. The Turks launched the first of their counter-attacks during the night of 6 August, and for three days thereafter wave after wave battered against the Australian defences. The cruel bayonet resolved most of these assaults, but the bombs roared ceaselessly as men stood face to face hurling the hissing missiles, catching them and hurling them back, catching them again and again returning them, until at last they exploded.

They take anything from one to five seconds to explode after landing and if you are close enough the best thing to do is to throw them back . . . The other day one of our men picked up three in quick succession and threw them back to the enemy, but the fourth one was too many. It exploded in his hand blowing it off and also injured two others, one losing one eye and the other two eyes.[59]

The dead piled four and five deep along the trenches; they

were lying everywhere, on top of the parapet . . . in dugouts & communication trenches and saps, and it was impossible to avoid treading on them. In the second line the Turkish dead were lying everywhere, and if a chap wanted to sit down for a spell he was often compelled to squat on one of 'em.[60]

The stench of the dead bodies now is simply awful, as they have been fully exposed to the sun for several days, many have swollen terribly and have burst . . . many men wear gas protectors . . . there has been no attempt up to the present to either remove or bury [the dead], they are stacked out of the way in

58. McAnulty, *D* 7-12/8/15.
59. Semple, *L* 12/8/15.
60. Bendrey, *D* 8/8/15.

*any convenient place sometimes thrown up on to the parados
so as not to block up the trenches, there are more dead than
living . . . [and] we have been too buisy to do anything in the
matter.*[61]

A visible miasma hung over the fallen, but still the slashing bombs
burst, and still men mounted the bodies of their dead comrades to
stab and shoot. One man recalled that Lone Pine was like being 'in
a cage with a few playful lions & Tigers for a year or two'.[62] For
Australian soldiers generally, it was the bloodiest hand fighting of
the war.

On the night of 9 August the Turks, worn by incessant activity
and realising that the main threat to them lay elsewhere, abandoned
their efforts. They had pushed back the new Australian line at
points, chiefly in the south of Lone Pine, but they had lost more than
6000 men in the fighting, and had expended most of their available
reserves. The Australians had also employed additional reserves,
sending the 12th and 7th Battalions into the Pine by 8 August, and
the 7th Light Horse Regiment and elements of the 5th Battalion by
9 August. The men had done more than was required of them, but
over 2300 Australians were killed or wounded at Lone Pine, and
again, as at the landing, small units of men completely disappeared,
and larger units were decimated. About half those packs stacked
before the battle were not claimed. Their owners lay at Lone Pine,
and the maggots dropping from their bodies there were swept up by
the bucketful.

The Australians were to make more feints, but next they engaged
directly in the main Suvla offensive. On the night of 6 August New
Zealanders, Australians of the Fourth Brigade, and Indians moved
from the northern Anzac perimeter towards the heights approaching
Hill 971. These commanded the Dardanelles, and also their possession would secure the southern flank of the English at Suvla.
They were planned to fall that night. The men advanced through
rough and scrubby country and made good headway at first, but
later they lost impetus in the dark gullies and struggled confusedly
forward, falling further and further behind their timetable. Some
units lost themselves until after dawn, and by daylight none had
reached their objective. The leading New Zealanders were closest,

61. de Vine, *D* 9/8/15.
62. Brett, *D* c.12/9/15.

on Rhododendron Ridge, a thousand yards from Chunuk Bair, and a mile and a half from 971. The rest were still in the gullies, and nowhere were they near the ridge lines.

Those ridges were the key to the peninsula. No Turk defended them, for the nearest reserves were fighting at Lone Pine. Few British soldiers, if any, realised this, few grasped the importance of their task, and most, wearied by a night of toil and months of sickness and exertion, were too tired for further effort. The Australians in particular suffered from confused leadership, and the Fourth Brigade stopped where morning found it. The Indians advanced a little, then halted. The New Zealanders breakfasted, their leaders debated, and finally, at eleven a.m., they moved to attack Chunuk Bair.

It was too late. The Turks occupied the Hill 971-Chunuk Bair line during the morning, and stopped the New Zealand attack.[63] Subsequent British assaults made some headway, but the Turks brought up more reserves, and shot and bombed the attackers away. '[T]he Charge of the Light Brigade couldn't have been much livelier than this', an Australian wrote as his brigade struggled towards 971, 'nearly every yard of that valley was being swept by rifle fire.'[64] Although the New Zealanders held Chunuk Bair for a few hours on 8-9 August, the critical heights were never gained, and by 10 August the Turks had won. The Suvla offensive was the last great Allied throw on Gallipoli, and it gained nothing.

Australians made four further feint attacks, all on the early morning of 7 August. Three hundred of the 6th Battalion attacked German Officer's Trench but were driven back, losing 146 men. The 1st Light Horse Regiment occupied Turk trenches on Dead Man's Ridge with 200 men, but were forced out by flanking fire after suffering 154 casualties. Fifty-four troopers of the 2nd Light Horse Regiment attacked Turkish Quinn's: all were shot but one. These were very gallant attacks, epitomising the high degree of bravery and battle discipline of which Australians were capable, but they achieved nothing, and they sank agonisingly to bloody and inevitable failure.

The most tragic feint attack, at once the most gallant and the

63. The Turks came from their line in The Nek area, an unexpected source. They had been sent by their commander, Mustapha Kemal, who thus twice on Gallipoli rendered great service to his country.
64. Pte F. Clune, 16 Bn, Seaman, of Day Dawn, WA. RTA 31/10/15, aged 21. *L* 20/8/15.

most hopeless, was made by the 8th and 10th Light Horse Regiments against the Turkish trenches at The Nek. The Nek was a ridge 50 yards wide at the Anzac line, narrowing to about 30 at the Turkish front. The opposing trenches on it were about 20 yards apart, and at least five Turkish machine guns covered the intervening ground. Four lines of the light horse, each of about 150 men, were to seize the enemy front line and the maze of trenches and saps behind it, on Baby 700. They would be preceded by a naval and artillery bombardment, and were to attack at two minute intervals. The light horsemen were eager and confident, for this was their first great battle, and they expected to break from the interminable trenches into the open. Sick men hid or escaped from their doctors to be in the charge, and every man was impatient to emulate the Lone Pine attack they had watched the evening before.

At four on the afternoon of 6 August the artillery began a gentle bombardment. It intensified early on the 7th, but at four twenty three a.m., seven minutes before time, it ceased. The light horsemen stood still in the silence. In the enemy trenches soldiers cautiously emerged from shelter, lined their front two deep, fired short bursts to clear their machine guns, levelled their rifles, and waited. At four thirty precisely the first line of the 8th Light Horse leapt from their trenches. As their helmets appeared above the parapet, an awful fire broke upon them. Many were shot, but a line started forward. It crumpled and vanished within five yards. One or two men on the flanks dashed to the enemy's parapet before being killed, the rest lay still in the open.

The second line saw the fate of their friends. Over their heads the Turk fire thundered undiminished, drowning out any verbal order. In front the slope was shot bare of foliage. Beside them lay dead and wounded of the first line, hit before they cleared the trench. But they waited two minutes as ordered, then sprang forward. They were shot down. The 10th Light Horse filed into the vacant places in the trench. They could hardly have doubted their fate. They knew they would die, and they determined to die bravely, by running swiftly at the enemy. 'Boys, you have ten minutes to live,' their commanding officer told them, 'and I am going to lead you.'[65] Men

65. Lt Col J. W. Springthorpe, AAMC, Physician, of Armadale, Vic. b. 1855. D 29/8/15. Springthorpe was in Egypt, and was here repeating the statement of wounded survivors of the charge. Lt Col N. M. Brazier (Pastoralist and surveyor, of Kirup. WA. b. 1866) commanded 10 LH Regt at The Nek, but did not charge with it. Possibly the statement refers to Lt Col

shook hands with their mates, took position, and when the order came, charged into the open. The bullets of their expectant foe caught them as before, and tumbled them into the dust beside their comrades. Moves were made to halt the fourth line, but too late, and these men, too, climbed out to be killed.

It was now a little after five fifteen a.m.

you can imagine what it was like. Really too awful to write about. All your pals that had been with you for months and months blown and shot out of all recognition. There was no chance whatsoever of us gaining our point, but the roll call after was the saddest, just fancy only 47 answered their names out of close on 550 men. When I heard what the result was I simply cried like a child.[66]

Two hundred and thirty-four dead light horsemen lay in an area little larger than a tennis court. Most were there still in 1919, their bones whitening the ridge to observers half a mile away. One hundred and thirty-eight others were wounded, and about the same number otherwise survived, almost all of them from the later attacking waves.

They never had a hope of success. When they realised it they were not deterred, but, remaining true to their ideals and their country, went bravely to a worthless end. '[I]t was heroic,' wrote one who watched them, 'it was marvellous . . . yet it was murder.'[67] All the tragic waste of the Great War was contracted into their passing, for as they died the English troops at Suvla, plainly visible from The Nek, were making tea.

A general despondency settled on the Australian ranks after August. Twice, by the most gallant efforts, they had fought to win a decision. Twice they had been baulked, not, they felt, by their own failings, but by the misdirection of their leaders. Their sacrifices had won nothing, and could win nothing unless properly directed. The realisation crippled their fervour, and they grew too weary and discouraged to welcome further fighting. As during the depressing days

A. H. White (Maltster, of Ballarat and Elsternwick, Vic. KIA 7/8/15, aged 33), the 8 LH Regt's CO, who led the first line and was killed less than 10 yards from the Australian trench. The statement would fit White's frame of mind at that time. See Bean, *Official History*, II, p. 612.
66. 2/Lt C. C. D. St Pinnock, 57 Bn, Broker, of Croydon, NSW. KIA 19/8/16, aged 30. *L* 15/8/15.
67. Cameron, *D* 18/8/15.

after the landing, a few men hoped for a wound to take them from Gallipoli; and a new type of comment began to appear: 'They are lucky who get away from here wounded . . . It is quite common for men to go mad here. The strain on the nerves is so severe',[68] and, 'Now is the time we feel what *war is*. Reaction is setting in—and I can notice several "old hands" cracking up',[69] and,

Ones nerves get very nervy . . . having to be on a continual strain of looking, watching and listening all the time. You will see some chaps walking along when all of a sudden they will duck behind something and get under cover when it is only a steam boat blowing off steam . . . everyone laughts at the time but still nearly everyone gets doing it some time.[70]

After August the Gallipoli campaign became almost entirely concerned with disease and its effects. The percentage of men reporting sick had fallen to 3.5 before the August battles: it rose to 8.6 in mid-August, and to 8.9 three weeks later. It fell when colder weather killed the flies, but it remained high for the rest of the campaign, so high that many sick were obliged to remain on the peninsula. Statistically the health of the troops had collapsed; in fact, more men were yielding to afflictions they had formerly defied. It was a certain indication of shaken morale.

Although the Anzacs were battered, few were broken. In September an expert survey judged three quarters of them totally unfit for active service, yet most stayed proudly in their trenches, determined to fight to the end. But for the first time they neither liked it nor felt obliged to like it, and they complained far more readily of discomforts they had scarcely mentioned before August:

One of the greatest difficulties here is the shortage of water . . . I had . . . the first [shave] for a week and my face was coated with the dust and grime I had got through all the recent fighting and trench digging. After I had finished the water in my mess tin . . . [was] muddy . . . and I washed my face in that and . . . [then] had my tea out of the same tin[71]

I have not had a wash now for 4 weeks, nor had my clothes off. I accomplish my toilet with the corner of a towel steeped in a

68. Devlin, *L* 2/9/15.
69. Armitage, *D* 24/11/15.
70. Lt S. P. Boulton, 2 FAB, Bank officer, of Sydney, NSW. DOW 3/10/18, aged 28. *L* 11/9/15.
71. Semple, *L* 13/8/15.

2 ounce tobacco tin. Water for washing purposes is out of the question . . .[72]

Tucker has been a drawback. Always the same bully and biscuits . . . if a cove is lucky by paying 2/- a tin for milk he can have luxuries in that way . . . [or] 3/- for an ordinary cake of chocolate[73]

I had the misfortune to break another tooth a couple of days ago a good back tooth . . . when I was trying to bite through a particularly hard biscuit.[74]

immediately I opened . . . [my tin of jam] the flies rushed [it] . . . all fighting amongst themselves. I wrapped my overcoat over the tin and gouged out the flies, then spread the biscuit, held my hand over it, and drew the biscuit out of the coat. But a lot of flies flew into my mouth and beat about inside . . . I nearly howled with rage . . . Of all the bastards of places this is the greatest bastard in the world.[75]

a wash would be a great luxury, lice and flies . . . [are] in everything, I wear my clothes inside out every few days, but still the brutes are scratched for.[76]

The worst things here (Turks excepted) are the flies in millions, lice . . . & everlasting bully-beef & biscuit, & too little water. Also it will be a good thing when we get a chance to bury some of the dead.[77]

On 28 November snow fell, the first cold weather most Australians had experienced for 16 months. '[W]e had no covering of any sort and just had to grin and bear it . . . [we stood] to arms . . . all night . . . it snowed on us all night and all the next day.'[78] Physically, this new trial was perhaps the hardest to bear: the blizzard froze soldiers to death, and 3000 men from Anzac (and 12,000 from Suvla) were evacuated with frostbite and exposure.

72. Capt F. Coen, 18 Bn, Barrister, of Yass, NSW. KIA 28/7/16, aged 32. *L* 12/8/15.
73. Lt E. S. Dowling, 1 LH Regt, Station overseer, of Narromine, NSW. DOW 18/11/17, aged 21. *L* 19/8/15.
74. Pte P. S. Jackson, 11 LH Regt, Book keeper, of Kynuna, Qld. DOW 19/4/17, aged 27. *L* 2/12/15.
75. I. L. Idriess, *The Desert Column* (Angus & Robertson), p. 46 (–/9/15). (Tpr, 5 LH Regt, Miner, of Grafton, NSW. RTA 15/2/18, aged 30.)
76. Hunter, *L* 6/10/15.
77. Capt D. G. Campbell, 5 FAB, Grazier, of Bombala, NSW. KIA 21/10/17, aged 30. *L* 11/8/15.
78. Hunter, *L* 8/12/15.

Above all the monotony of their lives and the lack of progress wore down the hopes of the Australians. An eternal round of patrolling, a little sniping perhaps, tunnelling, sentry duty, fatigues, and just sitting in trenches filled their days, and none of these things could bring victory. Few men were keen to risk a great battle under their present British generals, but most wanted to shake away the deadly stalemate that had settled upon them. '[T]he strain is gradually telling', a soldier admitted, '& if I stick it out for more than 3 months without a change I'll be agreeably surprised.'[79] From the end of August medical officers continually urged the relief of the Anzac Corps. In September men began to be sent to Lemnos or Imbros for rest, and as those remaining wearily waited their turn, 'the ever-repeated question [was] "When are we going to be relieved" . . . we all think weve earned a decent spell.'[80] Men promised relief were 'very thankful too, as . . . nearly all are feeling "run down" . . . we will have no difficulty carrying on, but at the same time, we are eagerly looking forward to be relieved.'[81]

But the luckiest soldiers were spelled for six weeks, and most for less than a fortnight. By late November some still had not gone, and many who had gone returned to Anzac looking as though they had not left it. A wound was the only passport to genuine rest, and after August the wounded were not anxious to return to Anzac. 'I have seen quite enough of the glories of war,' one wrote, 'now I am quite willing to have some of the curses of peace. If the Australians lose many more men there will not be many left in Australia. I hope that they will see reason shortly and stop it altogether.'[82] Another recalled early in 1916,

'Holiday wounds' were anticipated with great joy . . . I have seen [wounded] men . . . beam with smiles, when half an hour before that same face wore a haggard expression; but it must be remembered that these men were exhausted through months of service under awful conditions . . . I've heard . . . friends . . . say I would give you a fiver (or a tenner) for [your wound][83]

79. Capt E. A. Warren, 27 Bn, Bank manager, of Mt Gambier, SA. KIA 5/11/16, aged 29. L 17/10/15.
80. Lt J. M. Aitken, MC, 11 Bn, Accountant, of Kalgoorlie, WA. KIA 10/8/18, aged 27. L 13/9/15.
81. Ellsworth, L 11/9/15.
82. Sgt W. P. Beales, 4 Bn, Gardener, of Brisbane, Qld (b. England). KIA 3/3/17, aged 31. L 21/8/15.
83. Youdale, D –/4/16 (re –/10/15).

and a reinforcement in Egypt reported,

I was told by an A.M.C. man that the wounded soldiers from the early contingents were all eager to return to the front; but those who come now are glad to have done their bit and content to let others take their place.[84]

The unlucky, who were not wounded, were without comfort, and often their thoughts returned to peace and the homes they had left so willingly. One soldier confessed, 'if Johnie Turk was to declare the war over tomorrow I would be the happiest man on earth. I've had quite enough. If you ever catch me looking for gore again—well you can kick me.'[85] A private declared, 'we are all longing to be [home] . . . we're sick of the game of fighting & it will be a tremendous relief to know that its all over & we can go home & live in piece'[86], and Lance Corporal Mitchell thought of 'a land of sunshine warmth and happiness—a land of sweet scents and bright colours—home. But the track home is through a winding trail of smoke and blood, stench and torment. How many of us will reach there unbroken?'[87] These were not the men of August 1914.

Still they wished to see the war won before they went home. They were too weak to march, some veterans told Birdwood, but they would fight.[88] 'If England will only send us more men and ships. we can get through this job O.K.', Lieutenant Armitage decided, '. . . It's no good making a fuss now over the mess that has been made—that can wait—what should be done is a determined strong push . . . we'd be through this show in 3 weeks'.[89]

No buffet had broken their resolution. Some Australians felt transient doubts about the fighting ('The fact that they died well is no answer to the question as to why they should die at all'[90]), but these could not long survive, because they added pointlessness to discomfort and probable death. Men needed to find purpose in their

84. Pte T. L. Young, 28 Bn, Teacher, of Perth, WA (b. England). DOW 2/1/17, aged 32. *L* 16/11/15.
85. Maj W. T. Mundell, 15 Bn, Commission agent, of Moonee Ponds, Vic. DOW 19/8/17, aged 28. *L* 20/8/15.
86. 2/Lt E. W. Harris, 3 MG Coy, Civil servant, of Claremont, WA. KIA 5/5/17, aged 28. *L* 9/10/15.
87. Mitchell, *D* 12/11/15.
88. Letter from Birdwood to his wife, 18 August 1915, in R. R. James, *Gallipoli*, p. 303.
89. Armitage, *D* 21/10/15.
90. Richards, *D* 1/8/15.

actions, to make them bearable, and from the faiths of their past
they discovered several justifications which supported them. Private
Aitken admitted that a soldier's life was hard, but 'it also hardens
one . . . broadens ones outlook on life, and . . . teaches one one's
duty to humanity.'[91] After Lone Pine another wrote, '[We have all]
suffered some casualty. But we all have the knowledge of . . . brave
fighting for a just cause'.[92] 'It looks as if we are going to be here for
months & months & months', a third complained, '. . . we are going
to have a hell of a time here . . . each day Australia appears to fade
further & further away from my longing eyes. Still we are out to do
the job so must not complain if it is more arduous than we expected'.[93] 'What a gigantic conflict this has turned into', a fourth soldier
reflected,

*the loss of life is appalling; rivers of blood . . . the trenches red
with the life blood of my comrades . . . Sometimes I weary so
of it all and long for peace; it is only the fact that the safety of
our loved ones, the integrity of our Empire is at stake that lifts
ones spirits up again, to face the roughing and the grim horrors
of the battlefield.*[94]

The Australians remained convinced that what they did was worthwhile and necessary. Duty, although daily growing harder and
harsher, kept them firmly to the task they had undertaken.

Most of the new arrivals after August landed with their martial
enthusiasms intact, as though the war-weary men about them were
invisible. 'We are right in the soup now, and it is not half bad, in
fact we are having a real picnic',[95] a Victorian student declared, and
another student reported, 'Well as for the life. It certainly appeals
to me so far. The screaming shells and spluttering machine guns are
music I have dreamed of since childhood.'[96] About two months after
he landed a photographer commented, 'we have a tip top time here
the experience is all one could want but of course we have not had a
shot at hand to hand yet but I am looking forward to it and so are
all the boys'.[97] 'The military life suits me splendidly &, despite the

91. Aitken, *L* 18/8/15.
92. Cotton, *L* –/8/15.
93. McCrae, *L* 7/9/15.
94. Lt C. H. Ruddle, 9 Bn, School teacher, of Bundaberg, Qld. DOW 23/7/16, aged 30. *L* 5/12/15.
95. Alcock, *L* 27/9/15.
96. Worrall, *L* 19/10/15.
97. Sgt D. L. Bleechmore, 22 Bn, Photographer, of Brighton, Vic. KIA 5/8/16, aged 25. *L* –/10/15.

occasional hardships . . . I am tougher and fitter than ever before. There is no monotony in life out here and excitement is never lacking',[98] a recent arrival remarked in mid-November, and in December a late reinforcement wrote, 'Have at last reached my destination and am agreeably surprised with it and find the conditions exciting. So far the weather has been glorious and the food good.'[99] The veterans were reporting snow and hard biscuits about this time.

Men who reached Anzac after August were not given an opportunity to fight a great battle there. This contented a few:

My word war is a horror alright, until one comes right into it & sees the real thing he has no idea of what it means, glorious charges, magnificent defences, heroic efforts in this or that direction all boil down to the one thing, the pitting of human beings against the most scientific machinery & the result can be seen in the papers[100]

But most were disappointed by the mundane routine of the trenches. Several noted that the Gallipoli fighting was 'unreal', and 'didn't feel like real warfare', and was not much different from being in George Street, and a light horse reinforcement wrote,

It is funny war here—dug into the ground like great rabbit warrens, with the enemy only forty yards, in some places only five away, and also dug in, and often days elapse and you never see a Turk, in fact . . . lots of us . . . haven't seen one at all yet . . . really a feeling gets hold of you and you wish for the order [to charge] to come.[101]

A Second Division soldier commented,

Abdul is only about 60 to 200 yards off . . . We snipe at him and he snipes at us . . . This 'sit-down' style of warfare is different to what any of us anticipated. Nevertheless we are here as a garrison with a definite duty before us. We are hoping hourly

98. Lt O. R. Law, 48 Bn, Journalist, of East Torrens, SA. KIA 14/8/16, aged 26. *L* 18/11/15.
99. Capt R. J. Henderson, MC & bar, 13 Bn, Electrician, of Drummoyne, NSW. DOW 13/5/18, aged 32. *L* 12/12/15.
100. Capt W. H. Sheppard, 17 Bn, Insurance surveyor, of Summer Hill, NSW. RTA 23/7/17, aged 27. *L* 28/8/15. Lt H. V. Wood, 16 Bn, Carpenter, of Woodville, SA (b. Scotland). b. 1889. *D* 10/11/15 refers to a new arrival who deliberately shot off his foot. Self inflicted wounds were rare on Gallipoli.
101. Hunter, *L* 25/9/15.

that we may be attacked but the Turk is about as cautious as we are.[102]

'The zip, zip, zip of the bullets overhead and the occasional boom of the big guns, seemed . . . [not] to *herald that* other phase in this great game to which we have so anxiously looked . . . *our* Mecca . . . a *"Charge"*',[103] a man told his parents, and a young farmer concluded, 'What wouldn't we give for a go at Abdul. It seems to be our duty to continually watch him'.[104] The impatience of the new men contrasted markedly with the grim lethargy of most old soldiers.

Yet all soldiers still fought the war for similar ends. Their world rested upon King and country, upon duty, honour, patriotism, manhood, and courage, and they would die for their world. The folly of some generals had compounded their difficulties, but that had not lessened the justice of their cause, and they were determined to win victory, whatever it cost. If the Empire's lustre was tarnished it still meant a great deal, and few Australians on Gallipoli ever considered abandoning its defence. They remained willing to fight.

Early in December 1915 they learnt that they would no longer have to fight. Anzac was to be evacuated. In one respect, the troops welcomed the news. Daily they saw more and more of their comrades sickening in the trenches, and themselves growing weaker without prospect of alleviation, and the miseries of winter approaching. One soldier, a fit man in December, had lost four stone in weight since he landed in August, and he was one who had not fought the great battles on the peninsula. Many Australians were ready to seek a better land, which would give them rest from the trenches.

Some were glad to leave for other reasons. The campaign seemed hopeless: 'necessity is imperative. We can not do good by staying here',[105] and, 'We are all very sorry to have left Anzac without gaining our objective after 9 months hard efforts, but the position in front of us was impossible, and our position untenable during the winter months, the whole business has been a very sorry mess up and a sheer waste of men & material.'[106] But to most Australians

102. Capt H. F. Curnow, 22 Bn, Public servant, of Bendigo, Vic. KIA 5/8/16, aged 23. *L* 22/9/15.
103. Capt W. A. Cull, 23 Bn, Coachbuilder, of Hamilton, Vic. POW –/4/17 and RTA 8/4/18, aged 22. *L* 15/9/15.
104. Lt A. L. Dardel, 12 FAB, Orchardist, of Batesford, Vic. DOW 8/5/17, aged 24. *L* 1/11/15.
105. Coen, *L* 17/12/15.
106. de Vine, *D* 20/12/15.

these considerations were least important. Whatever their difficulties they were not men to flee from them. On Lemnos after the evacuation, the survivors of Anzac were given Christmas billies from home. On each a kangaroo was printed, pitching a Turk off the peninsula with his tail. That hurt, for defeat had not been the fault of Australian soldiers. On Gallipoli the men of the AIF learnt to put their trust first in themselves: they never forgot this lesson, and thereafter they fought not only for King and country, but to maintain their own reputations.

ANZAC

4 Nationhood, Brotherhood and Sacrifice

> 1915. Australia's entry into the Company of nations—no finer
> entry in all history ... to have leapt into Nationhood, Brotherhood
> and Sacrifice at one bound ... what a year:— never can Australia
> see its like again.
>
> Captain F. B. Stanton, 14th Battalion,[1] 9 December 1915

The Australians answered a vitally important question at the landing. They fulfilled their expectations about their fighting prowess,
and they proved their country to the world: they passed the test of
battle. Their own reinforcements, on first seeing the ground captured
that Sunday, recorded amazement and admiration at their feat, and
soldiers of the Empire hailed them not only as fit to rank with
Britain's heroes, but as having performed the finest deed in her
history. 'No troops in the world can have fought better,'[2] wrote an
old Scottish regular who had seen eight years' active service on the
Indian frontier, while a physician in Egypt, an Imperialist and
former critic of Australian indiscipline, exclaimed, 'The outstanding
fact—sunny Australians, careless in language, in many externals,
including discipline, have unflinchingly undergone a strenuous
preparation, faced its ordeal more than courageously, and ... come
out with a "victor's and a hero's crown".'[3] Men of the British navy,
the shield of the Empire, praised the Australian accomplishment,
'saying that they would take their hats off to the Australians after
that day ... They also said they never saw such gallantry and never
heard such language before'.[4] Indian soldiers called the Anzacs the
'white Gurkhas', a high accolade, for every Australian rated the
Gurkha among the best of the Empire's soldiers.

1. Bank clerk, of Stawell, Vic. KIA 11/4/17, aged 23.
2. Davidson, L 13/5/15.
3. Springthorpe, D 3/5/15.
4. Sgt D. J. Anderson, 8 Bn, Pharmaceutical student, of Bendigo, Vic. KIA
16/6/15, aged 19. L –/5/15.

The men of the AIF heard all this proudly. None could surpass what they had done, they believed, and the Empire knew it. Their new status placed them high, and for the first time in their lives an allegiance to Imperial traditions became inadequate. Men who once had persistently worn English uniforms now clung to their Australian issue until long after it was tattered to rags, and by late May wounded in Cairo were objecting to using the British Soldiers Club because of its name. An Australian NCO who had previously considered his associates 'malcontents' and criticised their drunkenness and brawling and indiscipline, wrote after the landing, 'the boys behaved steadier than many veterans would have . . . [they] acted on their own initiative, and . . . so saved a very critical situation.'[5] After reviewing the events of that famous Sunday, an ambulance-man on a ship off Anzac noted prophetically, 'I really believe [today] will mark an era in Australian history. On this day Australians proved themselves.'[6] Another Australian told his mother, 'it must be a comfort to know that we all have done our duty & held our own with the best troops in the world. Australia's rag time army is not so bad after all'.[7] It was more than a comfort to his countrymen. It opened the door to a new world, and it radically amended the former balance in Australian minds between nation and Empire, a change which endured in their own lives, and in the history of their country.

Australians accordingly looked more critically at the performance of English soldiers. They saw much to admire: the young English midshipmen who piloted the tows at the landing, the gallant and dogged Twenty Ninth Division fighting at Cape Helles, and the deeds of some of those who attacked with them during the August offensive. Yet few could accept the barrier between British officers and their men, and many considered the former's punctilios and the latter's docility inefficient in a fighting force.

At critical points during the fighting, events confirmed their disquiet. The Royal Naval Division, which had relieved part of the Australian line at the end of April, lost some trenches to the Turks soon afterwards, and although with Australian assistance they shortly regained them, the reverse shook confidence in their ability.

5. Aitken, *D* 29/4/15.
6. RQMS H. E. Gissing, 14 Fld Amb, Chemist, of Ashfield, NSW. b. 1888. *D* 25/4/15.
7. Pte A. J. Morrice, 13 Bn, Time keeper, of Dubbo, NSW. RTA 7/9/15, aged 41. *L* 11/6/15.

When the Second Brigade went to Cape Helles in May, at least one Australian private was 'quite astonished at the behaviour of the English troops while under fire, they are arrogant cowards in comparison with the colonials.'[8] These objections paled beside the bitterness directed against the Englishmen who had landed and dallied at Suvla. Australians regarded that blunder as the fault of English generals particularly, but some did not exonerate the British soldiery. An English university graduate in Egypt reported, 'The Australians who have returned here from the front profess to believe that the British soldier is not much good at fighting. They say that they take trenches and the British soldiers lose them again. They admit that the British regulars are good soldiers but not the New Army.'[9] This Englishman doubted the truth of the reports, but Australians at the front emphatically asserted them. One stated that he had lost his earlier respect for the Imperial Army because his comrades had to retake positions it lost,[10] and a corporal seconded to a British brigade at Suvla declared after returning to his battalion,

Glad we are, to get back here with the boys. Our army has been called a ragtime one, but never again will I think it so, after the poor miserable crowd we have been with. The lack of organisation, spirit and individual initiative was enough to break a man's heart.[11]

An Australian officer complained towards the end of the Suvla fighting, 'I wish Kitchener would send us *soldiers* not boys to do the business. If what I have seen (with a few glorious exceptions) are trained soldiers—well pack up and leave the Empire'. Yet, like almost every Australian, he remained loyal to his Empire, and he found a way to reconcile his loyalty with his contempt for the New Army. 'We call the Regulars—Indians and Australians—'British'—but Pommies are nondescript', he wrote, and later, 'The British Army contains many good ones—but there are others who lack initiative, endurance, and resource, and God help England if she relies on these last . . . this war has made me intensely British and absolutely Australian.'[12] Others in the AIF distinguished 'British'

8. Sgt R. L. Hampton, 5 Bn, Chemist, of Newport, Vic. RTA 23/7/18 and DOD 7/4/19, aged 26. *D* 13/5/15.
9. Young, *L* 26/11/15.
10. Lt H. E. Malpas, 7 MG Coy, Draughtsman, of Unley, SA. KIA 7/8/16, aged 22. *L* –/9/15.
11. Guppy, *D* 3/9/15.
12. Armitage, *D* 29/8/15, 29/8/15, 18/1/16.

from 'Australian', thus qualifying their Imperial ardour and reinforcing their pride in their own capacities. An English immigrant educated at Rugby School decided,

the right *type of Australian is a real firm fellow and can't be beaten anywhere, that does not include the street corner wowsers of the towns but chiefly the country lads. Any of Kitchener's men and Territorials look very awkward beggars beside the Australian, besides of duller intellect (that is judging the average by appearances). The British seem to be all boots, and gapes, but the Australian usually looks as if he knew what he was after.*[13]

This disturbed the assumptions of pre-war years.

Australian soldiers could now support their preference for a less rigid disciplinary code. The English system, when applied to citizen soldiers, had not proved itself in battle. Their system had. On 24 April a private of the 2nd Battalion was court martialled for indiscipline, but the finding was not made public before the battalion went into action next day. On 26 April the private was recommended for a decoration for courage and coolness during bayonet rushes on Russell's Top, in June he was again recommended and promoted to corporal, and in August he won a DCM at Lone Pine. But later in Egypt another court martial demoted him to private again, for indiscipline. Throughout the war similar apparent contradictions in AIF behaviour frequently bewildered British authorities, for success convinced many Australians that what they did out of the line—off the job—was their concern, and that parade ground drill in no way improved a man's fighting abilities. 'As long as they are safe or down at the base [the English troops] outclass our ragtime army', observed the private who had watched English soldiers with dismay at Helles, 'for when our work is done and mind relaxed we throw all cares to the wind & become an orderly rabble.'[14] 'What is a soldier?', asked Sergeant Aitken,

Roughly speaking, he is a component part of a huge machine which has been drilled & trained to such an extent that it obeys an order implicitly, unquestioningly . . . A soldier will think, maybe, but will not act without orders . . .

13. Sgt R. W. W. Adams, 11 Bn, Farmer, of Katanning, WA (b. England). DOW 26/7/16, aged 26. *L* 1/10/15.
14. Hampton, *L* 13/5/15.

> *... the Australian is not a soldier, but he is a fighter, a born fighter; each Australian has his separate individuality & his priceless initiative which made him ... infinitely better than the clockwork soldier.*
>
> *Discipline irks him, he is not used to it, & its a thing he can never be made to thoroughly understand; every man ... considers himself the equal of every other man, its not in his programme to take peremptory orders, but he looks upon a request ... almost ... [as] a command.*[15]

'The Australian is ... independent and high spirited,' Private Richards reflected,

> *and ... should the military folk succeed in breaking that spirit the Australian will no longer be the fearless fighting man that he is now ... Heart and soul [Australians] ... are here to fight, not simply to obey fruitless orders issued only for the sake of enforcing authority*[16]

'My men are the "Blind 50" in Camp or Barracks,' an officer recorded of his platoon, 'but they're grand soldiers in the trenches ... Active Serv. discipline is very diff. to Camp or Barracks.'[17] The subsequent English complaint, that Australians were good fighters in the line but bad soldiers out of it, was to most in the AIF a virtue.

After the landing Australians were less willing than ever to respect English officers. 'We were going along', recalled a trooper in 1916,

> *when we heard a fairy voice say 'Hey you men, why don't you salute?' We told him we were Australians, but the officer said he did not care who we were ... we would have to salute before we passed that way, so we said we would go another way ... [we] went nearly half a mile ... rather than salute him.*[18]

Some men would seldom defer even to Australian officers. Monash[19] reprimanded his brigade for its offhandedness, complaining that men kept pipes in their mouths or stood easy while superiors addressed

---

15. Aitken, *L* 29/8/15.
16. Richards, *D* 21/9/15.
17. Armitage, *D* 20/6/15.
18. Youdale, *D* –/4/16 (re –/9/15).
19. Gen Sir J. Monash, GCMG, KCB, VD. Commanded 4 Bde 1914-16, 3 Div 1916-18, Aust Corps 1918. b. 1865.

them, played cards on sentry duty, dressed carelessly, and left trenches untidy. Most officers tolerated many of these things, and more. 'Ullo—where'd yer get the prisoners?', men asked a private escorting three of the First Division's generals about the lines, and the story goes that another private informed a bristling General Walker[20] that judging by the crossed swords and battle-axes on his shoulders, the general was either a butcher or a pioneer. Birdwood was told to 'Duck, you silly old dill' while swimming under shrapnel fire at the beach one day, and he ducked. He knew the difficulty of enforcing a mere formal obedience, and how well his men fought in a real trial. Like many officers he accepted the standards of his men, and judged and was judged by the test of battle.

Yet, the significance they attached to their achievements in battle notwithstanding, many Australians behaved as though war were a game. Before the landing an old soldier in the 11th Battalion told his men that flying bullets sounded like small birds passing overhead. During the battalion's dash across the open water north of Ari Burnu to the beach on 25 April, a man recalled the comment, looked skyward, and remarked to his neighbour, 'Just like little birds, ain't they Snow?'. The whole boat collapsed into laughter. In other boats at the landing men played cards under fire, and talked and joked. 'They want to cut that shooting out,' a soldier protested, 'somebody might get killed.' 'They're carrying this too far, they're using ball ammunition', another exclaimed, and the merriment rose to mingle with the roar of the shells. As they touched the shore, one man climbed from his boat remarking that it was bloody poor farming country,[21] and at least two, while bullets kicked the sand around them, pulled out vest cameras and photographed the scene before strolling on. Other Australians, too eager to dally on the beach, laughed and sang as they charged up the hills, and their casual gait as they broke the dawn skyline on Plugge's Plateau first informed watchers on the ships that the covering force was ashore. They had come to their greatest and gayest adventure, and they were enjoying it.

Throughout the Gallipoli campaign no extremity ever shook their studied defiance. The beach at Anzac was always under aimed

---

20. Lt Gen Sir H. B. Walker, KCB, KCMG, DSO. Commanded 1 Div 1915-18. b. 1862.
21. Later another commented, 'This . . . is . . . scrubby country too poor for the most part to run one bandicoot to the square mile & then he wouldn't get fat.' (Sheppard, *L* 28/8/15.)

Turkish shrapnel fire, yet crowds swam there daily, 'just like Manly Beach on Sunday, there were hundreds of men swimming and diving off punts & things . . . we don't seem to take much notice of shells now.'[22] Swimmers were rarely forced ashore, and under fire entertained onlookers with remarks like, 'Hope there's no sharks about', or, when wounded, 'Cripes, I've been torpedoed.' After one day on Anzac some 2nd Battalion reinforcements, waiting to charge Lone Pine, watched the dust dancing in No Man's Land: 'Talk about shrapnel, it sounded for all the world like blanky hail . . . A shell burst in the trench just behind Roper and I, and upended both of us . . . but we [just] shook hands and sat down again. And then Mac had to have his little joke, and wanted to know [how] was it for a 2d car fare to Glebe.'[23]

Men used the language of sport to describe the game they were playing, comparing the tension before battle with that before a football match, or describing their time in the line as an innings. At Lone Pine a soldier looked at the calico patches on his mate's back and commented, 'Fancy going on the field without our numbers.' 'My word we do give the poor old Turks a terrible doing', a man noted on 19 May, 'I think it is wonderful how our boys love fighting. It is just the same as sport. Australia can hold its own against the world . . . in sport, and . . . in fighting',[24] and a private considered, 'War is a great game, and I wouldn't have missed our scrap for all the tea in China.'[25]

During the early weeks the game they played excluded the Turk. As boys they had learnt to hate their Empire's adversaries, and to revile the Turks for barbarous atrocities. At the landing many believed willingly that Turks had mutilated Australian dead and wounded, and some accepted the most improbable accounts of Turkish barbarity: on 27 April a wounded Australian wrote, 'We have one man here with his tongue cut out, another lay wounded and a Turk cried "Australian" and drove his bayonet in, but was shot and the bayonets work was not completed'.[26]

The invaders consequently showed their foes little mercy. They hunted down the Turkish snipers hidden in the scrub behind their

22. Ryrie, *L* 1/6/15.
23. Bendrey, *D* 6/8/15.
24. Lt W. H. E. Hale, 12 Bn, Commercial traveller, of Beaconsfield, WA. KIA 5/10/17, aged 29. *L* 19/5/15.
25. Buley, *Glorious Deeds*, p. 161.
26. Donkin, *D* 27/4/15.

front, and killed them. They shot every Turk on sight, firing on enemy burial parties which were doing the Australians good service by their labour, striking down men attempting to cross the lines in surrender, and exclaiming after a successful shot, 'Take that you black b-----s.' 'I shot 3 snipers dead to-day,' reported a New South Wales farmer, Archie Barwick, 'they were picking off our poor fellows who were hobbling down to the dressing stations, the first one I killed I took his belt off to keep as a souvenir of my first kill with the rifle. the other two I laid out beautifully I felt a lot more satisfied after that for I had got even'. Like many Australians, he described his bayonet work unhesitatingly: 'I can recollect driving the bayonet into the body of one fellow quite clearly, & he fell right at my feet & when I drew the bayonet out, the blood spurted from his body', and later that day he bayonetted another Turk, which made him feel very proud.[27]

Hatred of the Turk died suddenly from almost every Australian about a month after the landing. At dawn on 19 May, most of the 42,000 Turks in the trenches opposite attacked the Anzac line. Large numbers were shot in No Man's Land, and only a few entered the Anzac trenches before being killed. They had no hope of success, but gallantly they maintained their attempts, coming on to be slaughtered, their courage unshaken, until by noon 10,000 lay killed or wounded. Then, finally, their surviving comrades sank into the scrub, and late in the afternoon the Turkish leaders gave up the assault.

The Anzacs lost 160 killed and 468 wounded: they had evened the score. 'I'll admit to a certain savage pleasure in firing to kill,'[28] one stated that day, and later another recalled, 'we had a gorgeous time . . . for two solid hours we blazed away . . . our rifles got too hot to hold and the bolts jammed but we got others . . . as it got lighter . . . hundreds fell in a vain endeavour to make a bolt for safety—we had them before they got 5 yds.'[29]

This suggests sport, and there was that sense, but more importantly the bravery of their assailants profoundly affected the Australians. 'My rifle was in at the start, blazing at those shadowy forms,' wrote Corporal Mitchell, '"Oh you poor devils", was all I

27. Sgt A. A. Barwick, 1 Bn, Farmer, of Woolbrook, NSW (b. England). b. 1890. *D* I, pp. 106 (re 26/4/15), 108-9, 109-10 (re 27/4/15).
28. Aitken, *L* 19/5/15.
29. Duke, *L* 29/5/15.

could say, thinking only of the fate of the unfortunates if they got right up to us. It was a massacre.'[30] The Turk had proved a normal man and a brave soldier, displaying those same virtues Australians ranked highest. Animosity gave way to admiration, and the Turk became part of the game. 'Saida [goodbye]—play you again next Saturday,' Australians shouted to the retreating enemy after the attack, and that attitude, a friendly but determined rivalry, became part of life on Gallipoli.

Five days later, on 24 May, an eight hours armistice was arranged to bury the dead, for their stench permeated the entire Anzac area. Enemies met, saluted each other, and exchanged photographs and cigarettes.[31] '[T]he time was taken up by making friends with the Turks, who do not seem to be a very bad sort of chap after all', remarked Sergeant de Vine, 'After today most of our opinions on the Turks were changed, they certainly play the game better than the Germans do.'[32] When they had finished the work, and the time set had almost expired, each side waved a smiling goodbye before dropping back into its trenches.

The Turk 'played the game' by keeping the terms of the armistice, and thereafter the Australians regarded him almost affectionately, christening him 'Jacko', or 'Abdul', or 'Johnnie Turk', and communicating with him frequently during lulls in the fighting. Particularly after August, they threw bully beef and condensed milk in exchange for boiled onions, and swapped cigarettes, knives, photographs and badges between the lines. Men sometimes walked safely into No Man's Land and even to the opposing trenches to retrieve gifts thrown short, and garrisons wrote each other notes of friendly abuse or of commiseration for the life of a soldier. At Quinn's Post,

a note was thrown over by the Turks, evidently in answer to one from our chaps asking the distance to Constantinople . . . 'You ask how far it is to Constantinople. How long will you please be in getting There?' They used a knife as a weight when they threw the note and asked for it to be returned. It was thrown back but fell short . . . On being told where it was they asked our chaps not to fire while one of them got it . . . On

30. Mitchell, *D* 19/5/15.
31. The trenches opposite were also reconnoitred, and dead ground in No Man's Land used as graves to fill it in. (Pte G. E. Gower, 15 Bn, Grocer, of Brisbane, Qld. RTA 8/5/16, aged 25. *D* 24/5/15.)
32. de Vine, *D* 24/5/15.

another occasion there must have been a German officer approaching, for all of a sudden the Turks began signalling to our chaps to get down in their trenches. They immediately took the hint and then a machine gun began to play along the parapet from end to end. Of course, no damage was done. This shows something of the fairness with which the Turk fights.[33]

Another man, probably at Quinn's, recorded,

we got an interpreter up, and he sang out to [the Turks] . . . & finally got about a dozen . . . Up on the parapet having a 'yap' to him—and one of our chaps went over and got a cigarette case from them . . .

When we want to send a note over we 'ring them up' by knocking a stone on a tin periscope—& they answer by waving a periscope. Then if the note gets into their trench alright, they give another 'wave' as an acknowledgement.[34]

'Did I ever tell you of Ernest', inquired a third soldier,

Ernest was a gaunt old Turk who used to come out of his trench every morning to gather firewood (our chaps never fired a shot for a long while) They used to chuck him tins of bully and he'd salaam and thank them. Poor old Ernest died a sudden death one morning when a new lot come in the trenches.[35]

Anzac and Turk arranged shooting matches, each contestant in turn firing at a target waved above the enemy trenches. Scores were signalled back to the marksmen, and occasionally bets were made on the result. Opponents also exchanged verbal sallies: one night in June Australians at Quinn's put up some barbed wire in front of their trenches, only to find in the morning that the Turks had stolen it, and re-erected it before their own lines. 'Hey Turk', an Australian called. 'Hello Australia', came the reply. 'The John Hops are after you for pinching our wire.' Sometimes the jesting was more macabre: 'Hey Turk'. 'Hello Australia'. 'How many of you are in [i.e. will share] a tin of bully?' 'Oh Tousands. Tousands.' 'Well

33. Lt J. C. Price, MC, 2 Div Sig Coy, Turner and fitter, of Homebush, NSW. b. 1892. *L* 22/10/15.
34. Capt L. K. Chambers, 17 Bn, Clerk, of Mosman, NSW. KIA 29/7/16, aged 22. *L* 26/10/15.
35. Lt H. E. Moody, 3 FAB, Solicitor, of Yorketown, SA. DOW 27/8/16, aged 23. *L* 19/12/15.

divide that among you', and over would go a home made bomb. The Turks played this joke too, and the Australians appreciated it: 'This is the sort of thing that makes life here interesting,'[36] one explained.

In short, the Turk was a brave and resourceful but gentlemanly opponent who followed the rules. 'They are the whitest fighters that ever fought,' a 10th Battalion officer decided,

and are playing the game like men to the last post. Any of our wounded they pick up, they are said to treat skilfully, and humanely, and prisoners are treated in the best possible fashion. This is very different from the first round, when 'no prisoners' was the order of the day on either side, [*because each was under a misimpression about the other.*][37]

He was probably too generous to his enemy, for only seventy Australians were taken prisoner on Anzac, but his was a typical regard. Some Australians refused to wear gas masks, because they said Jacko would never use gas, and Anzacs today retain affectionate memories of their old opponents.

Nevertheless the Australians were determined to maintain their reputations in a craft in which they had such apparent proficiency. They felt themselves not merely sons of the Empire, but Australians, owning no masters, and if war was a game to them, winning was serious business. Despite their laughter and their jesting, they fought remorselessly, to win and to enhance their glory. Most had 'pre-match' nerves before a big battle, but 'the first few bursts of shrapnel' dispelled these, and the men became 'quite cool. Some smoking some having a few jokes, just the same as if they were at their usual employment.'[38] During the Turkish attack on 19 May, and again before Lone Pine in August, soldiers, their 'sporting instincts' roused, offered bribes and even fought for a place in the firing line, and until August very sick Australians remained in the trenches on the chance of participating in an approaching fight, or hid to avoid being 'sent away in the middle of the fun'.[39] Too many

36. L/Cpl R. Richards, 5 MG Coy, Clerk, of Homebush, NSW. DOW 26/11/16, aged 22. *L* 8/10/15.
37. Capt A. E. Leane, 48 Bn, Insurance inspector, of Adelaide, SA. DOW while POW 2/5/17, aged 23. *L* 22/8/15.
38. Pte W. G. McSparrow, 2 Bn, Chauffeur, of Annandale, NSW (b. England). KIA 6-9/8/15, aged.24. *L* 6/5/15.
39. Silas, *D* 1/5/15.

volunteered for raids and patrols, and most mined and sapped vigorously, or ceaselessly scanned the Turk lines for a target. Before August many thirsted for a charge, and even after that month's battles, when weariness and disillusion had curbed their zeal, they patrolled No Man's Land tirelessly, still stalking the Turk. Some were killed by their eagerness: they looked too long over the parapet to see the fabled enemy, pushed too readily into No Man's Land, or inquired too closely into the workings of home made bombs or duds.

Many declared their own private wars. '[T]he rifles are making a horrible row', exclaimed Colonel Ryrie,

I must find out what its about. later. *It was one of our men having a bit of a battle with some snipers, he has just come in wounded in the head, but he said he got three of them. he went into the scrub after them. his wound is not serious and he wants to go out again as soon as he gets it dressed.*[40]

A 3rd Battalion officer discovered his men watching over the parapet while one of them stood breast high above it, arms folded, gazing towards the Turks. He was duelling with a Turk opposite, each man taking his turn to shoot at his opponent, till one should fall.[41] The Anzacs felt they had the measure of their foe, and they lived for the game and for victory, some readily risking death for a chance to kill. What baffled them at last was not their own deficiencies, nor even the undoubted stoutness of the enemy, but the mistakes of their own generals.

Some Australians fought successfully in battle partly because they were so willing to kill. In May a Tasmanian private, imagining his victim's wife and children, refrained from shooting a Turk 100 yards away,[42] but this was exceptional, and, in a battle, perhaps impossible. Battle rouses many soldiers to unfamiliar frenzies, and most Australians were swayed by no more than this. Private Aitken, of the 11th Battalion, recounted of the landing, 'at last I've got war to write of to you; we're in the thick of it . . . we landed under fire. I quite forgot to be frightened . . . for some reason, I got quite annoyed and reckoned to have my money's worth if I were to be

40. Ryrie, *L* 14/7/15.
41. The Australian was shot, by a Turk on the flank. (Bean, *Official History*, II, p. 287n.)
42. Pte J. A. Kidd, 15 Bn, Carpenter, of Evandale, Tas. RTA 29/7/15, aged 27. *Narrative*, p. 9 (29/5/15).

shot so rushed ahead and did my bit with the rest'. He went on to
relate that after the first intoxication had died down it still gave him
a sort of blood-curdling satisfaction to shoot at men as fast as he
could, and that a bayonet charge was the acme of devilish excitement. Then, perhaps in a quieter moment, he reflected, 'war is hell
indeed—bloody hell; having to go through it, I think a man expiates
all his sins'.[43] Another soldier described his bloodlust in the Hill 971
fighting:

*a lot of our men went down, but one never stops to think of
them or oneself it is just a matter of keeping a few men together
& go on so as to keep the front line intact . . . I used often to
think what sort of feeling it would be to kill anybody, but now
it is a matter of who is going under first, the Turk or yourself &
you just . . . let him have the bayonet right through, but 'oh' the
misery & cruelty of the whole thing, 'but a soldier does not
want any sentiment.' The look on the poor devils when cornered
& a bit of steel about a foot off in the hands of a tempary mad
man, because the lust for killing seems very strong.*[44]

'I think I went mad for a while, at seeing so many hurt,' a third man
confessed, 'for we could not see how the Turks were getting on. I
wanted to get on top and charge the Turks . . . That was the only
time I was "Battle mad."'[45]

These men are admitting a transient passion, but other Australians, certain of their cause, trusting themselves entirely, and with
something of the harsh antipodean frontier in their souls, wrote of
killing without hint of remorse, and with every suggestion that their
murderous urge remained after the fire had died from their blood.
At the landing some carved their way up the hills with ferocious
exultation:

*I had the good fortune of trying my nice shinny bayonet on a
big fat Turk, he yelled out Allah, then on again we went & I
came across a sniper when he saw me coming straight at him
with cold steal he got up & started to run but my nimble feet
caught him in two strides I stuck it right through his back*[46]

43. Aitken, *L* 29/4/15.
44. Lt F. C. Yeadon, MC, 22 Bn, Engineer, of Darwin, NT. KIA 5/8/16,
aged 28. *L* 19/8/15.
45. L/Cpl J. B. Bell, 45 Bn, Plumber's labourer, of Sydney, NSW RTA
10/3/18, aged 48. *L* 21/10/15.
46. Pte L. E. Hyder, 6 Bn, Furniture packer, of Kew, Vic. RTA 15/8/15,
aged 24. *L* 27/7/15.

the Turks started to run those that did stop flung down their guns and cried mercy but the boys were not that way inclined and killed them all . . . we captured some German officers who got short shift one of them . . . shouted good old Australia . . . a lad pushed his rifle up to his head & blew it nearly off[47]

up the hill . . . we swarm . . . the lust to kill is on us, we see red. Into one trench, out of it, and into another. Oh! the bloody gorgeousness of feeling your bayonet go into soft yielding flesh —they run, we after them, no thrust one and parry, in goes the bayonet the handiest way.[48]

a soldier had 8 Turks (wounded) to guard he was placing them along in a row he said I am only going to bandage them up, finis Turk.[49]

A man of the Fourth Brigade recalled the night advance towards Hill 971 on 6–7 August:

We charged 3 hills that night. On the first hill I bayoneted a Turk who was feigning death, with a few extra thrusts. He was an oldish man & on the first thrust which did not go right home he tried to get his revolver out at me, but failed . . . coming up the third hill, a gigantic Turk . . . grabbed me round the chest . . . he was a veritable Samson . . . [and] slowly began to crush the life out of me, I was almost gone when a mate of mine called Tippen came up & bayoneted him . . . We made sure of him & then continued up the hill. Poor Tippen got shot just in front of their trench in the stomach with two bullets, he died groaning horribly. I killed his assailant however by giving him five rounds in the head. I . . . let him have it full in the face. It was unrecognisable[50]

One Australian, an ambulanceman, specifically linked the fighting effectiveness and the murderous inclinations of some of his countrymen:

47. Pte W. J. Gray, 5 Bn, Jockey, of Sale, Vic. DOD 30/5/15, aged 27. *L* 27/5/15. If there were German officers killed at the landing, which is highly improbable, it is unlikely that at that time they could have identified their assailants as Australians. The two men last quoted were writing to their mothers.
48. Francis, *L* 25/4/15.
49. Sgt H. B. Macarty, 50 Bn, Electrician, of Broken Hill, NSW. RTA 24/6/16, aged 30. *Notes.*
50. Sgt H. M. Jackson, 13 Bn, Builder's clerk, of Glebe, NSW. DOW 15/8/16, aged 23. *L* 21/8/15.

There are a lot of bush-whackers, copper-gougers, etc. from the Cloncurry district in the 15th Battalion and I believe they are the finest of all soldiers, fearing nothing and as full of dash and endurance as man ever was. I am inclined to think they make it too willing bayonetting and killing when mercy should be shown and prisoners taken . . . There is no doubt that our men are hard and even cruel.[51]

Perhaps because it made war a series of individual combats, a favourite Australian weapon was the bayonet: 'they will not face our bayonet' was a frequent boast. The Turks came to recognise their foes as both brave and merciless with the weapon, and rarely withstood the last minutes of an Anzac bayonet charge. 'Just to prove the Australians are enjoying themselves,' an artilleryman, Nigel Ellsworth, stated,

when there is going to be a night attack, one can't buy a place in the main firing trench, and men are known to have refused £2 for their positions during the fighting. They stand up in the trenches & yell out 'Cone on, we'll give you Allah', & . . . let some Turks actually get into our Trenches then tickle them up with the bayonet.[52]

Many AIF values related to personal achievement in war. The Australian heroes were the best renowned fighters—Jacka, who won the first VC by shooting five Turks and bayonetting two; Simpson, the man with the donkey, and men like him, who risked death daily to save the lives of their comrades; Sing, 'the Murderer', the sniper from the light horse, who shot over 200 Turks; Freame, the best scout on Anzac, who knew No Man's Land as well as his own trenches; Black, and Murray, machine gunners of the Fourth Brigade, and a dozen more of their quality.[53]

They were the peers, but Australians applied the standards they

51. Richards, *D* 11/6/15.
52. Ellsworth, *L* 3/7/15.
53. Capt A. Jacka, VC, MC & bar, 14 Bn, Forestry employee, of Wedderburn, Vic. b. 1893; Pte J. S. Kirkpatrick, 3 Fld Amb, Ship's fireman, of Melbourne, Vic (b. England). KIA 19/5/15, aged 22; Pte W. E. Sing, DCM, 31 Bn, Horse driver, of Proserpine, Qld. RTA 21/7/18, aged 32; Sgt W. H. Freame, DCM, 1 Bn, Horse breaker, of Kentucky, NSW (b. Japan). b. 1885; Maj P. C. H. Black, DSO, DCM, 16 Bn, Miner and prospector, of Southern Cross, WA. KIA 11/4/17, aged 37; Lt Col H. W. Murray, VC, CMG, DSO, DCM, 4 MG Bn, Bushman, of Launceston, Tas. b. 1884. Black was a L/Cpl when he landed on Anzac, the others were privates.

set to every soldier: to the English, whom they found wanting so often, to the Turks,

The last patient I brought in . . . was shot through the lungs and I fear had but little time to live, but on the way down he said several times 'By God, that Turk could shoot well. He got me a beauty, didn't he?' 'I thought I had him right enough but he beat me easily.' . . . 'I feel pretty bad and expect I'm done for.' 'But, strike me dead, that Turk could shoot all right.'[54]

and to themselves, and Australian standards impressed observers. On 8 May a British major watched the advance of the Second Brigade up the bare slope of Krithia Spur, at Helles, and recorded,

The enemy's shelling was shifted on to them in one great concentration of hell. The machine-guns bellowed and poured on them sheets of flame and of ragged death, buried them alive. They were disembowelled. Their clothing caught fire, and their flesh hissed and cooked before the burning rags could be torn off or beaten out. But what of it? Why, nothing! . . . They were at home in hell-fire . . . They laughed at it; they sang through it. Their pluck was titanic. They were not men, but gods, demons infuriated. We saw them fall by the score. But what of that? Not for one breath did the great line waver or break. On and up it went, up and on, as steady and proud as if on parade. A seasoned staff officer watching choked with his own admiration. Our men tore off their helmets and waved them, and poured cheer after cheer after those wonderful Anzacs.[55]

Out of battle, their standards impelled Australians never to bow before fear or hardship, and never to admit defeat. 'Are We Downhearted', a man repeated a popular catchcry, 'No we will beat these turks if we have to stay here 35 years'.[56] Old soldiers knew the shell from which to duck or run, but self-respect (or fatalism) required that they swim under fire at the beach, and walk unflinching if they must through the bullets of their enemies. Private Richards, a stretcher bearer, explained, 'It is a queer feeling to hear a shell approaching in your immediate direction, not knowing where it is

54. Richards, *D* 4/5/15.
55. In James, *Gallipoli*, p. 154.
56. Pte F. W. G. Bessell, 51 Bn, Miner, of Broken Hill, NSW. KIA 14-16/8/16, aged 26. *L* –/10/15.

likely to burst, and because a dozen others passed safely over, one hates to pay John Turk the compliment of ducking . . . he grips his courage and takes "no notice".[57] A light horseman recalled that on fatigue duty,

Johnny Turk started to shell us. Two of us were at each end of two long, heavy pieces of timber and it was practically imposs- ible to run. The timber was too valuable to us to let it go so we just had to shuffle along at the best rate we could until we got under a bit of cover, when we had a good spell. Fortunately no one was hit.[58]

This demeanour inspired those who watched. In August a recent arrival on Gallipoli observed, 'By golly it is a treat to see the cool way these men who have been here since the first landing go about their work they dont seem to worry a bit about anything bullets and shells might be so much cotton wool for all the notice they take'.[59] That was the impression they hoped to convey, but they would have behaved similarly had no-one been watching, to satisfy their own self-respect. 'Appleby and I were cooking tea', an infantry private remembered, 'and it was very funny despite the danger. We would cut an onion then duck into the dug out for our lives, then out again to give it a stir and in again as a shell would come whistling by . . . we were laughing all through because it was comical.'[60] While most of his mates bolted for cover from a barrage of Turkish shells, George Mitchell visited a cook's quarters and obtained a fortnight's supply of tea, a bag of spuds, and a bag of onions.[61] His comrades would have admired his gay defiance, because it mocked danger and so conformed to their code. It helped their predicament to be 'always happy and bright and joking and at times you can hardly believe that we are so next door to death. It is really marvellous . . . even when wounded you hear from many of them peals of laughter, while waiting for the Doctors'.[62]

Wounded Australians showed a particular spirit in adversity. Anzacs true to their code 'cracked hardy' when wounded, thus least

57. Richards, *D* 4/8/15.
58. Price, *L* 27/10/15.
59. Sheppard, *L* 28/8/15.
60. Grubb, *D* 14/9/15.
61. Mitchell, *D* 8/5/15.
62. Capt F. Moran, 15 Bn, Bank clerk, of Brisbane, Qld. DOW 20/8/15, aged 38. *L* 3/9/15.

inconveniencing their comrades, and best showing their manhood to the world. Doctors reported several instances of their nonchalant courage. After the Turkish attack on 19 May a man was brought into the beach hospital with his hard palate shot away. He could not speak, but he wrote, 'We gave the bastards hell'. After the doctor had wired his jaw and moved on, the man sent him another message: 'tell Doc there is a tooth loose.' He had uttered no sound.[63] Another came with a hand over his face, asking if the doctor were busy. He waited his turn, then removed his hand. A bullet had shot out his eye, and gone on through his head.[64] In September a private wounded on 25 April asked if the doctor might help him with 'a little trouble' he had. He had dysentery, a compound fracture of the arm, two bullets through his thigh, another through his diaphragm, liver, and side, and minor injuries.[65] 'You know a man is hit by the string of language, and he generally tries to have a look at who got him,' an artillery officer stated, 'and unless absolutely crippled, they almost invariably walk down to the Beach Hospital . . . Never a moan or a grouch. Always the question "How long before I can come back, Doc?"'.[66] This question almost disappeared after August, but throughout the campaign the hardihood of the wounded never faltered. Until the last day, they 'crack[ed] jokes if they only had their tongues left'.[67]

Their staunchness was its own reward, but it also lessened the inconvenience a man's mates were put to, and for Australians this was a basic consideration. War makes soldiers comrades, because comrades sustain hope in battle, mitigate despair in adversity, and relieve a monotonous existence. The Australians recognised this: 'Warfare breeds the spirit of good will . . . one chums up with any-one now no matter what unit he belongs to',[68] one wrote, and after the landing another confessed, 'in Cairo I was ashamed of [my comrades] . . . now I am proud to be one of them'.[69]

But mateship was a particular Australian virtue, a creed, almost a religion. Men lived by it:

63. Col. J. L. Beeston, CMG, VD, AAMC, Surgeon, of Newcastle, NSW. b. 1859. *D* 19/5/15.
64. Pte W. R. Reynolds, 3 LH Regt, Orchardist, of Hobart, Tas (b. England). RTA 11/4/16, aged 35. *D* 17/5/15.
65. Bean, *Official History*, II, p. 374n.
66. Coe, *L* 14/5/15.
67. Campbell, *L* 16/9/15.
68. F. W. Muir, *D* 30/4/15.
69. Silas, *D* 25/4/15.

*'Put this flour in your dixie old man and make my pancakes
with yours, will you?' 'Lend us yer fire after you mate' 'Usin'
that bit 'er fat, I'm short of a piece, lets have it will yer' . . . The
trench is no place for a selfish natured man where almost everything is common property, just for the asking.*[70]

They died by it, and it could become their finest epitaph: the man
who had asked about a twopenny tram ride to Glebe before Lone
Pine[71] was killed an hour later, and his mate wrote of him, 'he was
a jolly fine cobber, and always stuck to his mates.'[72]

Above all they fought by it. They fought because their mates
relied on them, and this and their own self-respect were the chief
causes for their continuing to fight after fighting had lost much of its
attraction. '[P]lease God I may die in the same manner and fight in
the same spirit that I know my comrades will display, for they know
not defeat',[73] Ellis Silas prayed, and Archie Barwick, caught during
the early fighting in a hail of bullets and with men dying constantly
around him, admitted, 'I had a terrible fight with myself . . . one
part of me wanted to run away & leave the rest of my mates to face
it, & the other part said no, we would stop & see it out at any cost'.[74]
He saw it out. '[W]hen you . . . think of your poor cobbers left
behind in the trenches,' stated a man in hospital at Malta, 'perhaps
not [eating], . . . or still worse lying wounded in some place and not
able to get a drink . . . you say to yourself "I'll play the game, I'll
go back and help the boys out"'.[75]

This sentiment could always rally Australians, and the man who
risked himself for his mates was the best sort of Australian. A light
horse scout told of a patrol into No Man's Land:

*We advanced to within about 150 yards of the Turks where . . .
[they] opened on us with shrapnel. I was slightly in advance of
the rest and ordered them to retire and King sang out to me
that Cooper was wounded . . . We carried him a few yards
under fire from the Turks trenches when King exclaimed 'My
God my poor old leg is gone' and dropped. Hewitt and I carried*

70. Capt L. C. Roth, MC, 2 Pioneer Bn, Surveyor, of Elsternwick, Vic.
DOW 6/10/18, aged 25. *L* 1/1/15.
71. See this chapter, at n. 23.
72. Bendrey, *D* 6/8/15.
73. Silas, *D* 1/5/15.
74. Barwick, *D* I, p. 102 (re 28/4/15).
75. Clune, *L* 20/8/15.

Cooper on to the trench and then went back for King. We were in plain view of the Turks all the time and could hear the bullets singing all round us and thudding into the dirt at our feet. How they missed us I don't know. We carried King into the trench . . . I then crept out and got . . . [his] rifle[76]

Not all Australians showed such spirit, but many did. 'One of our fellows goes out three times to bring in wounded comrades', an engineer wrote on 25 April, 'The third time he is shot through the head and pitches forward on his face within a few feet of his goal.'[77] On the exposed hillsides of the first day, that death was almost inevitable, as were others like it at Lone Pine:

I saw several men sacrifice themselves here, they went to certain death, one chap in particular I remember . . . we were chasing some Turk's round a little sap & they reached the bend first, everyone knew the first man round the corner was a dead one, but this chap never hesitated, he threw himself fair at them, & the six fired together, & fairly riddled him with bullets, that was our chance & we into them, & it was all over in a few minutes.[78]

That man shared completely, and died bravely. Perhaps he felt his mates expected it of him, and perhaps in different circumstances he would have expected it of them.

Only death had conquered his spirit, and the shadow of death hung continually over every man on Anzac. By tradition death was a part of war's romance, but no Australian had prepared himself for the horror and frequency of death on Gallipoli. They landed believing it unlikely that they would die, and until they fought a great battle most still imagined death in the vague and abstract terms of their boyhood. Shooting a Turk, for example, if he were not too close, was to many much like striking down some shadowy foe of the Empire's past. '[I] . . . have shot 1 Turk, that is for certain', a young soldier told his mother, '. . . he grasped his side & rolled down the hill. I was awfully excited, it is just like potting kangooroos in the bush.'[79] 'I am getting a hot shot', another announced, '. . . I hit at a face at 200 yards . . . the sergeant swears I scored a bull'.[80]

76. Cpl E. L. Magill, 7 LH Regt, Farmer, of Bogan Gate, NSW. DOW 20/10/15, aged 22. *D* 10/7/15.
77. Turnley, *D* 25/4/15.
78. Barwick, *D* I, p. 153 (re 6/8/15).
79. Guest, *L* 28/5/15.
80. Roth, *L* –/9/15 (second letter).

A third remarked that he 'did a bit of sniping this morning . . . [and bagged] my first Turk, getting him through the neck or shoulder, he threw up his hands and went down like one shot, the distance was 500 yards.'[81]

These soldiers saw their foe as targets, not men: death had no reality, and so they could assume their own continued immortality and miss the menace of the grim Reaper. They expected to go to war, kill, and go home: one predicted, 'with a bit of care . . . Ill be home to ride in the train . . . as long as a man doesnt act the goat & expose himself unnecessarily he cant have a tumble.'[82] Three years later he was mortally wounded advancing into German machine guns in France.

Long before then, death demanded the consideration of his comrades. It challenged some unexpectedly, materialising on a quiet morning. 'A man was just shot dead in front of me', a trooper related,

He was a little infantry lad, quite a boy, with snowy hair . . . I was going for water. He stepped out of a dugout and walked down the path ahead, whistling. I was puffing the old pipe . . . he suddenly flung up his water-bottles, wheeled around, and stared for one startled second, even as he crumpled to my feet. In seconds his hair was scarlet, his clean white singlet all crimson.[83]

The sniper could have shot the trooper had he so chosen, while the infantry lad passed on to the water cart. 'I killed my first Turk on Saturday', a soldier reported, 'I was firing at a sandbag on the Turkish parapet and this chap must have been trying to prop the bag up. I fired at the bag, and, to my surprise, I saw a man jump in the air and then fall'. The thought that he had killed a man distressed this soldier, and he tried to justify the deed: 'It was just this Turk's bad luck . . . Anyway that is what I am here for.'[84] These were old defences, eternally relevant to the business of war, but only now did this soldier advance them.

Death appeared before other men when they killed their foes at close range during a pitched battle. 'I got [a Turk] in the neck,' an

81. Lt C. H. Dakin, 5 MG Coy, Orchardist, of Woodford, NSW. KIA 15/4/17, aged 23. *D* 26/10/15.
82. Roth, *L* -/9/15 (second letter).
83. Idriess, *Desert Column*, p. 25 (30/5/15).
84. J. B. Bell, *L* -/8/15.

infantry private wrote after a trench fight in May, '. . . made me feel
sick and squeamish, being the first man I have ever killed . . . I
often wake up and seem to feel my bayonet going into his neck.
Ugh! it does get on a man's nerves.'[85] Or death became real when
friends were killed unexpectedly during the daily round of trench
warfare. Sergeant Cameron, a Victorian farmer in the 9th Light
Horse Regiment, recorded,

*This afternoon we lost our brave little officer . . . than whom
the Regt. boasted no better. He was on the observation post and
just turned round to give an order when a bullet struck him in
the left side of the head, coming out on the right. Mr. Mac as
he was called, died giving his orders—his last words were
'Stand to arms, Twelve hundred, Five Rounds—Oh God! and
fell back . . . I feel a great loss keenly. The first officer of the
9th to go. Poor Mac!*[86]

A visit to a cemetery, the stench of chloride of lime, or the sight of
bodies could also lead men to consider the possibility of dying:
'8 a.m. 9 hours armistice granted to bury dead . . . Will have a look
over battle field while it lasts', Sergeant Cameron decided eight days
after he reached Anzac, and later he wrote,

*Have done so and . . . Its awfulness is appalling. Thousands of
bodies lie rotting in the intervening space between enemy's and
our trenches . . . and the stench is sickening. The burial party
has indeed a horrible job, yet the whole thing is peculiar in that
Turk, Britain or Australian are intermingled in the common
task of placing out of sight the bodies of dead comrades, and in
a few short hours this will cease and each will be in his own
trench, each doing his best to add to the already large list.*[87]

For a time some Australians protested against death. After his
mate was shot an infantry sergeant burst out, 'Oh my God this is
too horrible this bloody war—every day someone getting killed',[88]
and when his brother was killed a trooper declared, 'I am going to
have some more shots at the bloody Turks now. I suppose they will

85. Pte A. M. Simpson, 13 Bn, Electrician, of Sydney, NSW (b. England).
DOD 17/6/18, aged 39. *L* –/5/15.
86. Cameron, *D* 31/5/15.
87. Cameron, *D* 24/5/15.
88. Coulter, *D* 28/7/15.

get me in the end but I intend to avenge Reg.'[89] But grief and revenge were inadequate responses to a threat so relentless and an end so probable. Some soldiers, seeing the toll mount, pondered their own futures. 'Frankly speaking no man has the firm conviction that he will return',[90] Corporal Mitchell wrote early in June. '[W]e have not much time to think of [death] . . . here,' Corporal Ranford claimed, yet he was thinking of it: 'especially as we never know from one minute to another when our turn is coming.'[91] Private Richards commented,

in front of me now . . . there are ten bodies lying in line . . .
Yesterday these were fine specimens of Australian manhood.
Men that any nation would be proud to claim. It is a sickly
sight if one is willing . . . to dwell on [it] . . . but this we must
not allow as there is so much blood and slaughter about to face
that one cannot be sentimental.[92]

Sooner or later most Australians were forced to accept that the dead were normal to life on Gallipoli, and unless the victim was a close mate or a relative, they soon were not sentimental. Three months after he had described the killing of his officer, Sergeant Cameron noted simply of a man of his troop, 'Poor old Maude got one in the head today.'[93] At the landing a 10th Battalion soldier called several times to a mate without response, then crawled up to his position: 'The poor fellow had been shot through the heart, and was quite dead. At first these things fill you with horror, but after awhile you become accustomed to them and take little notice.'[94] A 1st Battalion officer stated, 'the expression at 1d shy shows "Another doll over" is . . . [what] you experience . . . in seeing even one of our own men go over.'[95] At Lone Pine a man told his family, 'The dead were 4 & 5 deep & we had to walk over them: it was just like walking on a cushion . . . I daresay you will be surprised how callous a man becomes: a man may have a very close chum well if some-body tells him his chum is killed all he says is—"poor chap"—& he

89. Sgt. A. S. Hutton, 3 LH Regt, Collector, of Adelaide, SA. b. 1888. *D* 20/5/15.
90. Mitchell, *D* 4/6/15.
91. Ranford, *D* 13/6/15.
92. Richards, *D* 1/8/15.
93. Cameron, *D* 19/8/15.
94. B. B. Leane, *D* 28/4/15.
95. Lt Col H. G. Carter, DSO, 5 Pioneer Bn, Electrical engineer, of Neutral Bay, NSW. b. 1885. *L* 25/5/15.

forgets all about him',[96] and towards the end of the campaign an infantry private repeated, 'its no surprize to tell a fellow that so & so was killed last night one get so use to hearing of death's that the look of unconcern is all that one gets'.[97]

Of necessity dead men were often ignored, or treated as refuse:

The dead that are left unburied are tossed over the rear of the trench, and are now smelling very badly being a menase to our general health, in fact the whole of the ground in front is covered with the dead who have been lying there for a week in the sun.[98]

Men must be prepared to see things here, and . . . carry on with the job . . . my sub & myself were sent out burying soldiers who had been dead for weeks . . . I had to undo their clothes to search for the Identity disc & Pay book, & the bodies were that swollen & rotten that their clothes are bursting at the seams. We work with handkerchiefs around our noses & . . . hook a couple of drag ropes around his ankles & drag him in & chop his arms in & fill up lively . . . speed at 'filling in' is essential.[99]

our new firing line . . . is a most gruesome sight . . . as they have made it under where all the Light Horse bodies are lying and just on the parapet of the trench may be seen legs, heads and bodies of our men who died in the [Nek] charge . . . and are still there.[100]

A few men were even callous to the dying—'A [wounded] Turk . . . the other night . . . let out some heart rending yelps—but our chaps roared and laughed at the poor devil'[101]—but this was not usual on Anzac, even towards the Turk, and where they could Australians tended the dying gently.

Perhaps they saw their own ends in the surrounding dead. They clung while they could to notions of their immortality, but they came to realise that at any moment chance might stretch them alongside the still shapes about them, and at last many were forced to admit

96. Lt J. H. Dietze (real name J. H. Sandoe), 45 Bn, Engineer, of Marrickville, NSW (b. England). KIA 18/9/18, aged 24. *L* 19/9/15.
97. Bessell, *L* –/10/15.
98. de Vine, *D* 2/5/15.
99. Ellsworth, *L* 25/7/15.
100. Dakin, *D* 15/10/15.
101. Armitage, *D* 4/11/15.

the probability of dying. With varying degrees of reluctance, they became fatalists.

Their fatalism took different forms. Many who among the habits of peace had served their Maker now took strength from His comfort. 'What is it to me, if I am killed?' one man asked,

I am not left to worry over it . . . I think war is sent with a purpose by God, and I think it has its effect. Men are here who are immoral to a degree or were and after a time there is a change in them, one becomes more thoughtful for a time and . . . [we] direct our thoughts to our homes and from there to God . . . Men, who months ago, would have been ashamed to have it known that they had a bible are seen reading it often in their posies . . . all [is] designed to draw men nearer to God.[102]

Lance Corporal Mitchell, who was certainly not religious, supported him.

taken all round the moral tone of our men has improved wonderfully with the advent of action. Swearing has diminished (except when close to the enemy) and the most hardened turn their minds to divine things. As one man put it, 'when you are talking to your pal, look away, and when you look back see him in a heap with a bullet through his brain, it makes you think.'[103]

But most Australians found their surroundings too horrible to see the workings of divinity in them. They came to prefer a more mechanical manipulation, to accept the illogical and hence understandable vagaries of fate, or chance, or destiny, or luck. ' 'Tis no good being anything but a fatalist', Lieutenant Coe decided after the first violent week on Anzac, 'When your time comes, so does your bullet. And if my time is not up for years yet, well, I shall get back all right, and thank God for my narrow escapes'.[104] In October another lieutenant observed, 'What . . . appear marvellous escapes . . . one soon takes as a matter of course which is I think a wise dispensation of providence as were a man to dwell much on what might have happened if such & such a shell burst in such & such a place, his nerves would undoubtedly go to pieces in no time.'[105]

102. Hunter, *L* 15/10/15.
103. Mitchell, *D* 13/5/15.
104. Coe, *D* 2/5/15.
105. Warren, *L* 17/10/15.

Although these men were obliged to accept the partnership of death in their enterprise, they would not submit their spirits to it. One soldier bathed under shrapnel fire because he needed a wash, and because it was 'useless and impossible' to dodge the shells which exploded regularly above him. Another, crossing an area swept by machine gun fire, felt simply as though he were hurrying home through the rain with a new straw hat on. Their fatalism fortified the defiance of such men—they could ignore bullets if being shot at was unavoidable.

More than this, because death menaced them, men strove against its oppression. Usually a man could not choose the manner of his passing. When he could he tried to die well, to defy the great unknown and show its palsied hold on his memory even while it bore his soul away. The death of Fred Lowry, the bushranger shot into fame by 'dying game' fifty years before, was several times re-enacted on Anzac. 'I'm dying,' a twenty year old artilleryman muttered after a Turk shell had blown up his battery, 'but by God I'll die game.'[106] 'Mafeesh . . . missus and kids—dirty swine', a wounded Australian murmured before he dragged himself to his knees, fired a last shaky shot at the sky, and collapsed.[107] 'Tell Marjorie how I died,'[108] requested a soldier shot on the first day, and in July a dying infantryman kept repeating, 'Oh well we've had some good times together.'[109] Some claim that Ned Kelly said almost the same thing, before he died.

Their earthly farewells dignified the lives and memories of these men, and effaced their failings in the minds of those who saw them die. They became both inspiration and example, because in dying they had struck the best possible bargain with their last enemy. Those who remained walked perpetually along the edge of a great shadow, separated only by time from those who had already passed into the darkness. They hallowed the memories of dead mates, especially if they had died well, because at any moment death might be their own destiny, and only the memories they left would survive their passing. So the living prepared themselves, hoping, if

106. Dvr D. Barrett-Lennard, 3 FAB, Vigneron, of Guildford, WA. KIA 17/7/15, aged 20. *L* re death, 17/7/15.
107. H. W. Cavill, *Imperishable Anzacs*, p. 81 (re 25/4/15). (Pte, 2 Bn, Artist, of Ashfield, NSW. RTA 10/5/16, aged 25.) 'Mafeesh' is Australian Arabic for 'finished'.
108. Mitchell, *D* 25/4/15.
109. Sgt C. H. Lewis, 13 Bn, Clerk, of Sydney, NSW (b. England). DOW 4/7/18, aged 25. *L* 15/7/15.

it was their lot to die, to die well, and thus come nearest to straddling the great divide.

News of the evacuation upset this thinking, because it would separate the survivors from their dead comrades forever, as nothing else could. 7594 Australians and 2431 New Zealanders lay slain about those Turkish ridges, and now, for the first time, most of their surviving mates felt the real pain of parting. The strongest Australian reaction to the news of that December was sorrow and regret at leaving their dead in enemy hands. 'I hope *they* won't hear us marching down the deres', one said, and during the final days men carefully tidied the graves of their friends, fencing them and placing stones and crosses above them. After he left Anzac a man who had landed on the first day wrote,

It was a sad day for us that the order for the evacuation was issued. Every man of the good old 1st division has someone, whom he honoured and respected, lying in one of those solitary graves at Anzac, the thought of having to leave these sacred spots to the mercy of the enemy made the spirit of the men revolt and cry out in anguish at the thought of it. It has even been said that some of the men broke down and cried ... when they heard the order ... It drives me almost to despair[110]

Another veteran wrote out a sad goodbye to his dead mates:

> *Not only muffled is our tread*
> *To cheat the foe,*
> *We fear to rouse our honoured dead*
> *To hear us go.*
> *Sleep sound, old friends—the keenest smart*
> *Which, more than failure, wounds the heart,*
> *Is thus to leave you—thus to part,*
> *Comrades, farewell!!*[111]

At the evacuation the Australians summarised the ways in which the Gallipoli campaign had influenced their thinking. Their sorrow at abandoning their dead increased their disgust with English New Army troops. 'I have seen at least two hardened soldiers—(Boer war

110. Pte A. L. Smith, 1 Fld Amb, Railway signalman, of Hornsby, NSW. KIA 17/8/16, aged 25. *L* 30/12/15.
111. Guppy, *D* re 19/12/15.

men too) weeping over the news [of evacuation],' Lieutenant Armitage stated on Lemnos, 'We all feel extreme disgust at the weakness of K's army—who bungled up the 'Sari Bahr' action,[112] and fuddled Suvla Bay . . . inefficient, incapable, and badly led troops . . . If they had been shoved in right, we would have finished Jacko'.[113]

Private Mitchell, sick with enteric in England, thundered,

All that sacrifice, all that labour, all that suffering for nothing at all . . . the flower of Australia's manhood [dead] . . . Wandering parties of Turks in search of loot will trample over them . . . I feel bitter about it. Had experienced troops been put in. instead of Kitchener's army—men fresh from the old country who had never heard a shot fired— . . . the tale would have been different.[114]

Australians absolved themselves from any blame for their defeat, but they suffered it with the rest, and they felt the disgrace keenly. 'Hill voiced the feeling of us all', a man declared after the news was first broken,

when he said, 'God help us if such a thing comes about. may it never be that, far better we should stay here and suffer hardship and privation, as we have done before, or better still throw everything into the scale and strike one great blow for victory or death with honour.'[115]

An officer wrote,

the Turks have beaten us . . . Tonights . . . the last night at Anzac . . . it hurts to have to leave that place. I . . . was undoubtedly sick of it and needed a rest, but . . . to absolutely chuck the whole thing cuts right in. And I'm damned if they can say the Australians failed to do what was asked of them. They did everything . . . more than they were asked. We feel it very much believe me. We haven't had a fair chance.[116]

Many Australians, proud, shamed, and brave, determined to fight to the last. Even though they believed death or capture certain there

112. Not only Kitchener's army was responsible for this. See the account of the night attack on 6 August, in chapter three.
113. Armitage, *D* 19/12/15.
114. Mitchell, *D* 21/12/15.
115. Guppy, *D* 14/12/15.
116. Moody, *L* 19/12/15.

they begged to join the rearguard, and if they were refused they paraded before their officers demanding to know what dishonour had excluded them. If they were selected they were glad, and prepared themselves as befitted men of the Empire. 'It will be a serious business,' one of the chosen predicted, 'and we will be very lucky if we ever reach the Beach and boats, but at school I learnt this motto: "Dulce et decorum est pro patria mori," and I feel composed, and, if possible, happy . . . I take this opportunity of saying farewell to all the loved ones at home and all my intimate friends.'[117]

His manhood was guided by the traditions of his Empire, yet the evacuation of Anzac and Suvla was one of the few intelligent military operations conducted on Gallipoli, and it was planned by his own countrymen. 35,445 men were got safely off Anzac in eleven nights, 20,277 of them on the last two nights, 18 and 19 December. There was one casualty, a man wounded by a stray shot, and the last Australians were in their ships before the first Turks ventured into the open. It was a brilliant withdrawal, hailed at the time as 'an achievement without parallel in the annals of war'.[118]

The men left without hating the Turk. He had fought a good and generally chivalrous fight. Gallipoli had been a game to the end, played on both sides by sportsmen. Symbolically, men played a cricket match on the last day, on Shell Green, 'just to let them see we were quite [un]concerned . . . & when shells whistled by we pretended to field them. The men were wonderfully cheerful and seemed to take the whole thing as a huge joke.'[119] Some soldiers laid out food and wine for Jacko in their dugouts, and left him messages, saying goodbye, requesting respect for the Anzac dead, and sharing with him the serious and the comic, the great and the petty, as they had since May. In the headquarters dugouts of the Third Light Horse Brigade someone addressed a note to the Commander of the Turkish Forces on Gallipoli:

The Brigadier presents his compliments to our worthy TURKISH opponents and offers those who first honour his quarters with their presence such poor hospitality as is in his power to

117. Worrall, *L* 16/12/15.
118. *Special Order of the Day*, 21 December 1915 by Sir Charles Monro (C in C, Mediterranean Expeditionary Force).
119. Ryrie, *L* 23/12/15.

give, regretting that he is unable personally to welcome them.

After a sojourn of 7 months in Gallipoli we propose to take some little relaxation at that period in which we are instructed by a Higher Power to observe 'Goodwill towards all Men' and in bidding 'Au revoir' to our honourable foes we Australians desire to express appreciation of the fine soldierly qualities of our Turkish opponents and of the sportsmanlike manner in which they have participated in a very interesting contest, honourable, we trust, to both sides.

For a little while we have been with you, yet a little while and you shall see us not. For us it is a matter of deep regret that the ancient friendship so long existing between the British and Turkish Empires should have been thus disturbed and broken by the insidious machinations of the Arch-enemy of humanity.

We have left this area and trenches in which we have taken considerable trouble and pride, clean and in good order, and would be grateful if they may be so maintained until our return, particular care being asked in regard to matters of sanitation, so vital to the health and well being of an army.

We hope that you will find the Wine, Coffee, tobacco, cigarettes and food to your taste, and a supply of fuel has been left in the cupboard to ameliorate in some measure the discomfort during the cold watches of the winter.

Our only request is that no member of the nation who was guilty of the inhuman murder of that noble woman Miss Edith Cavell to whose photo this message is attached, will be permitted to pollute with his presence the quarters of soldiers who have never yet descended to such barbarous and rutless methods.[120]

The Third Light Horse Brigade had suffered much on Anzac. Its troopers had charged The Nek. Yet none felt rancour for that. Their malice, and the malice of every Australian soldier, was reserved for the Hun, for he had caused the war.

120. From Supplementary Material for 3 LH Bde War Diary, in the AWM Library.

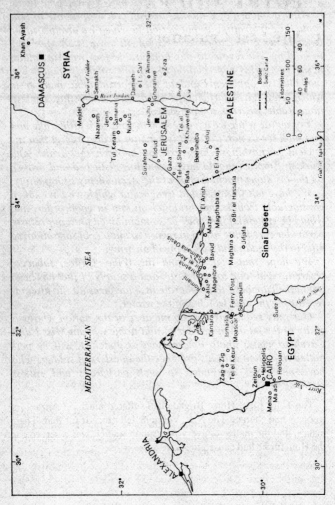

Egypt and Palestine

EGYPT AND PALESTINE

5 The Last Crusaders

[T]he Anzac Mounted Division swarmed out across the wadi,
thousands of mounted men thundering across the plain—guns going
hell for leather—neigh of horses—spin of wheels—far-flung shouts
of laughing excitement—everyone anticipating a big fight. It was a
grand sight. But it was nothing serious. Only five thousand Jacko
infantry with twenty guns.

Trooper I. L. Idriess, 5th LH Regiment, c.17 July 1917

The Anzacs bequeathed a memorable heritage to their country. To
many, Gallipoli was Australia's Westminster Abbey, the fount of
her traditions, the shrine of her nationhood, the tomb of her kings.
'Australia's best and bravest. Heroes all!', a soldier hailed his
comrades slain on Gallipoli, 'The memory of their magnificent
achievements shall ever be fresh in the minds of their own countrymen. The story of their heroism shall be told to Australians for
generations to come'.[1] The survivors of Anzac were a select frater-
nity, which could never admit new members, and for the rest of their
lives they would take pride in their distinction. To have fought on
Gallipoli conferred special renown, officially recognised by a gold
'A' veterans wore over their colour patches, and universally evi-
denced by the deference other Australians accorded a man who
had been on Anzac.

Yet the Gallipoli men were returned to Egypt, and most of them
resented another incarceration in the land of sorrow. Time faded
Anzac's discomfort—'It's the humour that they always remember.
They forget all the troubles and hardships'[2]—but the Egyptian
wastes seemed eternally to be with them. Those who hoped to be-
labour the Hun were especially irked. 'I don't know how long we are
here for', a man with four months' service on Anzac wrote, 'Myself I
would sooner be fighting & at the Germans. If I get the opportunity

1. Coen, *L* 28/1/16.
2. Chinner, *L* 16/2/16.

I will drive it in',[3] and a soldier just returned from the Dardanelles predicted, 'there is a job for us and our fellow Anzacs near by—and by God . . . we'll make our names stand out in Hunnish blood then . . . if only we get put against the God damned Huns—well things will move.'[4]

As the months passed, monotony and a sense of futility corroded the patience of almost every veteran, and soon many, including some who had survived the fiercest fighting on Anzac, were ready for a second spell in the trenches. Lieutenant Armitage typified the growing discontent of such men. In January he wrote, 'my new men are all frightfully keen and anxious to get into a scrap—and I will admit that many of us "old hands" are beginning to hanker after powder again. This life seems to slow'; in February, 'It's about time we had another scrap. Our last was on Nov. 16—so we are getting the fighting itch again'; and in April, 'A big mistake is being made keeping us here too long, for we are "over-trained", and we have the d----s own job to keep our men from "going to the pack" through staleness. It is so monotonous here—that we all long for orders to get away to the Firing line—as Trench work is never dull there.'[5] 'Well I suppose we will be into it again soon . . .', another veteran speculated, 'I don't suppose they will keep *old soldiers* out of it for long',[6] and Birdwood asked a soldier digging trenches by the Suez Canal 'if I thought I was at Anzac, digging trenches again? I answered him saying oh, no there is nothing flying about overhead —he cheered me by saying there might *soon be*—something!'[7]

Because they thus ignored its hardships, veterans probably did not believe themselves greatly changed by their stay on the peninsula. Lieutenant Armitage claimed, 'I have been through a fair lot during the last year—have seen many sights, pleasing, horrible, awe inspiring, hellish, but as far as I can say, the effect has only been to broaden my experience, make me a little more serious . . . I think I am . . . as of yore.'[8] This was the feeling of many old soldiers. They were proven fighters, but their purpose had not altered, and

3. Sgt T. H. Hill, MM & bar, 19 Bn, Woolclasser, of Neutral Bay, NSW. DOW 22/9/17, aged 33. *L* 14/1/16.
4. Armitage, *D* 12/12/15.
5. Armitage, *D* 18/1, 15/2, and 17/4/16.
6. Sgt W. N. Berg, 18 Bn, Press photographer, of Glebe, NSW. RTA 10/4/18, aged 21. *L* 17/1/16.
7. 2/Lt H. Attwood, 7 Bn, Accountant, of Bendigo, Vic. KIA 20/9/17, aged 35. *L* –/3/16.
8. Armitage, *D* 23/4/16.

they still fought to humble the Hun. Their ideals and their senses of right and manhood remained secure, and their love for Australia was at least as strong as formerly. 'Australia's future as a free country is inextricably bound up with the successful issue of this conflict', one man declared, '. . . should my life be sacrificed . . . [I make the sacrifice] willingly and cheerfully . . . my country is my life, my life is my country's.'[9] Their faith in their Empire, though questioned, was firm. 'Talk about Empire sentiment,' a frequent critic of English troops exclaimed after a review of Australians by the Prince of Wales,

well it was not till then that I realised what loyalty and royalty meant. To see a mere lad . . . [provoke] one continual roar of cheers, was a wonderful sight. Cheer—never have I heard such cheering. The Son of our King saw us . . . and we can say 'God Save the King'—'Bless the Prince of Wales'—'Damn their and our enemies.'[10]

The Anzacs were ready to soldier on, and do what honour and duty required.

But Gallipoli had wrought changes. Some soldiers now preferred even the desert to the trenches, and one or two schemed for repatriation: 'Some of the Malingerers . . . have a method of making their knees swell by binding them tightly with a towel and continuously knocking at each side of the knee unfortunately that swelling only lasts about 24 hours. chewing cordite for a temperature is another scheme but a very old one.'[11] More generally, the adventurous enthusiasms prevailing a year earlier had disappeared. Though they still rated victory most important, more men were ready to see the war end and go home, and many ruefully remembered their former innocence. A veteran stated of a new arrival,

He was not—much to his chagrin—on Gallipoli . . . The best wish I could give him was that he would never see a shot fired. However, I was of the same mind as he until I had the experience of being under fire. I do not care if the war ended tomorrow. While it is on, of course, I would never be happy

9. Coen, L 2/2/16.
10. Armitage, D 23/3/16.
11. Pte T. J. Cleary, 17 Bn, Electrician, of Annandale, NSW. b. 1876. D 22/4/16.

unless at the front line but the sooner it ends the better for us all.[12]

In May 1916 Lieutenant Armitage admitted, 'As for V.C., D.S.O. . . . there's not too much satisfaction in getting one—so long as one does his job thoroughly as a . . . soldier . . . and leaves or goes through this show with a white name—that's all that counts,'[13] and in the preceding September a soldier had concluded, 'I have never once regretted joining the Army and if I have a bit of a rest & decent food I will go back . . . with a good heart: *but* if they say would you like to go to Australia . . . I guarantee I would not miss the boat.'[14]

But the boats were carrying reinforcements from Australia, and by early 1916 enough troops had arrived to create two new divisions.[15] This was begun in February, by mingling the new arrivals with the veterans: in the infantry for example, the original 1st to 16th Battalions exchanged half their strength for half the strength of their respective 'daughter' battalions among the new formations, the 45th to 60th Battalions. The move distributed the experienced men evenly through the force, and so facilitated training, but it was strongly resented by old soldiers. 'I felt as though I were having a limb amputated without any anaesthetic,'[16] a 12th Battalion officer stated after watching his comrades march away, and Anzacs torn from the ranks of their friends and memories were especially bitter, for already their old units had won a loyal allegiance from them.

The men whose arrival thus disconcerted the veterans were better warned of their futures than their predecessors. They had read the Gallipoli casualty lists, they heard the tales of the old soldiers. If they heeded these cautions, they soon forgot them. In December 1915 Eric Chinner observed that the year had been a red one, and hoped that in 1916 peace would settle the sadness of the nations. But in January he declared, 'it makes me green with envy when [old soldiers] tell me stories of battle . . . Our hopes [of a fight] are continually raised—only to be dashed to the ground again'.[17]

12. Coen, *L* 30/1/16.
13. Armitage, *D* 14/5/16.
14. Dietze, *L* 19/9/15.
15. 4 and 5 Divs. 3 Div was being raised in Australia.
16. Bean, *Official History*, III, pp. 48-9.
17. Chinner, *L* 31/12/15 and 23/1/16.

Most new soldiers wished to experience their own battles, what-ever the risk. Some repeated the impatient ardour which had marked the First Division a year earlier: a trooper languishing in the details because his regiment was at full strength hoped it would be 'smashed up' in a battle, so that he could reinforce it.[18] Others were made eager by the desert. One sailed reluctantly from Sydney in September 1915 and confessed to homesickness in October and November, but noted in January 1916, 'Great possibility of remain-ing here till end of war which would be disappointing. Would like to have a scrap and put up with results.'[19] 'I wish they would let us get to business instead of fooling around here, everybody is sick of it',[20] an infantry private complained, and with mounting impatience another wrote, in February, 'Things are very slow here, and I will be very glad when we get a move on . . . I wish they would let [us] . . . have a cut at someone—I don't mind who it is—as long as we get away from this inactivity'; in May, 'the sooner we are out of this the better. Surely they cannot keep us here, doing nothing, much longer'; and as he left Egypt later that month, '[I] have had a long stretch of inactivity and a more or less easy time for many months now, so am quite ready to go "into it", in fact will relish the idea.'[21]

Yet, unlike the earliest enlistments, these men restrained their exuberance, tending to direct it less towards adventure, and more towards duty. Some wrote of God and Empire: 'We who are out here have a double duty to perform: to help our British brothers in the great cause, and to wipe out a debt to those who have given their lives for us earlier in the war. But God is with us. He will repay: vengeance is His. In His good time we shall win.'[22] Others had a more pragmatic concept of their mission: directed by the Australian press and alarmed by the power of Germany's war machine, they longed to assail the Hun,

to get to grips with the kasiers horde I think they would get a rough time of if we could get at them as it is a fault of ours to go & we do not take much notice of orders when we are in a

18. Capt C. E. Gatliff, 13 FAB, Business manager, of Carlton, Vic. RTA 9/8/18, aged 36. *L* 5/3/16.
19. Sgt L. R. Elvin, 1 Bn, Engine driver, of Lithgow, NSW. KIA 5/5/17, aged 26. *D* 30/9, 10/10 and 2/11/15, 7/1/16.
20. Armstrong, *L* 27/12/15.
21. L/Cpl A. F. Fry, 13 Bn, Supercargo, of Lindfield, NSW. DOW 14/8/16, aged 23. *L* 20/2, 3/5, and 26/5/15.
22. Chinner, *L* 28/3/16.

*tight as it is each man for himselfe different to the home lads
who do not know what freedom is like we are used to in the
bush . . . [I had to sell my farm to get here, and lost a bit of
money] but I do not mind the sacrafice as I am happy to be able
to do my duty for the dear old flag & I could not rest or give
my mind to work so had to go*[23]

and shortly after leaving Egypt an untried soldier asserted, 'we are
helping to save [France] . . . from the un-"Kultured" modern
"Hun", who has, with the Kaiser & War Lord's sanction, done his
best to out-do the savage tribe of Attila of old, in the wrecking of
God Almighty's Laws, made for the good of humanity.'[24]

Although new and old soldiers thus differed in their attitudes to
war, they diverged only slightly in their respective responses to
discipline. New soldiers tended to react against minor irritations
which veterans tolerated, and old soldiers who knew the 'lurks' did
as they pleased more easily, but their monotonous existence and
the proven worth of their army in battle made every Australian
impatient of seemingly pointless restrictions. On Lemnos an Anzac
explained, 'its nice and quiet here, no danger and all that but I
really think I'd rather be back on the Peninsula; camp life with its
rules and regulations, red tape and ceremony is very distasteful
after having been thro' the real fighting'.[25] Entertainment facilities
still hardly existed in Egypt, and absence without leave, untidy dress,
venereal disease, refusal to salute or to pay train fares, and attacks
on natives and native property remained prevalent offences in the
AIF. 'If they take my advice they will take "Gallic leave",
"in moderation" whenever they need it', a private on Gallipoli had
written about two recently enlisted brothers, and despite the censor
(his platoon commander) he added, 'The penalty is nothing much.
I have never "put in" for leave since I joined the military and I
never went short for leave either in Victoria or Egypt.'[26] Many
Australians, believing that Gallipoli proved the worthlessness of a
strict code of discipline, thought as he did, and passed their off-duty
hours almost as they liked.

23. Pte L. B. C. D. Bibbs, 57 Bn, Farmer, of Mirboo South, Vic (b. England). KIA 28/4/18, aged 35. L 20/2/16.
24. L/Cpl H. J. Cave, 1 Bn, Customs clerk, of Balmain, NSW. b. 1892. L 2/4/16.
25. Aitken, L 19/11/15.
26. Gnr E. Burgess, 14 FAB, Insurance clerk, of Geelong, Vic. KIA 4/10/17, aged 22. L 18/10/15.

The practice of saluting roused their particular opposition. A private explained,

if we are to salute each and every . . . officer we meet . . . a chap will get the equivalent of housemaid's knee in his elbow . . . Can't see how being all the time as stiff as a poker is going to win the war. We came here to fight for freedom, not to be slaves to our superiors—we haven't got any. If I salute an officer I like to feel that we are exchanging man-to-man compliments, and I reckon the officers worth saluting feel the same way.[27]

This was one manifestation of the unrelenting egalitarianism of Australian soldiers. An officer described another:

After breakfast I put my head outside my hut and rap an order. Do I see men running to obey? No. We are Australians. There are curses and growls everywhere . . . and in about a half-hour the men are on parade. I know all about it so I always call out half an hour before I really want them. Then a job is given them. Do they smartly obey? No. They gather in cliques and finally slouch off, swearing and smoking . . . a dirty black pipe (I have one myself.) Parade is over. I look at the work . . . they have done more than I expected. So they go on day after day. A better lot of men could not be found.[28]

The comradeship of the trenches reinforced the independent outlook natural to many old soldiers, and, because inexperienced men tended to imitate the veterans, also united almost every soldier in a more forceful opposition to authority. Men acted with a directness, even a violence, that might have daunted them a year before. Australian prisoners evolved a system to escape from their escorts which worked because 'the escorts will not use their bayonets against their fellow soldiers.'[29] A private detached to police duty recorded,

This morning the prisoners were very troublesome so the Sergeant of the Guard called me and another chap in (with fixed Bayonets) to take their Bedding, Blankets etc. They refused to give them up when asked So I turned to the Sergt. gave him

27. 'A. Tiveychoc' [R. E. Lording], *There and Back*, p. 115 (2/6/16). (Pte, 30 Bn, Book keeper, of Burwood, NSW. RTA 22/2/17, aged 19.)
28. Chinner, *L* 31/12/15.
29. Raws, *L* 8/5/16. See diagrams over page.

```
o o o o          o o o o          o o o o
o x x o          o x x o          o x x o
o x x o          o   o            o    o
o x x o          o x x o          o    o
o x x o          o x x o          o x x o
o x x o          o x o            o  x o
o x x o          o xxx o          o xxx o
o x x o          o xxx o          o xxxx o
o x x o          o xxx o          o xxxx o
ooooooo          ooooooo          ooooooo
```

1. *March off.*　　2. *Prisoners wedging*　3. *More pressure.*
　　　　　　　　　　back, saying they have
　　　　　　　　　　bad feet or escort is
　　　　　　　　　　marching too fast.

```
o o o o                                    o o o o
o     o                                    o xxx o
o     o                                    o x o
o x x o                                    o o o o
o     o                                    o
ox    xo              o
o      xo             x
xx                         o
o x x xo                         o
x                          o  o      o x x
   o xxxx x                      o
o                        o    x
     oo oo o             o        o o
                     x        o
                     x  o    o
                     x  x    x
                          x     o
                                 x
```

4. *Breaking off.*　　　　　　　5. *Off.*

(x = Prisoner : o = Escort)

Diagrams showing the method used by Australian prisoners in Cairo to
escape from their escort, early 1916. From Lt J. A. Raws, 23 Bn, *L*
8/5/16

*my Rifle and Bayonet and told him to put me in. That I didn't
enlist to do a Policeman's work.*[30]

A young lance corporal noted,

*Some Red-Caps (Military Police) raided a harmless Two-up
School right away from the lines. The news spread like magic,
and soon hundreds of chaps were around them—exit the Military Police. Everyone thought some damage would be done to
them, but they thought discretion better than valour, and left
calmly*[31]

and on a troop train between Heliopolis and Tel el Kebir,

*some silly ass . . . uncoupled the last truck (on which the
officers were) and of course others followed suit, we were on
the down grade and very soon the train was coming along in
four parts. Talk about laugh, the front part of the train went on
about two miles and then had to come back. There was a big
row about it of course.*[32]

Not even Australians could defend some transgressions. Venereal
disease clearly impaired battle efficiency, yet Australians in Egypt
were particularly susceptible to it. In every army the sole effective
counter to venereal disease was removal from sources of infection,
but to Australians no area was out of bounds, and the higher rates
of pay they enjoyed increased the disease rate among them. Australian soldiers also mistreated local Egyptians, whom they despised.
As they had in 1915, men gave Egyptians 'references' in English
advising readers to kick the bearer, upset trays of food and fruit,
and burnt Egyptian stalls; but by 1916 months of warfare had
weakened Australian respect for civilian niceties, and the slouch hat
terrorised the natives. One man stated,

*We put in most of the day in the Wassa and explored most of
the Joy houses but didn't do any business with them. The
Aussies have got these people bluffed alright. I don't think
there is any other place on Earth where a man can go into a
house of this character do almost as he likes and walk out with-*

30. Cleary, *D* 13/5/16.
31. Champion, *D* 6/3/16.
32. McWhinney, *L* 16/1/16.

*out cashing up or getting 'flattened out' but these people fear
the Aussies more than they fear their God.*[33]

Men of the Eighth Brigade on a route march near Tel el Kebir
sniped at passing 'Gyppos' until their targets fled over the skyline,
Egyptian conductors were thrown from moving trains, and Egyptian stationmasters and minor officials were assaulted. 'The British
soldiers are a sedate lot in comparison with ours,' boasted a Victorian private,

*they don't knock the baskets of oranges off the heads of the
natives, or pull the boys off the donkeys by curling the head of
their walking sticks round the heads of the said boys and pulling, but walk along the streets as if they had the reputation of
the whole Islands at stake . . . I think they imagine us to be a
lot of hooligans and something to be well avoided.*[34]

Predictably, the authorities retaliated. In October 1915 Sir John
Maxwell, General Officer Commanding in Egypt, wrote sympatheti-
cally of AIF discipline in a private letter to the Australian Governor-
General,

*The men are splendid! as fighters, the best the World has seen!
no words can overpraise them. In the trenches their discipline is
excellent, for they see the reason* why! *but here in Egypt they
get impatient, and the officers have no real hold on their men.
The men do not see the necessity for either training or restraint.*[35]

But Maxwell several times asked AIF leaders to tighten the discipline of their force, and early in February 1916 his successor, Sir
Archibald Murray, who had daily to suffer the disrespect of Australian soldiers, complained of their indiscipline to the Imperial
General Staff in London, and to Birdwood. Birdwood endorsed
Murray's complaints and passed them on to his subordinate commanders, observing that 'other qualities besides actual fighting are
necessary', criticising Australian slackness in saluting and dress,
and warning that these things might bar the AIF's transfer to

33. Cleary, *D* 15/4/16.
34. Pte J. T. R. Easton, 14 Bn, Shipping clerk, of Kensington, Vic. DOW
4/7/16, aged 25. *L* 5/12/15.
35. Novar Papers, 3590, NLA.

France.[36] Wise commanders saw nothing malevolent in the most frequent abuses, refusal to salute and absence without leave, and disciplined them accordingly, but a spate of orders to improve every aspect of discipline followed Birdwood's letter. One hopeful commander even ordered his division to 'drop the use of two words in particular . . . f--- and b-----; They are both beastly especially the first.'[37] Some units held saluting parades, others introduced 'saluting raids' (an officer followed at a discreet distance by military police detailed to arrest men who failed to salute him), military police were posted on trains and stations, Australian units were sent to garrison the Canal, and training was intensified.

On one or two occasions, perhaps because some officers mistrusted the discipline of their men, training was overintensified. In March 1916, ostensibly because train transport was not available, the majority of the Fourth and Fifth Divisions were sent to march the heavy sand between Tel el Kebir and the Canal, about 39 miles, in three days. It was already hot, the men carried full packs and the meagre water ration laid down for battle conditions, and most had recently been given typhoid injections. Too much was asked of them. Numbers early fell out, and more as the march continued, chiefly from the Fourth, Twelfth, and Fourteenth Brigades, which first began it. The Fourteenth attempted the most arduous route, and was particularly distressed. The men lost all formation, wandered dazedly over the scorching sand, and shambled to their destination in exhausted ones and twos. 'Men fell unconscious in the sand and were left lying where they fell', a man of the 56th Battalion related,

Some became delirious and raved. The strongest among us felt that his strength had been taxed to the utmost . . . At each halt we looked back. Away to the skyline, we could see forms of men lying huddled in the sand, as though machine-gun fire had swept the columns . . . some would rise and totter a few paces, to collapse again . . . We were . . . marching on our determination, foaming at the mouth like mad dogs, with tongues swollen, breath gripping our throats with agonizing pain, and legs buckling under us.[38]

36. 12 February 1916, in AWM File No. 265/1.
37. 12 May 1916, in AWM File No. 265/2.
38. H. R. Williams, *The Gallant Company*, pp. 24-5. (Lt, 56 Bn, Warehouseman, of Croydon, NSW. b. 1889.)

Thirty-eight of the battalion's 900 men completed the trek on time, yet for several days afterwards the 56th was marched for two hour periods carrying full packs, to improve its march discipline. Their brigadier was relieved of his command.

The Fourth and Fifth Divisions went to the Canal to release the First, Second, and New Zealand Divisions for France. This move began in March, and later the Fourth and Fifth Divisions followed, the last units quitting Egypt in June. A few soldiers disliked the change, but most agreed with the Australian who exclaimed, 'Thank goodness we have at last left . . . the land of Desert and Dirty Niggers.'[39] As the men broke camp and marched to Alexandria for the last time, they sang farewell to the land of the Pharaohs:

> *We have written letters to our folk in Aussie land,*
> *Saying we are leaving Gyppo s--- and sin and sand;*
> *We are off to France to fight a much more worthy foe*
> *Than the Gyppo—from whom we are mighty glad to go.*
> > *It's a long way to fight the Fritzie,*
> > *Where we might stop a shell;*
> > *But before we leave you spielers,*
> > *Here's a soldiers last farewell!*
> > *Good-bye saida Wallahed!*
> > *And all your rotten crew;*
> > *It's a long, long way to hang the Kaiser,*
> > *Good-bye and ---- you![40]*

They were bound, at last, to meet the Hun.

One arm of the AIF, the light horse, remained.[41] This upset some light horsemen, because although the Turks would probably capitalise on their Gallipoli triumph by attacking Egypt, by 1916 the decisive battles were certain to be against Germany, on the Western Front. A number of men transferred to artillery or infantry

39. Richards, L 21/3/16.
40. 'Tiveychoc', *There and Back*, p. 188 (16/6/16).
41. 13 LH Regt and a troop of 4 LH Regt went to France, principally as traffic police. In the desert campaign Australians also served in the Australian and Anzac Sections of the Imperial Camel Corps (formed early in 1916) and in the Australian Flying Corps. British forces in Egypt by mid-1916 were a (mounted) Yeomanry Division, two infantry divisions, and supporting units.

THE LAST CRUSADERS **127**

units, and many were uneasy about the possibility of uselessly garrisoning a back area.

They had no cause for concern. By March 1916 it was clear that the Turks would attack Egypt, and in that month the British began building a railway and a water pipeline into the Sinai Desert, while the light horse began long patrols to harass the enemy. In mid-April men of the 9th Light Horse Regiment destroyed a small Turkish outpost at Jifjafa, about 60 miles from the Canal, but most patrols were uneventful. The Turks struck the first effective blow, late in April, when their infantry overran Fifth Yeomanry Brigade outposts at Katia and Oghratina, inflicting more than 350 casualties. The Yeomanry were English troops, led/principally by idle and incompetent officers, many of whom, while their comrades resisted until killed, fled the area with unreasonable haste, and also abandoned their positions at Romani, seven miles away. They had been covering the railway, and on 23 April the Anzac Mounted Division[12] crossed the Canal and advanced to Romani to relieve them. The Turks had not approached, and light horse patrols found Katia and Oghratina unoccupied.

At Romani the Australians discovered evidence of the flight of the British garrison. Yeomanry officers had abandoned beer, soda water, whisky, gin, champagne cooling in buckets of water, unopened letters, golf balls, sticks, and links, dressing tables, chamber pots, camp stretchers, carpets, cake, and tinned food. General Ryrie listed five English lords whose effects were recovered, and commented, 'They were not the right people to put at this sort of job.' The luxuries had been transported from the Canal by camel, and to enable this soldiers had been put on water rations. On 26 April light horse patrols found six wounded Yeomanry lying in the desert near Romani. The Turks had bound their wounds and given them food and water, but the Arabs had stripped them, and they had been left by friend and foe to die. Three Yeomanry in a similar plight were found the following day.[43] These incidents probably weakened the Imperial enthusiasm of some Australians, particularly since Yeomanry officers had been among the most disparaging critics of Australian indiscipline in Egypt.

42. That is, 1, 2, and 3 LH Bdes, and the New Zealand Mounted Rifles Bde.
43. For this paragraph, Sgt G. Macrae, 6 LH Regt, Farmer, of Dorrigo, NSW. b. 1889. D 25-27/4/16; Ryrie, L 27/4 and 1/5/16; H. S. Gullett, Official History, VII, pp. 82-8, 91, 92.

By May the railway and an infantry division were at Romani, and during the following months, while the British strengthened their defences, the light horse searched the desert for Turks or Bedouins. The Arabs had no love for the Christians and much for their equipment, but usually attempts at their capture failed, because on the open sand they could easily observe and evade any searching force. Yet it rarely came even to that, and most light horsemen did not see an enemy. An officer outlined a typical patrol:

We were called up at 2.25 this morning fed up & break-fasted in a hurry & were headed into the desert at 4 AM; We arrived at Qatia before 8 oclock where C Troop put in the day & was our base, the other Troops were sent to various points on patrol with orders to be back at Qatia by 3 o'clock . . . A troop did not turn up & men were sent out in pairs to try & pick them up; . . . [they had] put themselves on guard over some Signallers who were repairing the telephone line to Ogratina . . . [we returned to camp] at 8.30 watered & fed our horses & finished tea by 9.45: For the 16 hours we were away we only had a little bully beef & a piece of bread.[44]

The inconsequence of these excursions accentuated their severity. May and June were the hot months of summer, and the desert forays often prostrated those who undertook them. The temperature reached its peak on 16 May, 124.5° in the shade, and leather burnt the fingers at touch. The day before, a large force reconnoitred near Katia. They left Romani after lunch on 14 May, camped east of Katia for five hours during the night, patrolled the desert next day, and returned to Romani that evening. The trek was across heavy sand, a hot wind blew, and it was over 120° in the shade. By eleven on the morning of the second day the water was too hot to drink, and troopers began to faint. At half past one the patrol reached brackish water, and the men rushed it, 'a lot of them half silly. Some were frothing at the mouth & I saw one man put a bucket of water to his lips & finish the lot.' Then they struggled on, their horses taking two hours to travel six miles to Katia. There horses and men drank, and the men vomited the water, and drank again. After the patrol reached Romani over 100 soldiers went sick with

44. Lt F. H. Tomlins, 1 LH Regt, Farmer, of Cowra, NSW (b. England). b. 1891. D 27/5/16.

sun stroke and heat exhaustion, and several horses died.[45]

In mid-July the enemy began his expected advance into Sinai. The lines of sick vanished from the light horse camps, and patrols eagerly raided the advancing foe. The Turks came slowly, patiently toiling their equipment across the sand. East of Katia they halted to build defences, but on the night of 3 August they moved against Romani. Everything was against them. Their supply lines were extended across a waterless desert, they had few mounted troops and no superiority in artillery or overall numbers, the desert march had wearied them, and their opponents were well fed and well watered, with the infantry behind good defences. Despite their bravery and evident weaknesses in the British command, the Turks never had a real chance of success at Romani.

It hardly seemed so to the defenders. The enemy's assault fell on the southern flank of the Romani positions, where the light horse held a thin line of posts, and for a night and a morning the out-numbered horsemen fought a gradual withdrawal, holding back the attackers until the heat of the day should exhaust their efforts. The Turks advanced bravely, some throwing off their boots to move more swiftly over the clutching sand, and by evening they had won Mount Royston, a commanding hill, from the New Zealanders, and obtained some control of the southern Romani area. But they had lost over 2000 men, their strength was spent, their water seven miles away at Katia, and their foe unbroken. When the Australians and New Zealanders counter-attacked the following morning, they turned and fled. Many were captured, but at Katia their rearguard stood. 'The Turk was a snarling fury over every yard of ground . . .', Trooper Idriess wrote,

From palm to palm, from mound to mound, we fought forward, sweat creasing rivulets of sand down our faces, matting the hair on bared chests . . . Over every bare patch the Turks had machine-guns trained . . . the men . . . simply had to rush through a continuous stream of bullets . . . [or] several streams of bullets criss-crossed . . . We fired back, split up into many little groups, nearly all in sections. We'd jab our bayonets through the bushes, and the Turks would stab back—we'd burst in around the bushes and glimpse the Turks' gasping mouths as they hopped back behind the next mound.[46]

45. Macrae, *D* 15/5/16; Ryrie, *L* 15/5/16.
46. Idriess, *Desert Column*, pp. 103-5 (5/8/16).

At dusk the Anzacs retired, and the Turks then withdrew to Bir el Abd. There they resisted further assaults and even counter-attacked, and on 9 August the British fell back to Romani.

The Australians and New Zealanders, a small proportion of the British force, won Romani. They lost about 1100 men, yet they made Egypt safe, and they gained the initiative for their side. They reported the great victory calmly: 'for two weeks we have been engaging the Turks, and the last couple of days put the finishing touch to it. very strenuous, and quite the hottest time ever I experienced. but it is good to know the Turks were very well "hit up." '[47] More had been possible at Romani, for during most of the battle the bulk of the British force had remained idle, moving only when the Turks had fled, and then following cautiously. They lost an opportunity to destroy the entire Turkish army in Sinai.

On 12 August light horse patrols found Bir el Abd evacuated. The enemy had withdrawn to El Arish, the nearest water, 50 miles to the east. The British followed slowly, building the railway and water pipeline as they came. Twice during this time mounted troops raided Turkish desert posts, Mazar on 16 September and Maghara on 15 October, but neither raid achieved much, and the Australians were generally obliged to confine their activities to the wearying monotony of their desert patrols. 'I was unable to stop falling asleep in the saddle', a man recorded of a four day patrol, 'The first time I fell asleep I landed up against a wagon wheel, the second I got nearly kicked by a draught horse. The third time . . . my cussed little pony took me right ahead alongside our worthy Colonel & Major & my innocent slumber was broken by bitter words'.[48] The work was boring, yet in camp almost the only diverting activities were dodging an occasional German 'Taube' (bomber), or searching clothes for 'wogs' (lice). Despite rests on the Canal the brigades grew rapidly sick of Sinai. One trooper complained, 'All food one eats seems to contain sand, one can feel it grating on ones teeth & lately there has been a strong wind blowing continuously & sand has been whirling around us all the time. This Sinai Peninsula is a dreary waste of desert; one longs to see timber and green grass once again.'[49] At last orders came to attack El Arish, and on the night of

47. Dowling, *L* 6/8/16.
48. Cpl M. C. Evans, 1 LH Fld Amb, Agricultural student, of Kyogle, NSW (b. England). b. 1895. *D* 19?/9/16.
49. Jackson, *L* 18/11/16.

20–21 December the Anzac Mounted Division and the Camel Corps Brigade silently surrounded the village. It was deserted. Without a fight the Anzacs had come from the wilderness, on to the firm ground and the flower covered hills bordering the Holy Land.

The Turks had retired to Magdhaba, 23 miles inland, and there offered the British an unenviable challenge. The Magdhaba defences were well sited, yet an attack would have to succeed within a few hours or be forced by lack of water to return to El Arish. Light horse and cameliers assaulted the place on 23 December, and broke the enemy's resistance just as orders came to retire. Only 146 attackers were made casualties, but the wounded were made to suffer a fearful ordeal: an incompetent British staff kept them languishing at El Arish, and they did not reach hospital in Egypt until late December or early January. Men had feared wounds in Sinai, because transport there was always agonising and often fatal; it appeared they still had much to fear, from their own staff.

The advance continued. Rafa fell on 9 January 1917, after a hard fight, and by March the British had arrived opposite the Turk line between Gaza, on the coast 40 miles north-west of El Arish, and Beersheba, 30 miles inland from Gaza. This was the strongest Turkish position in the Middle East, and the gateway to Palestine. It was defended by about 15,000 well entrenched men, it took advantage of high ground to command its approaches, and it was flanked by waterless desert. It had to be breached before nightfall on the first day of an attack, or want of water would force a retirement.

The British attacked at Gaza on 26 March 1917. Led by the Second Light Horse Brigade, the mounted men raced east and north of the town to surround the defenders:

One squadron was sent ahead to reconoitre while the main body advanced slowly . . . We could see the road to Beer Sheba running away to our right & a cloud of dust . . . travelling in a hurry . . . Two or three of our boys . . . galloping across country . . . cut off the fugitives . . . It was a great race, lasted some time & our lads won in the finish[50]

The soldiers had captured the relieving commanding officer of Gaza and his staff; the mounted brigades then took up position and

50. Sgt B. Baly, MM, 7 LH Regt, Foreman, of Liverpool, NSW. b. 1887. L 2/4/17.

settled to wait the main attack, from infantry, south of Gaza.

This was spearheaded by the Fifty Third Division, but incompetent leadership marred its attempt; it began four hours late, and at crucial points was not given artillery support. The men advanced gallantly, but slowed among cactus fences in the area, and almost halted before the slopes of Ali el Muntar, a commanding knoll 1500 yards southeast of Gaza. When time expired at dusk, a costly advance had won Muntar, but Gaza remained in Turkish hands.

General Chetwode, commanding the 'Desert Column' (roughly, the mounted troops), had foreseen the infantry failure, and soon after midday ordered General Chauvel[51] to attack the town. The scattered ring of horsemen were gathered together by about four in the afternoon; then they

galloped in from the rear . . . dismounted & advanced on foot . . . [through numerous] Prickly Pear Hedges, 6 ft high & 4 or 5 feet through, it was just like going through a maze, little narrow lanes running in all directions, with Turks hidden all through it. We had to cut our way through the wretched stuff with our bayonets & got smothered with prickles and thorns.[52]

I saw our men & Turks firing at each other through cactus not more than 6 ft apart & some of our fellows were shooting off their horses like shooting rabbits. they said they could see them better from up there.[53]

The going was hard and furious, but shortly after nightfall men of the Second Light Horse Brigade from the north and New Zealanders from the east were entering Gaza. They had won.

We had captured & killed a lot of the enemy & thought things were going well with us . . . [when] word came through for a general & speedy retirement. Then the fun began, we had got so far into the maze of Prickly Pear & mud huts that we did not know which way to get out. So just had to do the best we could cutting & slashing to get through the cactus & dragging our prisoners along with us. However we got out & found our horses & got away.[54]

51. Lt Gen Sir H. G. Chauvel, GCMG, KCB. Commanded Anzac Mtd Div 1916-17, Desert Mtd Corps 1917-19, and AIF troops in Egypt 1916-19. b. 1865.
52. Baly, *L* 2/4/17.
53. Ryrie, *L* 30/3/17.
54. Baly, *L* 2/4/17.

The order to retreat was the most unfortunate of a series of blunders perpetrated by a careless and poorly organised British staff. All ranks of the light horse received it with dismay, and withdrew reluctantly, the Turks rarely pursuing them. Later the reverse hardly disturbed the equanimity of some light horsemen—one wrote, 'It was a ticklish job and risky . . . However we are nearly ready for another go for it & this time I think we'll take it'[55]—but others for long carried bitter memories of the first Gaza battle.

In mid-April a second attempt on Gaza, in which Australians took little part, failed, and not till October did the British again assail the Turkish positions. Until then the Anzacs patrolled No Man's Land and the desert wastes east of Beersheba, and raided Turkish installations, the most notable raid destroying railway track between Auja and Asluj, on 22 and 23 May 1917.

General Allenby, the new British commander, used the summer of 1917 to build up his resources, until by October he outmatched his opponents in every respect. Then he struck. On the morning of 31 October, three infantry divisions attacked the western approaches to Beersheba. When they had embroiled the defenders in battle, the horsemen swept forward, cutting the roads leading east from the town, and scattering the Turkish outposts. The infantry advanced, but the defence held, and once more time and want of water pressed the attackers. The methodical, casualty saving tactics usually employed were too slow to win the day, and in mid-afternoon Chauvel ordered two comparatively untried light horse regiments, the 4th and the 12th, until then in reserve, to charge Beersheba.

At four thirty p.m. the chosen regiments drew up behind a small hill southeast of the town. When their lines were ready they trotted forward, and as they crested the rise they saw Beersheba four miles away, and between an open and gentle slope, cut across by an unknown number of enemy trenches. As the first Turkish shrapnel shells burst above them the men drew their bayonets, urged their mounts to a canter, and then galloped across the slope. At first men and horses crashed regularly to the ground as shrapnel and machine gun bullets caught them, but during the last half mile the excited Turks forgot to lower the sights of their weapons, casualties almost ceased, and soon the thundering lines were home. Some struck down at the men in the trenches, others charged on, into the town and beyond.

55. Baly, *L* 2/4/17.

Perhaps this was the last great successful mounted charge in history. Certainly it ruined the Turkish hopes, for it smashed open the gate to Palestine. Half an hour before the barriers which had so long defied assault had been secure, now all was confusion and disaster. 'We did not believe,' a captured German officer confessed, 'that the charge would be pushed home. That seemed an impossible intention. I have heard a great deal of the fighting quality of Australian soldiers. They are not soldiers at all; they are madmen.'[56] The stroke of the Australians converted defeat to victory, secured the morale of their side, and injured the will of their enemy, who never afterwards withstood a mounted charge. For that gain thirty-one Australians were killed, and thirty-six wounded. Yet, as almost always, light horsemen reported the incident laconically. 'I enjoyed the whole turn out it was very interesting', one stated, 'A man could get any amount of good souvenirs'.[57]

Next day the victorious British surged north through Beersheba, and then swung east to encounter the Turkish reinforcements rushed from Gaza to halt them. Determined enemy resistance at Tel el Khuweilfe and near Tel el Sheria between 1 and 8 November prevented the complete rout of the Turkish armies, but everywhere the British advanced, slowed only by thirst, exhaustion, and a rearguard of German machine gunners. By 9 December they had taken Jerusalem, and shortly afterwards they halted.

Before this offensive, in July 1917, 22 per cent of the Anzac Mounted Division had 'Barcoo rot', or septic sores caused by food deficiencies, and the original members of regiments were showing a general lassitude and enfeeblement which easily enabled doctors to distinguish them from later reinforcements. Allenby's tireless advance had further exhausted the men, until their condition was

not the tiredness that comes from one or two days hard work but the exhaustion that comes from weeks of long trecks sleepless nights anxious severe scrapping little food and cold nights . . . at least 90% [of the Camel Corps] had caught mange from the camel. This . . . greatly interferred with the mens sleep. Continual scratching broke the skin and this led to septic sores.[58]

56. Gullett, *Official History*. VII, p. 404.
57. Cpl A. J. Anderson, 4 LH Regt, Farmer, of Mount Egerton, Vic. KIA 12/4/19 [sic], aged 25. *L* 4/11/17.
58. Col A. J. Mills, DSO, VD, 15 LH Regt, Dentist, of Parramatta, NSW. b. 1884. *D* 29/12/17.

Allenby therefore rested his squadrons, while he reorganised his supply lines and planned his next stroke.

He delivered it on 19 February 1918, west of the Jordan River. His men broke quickly into the open, within two days advancing 26 miles to their objective about the Wady el Auja, north of Jericho. Again Allenby halted, and while he prepared another general assault, the raid on the railway at Amman took place. Amman was roughly 30 miles east of Jericho, deep in Turkish held mountains beyond the Jordan. To reach it attackers had to win bridgeheads across the flooded river, then fight forward over narrow mountain tracks. The Anzac Mounted Division[59] and English infantry began the attempt on the night of 21 March 1918. By the 23rd they had seized three bridgeheads on the Jordan's Turkish bank, and the mounted troops were struggling forward against rain and resistance to Amman. They arrived on 27 March, and found the village defended by about 4000 enemy soldiers: Arabs had told the Turks of British plans. The raiders inflicted minor damage, but Amman held firm, and on 31 March they withdrew. By 2 April the men had recrossed the Jordan, retaining only one bridgehead beyond it, at Ghoraniye.

The Amman raid was an ill conceived enterprise. The raiders assailed an alerted enemy, superior to them in numbers, and entrenched in good defences. They caused the Turks trifling inconvenience, but lost 177 Australians killed and 1023 wounded or missing. This was as many as at Romani, and almost a quarter of those suffered by Australians during the entire campaign. No reverse in Sinai or Palestine affected the light horsemen so deeply.

A month later British forces once more raided east of the Jordan. On 30 April the Australian Mounted Division[60] and the Sixtieth Division attacked and captured Es Salt, on the track to Amman. But behind the attackers the mountain trails leading back to the Jordan were precariously held, and the Turks pressed their opponents closely. Early on 1 May they attacked at Damieh, near the river, drove back the light horsemen, and only by the slightest margin failed to cut the main Es Salt track.[61] On 2 May Turkish pressure

59. Now comprising 2 LH Bde, the ICC Bde, and the NZ Mtd Rifles Bde. On 30 March 60 Div (London infantry) reinforced the Anzacs at Amman, and contributed materially to the few advances made.
60. That is, 3 and 4 LH Bdes, and 5 Yeomanry Bde.
61. The Turks captured nine English guns protected by 4 LH Bde, which, save for the pieces left on Gallipoli, were the only guns lost by Australians

increased at all points, and by the 4th they had forced the British once more behind the Ghoraniye bridgehead.

The Australians reported this fight with predictable brevity. 'Well here we are back again after another trip to Es Salt and mighty lucky we are to be back, we were nearly all collared',[62] General Ryrie noted, while at Es Salt a man of Ryrie's brigade remarked, 'Our position is serious as Jacko is giving our chaps a bad time further back & we are pretty well cut off & can't get rations. During the evening we were told that we had to get out at dark . . . we . . . got away two in the morning.'[63]

It was now high summer, and the front quietened while the soldiers suffered the heat. Few even among the local populace remained in the Jordan Valley during summer; the Australians were kept there, in a moist heat varying between 100° and 125° in the shade. A light, powdery dust perpetually frayed their tempers, they rarely tasted fresh food, and flies, mosquitoes, spiders and scorpions plagued them. The number of sick evacuated rose alarmingly,[64] for even Egypt was civilisation beside the barren monotony of that hot, sticky, dusty, lonely valley.

On 19 September 1918, after a delay made necessary partly by the transfer of several British units to France, Allenby launched his final offensive. He attacked away from the Jordan and along the coast, up the Plain of Sharon towards Tul Keram, Samaria, and Nablus, and his direction completely deceived the Turks. English infantry quickly overran their defences, and early on the first morning horsemen broke through to their rear, within 24 hours virtually trapping two Turkish armies. Nazareth, 40 miles north of the start line, fell on 20 September, and Nablus and Samaria a day later. The great chase had begun.

Everywhere the enemy was demoralised. The Turkish armies west of the Jordan lost general formation as every man, seeking his own salvation, turned to dodge the flying hoofs of the horsemen, or

during the war. Men censured 4 LH Bde for their loss: one trooper wrote, 'the 4th got the order "every man for himself" leaving the guns without an escort or horses & became completely demoralised . . . [they] absolutely showed the white feather'. (Tpr G. T. Birkbeck, 1 MG Squad, Printer, of Ashfield, N.S.W. b. 1892. *D* 1/5/18.) The men responsible were among the victors of Beersheba.

62. Ryrie. *L* 6/5/18.
63. J. G. Burgess, *D* 2/5/18.
64. A quarter of the light horse were evacuated with malaria during 1918, and 101 died of the disease.

cowered from the bombs and bullets of airmen who cut the Turks down as they crowded through the narrow mountain gorges in retreat. On the night of 20–21 September, twenty-three Australians straddled the Nablus-Jenin road and bluffed 2800 Turks and Germans with four guns into surrender:

They had no idea we were there and came along in batches of 100 or so. The road ran between high hills, passed over a bridge, and then on to about 10 acres of clear, flat ground . . . We would allow the enemy to pass over the bridge, then bail them up and disarm them, and then turn them out to the flat. There was a great amount of booty . . . and . . . We struck some good cigars and there we were with about six revolvers each smoking cigars bailing them up. We must have looked like the Kelly Gang . . . I got an Iron Cross and several other medals, also . . . thousands of pounds of Turkish notes . . . also a number of stamps. They had a large stack of champagne . . . which was pretty decent . . . also a good pair of binoculars . . . Also a waterproof coat also a couple of green Turkish towels.[65]

By 24 September only a few hundred Turks remained free west of the Jordan, and east of the river mounted troops, sweeping easily through Es Salt and Amman, took 10,000 prisoners and fifty-seven guns.

Some hard battles were fought later, notably at Semakh on the southern shores of the Sea of Galilee, on 25 September, but Allenby's triumphant progress could not be halted. On 1 October light horsemen took Damascus, and on the 2nd Khan Ayash, 17 miles further north. Near this village on that day, 100 men of the Third Light Horse Brigade captured 1500 prisoners and three guns, and two light horsemen took eighty-eight prisoners and a machine gun.

This was the last light horse action of the war. Since 19 September twenty-one Australians had been killed and seventy-one wounded, and light horsemen had taken 31,355 Turkish prisoners. They reported their victories soberly. '[T]he boys have enjoyed the stunt pretty well so far,' a corporal noted, 'of course they had a pretty rough time coming up; some reckon they are sick of the look of Turkish prisoners'.[66]

65. Lt H. H. Stephen, 9 LH Regt. Farmer, of Glenelg, S.A. b. 1889. *L* 17/10/18.
66. A. J. Anderson, *L* 27/10/18.

On 30 October, after Allenby had reached Aleppo in Syria, the Turks signed an armistice. The Australians heard this news and the more momentous announcement of 11 November with little demonstration. The long years were over, and home was near, but the end had been too swift for men to give thought to the future, and some even found it difficult to recall properly their civilian past. So they waited, quietly but expectantly, until the army should order them back to Australia.

Not all went home. Some light horsemen died of malaria in Damascus after the Armistice, and some were killed during the Egyptian uprising early in 1919. And the horses stayed: the old horses were destroyed, the able were sold in Egypt and Palestine. Most troopers had brought their horses from Australia, and thereafter man and horse had shared many a hard hour together. 'Here, a man thinks more of his horse than he does of anything,' a trooper had written in 1917, 'and it is our first consideration that he gets the best of everything.'[67] The Australian walers had been good campaigners, loyal and game through the parched desert marches, during the cold, wet treks over the treacherous mountains, and in the wild, galloping rides of battle. They were acknowledged generally superior to other horses serving in the Middle East, and their riders thought them fit to share Heaven, yet they were sold into the slavery of the Arabs. It was a bitterly resented decision, and some light horsemen shot their horses rather than accept it. Major Hogue wrote,

I don't think I could stand the thought of my old fancy hack
Just crawling round old Cairo with a 'Gyppo on his back.
Perhaps some English tourist out in Palestine may find
My broken-hearted waler with a wooden plough behind.

No; I think I'd better shoot him and tell a little lie:—
"He floundered in a wombat hole and then lay down to die."
May be I'll get court-martialled; but I'm damned if I'm inclined
To go back to Australia and leave my horse behind.[68]

Most light horsemen were countrymen,[69] and almost all con-

67. Stephen, L 19/3/17.
68. In H. S. Gullett and C. Barrett (eds). *Australia in Palestine*, p. 78.
69. The embarkation rolls for the original complement and the last two reinforcement sections of 1 LH Regt (NSW), 5 LH Regt (Qld) and 10 LH Regt (WA), show that about 85 per cent of these men came from rural areas and were chiefly in rural occupations. Few of any occupation in country towns in 1914 could have isolated themselves from rural influences.

THE LAST CRUSADERS **139**

sidered themselves bushmen. Those who by necessity or inclination rode horses in civil life were attracted to the mounted arm of the AIF, and from these a difficult riding test selected only the best horsemen. Many of the chosen were accustomed to an outdoor existence, and were at least susceptible to the skills and attitudes of the bushmen. They thought themselves the sturdiest and freest of their race, well able to ride, shoot, and live off the country.

Bush types persist in an army, and they did particularly in the Australian Light Horse. Bushmen among the Australians introduced to all the British Middle East forces several innovations learnt in Australia, and they were good horsemen usually, and did have a good eye for ground, and could exist under harsh conditions. The heat, the long days in the saddle, and the outdoor camps were much the same in Sinai, in Palestine, and in Australia, and if the light horseman lost by his separation from home and his subjection to discipline, he gained like minded companions and the sense of an elevated purpose, and he was able to display many characteristics natural to his countrymen but more or less suppressed among Australians on the Western Front. Light horsemen performed dashing and chivalrous feats and won some of the most complete victories of the war, yet they behaved as though nothing they did was exceptional, and they wrote little about it. They advanced almost 400 miles in two and a half years, but some at least thought they made ground slowly. Theirs was a most serious task, and seriously they engaged in it, yet they never admitted that it was more than a sort of game, and they encountered every menace carelessly and confidently. During the Turkish advance on Romani in July 1916, an Australian patrol rode into a superior enemy force. The Australians retired two or three hundred yards, dismounted and engaged their advancing foe, then retired as the Turks drew near. Several times they played this game, and once they boiled their billies and made tea while their enemy laboured across the sand towards them. In December 1916 General Ryrie remarked, 'I tried to shoot a big vulture yesterday. if I had, I would have chopped his head and claws off and dressed him & sent him out to Col[onel] Fuller for a Xmas turkey.'[70] These antics became almost impossible to Australians in France.

With similar levity and resolution, light horsemen mocked apparently superfluous spiritual and temporal usages. They derided

70. Ryrie, *L* 17/12/16.

the conventions of God. They followed the Crusaders, and they helped liberate the Holy Land, but they never admitted a serious zeal, they were not religious, and they showed only an active tourist's interest in the birthplace of their faith. 'Had a good look round Jerusalem . . . ,' a trooper told a mate in 1918, 'Don't think much of the crib, Of course the old historical sites & buildings are interesting & beautiful in cases, but the yarns about lots of em are guesswork & some all balls. Anyhow one think I do know & that is the Cognac sold there is murder & worse'n anything you or I ever drank.'[71] Australians also objected to the prices asked by boatmen for transport across the Sea of Galilee by observing that it was no wonder 'that other bloke' walked, and delighted in the story told of the cameliers, that, had they been in Palestine when Christ was crucified, they would have been blamed for it. And at Bethlehem in 1918 a light horseman was shown the tomb of St Jerome, and told that the oil lamp on top had been burning for 500 years. 'Well, its high time it had a rest', he exclaimed, and blew it out.

Light horsemen also derided the conventions of men, and like the infantry developed distinctive attitudes towards discipline. Many, the sons of landowners or professional men, had been bred to a gentlemanly restraint, so that originally they were 'remarkable among the Australian force . . . for punctilious observance of formalities',[72] but in time they became as averse as any Australian to army ceremonial. Few light horsemen had heard a word of stark command in their lives, and, though deferring initially to the romance of army life, they quickly came to judge the merits of every order by their own standards. Sometimes they were obliged to accept instructions they resented—'compelled to go to Football match . . .', noted one man, 'it went against the grain to be compelled . . . but it turned out a very interesting game'[73]—but where possible they ignored useless impositions, and regulated their lives by accustomed and independent ways. 'Tom . . . was up before the Major this morning . . .', a trooper in Sinai related, 'he was doing a galloping stunt on a donk in the village here & rode express into a cafe where the Brigade Major was having some eggs etc. The donk propped & slid along the floor knocking the B.M.'s table over. Tom

71. Tpr A. C. Lumley, 5 LH Regt, Trader and pearler, of Samarai, Papua. b. 1882. *L* 6/4/18.
72. Gullett, *Official History*, VII, p. 34.
73. Sgt. S. V. Hicks, 8 LH Regt, Farmer, of Rushworth, Vic. RTA 12/7/18, aged 27. *D* 6/3/17.

was told to be more careful in future.'[74] And in Palestine a general commented, 'I went out last night and shot two dogs which were always barking. The owners hav'nt said anything about it, I think they are afraid. I never did like barking dogs much.'[75]

Apparently the cameliers were especially unruly, and were proud of it. Their Corps had been formed partly by enrolling 'bad characters' from other Australian units: 'I doubt if so many "hard-doers" could have been found in any other Australian fighting unit . . .', Frank Reid, a camelier private, wrote after the war,

hardly a day passed without at least half a dozen of the Cameliers being paraded at the orderly room for disorderly conduct . . . Nearly every night there was a stoppage of the [Cairo tram] service because the Cameliers would not pay their fares . . . a conductor would be pushed off the tram and the driver would follow him. Then . . . wild rides, with gongs clanging as the trams proceeded full speed across intersections with natives, fowls, and donkeys scattering in all directions to escape injury.[76]

This was an old Australian game, but occasionally cameliers threatened to shoot unpopular officers, and once an officious camelier lieutenant lost his patrol in the desert and then asked his men where they were. A private rode up alongside him and whispered hoarsely, 'Sir, something tells me we are on active service abroad.' Cameliers preferred to give officers a wave or a nod rather than a salute, and, as did most Australian soldiers, they admired the officer who led well in battle, lived as a soldier in camp, and respected the dignity of his men.

Almost every light horseman resented saluting. The salute was a difficult exercise of obscure necessity, particularly when performed from horseback, in the desert, before neatly dressed staff officers rarely seen about the business of war. Many Australians considered that those who most demanded the salute usually least deserved it, and generally they ignored any but their own officers. 'Not only do your men fail to salute me when I ride through your camps,' one British general complained, 'but they laugh aloud at my orderlies.'[77]

74. J. G. Burgess, *D* 5/4/16.
75. Ryrie, *L* 27/2/18.
76. F. Reid, *The Fighting Cameliers*, pp. 3-4. (Pte, ICC, Journalist, of Pring, Qld. b. 1885.)
77. Gullett, *Official History*, VII, p. 533.

Most English leaders were led to make similar complaints, but no admonition produced improvement: General Ryrie observed, 'Our men are not popular with the Imperial men as they *will not* salute them, we are always trying to drum it into them, but they are very tough.'[78] Gradually, as the light horse displayed its excellent battle discipline and won an unending succession of victories, the demands of the Englishmen diminished.

Perhaps because of his victories, the light horseman's war was not severe. Between April 1916 and December 1918, 973 Australians were killed in action or died of wounds in Sinai or Palestine, 430 died from other causes, 3351 were wounded, and only seventy-three, none of them officers, were taken prisoner. In France more fell in a day. There were periods of privation, and some hard battles, but little to approach the fearful conditions on the Western Front, and most light horsemen knew it. Although in the end many wearied of war, some did not, and the senses of glory and romance continued throughout to mark their brief accounts of battle. Near El Arish an officer listened to the rumble of the guns bombarding Gaza, and thought it quite pleasant, awakening good old memories of the past on Gallipoli.[79] Men in France came to hear only menace in that rumble. A brigadier at Magdhaba,[80] suddenly confronted by the rifles of five Turks, raised his cane and shouted at them in Zulu, and they surrendered. No-one in France would have tried that. In June 1916 a light horse patrol attacked a small Turkish outstation near Bayud:

a long range duel ensued in a desultory manner for about 3 hrs: the only casualties—on our side at any rate—being two horses slightly wounded by strays.

I myself heard three bullets whistle over, the first I have heard since Anzac,—I was forgetting that there was a war on.

The whole thing was very funny officers would ride up smiling & rubbing there hands

'There is a beautiful little engagement going on up the hill there'

'Anybody hit yet?'

78. Ryrie, *L* 20/3/17.
79. Lt F. J. Burton, 4 LH Regt, Farmer, of Nullan, Vic. KIA 31/10/17, aged 23. *D* 7/4/17.
80. Brig J. R. Royston, CMG, DSO. Commanded 12 LH Regt 1915-16, 3 LH Bde 1916-17. Returned to South Africa November 1917, aged 57.

Anzac Cove in early May 1915, looking north towards Ari Burnu (top left), where the first landings were made

Eighth Battalion men in a reserve trench on Anzac in May 1915

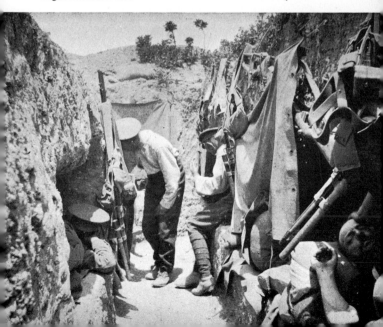

First Division artillerymen on water fatigue, Anzac, c.July 1915

Men of the First Brigade in the Lone Pine trenches on Anzac,
8 August 1915

A section of Shrapnel
Gully cemetery, Anzac,
November 1915

First Light Horse Brigade troops at Esdud, Palestine, on
10 January 1918

Light horsemen in the Ghoraniye bridgehead across the Jordan,
May 1918

Pozières village: the main street before the war [above] . . . and on
28 August 1916 [below]

Second Division men coming out of the line, c. March 1917

Fifth Division soldiers on the 'Jabber Track' in the Passchendaele area,
c. November 1917

A platoon of the 29th Battalion before the 8 August battle, 1918

Photograph of a group of ten
Australian deserters which was sent to the A.P.M.
Havre, with the following letter:-

"Sir,
        With all due respect we send you this P.C.
as a souvenir trusting that you will keep it as a
mark of esteem from those who know you well. At the
same time trusting that Nous jamais regardez vous
encore.   Au revoir.
                        Nous"

        Information regarding any of these men
should be addressed to Provost Marshal, G.H.Q.,
reference his No. M/4292/924
(see "KEY" given in P.G. No.19 para. A.1.)

Australian deserters hope never to see the military police at Le Havre
again

Oh no not when I left '
'It seems so incongruous after the peninsular.'[81]

In July 1916 Ion Idriess was one of a patrol ambushed at Mageibra: '[We] . . . rode like laughing madmen . . .', he related,

half our bodies were in view of the Turks. How their rifles rattled from across the valley! . . . Quickly we gained on the rest of the patrol, the wind swished back their excited laughter . . . Soon after the others had sped out into the desert from the bottom of the hill we caught up to them, steadying down to a swift hand canter. Everyone was laughing . . . [and] enjoying the joke immensely.[82]

Despite its discomforts, this was often a gay war. Although men fought it seriously, in a sense it was not a serious war: it was a sideshow, fought against an enemy who was deluded, not fiendishly bent on the destruction of mankind. Success persuaded a few Australians to discount the Turk as a soldier, but the Turks were infantry fighting against horsemen, and they were badly fed and equipped, and shockingly treated when ill or wounded. They lived and fought gallantly under conditions insufferable to European soldiers, and while most light horsemen assumed a racial superiority over their opponent, few despised him. He was always Jacko to them, dedicated to the destruction of his country's enemies, and fighting gamely and fairly through every reverse. For example, to reach Romani the Turks had to march across 70 miles of sandy desert, and over every yard of the way they laid planks and bushes to support their 60-pounder guns, thus laboriously inching the ponderous machines forward. This by itself won Australian admiration, but then the Turks made a forced march over the last 10 miles to Romani, and conducted a spirited assault as soon as they arrived. The Australians attempted nothing like it, and 'every man in his own fashion, by praise or jest or grim curse, expressed admiration for the willingness, the determination, the bitter stubbornness of the Turk.'[83]

That admiration never slackened. After Romani a patrol near Salmana Oasis found

68 Turks who had been left behind in the retreat & who were almost perishing from thirst. They had been four . . . [or] five

81. Evans, *D* 12/6/16.
82. Idriess, *Desert Column*, pp. 93-4 (–/7/16).
83. Idriess, *Desert Column*, p. 100 (5/8/16).

*days—without water and . . . were all very weak & could not
walk any distance . . . & were beyond . . . offering any resistance . . . We gave them what [water] we could & . . . there was
nothing for it but to put them on our horses while we led them!
This was a very queer sight . . . From the Colonel downwards
giving up our horses to prisoners of war while we trudged along
the sand for about 5 miles . . . It was hot & heavy work. But we
got the poor beggars all in. You see that it is not true that we
shoot all our prisoners!*[84]

In September 1918 about 6000 Turks were trapped by Allenby's
advance in waterless country south of Amman. They were at the
mercy of English and Australian airmen, but would not surrender,
and entrenched themselves at Ziza. Squadrons of the 5th Light
Horse Regiment went to meet them, and learned that the Turks were
willing to surrender, but mistrusted 10,000 Arab tribesmen who for
days past had prowled on their flanks, thirsting to plunder. General
Ryrie shared their mistrust, and galloped the rest of his Second Light
Horse Brigade to Ziza, took three sheikhs hostage, broke through the
Arab cordon, and joined the Turks. Australian and Turk bivouacked
together that night, dissolving years of conflict in hours of armed
alliance. Both fired at the Arabs and killed a few, but they were not
attacked, and when the New Zealand Brigade arrived in the morning, the Turks surrendered.

The Turkish commander at Ziza had offered to destroy the
Arabs, then surrender. The offer might have appealed in other
circumstances, wrote an official historian later, because the British
general who received it 'was strong in his respect for the Turk and
his scorn for the Arab, but it was impossible at the time'.[85] To a
man, light horsemen vehemently hated the Arabs. The desert
Bedouin hung like jackals about the Australian camps, begging and
thieving. They were of no consequence racially, they were black and
dirty, and they smelt. Like Ryrie at Ziza, the Australians hardly
thought it worth mention if a few were killed.

But the Arabs were also considered treacherous and cruel,
readier to pillage than to fight, spies for the Turks, savages who dug
up British dead for their equipment, who attacked weaker patrols,

84. Capt H. Wetherell, 5 LH Regt, Farmer, of Rylstone, NSW. b 1894.
L 20/8/16.
85. Gullett, *Official History*, VII, p. 725.

who stripped and left to die men lying wounded on the field. British policy protected them to encourage their allegiance: the Arabs used this to license their brigandage. Their claim to have been wronged by 'men in big hats' usually brought official retribution and orders to pay damages upon Anzac heads, yet counter claims were ignored. Reason and bigotry developed in the horsemen a murderous hatred towards the desert nomads, which sometimes exploded into action. At Hassana, in Sinai, men were sent out to round up Bedouins who had fired on Camel Corps patrols,

but when they approached . . . a Bedouin fired at close range, and Lance-corporal MacGregor fell badly wounded . . .

Later in the day a party of silent, grim-faced Cameliers captured the Bedouin who had shot the lance-corporal . . . With picks, shovels and rifles they marched out to a sandy hillock, and the Bedouin was forced to go with them. Half an hour later they returned—without the Bedouin[86]

At Mejdel, on the Sea of Galilee, in September 1918,

The ghoulish inhabitants . . . used to gather rifles from the road and snipe at our column, or shoot from a distance into a camp at night, in the hope of dropping a straggler whom they might plunder and strip. At last a party of road engineers . . . sent out scouts, who caught and brought in six of these foul vermin, caught . . . lying in wait with rifles in their hands. In the presence of the muktar (headman) . . . they were stood in a row and shot, giving the local inhabitants a wholesome object lesson.[87]

After the Armistice the insolence of the Arabs rose at last to blatant murder. One night in December 1918, near Surafend, a New Zealand machine gunner was wakened by an Arab tugging at his equipment. He sprang up and chased the thief, shouting for aid as he ran, but as he overtook the native he was shot through the stomach with a revolver, and died as his friends reached him.

This was one of several thefts and murders in the area. Grimly the dead man's comrades tracked his murderer to Surafend, placed a small picket around the village, and waited for dawn. When they

86. Reid, *Fighting Cameliers*, p. 85.
87. Lt J. R. B. Love, MC, DCM, 14 LH Regt, Missionary, of Strathalbyn, SA (b. Ireland). b. 1889. *L* 10/11/18.

demanded the killer, the sheikhs were evasive, and appeals to the British staff for action proved fruitless. At dusk, therefore, a large number of Australians and New Zealanders surrounded Surafend, passed out the women and children, and fell upon the men. Many Arabs were killed, most of the remainder were injured, and the village and a nomad camp near it were burnt. When the work was done, the soldiers returned to their lines.

'In the morning all the disciplinary machinery of the army was as active as hitherto it had been tardy',[88] but no culprit was found. Allenby abused the Anzac Mounted Division for the offence and caused much resentment thereby, but relations between Arabs and Australians did not improve. In March 1919, during the Egyptian uprising, a Gurkha sentry attached to the Second Light Horse Brigade was murdered by Egyptians. General Ryrie asked the village nearby to produce the murderer for execution; on receiving no response, he burnt the village.[89]

The fierce individualism with which he fought Turks, Arabs, and English staff officers lay close to the heart of the Australian light horseman. He lived under few restraints, and was equally careless of man, God, and nature. Yet he stood by his own standards firmly, remaining brave in battle, loyal to his mates, generous to the Turks, and pledged to his King and country. His speech betrayed few of his enthusiasms, and he accepted success and failure equally without demonstration, but the confident dash of the horseman combined with the practical resource and equanimity of the bushman in him, and moved him alike over the wilderness of Sinai and the hills of the Holy Land. Probably his kind will not be seen again, for the conditions of war and peace and romance that produced him have almost entirely disappeared.

88. Gullett, *Official History*, VII, p. 789.
89. Ryrie, *L* 29/3/19.

FRANCE

6 The Fighting in France

> For Christ's sake write a book on the life of an infantryman, and
> by so doing you will quickly prevent these shocking tragedies.
>
> Corporal A. G. Thomas, 6th Battalion, under
> fire at Pozières, 25 July 1916

1916

The Australians landed at Marseilles,[1] belied their reputation by
almost faultless behaviour in the port, and in a few days entrained
for billets in northern France. The journey was their most pleasant
since leaving Australia. The green countryside and the cheers and
kisses of the populace seemed paradise after Egypt, and second
only to one other land and people on earth. But it was not the
Western Front, and almost every Australian was eager to man that
legendary line.

By now many old soldiers were ready to re-enter the fray. Dreams
of glory still enticed some, boredom or a sense of duty prompted
many, and almost all, knowing that further fighting was inevitable,
compromised with fate and persuaded themselves that their experiences on Gallipoli would not be repeated. Sergeant de Vine
observed, 'We are all anxious to see the front line on this sector,
which we are told is quite different to the trenches of Gallipoli',[2]
and another Anzac exclaimed, 'In twelve days should God spare
me, I shall celebrate my 22nd birthday! How? Where? As a Soldier
I could ask for nothing better that to be Merrily in Action, and
doing well.'[3] The veterans also hoped to help destroy a monstrous
enemy. A young Queenslander told his family,

1. The first troops, 25 Bn and 7 Bde HQ, arrived from Egypt on 19 March
1916; the last, elements of 5 Div, soon after 8 July 1916. Thereafter most
Australians went from Australia to England, via Durban, Suez, or occasionally Panama, and then to France.
2. de Vine, *D* 10/4/16.
3. Cull, *L* 19/7/16.

France

*I'll do my best to return to you but if I do get a smack you'll
have nothing to be ashamed of and nobody will be able to say
that you gave birth to a son who was afraid to die and would
rather promenarde the street than fight for the Honour of their
Parents and sisters, for as sure as night follows day Belgium's
fate would have been Englands & Aust. had the Germans their
own way.*[4]

'I have not yet had the close quarter opportunity', Lieutenant
Armitage stated, 'but if God permits—when I do—I will show I
have not forgotten . . . Belgium, Servia, and Gallipoli.'[5] 'I expect we
are going to tackle them & drive 'em well back', predicted Private
Tom Hill, 'If so you can bet your son will be well in it. I hate them
that much . . . I am quite prepared to meet my maker . . . I am glad
to be fighting & upholding the good old British race.'[6] Since the war
began Australians had detested the Hun, and the grim days on
Gallipoli had committed the veterans deeply to their duty, so that
now a fierce hatred and a firm purpose animated them.

But the belief that war was a shining adventure continued to lure
some novices. 'I am very eager to get up "there" ', a lieutenant
wrote from southern France, '. . . I am very keen to reach some
finality after so many months training',[7] and just before he entered
the line another soldier announced,

*The long-looked-forward-to day has arrived, and it has brought
with it no apprehensions. The prospect of a term in the 'first
line' fills me with all sorts of anticipations. What will the actual
trenches be like? What is the feeling of one 'under fire' for the
first time? Are we to occupy a 'hot' part of the line, or a place of
comparative quiet?*[8]

A man who had reached Gallipoli in mid-December commented in
France that he could get leave to England, but would defer it 'until
I had a smack at the Germans. then after a flutter shall apply . . .
if still in the land of the living',[9] and Arthur Brunton declared,

*I don't seem to worry over it, but just look at it as a matter of
course. I will be frightfully wild if I get knocked out right at the*

4. Mann, *L* 1/6/16.
5. Armitage, *D* 5/4/16.
6. Hill, *L* 30/5/16.
7. Capt L. G. Short, MC, 23 Bn, Journalist, of Hawthorn, Vic (b. England).
b. 1885. *L* 16/6/16.
8. Sgt J. J. Makin, 21 Bn, Clerk, of Middle Park, Vic. b. 1895. *D* 11/6/16.
9. Henderson, *L* 11/6/16.

*start without having had a chance to damage the Germans . . .
one thing only . . . depresses me . . . the terrible blow it would be
to my little sweetheart if I never returned. Otherwise I am glad
that I am here to do my little bit towards avenging the wrongs of
Belgium and France*[10]

Yet probably most recruits at this time, in contrast to the 1914
volunteers, thought they were approaching a difficult and demanding duty. Just before his first 'tour' in the front line a young Englishman told his parents that he had never regretted joining the AIF,
that he had done the only thing possible, and that he knew their
trust and hope in him would never be misplaced.[11] A Victorian
officer enlisted to defend the Empire, and considered Kipling's
poetry 'very applicable to those of our boys who fall, giving up
their lives in God's cause for God's principles . . . Such a death
must wipe out all stains',[12] and for the first time in the war a few
untried men confessed themselves prepared to enter the line simply
because they could not avoid it. 'All the boys will be glad to get
into action I think,' a private observed, 'being close to it now and
knowing that it must come'.[13]

Nonetheless, even if they guessed at the ordeal ahead, new
soldiers were ready to fight. One reported,

*we are going to take our place alongside of the rest of the
Australians who have been fighting here for a few months. I
hope I get through all right and get back to Australia again.*

*I am in the best of health and spirits and not at all nervous
about the ordeal we have to face and hope we all keep up the
grand reputation the Australians have for bravery*[14]

Another claimed, 'our losses heavy. There is not a man though
who does not . . . [say] he is out to do his bit and if it's his stiff luck
to get cracked then those dear to him have the satisfaction of knowing he gave himself in the cause of humanity and freedom

10. Brunton, *D* 8/7/16.
11. Lt W. G. Blaskett, 48 Bn, Civil servant, of Bowden, SA (b. England).
KIA 11/4/17, aged 21. *L* 30/5/16.
12. Lt H. C. Howard, 59 Bn, Photographer, of South Yarra, Vic. KIA
19/7/16, aged 23. *L* 2/7/16.
13. Cpl H. K. Jackson, 8 Bn, Orchardist, of Hawthorn, Vic. KIA 27/7/16,
aged 24. *L* 9/4/16.
14. Lt F. W. Appleton, 14 Bn, Clerk, of St Kilda, Vic. KIA 8/8/18, aged 35.
L 27/6/16.

generally',[15] and when the new men first heard the guns, most saw the prospect of exciting adventure rising before them. On the day he joined his battalion in billets behind the line an officer recorded,

we were under shrapnel all day. The bursts did no harm to our men, although at times the dust rose within a hundred yards. The effect is at first a little startling, but . . . on the whole I rather enjoyed my first experience of a battlefield and regret very much that I was not in the big Pozieres stunt[16]

A succession of entries in a stretcher bearer's diary reflect similar ardour. On 31 July he noted, 'We are now under 20 miles from the firing line'; on the next day, 'We [are] . . . too late for this last big push. Eager to go up and see what the game is like. Well it will not be long now'; and a fortnight later, 'Just about a mile from the trenches now . . . It has taken me from October 20th, 1915 to August 15th, 1916, to get to the firing line.'[17]

The first months on the Western Front were not severe. The Australians were introduced into the line at Fleurbaix, near Armentières, where the trenches were

not dug, as it is impossible to dig more than 1 foot without striking water, sand bag breast works are erected about 5 to 6 ft high & 3 to 4 ft thick which gives very solid cover & protection from rifle shots, but would not last very long under artillery fire . . . Everything is remarkably quiet on this sector, which is at present being held by an English regiment, very seldom is a shot fired . . . A considerable amount of movement is taking place all day long to which the Germans apparently take no exception, the idea being 'Don't fire at me and I will not fire at you' these sentiments were expressed to me by a British tommy.[18]

Their gentle reception relieved many veterans. They contrasted it favourably with the dark days on Gallipoli, and agreed with the new soldiers that war was pleasant in France, because there were no great battles, but short stays in the line, comparative immunity, and

15. Bartlett, *D* 20/7/16.
16. Capt G. Stobie, MC, 6 Bn, Accountant, of Kew, Vic. b. 1892. *D* 27/7/16.
17. Pte A. M. Kilgour, 1 Fld Amb, Mint official, of Sydney, NSW. b. 1892. *D* 31/7, 1/8, and 15/8/16.
18. de Vine, *D* 27/4/16. The normal routine of the trenches is described in A. T. Paterson et al., *The Thirty Ninth*, pp. 75-8.

comfort in the back areas. 'I had the best of times in the trenches and I wish I was back again . . .' a soldier declared, 'I did 3 hours work laying wire at night, and had the rest of the 24 hours to myself, and . . . It suited me down to the ground . . . We also had splendid tucker.'[19] A private wrote, 'I am having good time over here . . . every thing being in our favour and every thing very quiet. I can tell [you] that if that was all we were to be affaraid of it would suit me untill after the war'.[20] A third man decided, 'coming across [to] the trenches is not to bad after all. I reckon it is a bally fine place now and again you have to duck from a 75 german shell but you get used to that'.[21] There were minor inconveniences, but also compensating diversions:

I broke a German periscope this morning from our snipers loop hole. The Hun waved the broken end up in the air. They always do that when we hit them and we do vice versa. I placed a tobacco tin up on the parapet for him to fire at and I got into the sniping post and scan their loopholes with the field glasses. After a while I saw one opened very cautiously and a rifle stuck out and before he fired I put a shot on the iron plate which is used to make the loopholes, he withdrew his rifle and closed up his loophole so of course I claimed a victory.[22]

Wounded in head & left eye @ 3.30 p.m. by German sniper. Just put my rifle through the Loophole & was drawing a bead on him when—Bang—his bullet smashed on to the iron plate of my loophole. Hardly knew what had happened at first but the blood soon put me wise.[23]

In a relatively tranquil atmosphere, the soldiers manned their breast-works, watched aeroplane 'dogfights', patrolled No Man's Land, sat out the German artillery's daily 'strafe',[24] waited for the victory most thought imminent, and willingly undertook the formal raids to which their leaders shortly introduced them.

19. Sgt C. C. H. Baldwin, MM, 3 Bn, Accountant, of Rose Bay, NSW. KIA 2/3/17, aged 23. *L* 21/5/16.
20. Anon. pte, 46 Bn, *L* –/7/16.
21. Lt J. H. McKenzie, 20 Bn, Labourer, of Taralga, NSW. b. 1894. *L* 12/4/16.
22. Lt T. Brew, DCM, 2 Bn, Fellmonger, of Ballarat, Vic (b. England). KIA 4/10/17, aged 20. *D* 29/4/16.
23. Bendrey, *D*.25/4/16.
24. Bombardment. The best known German shells were the 'whizzbang' (77 mm), the 'woolly bear' (the so-called 5.9 inch). and the 'coalbox' (15 or 18 cm). Artillery played a vital role in fighting on the Western Front.

Raids were vicious and bloody affairs. Later they became the least popular infantry tactic: within a few months of this time men were writing, 'they are not worth the cost . . . None of the survivors want to go in any more. Mac's nerves are very jumpy now, and many of the others are the same',[25] and 'my word it was hot. My mate was killed alongside me . . . the bulletts were like hailstones. No more raids for me if I can help it.'[26] But during the first half of 1916 the Australians were fresh, confident, and eager to match themselves against the Hun.

The enemy raided first, on the night of 5 May 1916, against a sector held by the 20th Battalion. They laid down

a shocking bombardment, hell let loose . . . it seemed as though every gun the enemy possessed was ranged against us & then when our artillery got going behind us, it was God darn awful, & . . . the Germans set up a cheering & shouting, the like, I have never heard before & simultaneously charged us in mass formation . . . they reached our left flank & got in amongst our fellows. It was fearful yet awe-inspiring, for the first few minutes I felt sick, then as steady as a rock, I was right in the line of fire & the shells came straight for my bay . . . some fellows nerves gave way & they became gibbering idiots Seargeants & all sorts, god it was little wonder for . . . fighting here is just simply massacre.[27]

The raiders inflicted 131 casualties, and apparently suffered none.[28] Worse, they captured two Stokes mortars, then so secret that Haig[29] had ordered that they never be left in the front line. Their loss embarrassed the AIF along the entire British battle front, and made the Australians eager for revenge. A month after the calamity a 27th Battalion NCO related,

25. Brunton, *D* 23/8/16.
26. Spr L. J. McKay, 15 Fld Coy, Fibro plasterer, of Fitzroy, Vic. b. 1897. *D* 17/9/16. Yet McKay added later that day, 'But taking it all round it wasn't bad & I got two days off for it. I am back so why worry.' Men commonly recovered from bad experiences in this way, otherwise they could not have continued.
27. Cpl A. G. Thomas, 6 Bn, Tailor manager, of Toorak, Vic (b. England). KIA 8/6/18, aged 40. *L* 9/5/16. Thomas's 6 Bn was in the line on the right of 20 Bn during the raid, and he is describing only the artillery bombardment which accompanied it.
28. In fact four Germans were killed and fifteen wounded. Ten Australians were captured.
29. Field Marshal Earl Douglas Haig, OM, KT, GCB, GCVO, KCIE. C in C British Expeditionary Force in France 1915-19. b. 1861.

*I was going to England on my leave on June the second. But
I volunteered to go on a raiding party & I have been picked &
I wouldn't miss that for anything. We are going to go into the
German Trenches & suprise them or else bomb them out. It
will be a fairly risky job but I think we can carry it out alright
. . . The Germans made a raid on our Trenches down at the
20th Batt. & killed or wounded a hundred men. so I may assure
we won't take no prisoners.*[30]

The first Australian raid, on the night of 5 June, succeeded, and
soon the Australians, never lacking volunteers, were raiding almost
nightly, agitating every quiet sector they held, and winning an
ascendancy over the enemy which they retained for most of the
war.

Usually, when a raid was decided upon, a raiding team would be
selected, withdrawn from the line, and trained against a model of its
objective:

*Each man in the raiding party had a certain job to do [for ex-
amples, demolition, collecting booty, taking prisoners, killing,
building defensive barriers, and looking for mine galleries] . . .
and he had to be a specialist in [it] . . . We were trained . . . for
three weeks just like a football team.*

*We don't take a single thing with us to show who we are if
Fritz gets our bodies. We wear Tommy uniforms . . . Only
about 4 men out of the 66 carry rifles and bayonets . . . The
rest carry weapons according to their job.*[31]

When all was ready, an artillery barrage saturated the objective, and
the raiders struck:

*when we did our dash all went like clockwork except one thing,
and that mistake proved very costly to us . . . the artillery had
been firing just too far, and nearly all their shells had landed in
Fritz's front trench instead of in his wire (which was uncut). I
don't know how we did it, but we got through into the German
trench and did our job in full. A piece of shrapnel got me*

---

30. Lt D. W. Caldwell, 27 Bn, Carpenter, of Semaphore, SA. KIA 2/3/17,
aged 23. *L* –/6/16. Possibly Caldwell took part in the raid made near
Messines by 25 and 27 Bns on the night of 28 June.
31. Sgt H. M. Davies, 57 Bn. Farmer, of Heidelberg, Vic. DOW 22/7/16,
aged 24. *L* –/7?/16. Bean, *Official History*, III, p. 245, also compares training for raids with that for football.

*through the left thigh . . . one of our chaps . . . managed to
get me out to a drain about the centre of No Man's Land. It
was impossible to get back to our own trenches until Fritz's
bombardment lifted . . . [and] The beggars . . . started spraying
with machine guns and shrapnel . . . We had to lie there for an
hour and three quarters before their guns lifted off our trenches
. . . my leg was quite stiff by this time . . . and as they were still
playing the search lights and machine guns all over us, our only
way out was along the drain . . . I hung on to [a fellow's] braces
and tried to keep my face up out of the mud as he dragged me
through . . . [At] the end of the drain a big sergeant of ours was
waiting . . . he picked me up and carried me right across to our
trenches with the bullets snapping all around . . . he brought in
four more*[32]

It is not surprising that raids became unpopular, for few succeeded faultlessly. When they did succeed, men often enjoyed
them. In the last year of the war, when the tactics of raids had
improved a little, a 1918 reinforcement reported,

*we advanced out into No Mans Land In the Dark as stealthy
as Red Indians & Took up Positions In Shell Holes Quite close
to the Hun Trenches[33] . . . [Then] our Artillery opened into the
Germans and Belted Hell & Blazes Into them—we sneaked up
under the Barrage & It was lovely shells Bursting & Lights
shooting all over the sky . . . all of a Sudden It lifted back a
couple of Hundred yards & away we charged yelling like devils
right Into His Trenches Fritzey Bolted & we after Him I was
directly after my officer & a couple Dodged Into a Dugout. we
Fed Them on Bombs etc & on To the next. Gee you should
Have been In the Fun our Boys Got Busy Bayonets, Bombs &
Rifle Fire. We First Bombed It & Finished off a couple & took
a couple Prisoners. Then we Into it & got all the Mail & So on.
I got a Bonzer Coat . . . also a Fritz Rifle . . . Its Good Fun & I*

---

32. H. M. Davies, *L* –/7?/16. But Bean, *Official History*, III, pp. 328-9,
states that no raid was launched by 5 Div (of which Sgt Davies's 57 Bn was
part) before 22 July (the date Sgt Davies died), and neither the 15 Bde War
Diary nor the 57 Bn War Diary mention a raid at that time. Probably the
records wrongly ascribe this account to Davies, in which case my assigning
the letter to July might also be inaccurate.
33. 'Silent' raids, relying on stealth, later often replaced those employing a
preparatory artillery barrage.

*Hope To Have a Bit more of the Raiding Stunt It will do me . . .
I . . . really enjoyed it.*[34]

Australians became notedly proficient raiders.

On 1 July Haig began his offensive on the Somme. 60,000
British soldiers were killed or wounded that day, and perhaps
650,000 before the generals halted in September; in return, less
than three miles of ground were won. The Somme was the supreme
ordeal of the British Army during the war.

Australians were not employed in the offensive during its first
weeks, and press reports led them to exaggerate its ease and success,
so that some, particularly the inexperienced, looked forward confidently to their first big battle in France. A West Australian ordered
to remain while his battalion went into the line felt it 'very much
again the grain. Going in again to night by hook or crook. Its too
awful to comtemplate being left out of the stunt.'[35] A young
lieutenant wrote,

*At last the day is near when Australia's boys will once again
be given an opportunity to show the World what we are made
of . . . to-morrow we hope to be on the road to Berlin . . . we
are ready, fit, and well, and with God's help will punish the
Bosh for his cruelty to the weaker races . . . to-day, you should
have seen the look of determination on the faces of all. I am
sure that the Hun will be sorry for the day when Australia sent
her sons to France.*[36]

'This is my last letter before going into a stunt,' an Englishman from
Victoria, Arthur Thomas, told his wife and children, 'I feel quite
cool and collected, of course being cool will not avail much . . .
[but] I am quite well & fit so will put up a merry fight for Old
England so three cheers for the Anzacs & the early ending of this
sinful game. God bless you all my loved ones pray hard for me.'[37]

Most Australians knew that a great battle lay ahead, guessed its
intensity from the trains of wounded and the casualty lists, and
prepared to do a necessary but uncomfortable duty. '[W]e are in
for a stouching up for a certainty,' Archie Barwick predicted, 'for

34. Molesworth, L 6/3/18.
35. Capt C. S. Dawkins, 51 Bn, Warehouseman, of Subiaco, WA. KIA 3/9/16, aged 24. D 14/8/16.
36. Malpas, L –/7/16.
37. Thomas, L 22/7/16.

we are going to try and do what English troops have so far failed to do . . . I don't expect many of us will come out alive . . . whether we take or fail in the charge however the boys are all very confident over it.'[38] Lieutenant Armitage recorded, 'I'll go into action with the calm assurance that I have done my duty to my men and my Country. If I happen to fall,—rest content with the knowledge that I have played the game, and done my job thoroughly,'[39] and Major Geoff McCrae, commanding the 60th Battalion, told his family, 'To-day I lead my battalion in an assault on the German lines and I pray God I may come through alright and bring honour to our name. If not I will at least have laid down my life for you and my country which is the greatest privilege one can ask for.'[40] He was killed at Fromelles, shot through the neck before he reached the enemy lines. Lieutenant Eric Chinner, bombing officer of the 32nd Battalion, resigned his fate to the care of his God: 'I am not afraid,' he told his parents, 'Of course, I'm a bit shakey, but not very scared . . . I'm writing this to you because you will [then] know something of what is doing should anything happen . . . I feel sure God will watch over me and pull me through. Cheerio anyway.'[41] He died in the German trenches, trying to smother a bomb he had dropped when wounded. Lieutenant Jacques d'Alpuget, a former Rugby Union international, wrote two days before he was killed,

we . . . are preparing for something big . . . the biggest move any Australians have done in France . . . long before this letter reaches you you will know the result, which I feel certain will be to the credit of Australia, if I happen to be one of the un-lucky ones you will know I have done my best and lead a straight life right up to the finish.[42]

The old confidence was still there, but the light had faded since 1914.

Although the First, Second, and Fourth Divisions, comprising 1 Anzac Corps, were ordered south to the Somme early in July, Australia's first major enterprise on the Western Front, a 'feint' designed to divert German reserves from the Somme, was entrusted

38. Barwick, *D* III, pp. 248-9 (17/7/16).
39. Armitage, *D* 30/7/16.
40. McCrae, *L* 19/7/16.
41. Chinner, *L* 15/7/16.
42. Lt J. M. d'Alpuget, 54 Bn, Accountant, of Edgecliff, NSW. KIA 17/7/16, aged 30. *L* 15/7/16.

to the Fifth Division, which had remained in the north, before the small town of Fromelles. As twilight faded upon its tenth day in France, 19 July 1916, this division, with the English Sixty First Division, moved forward to destroy the Hun.

The German artillery caught them before they reached their own front line. Shell after shell burst among the packed columns, cluttering the trench floors with dead and wounded. 'They lay in heaps behind the parapet . . .', a stretcher bearer related,

[or] crouched close under cover . . . Chaos and weird noises like thousands of iron foundries, deafening and dreadful, coupled with the roar of high explosives . . . ripped the earth out of the parapet, . . . we crept along seeking first of all the serious cases of wounded. Backwards & forwards we travelled between the firing line and the R.A.P. with knuckles torn and bleeding due to the narrow passage ways. 'Cold sweat', not perspiration, dripped from our faces and our breath came out only in gasps . . . By the time we had completed 2 trips [each of three miles] . . . we were . . . completely exhausted.[43]

A machine gunner, Sergeant Martin, recalled,

we had to get up as close to the parapet as possible anybody who did not do this was simply courting death for shells were falling all round . . . there were dead and wounded everywhere . . . I had to sit on top of a dead man as there was no picking and choosing . . . I saw a shell lob about twelve yards away and it . . . lifted [two men] clean up in the air for about 6 feet and they simply dropped back dead . . . one or two of the chaps got shell shock and others got really frightened it was piteous to see them . . . One great big chap got away as soon as he reached the firing line and could not be found . . . I saw him in the morning in a dug out he was white with fear and shaking like a leaf. One of our Lieuts. got shell shock and he literally cried like a child, some that I saw carried down out of the firing line were struggling and calling out for their mother, while others were blabbering sentences one could not make out . . . [a] badly wounded [chap] . . . had his body partly in a small hole that had a good deal of wood work about it, this

43. Pte W. J. A. Allsop, 8 Fld Amb, Clerk, of Mosman, NSW. b. 1893. D 20/7/16.

somehow got alight and all I could see was the lower parts of his legs and a piece of his face, all the rest was burned[44]

The men had not yet passed beyond the front trench, and as the awful toll mounted they began to realise the terrible ordeal before them. '[T]he shells are flying round like ants its awful,' one wrote, '. . . God knows how many of us will come out of it alive.'[45]

Shortly before six p.m. the leading Australians advanced into No Man's Land. Sergeant Martin continued,

We lost some men going over to the enemy's lines and you could hear the moans of the wounded and dying wherever you went. I got over the parapet . . . [and] made for a big hole and rested there while we got our breath . . . after that we made a dash but had to drop into any sort of hole we could find for machine guns were turned on to us and the bullets were just skimming over our heads . . . We got to Fritz's front line trenches eventually . . . [and then] to the portion of trench which was behind their front line . . . and stayed there till 5.30 a.m. when we were forced to retire . . . The Germans got somehow or other into their own front line while we were between their first and second lines and there was grave danger of our being cut off, so we had to make a bolt for it and a good few were hit coming back . . . but the bullets happened to miss me somehow or other[46]

This account well outlines Fromelles. Two of the six Australian battalions attacking and almost all the Englishmen were halted in No Man's Land, and an eager and confident enemy picked out and shot down almost every attacking officer. The survivors were without support, but they charged into the German line, and some advanced beyond. During the night they resisted several counter-attacks, but at last, depleted in strength and numbers, they gave way, and as dawn broke those not captured sprinted desperately through a merciless fire back to their own lines.

Australians had never experienced a more calamitous or tragic night. 5133 men had fallen, about 400 were taken prisoner, and

44. Lt L. J. Martin, 1 MG Bn, Warehouseman, of Dulwich Hill, NSW. b. 1889. *L* 31/7/16.
45. Cpl H. H. Harris, 55 Bn, Lift controller, of Redfern, NSW. b. 1873. *D* 19/7/16.
46. Martin, *L* 31/7/16.

some battalions had almost disappeared and for long were useless as fighting instruments. The wounded crowded the trenches, moving to tears a general who saw them, or lay out in No Man's Land, and were sniped by their jubilant foe. Soldiers attempted to arrange a truce to help them; the staff of both sides quashed the attempt. Some crawled to safety: Private A. F. Bell scribbled in his diary, 'Wounded in arm and leg. Going to try and crawl back to trenches tonight'.[47] He reached them, but died of his wounds four days later. Many wounded could not crawl, and lay with their pain for several days. Brave men risked the enemy fusillade to rescue them: one who made such a journey was Arthur Brunton, and before he set forth he prepared to die. 'This may be the last entry in this book,' he told his wife,

for tonight after dark I go out between the lines to bring in the wounded. They have laid in No Man's Land all day. Fritz will probably fire upon us, though we will be unarmed. We drew lots who should go so that it was fair to everyone . . . And now I must bid my little wife farewell, perhaps for the last time, though I hope not. I will do my best[48]

Another was Sergeant Elliott, from New South Wales:

we heard a wounded chap crying out, he was in 'No Man's Land' . . . I said 'Who's coming over' another chap said 'I'm on' so over the parapet we crawled and out to the wounded man, we got to him without anything happening, but as soon as we lifted him to bring him in 'ping' a bullet went through the top of my hat,[49] barely touching the scalp, so we had to lie low for awhile. when we started off again three shots were fired, so I thought it best to leave him until night. A Machine Gun had got him in the legs (4 wounds). He said he would be O.K. if he could get some water, and he wanted a smoke bad, so I gave him cigarettes and matches and promised him water and food, and then we run and crawled back to safety. The water and food went out as soon as we got back. I was a bit narked at not

47. Pte A. F. Bell, 59 Bn, Fireman, of Lakes Entrance, Vic. DOW 24/7/16, aged 25. *D* 19(= 20)/7/16.
48. Brunton, *D* 19(=20)/7/16.
49. During the battle Australians in the later attacking waves had worn slouch hats rather than steel helmets, the only important occasion in France when this was so.

getting him in, but it would have been suicidal to attempt any further.[50]

A third was Simon Fraser, a Victorian farmer:

we must have brought in over 250 [wounded] men by our company alone. It was no light work getting in with a heavy weight on your back especially if he had a broken leg or arm . . . You had to lie down & get him on your back then rise & duck for your life with the chance of getting a bullet in you before you were safe: one foggy morning . . . we could hear someone over towards the German entanglements calling for a stretcher bearer; it was an appeal no man could stand against; so some of us rushed out & had a hunt; we found a fine haul of wounded & brought them in, but it was not where I heard this fellow calling so I had another shot for it & came across a splendid specimen of humanity trying to wriggle into a trench with a big wound in his thigh . . . another man about 30 yds out sang out 'Don't forget me cobber,' I went in & got four volunteers with stretchers & we got both men in safely.[51]

Many wounded were not rescued. Some died at last; others, like the blind man who stumbled in circles about No Man's Land for several days before being struck down,[52] ended their miseries under the bullets of their enemies. Such men were within seconds of salvation, but were doomed. Their cries were awful, one who watched them wrote, '& every move they make the German puts the Machine guns on them some are calling for him to do it to end their misery & this only 50 yards from us & there are hundreds there'.[53]

Thus terminated Fromelles. Few who survived ever forgot it. Many were for a time 'absolutely unnerved', and 'unfitted for further resistance',[54] and the least affected, whose nerves lasted out the strife and the slaughter, lamented, 'we thought we knew something of the horrors of war, but we were mere recruits, and have had our full education in one day',[55] and,

50. Sgt L. F. S. Elliott, 56 Bn, Compositor, of Newtown, NSW (b. England). b. 1890. *L* 3/8/16.
51. 2/Lt S. Fraser, 58 Bn, Farmer, of Byaduk, Vic. KIA 11/5/17, aged 40. *L* 31/7/16.
52. Bean, *Official History*, III, p. 441n.
53. Spr R. A. Muir, 15 Fld Coy, Architect, of Manly, NSW. b. 1881. *L* 21/7/16.
54. Bean, *Official History*, III, p. 438.
55. Lt R. A. McInnis, 53 Bn, Surveyor, of Brisbane, Qld. b. 1891. *D* 19/7/16.

Thank God I am still alive and not murdered . . . My Steel Helmet saved me five times & how many escapes I had could not be counted . . . it was like a butchers shop . . . We look a sorry crowd covered with mud from head to foot arms, legs, eyes, noses, fingers bound up. Yes by hell we caught it & those who think this war is nearly over are in for some surprises.[56]

There was a further consequence. Australians blamed the British staff and, with less justice, the English soldiers beside them for the disaster. One believed that the generals had cancelled the truce arranged to rescue the wounded because Australians were 'common fellows' and not 'British aristocracy', and he wrote bitterly about the Sixty First Division's performance.[57] A few at Fromelles would have supported his first opinion, and most his second—and fifty years afterwards some had not relaxed their judgment.

On the Somme, the First Division had its objective. It was Pozières village, a German artillery position protecting their strongpoint at Thiepval. The place had already withstood several assaults, but it had to fall if the British advance was to continue, and on 23 July 1916 the First Division made ready to attack it. The men filed through the debris of a recent battlefield to reach their start lines, and an NCO remembered that as they lay waiting on the tapes,[58]

The tension affected the men in different ways. I couldn't stop urinating, and we were all anxious for the barrage to begin. When it did begin, it seemed as if the earth opened up with a crash. The ground shook and trembled, and the concussion made our ears ring. It was impossible to hear ourselves speak to a man lying alongside. It is strange how men creep together for protection. Soon, instead of four paces interval between the men, we came down to lying alongside each other, and no motioning could make them move apart.

But when the order came, the men went forward eagerly: 'In the meantime,' the NCO continued, 'the next waves had gone through us, and, being over-anxious, quite a number of our wave went with

56. Harris, *D* 20/7/16.
57. Capt N. A. Nicholson, 14 FAB, Grazier, of Campbell Town, Tas. b. 1886. *L* 21 and 20/7/16.
58. Before an attack lines of white canvas tape were commonly laid across the ground on which the assaulting troops were to line out.

them to be in the fun',[59] and during the advance Private Barwick wrote,

A & B Coy. were supposed to stay in this trench but no fear on they went like a pack of hungry dog's now they had tasted blood . . . the shellfire was now hellish & the noise deafening, but just to show you how cool the boys were, why, some of them were walking up with rifle's at the slope & singing 'I want to go home'[60]

The Australians easily penetrated the enemy's defences, and took most of the village in a few hours. They were exultant, for they had passed a critical test, and shown their superiority over the German infantry. Happily they prospected Pozières for souvenirs, or lay down to rest.

Then the storm burst. A furious bombardment fell upon the captured positions, pounding the earth, and tearing the fragile air with noise. For seven weeks the merciless shells rained almost continuously, the men powerless beneath them. They dug trenches; the guns obliterated them. They crouched in holes; the guns found them and blew them to oblivion, or buried them, and dug them out, and buried them again. Slowly the broken village and the green fields gave way to a desert of brown earth, and still the guns roared. A wall of shells constantly confronted men passing to the front or the rear carrying wounded, messages, food and water, or ammunition:

We . . . were given the job of delivering [bombs] . . . each of us carried our own equipment, 220 rounds of ammunition, 3 day's rations, rifle, and in each hand a box of bombs weighing about 30-lbs. I suppose the full load was about a hundredweight, and with this we had to travel about half a mile through a narrow sap, with a veritable hail of shells falling round us the whole length of it . . . Some of the fellows dropped out, others dropped part or the whole of their load, but most of us saw the distance out, realising that the delivery of the bombs was . . . life or death to the men in the line.[61]

The German gunners sniped at almost any movement; the shells chased men as they ran, churned every yard of ground, sometimes

59. Champion, *D* 23/7/16.
60. Barwick, *D* III, p. 279 (23/7/16).
61. Semple, *L* 13/8/16.

threw up dust visible for ten miles, and hung a perpetual fume fog over the battlefield. '[I]t seems almost impossible that a mouse should be able to live through it',[62] Birdwood declared. Australian soldiers have never endured a more terrible bombardment.

Through it all the Australians maintained their attacks, pushing the German infantry before them. Sometimes they failed, although not often, and always they paid heavily for success. The Second Division relieved the First on 26 July, and gave way to the Fourth Division on 5 August. The incoming battalions were quietened by the ruin they saw: by the dead, 'dozens and dozens . . . all distorted and frozen looks of horror on their faces',[63] and by the storm of shells, which 'became too awful for words, burying men alive and blowing up trenches, and making the whole place a shambles like a huge ploughed field'.[64] Yet, though every yard won multiplied the number of guns that could fire upon them, they slogged doggedly forward, driving a wedge deeper and deeper into the enemy's line.

The strain was almost too great, and every man battled quivering nerves. From an English hospital an officer told his parents,

After your loving words I could not have turned coward, though God knows what we went through, was Hell itself. We just had to grit our teeth and go ahead and do our job. I am not going to tell a lie and say I wasn't a-fraid because I was and who wouldn't be with Death grinning at you from all round and hellish 5.9 shells shrieking through the air and shrapnel dealing death all round. I don't know how I stood it so long without breaking[65]

A lance corporal wrote,

I can tell you I should never have got out alive. Most of the stretcher bearers were killed and wounded and the wounded could not get out . . . there were some wounded [Germans] down in the dug-outs that could not move, so we left them there to die . . . I think I will be away from the Batt about 2 months, then I hope the war will be over. I had a terrible shaking up, though I never lost my nerve for a moment. Some of the

62. Letter to Colonel D. Rintoul, 9 August 1916, WRB Original Document, Imperial War Museum, London.
63. 64. Capt A. J. Cunningham. MC. 2 Fld Coy, Mechanical engineer, of Upper Macedon, Vic (b. England). RTA 13/3/18, aged 32. D 27/7/16.
65. Maj W. G. M. Claridge, 22 Bn, Woolclasser, of Glen Iris, Vic. b. 1886. L 10/8/16.

men went mad. The Australians . . . took a village . . . the English had 3 goes [at] . . . and they stop in a trench while 15 inch shells are landing and very few of them show any fear . . . I hope the war is over very soon for if I ever get a spot like I was in I do not think it is possible to get out alive. It was perfect Hell. Two minutes before I was hit 50 men [were] left out of my company of 220 strong. When I was hit, 18 others were hit at the same time.[66]

In the trenches Sergeant Elvin noted, 'Heavy firing all morning— simply murder. Men falling everywhere . . . Expecting death every second. 23 men smothered in one trench. Dead and dying everywhere. Some simply blown to pieces. Shells falling like hail during a storm. Five left in trench',[67] and Sergeant Anderson prayed, 'If only the barrage will lift and we could get relieved, already our relief is late, the suspense is awful. At last the 21st Battalion has . . . appear[ed] . . . The barrage has lifted, and half dazed, we climb from the trenches and make a wild rush to get away while we have the chance.'[68] His thoughts rambling, Corporal Thomas scribbled as the shells burst ceaselessly about him,

If we can get these blighters back another mile or so then the Cavalry can hop into the bloody inferno and chase 'em right back eight miles or so. I shouldn't bother to take impressions for I want to forget it if possible. I am loaded like a pack horse carrying twelve bombs, 250 rounds am[tn]*, haversack, coat, two gas helmets, rifle. I am Corporal of the bombers and I will do some damage to these bloody huns I have seen things here that will make the bloody military aristocrats' name stink for ever. The soldiers I pity as they have been ruled into this farce . . . God, it is cruel. What humans will stand is astounding . . . To-night will be another long vigil gazing into death, this is truly the Valley of the Shadow. God help us,*

and,

God the whole chaos is too terrific for my pencil, it has been the most ominous time in our lives, God we have been playing tig

66. L/Cpl J. Cohen, 24 Bn, Diamond setter, of Princes Hill, Vic. KIA 4/3/17, aged 23. *L* 29/7/16.
67. Elvin, *D* 25/7/16.
68. Lt K. S. Anderson, MC, 22 Bn, Clerk, of Portland, Vic. b. 1892. *D* 30/7/16.

with death for seven days & nights . . . it has been too terrible, too fiendish . . . God I have seen the most gruesome sights the most awful tragic scenes it has been my cruel lot to witness, however, take it from me none of mine will ever tackle this job again . . . if men refuse to fight all the world over war will cease.[69]

Some men shot themselves, others went mad. Archie Barwick reported that within five minutes seventy-five shells, each 9.2 inches or larger, landed on an area of less than four acres:

All day long the ground rocked & swayed backwards & forwards from the concussion . . . [like] a well built haystack . . . swaying . . . about . . . men were driven stark staring mad & more than one of them rushed out of the trench over towards the Germans. any amount of them could be seen crying & sobbing like children their nerves completely gone . . . we were nearly all in a state of silliness & half dazed but still the Australians refused to give ground. men were buried by the dozen, but were frantically dug out again some dead and some alive[70]

A 20th Battalion officer stated that one of his sergeants,

who was leading the way commenced to roll about in an uncontrollable manner, and at length broke into a frantic rush, cursing and swearing at the huns. He was apparently suffering from overstrain . . . His memory had gone, and we had difficulty in getting him along. He recognised me, and said 'Is that you, Captain Fox. I will follow you to death. No one ever yet found D—— a coward.' . . . [he] would persist in sitting down and talking to a man who had apparently died on a stretcher . . . [he] again started a charge all on his own, charging down the road at full speed, . . . [and] came across some Tommy machine gunners whom he started to lash into; fortunately he was unarmed. When the others came up he set about them as well[71]

Those whose nerves survived the torment suffered unforgettable horrors: 'Our trenches very shallow in parts and full of our and

69. Thomas, *D* 27/7/16, *L* 3/8/16.
70. Barwick, *D* IV, pp. 11-13 (24/7/16).
71. Capt S. J. Fox, 20 Bn, Schoolmaster, of Sydney, NSW. b. 1893. *D* 14/8/16.

24/8/16.

Dearest Beat and Bill,

Just a line you must be prepared for the worst to happen any day. It is no use trying to hide things. I am in terrible agony. Had I been brought in at once I had a hope. But now gas gangrene has set in and it is so bad that the doctor could not save it by taking it off as it had gone too far and the only hope is that the salts they have put on may drain the gangrene out otherwise there is no hope. The pain is much worse today so the doctor gave me some morphia, which has eased me a little but still is awful. Tomorrow I shall know the worst as the dressing was to be left on for 3 days and tomorrow is the third day it smells rotten. I was hit running out to see the other officer who was with me but badly wounded. I ran too far as I was in a hurry and he had passed the word down to return, it kept coming down and there was nothing to do but go up and see what he meant, I got two machine gun bullets in the thigh another glanced off by my water bottle and another by the periscope I had in my pocket, you will see that they send my things home. It was during the operations around Mouquet Farm, about 20 days I was in the thick of the attack on Pozieres as I had just about done my duty. Even if I get over it I will never go back to the war as they have taken pounds of flesh out of my buttock, my word they look after us well here. I am in the officers ward and can get anything I want to eat or drink but I just drink all day changing the drinks as I take a fancy. The Stretcher Bearers could not get the wounded out any way than over the top and across the open. They had to carry me four miles with a man waving a red cross flag in front and the Germans did not open fire on us. Well dearest I have had a rest, the pain is getting worse and worse. I am very sorry dear, but still you will be well provided for I am easy on that score. So cheer up dear I could write on a lot but I am nearly unconscious. Give my love to Dear Bill and yourself, do take care of yourself and him.

Your loving husband
Bert.

Letter from Lt H. W. Crowle, 10 Bn, Builder, of North Adelaide, S.A. DOW 25/8/16, aged 32, to his wife and son, written a few hours before he died

enemy dead on which are swarms of black flies and maggots—
trenches reeking and crawling';[72] and sickening sights, 'brains hanging out, heads bashed in, arms and legs apart from bodies',[73] were
seared into their minds forever. They came to fear the battle area
as a 'Valley of Death' or 'the Jaws of Hell', they quit it thankfully,
and they received the order to return almost as a death sentence,
for they considered fighting at Pozières not war, but murder.[74]

Although the Australians never doubted their superiority over
the enemy, only a sense of duty and their own manhood induced
them to fight on. Corporal Thomas wrote, 'orders came through to
stand to and here we are all ready, eh steady, for some big stunt.
Our morale is excellent and the boys know the sacrifice, and also the
reward.'[75] A South Australian sergeant told his parents, 'When you
see this I'll be dead; don't worry . . . Try to think I did the only
possible thing, as I tell you I would do it again if I had the chance.
Send someone else in my place,'[76] and a young West Australian,
five months married, wrote farewell to his wife,

Well Darling one at 12 oclock tonight . . . we go over the
parapet & then our fate is sealed—if I am lucky we'll be
relieved I suppose within a week . . . The place is like Hell
darling but the sooner we get it over the better . . . remember
it is better to die for you & Country than to be a cheat of the
empire. I'll try love for your sake to do well & come through
. . . God be with you Love for all Time . . . Remember me to
baby when she is Born—if a boy dont make him a tin soldier
but should war break out, let him enlist & do his bit if not he'll
be no son of mine.[77]

The unparalleled intensity of Pozières forced Australians to find
additional reasons for continuing to fight. They took comfort from
the inevitability of battle, their superiority over the enemy's infantry,
and their success, for few troops achieved as much as they. Before
he entered the fight a timber getter commented,

72. Capt N. M. Cuthbert, MC, 2 Bn, Student, of Lindfield, NSW. b. 1896.
D 17/8/16.
73. Cohen, L 31/7/16.
74. For example, Kilgour, D 17/8/16.
75. Thomas, D 6/8/16.
76. Sgt D. G. J. Badger, 10 Bn, Bank clerk, of Peterborough, SA. KIA
21/8/16, aged 20. L –/8/16 quoted Bean, *Official History*, III, p. 797n.
77. Capt A. McLeod, 16 Bn, Bank clerk, of Katanning, WA. DOI 5/12/16,
aged 25. L 9/8/16.

*The Australians have been in the thick of it at last and . . . have
actually excelled themselves. What a reputation we will have
if we keep on going. But I am sure I have no desire to keep at
this game much longer. I'd sooner be slicing hunks off a tough
old Gray Box, than poking holes in a Prussian, any day. But I
suppose that will have to wait till the other job is finished.*[78]

Another soldier thought his experiences too awful to describe, but
found refuge from them in prayer and the expectation of being
decorated.[79] A third reported that the battle was a 'roaring boiling
hell of shot & shell & mangled men', but thought that the excitement
of hand to hand fighting and the 'walloping' given Fritz compensated
for this.[80] A fearful ordeal had tortured these men, and they had to
explain it, to justify its blood and pain and suffering. In this way, as
the war became less and less bearable, so it seemed more and more
necessary, and duty, honour and manhood more and more committed men to fight it. Pozières concluded for many Australians
what Gallipoli had begun, and channelled every motive for which
men had enlisted into a single objective: at any cost, to win the
war, and save the world from Teutonic darkness. Therefore they
struggled on: the First Division returned to the line on 15 August,
on 22 August the Second Division replaced it, on 30 August the
Fourth relieved the Second. On 5 September, after an advance of
not quite two miles to the edge of Mouquet Farm, the Australians
gave way to the Canadians, and for them the bloodbath of the
Somme was ended.

22,826 Australian soldiers fell to win a few yards of ground; and
only a minority, by great fortune, survived. It was a monstrous
sacrifice, which tumbled the romances and grand illusions of the
past into the dust, whence they rarely rose again. After Pozières
many soldiers looked back to their boyhood, and saw an unfamiliar
world. 'The actual realities of what modern war is like cannot be
described by pen', a soldier explained, 'One has to *live* it through
all its phases to understand anything about it.'[81] 'Ten months ago I

78. Sgt A. W. Armstrong, 24 Bn, Timber worker, of Swan Reach, Vic.
DOW 29/7/16, aged 26. *L* 24/7/16.
79. Capt W. G. Boys, 25 Bn, Master draper, of Maryborough, Qld. DOW
5/8/16, aged 26. *L* 2/8/16.
80. Lt J. T. Maguire, MC, 8 Bn, Public servant, of Bowenvale, Vic. KIA
4/10/17, aged 21. *L* 1/8/16.
81. Cpl J. R. Allan, DCM, 19 Bn, Dairy farmer, of Comboyne, NSW.
DOW 3/10/18, aged 41. *L* –/8/16.

was eager to get to the firing line', another asserted, 'My eagerness has been well fulfilled and well I know it.'[82] The Australians never forgot Pozières, nor the English staff which had sent them there, nor the mates killed, nor the New Army divisions which had failed so often on their flanks, nor a thousand scenes of horror and heroism, nor, most terrible of all, the ceaseless, merciless, murdering guns.

After the battle a narrower concept of duty generally prevailed. The AIF's severest penalty for indiscipline, repatriation to Australia in disgrace, became no longer effective, and wounded men, though usually prepared to return when the time came, gladly accepted the fortune which had struck them down. A serious wound—a 'blighty' —became an honourable escape from battle, a chance to rest, an offer of life, and a blessing many ardently desired. 'It was a bad night alright', Private Cleary wrote after the bloody fighting on 4 August, 'I was dead beat and wishing to goodness something would hit me so that I could go down with a clear conscience',[83] and an ambulanceman related,

Many a man smiles when he is told he will never be able to fight again or that he won't be right again for some months. Its Blighty for a spell anyhow, and probably back to Australia again, he may casually remark. The fellows shake hands with and congratulate their mates and brothers when they find that they have a wound that . . . will most likely keep them away for a few months.[84]

With these adjustments, the Australians passed through the agony and despair of Pozières. It had been their sternest test, and it broke much in them, but not their resolve, and gradually time and their sense of purpose restored most of their elan. 'Tramped back from the slaughter ground to scenes of peace and grandeur', Corporal Thomas noted, 'What a relief. The men soon forget everything and they soon started into song',[85] and a Tasmanian farmer observed, 'Fritz makes us wish we had stayed in Australia when he is aroused but we get quite cheeky again when we get out of range.'[86]

82. Kilgour, *D* 20/8/16, and compare with this chapter, at n. 17.
83. Cleary, *D* 5/8/16.
84. Richards, *D* 30/7/16.
85. Thomas, *D* 21/8/16.
86. Lt A. E. Gaby, VC, 28 Bn, Farmer, of Scottsdale, Tas. KIA 11/8/18, aged 26. *L* 2/9/16.

Yet men reinforcing the Australian battalions after Fromelles and Pozières came into a cheerless world. Some had been warned by the lists which lengthened endlessly in the daily press; all found the ranks of their units greatly depleted, and read a fearful tale in the faces about them. They arrived in the wake of great battles, and on the eve of a dreaded winter. They were noticeably less keen to fight than their predecessors. A machine gun private admitted,

I am not altogether in love with the business but it has to be done and we are trying to be as cheerful as we can be and at times it is pretty hard work. It is not altogether a nice sensation to have bullets and shells dropping all around you but I am gradually getting used to it and try not to mind.[87]

The new arrivals found their countrymen manning inactive sectors, and to a large degree this relaxed their fears. 'I used to wonder whether I'd be scared at my first experience in the trenches, but it was too interesting and exciting', a recruit wrote, 'Everything was novel. and hence enjoyable and the hardest thing was not to be able to get on top and see what was going on properly.'[88] Another commented, 'I like it immensely . . . it's not nearly so bad as I should have expected'.[89] '[I]ts a rough life pater', a third stated, 'but . . . it will be a great experience.'[90]

After the Somme fighting I Anzac Corps moved to a quiet front along the Ypres-Comines canal, where Private David Harford, a West Australian miner, recorded a

terrific bombardment by enemy batteries. as . . . [it] increases . . . we retire into our dugouts not that they afford much protection as they are shallow and the roof is thin but they are some protection from flying splinters. we lie flat on the floor of our dugouts, most of which are only built for one man, and listen to the awful bombardment, which is rapidly merging into a continuous roar. the ground trembles beneth me, and the air is charged with the acrid reek of high explosive fumes in all this overcharged horror there comes, as by a merciful despensation

87. Lt A. E. C. Atkinson, 9 MG Coy, Bank clerk, of Deniliquin, NSW. DOW 13/10/17, aged 21. *L* 8/12/16. I am here also describing men in 3 Div, which entered the line in December 1916 but which was not associated with the other Australian divisions at that time.
88. Adcock, *L* 10/10/16.
89. Alexander, *L* 3/12/16.
90. Gration, *L* 16/12/16.

*of nature a certain insensibility to all fears, quite simple
thoughts pass through ones mind, so it is to end here: Here in
this dark mildewed hole in the earth. I am to go out I look
round me at my damp rat-hole the sides and roof of which are
lined with sand bags . . . the lower bags are green with mildew
and the upper ones up near the sun and air are sprouting grass.
halfway up in the corner a cluster of poison mushrooms or
toadstools peer down at me. the center one a little taller than
the rest seems to nod at me as it sways and trembles to the con-
cussions . . . one simply notes these things, fear of death having
left one: and one prays that at least IT may prove one well
placed shell. a crash of thunder and a lightning flash, to thrust
us through the dark gates into eternity. only let it not be
crippling and yet life . . . one wonders whether that last light
explosive was a gas-shell how one's comrades are faring,
whether ANY of us will be alive when the bombardment ceases.
suddenly there is a concussion that seems to shake the breath
out of my body. a big shell has burst very near. Already a man
feels in his inmost self half-way to the other world, hopeless but
without fear. Hark! is the bombardment really getting less
violent or is it only fancy? it is not fancy? it is reality overhead
is a new note. the scream of shells, our shells, passing over us
on their way to the enemys batteries. one is astonished still to
be living, and then one hopes one may be alive not only tonight but also to morrow, a month hence, yes, even till
the troops go home. and then we creep out and take stock of
the damage and set to work to assist the wounded, and remove
the dead. everywhere can be heard the cry 'Streacher bearers
at the double' After which we set to work to repair our wrecked
trench. a heart breaking task. Far into the night we labour . . .
at last . . . we post sentries and lie down to get an hour or two's
sleep. in four hours time . . . there is . . . a bit of night sniping
going on and I take part in it.*[91]

During October the AIF voted on conscription, which, as in
1917, the majority of front line troops rejected. But conscription
interested few soldiers seriously, for in mid-October I Anzac Corps

91. Pte D. B. Harford, 51 Bn, Miner, of Ravensthorpe, WA. DOW 31/3/17, aged 31. *D* 14/10/16.

returned to the Flers-Gueudecourt sector in the Somme area; there the Fifth Division joined it from II Anzac Corps, and the Australians braced themselves to meet a new menace, which most knew would be severe, and some feared would defeat them. They were about to undergo a northern winter.

The 1916–17 winter was the harshest in France for forty years. Rain began in October, and shellfire churned the soft ground to a waste of mud and water. In the back areas movement quickly became difficult: an artilleryman reported,

about the MUD here . . . on foot one has to go very cautiously. Last time we were here one of our officers rode into a Shell hole. His horse disappeared in the mud & he was only rescued with great difficulty. He had to be pulled out with ropes & in doing so they strained his internal organs. He is now in Blighty & it will be 3 months before he is fit to rejoin his unit. It is a common sight to see men pulling one another out of the mud— it clings like glue[92]

and Private Cleary wrote,

Arrived at Bernafay wood after a long march in pouring rain. What made things worse was the fact that we . . . had to march through the muddy fields . . . because the Road was required for Vehicular Traffic . . . We were halted on the Hill facing Bernafay in pouring rain with no shelter, no Tucker and told to do the best we could and I put in easily the worst night I ever did or expect to put in. I absolutely threw my marble in and if it wasn't for the thought that I was on active service I think I would have wasted a cartridge on myself.[93]

In the line it was worse. Men already exhausted crouched in waterlogged shell holes, or stood and slept upright in the trenches thigh-deep in soupy mud, or crept into a hole dug from the side of a trench, hoping that the walls would not collapse and bury them:

a salvoe of shells landed near. I glanced up to try and locate the bursts by the flying mud, when I noticed that the whole side of the shell-slit was falling in . . . It struck me in the act of rising and completely buried me. The weight on my tin hat pressed

92. Gatliff, *L* 31/12/16.
93. Cleary, *D* 31/10/16.

*me down irresistably and forced my chin into my chest. After
struggling a little I found that it only settled the earth closer
around me. The brim of my hat kept the earth out of my nose
but the weight gradually forced it further down on my head, the
head band gradually travelling down my nose and taking the
skin with it . . . Then the realization came of what was gradually
but surely ending things. The soft earth at first yielded slightly to
my struggles, but was slowly settling down and compressing
under the weight above, so that the movement of my ribs was
becoming more and more constricted. It was as though an iron
band were tightening round my chest and preventing any movement. Then I heard the Sergeant Major speaking, and calling
me, as though he were a long way off . . . I heard him say, 'Good
God, I believe the man's buried! Come here two men with
shovels.—Now gently—don't maim him.' At last the terrible
weight was relieved, and they lifted me out and laid me on the
floor of the trench.*[94]

There were other discomforts. Behind the line, near Montauban, a
machine gunner recalled, 'The Trenches are very bad, and the
mud in them is three or four feet deep; men have to be pulled out of
it by ropes. The men have to sit in this mess all day and night, and
it is awful, everywhere dead lying about'.[95] The mud often prevented
the delivery of fresh water, so that the men were sickened by drinking fluid contaminated by dead bodies, and it delayed ration parties
so that they gave up, or lost their loads to shellfire. 'Very short of
tucker yesterday. Short again today. No Breakfast. The Ration Cart
has been gone 36 hours and not returned yet. Very cold and miserable', a soldier at Bernafay Wood recorded. On the following day
he noted, 'No Biscuit or Bread for Dinner but that is common now',
and on the day after that, 'Breakfast 2 inches of Bacon and a couple
of Spoonsful of suger. No Bread No Biscuits nothing else. Dinner
Small Spud ½ Tin of Bully.'[96]

Hunger and thirst were at least bearable, but during the winter
over 20,000 Australians were evacuated with exhaustion, frostbite,
or trench feet:

*I am on my way to hospital, suffering from trench feet due to
being in water up to my knees for 72 hours without a break.*

94. McInnis, *D* –/11/16.
95. Dakin, *D* 6/11/16.
96. Cleary, *D* 1, 2, and 3/11/16.

There was not a place anywhere in the trench where we could stand clear of water . . . as soon as I took my boots off my feet swelled rapidly so that I could not put my boots on again & I had to make my way to the ambulance station, barefooted. The distance was something like two miles and I had some difficulty in negotiating it.[97]

In the face of such trials soldiers in the line found it easiest, if the cold would permit them, to remain immobile in their trenches, enduring the hopeless desolation around them, clutching their comfortless rifles, and praying that relief or the rum parties would come to them and mitigate their misery.

The men at the front suffered less than those who moved between the line and the back areas, for ration parties, rum details, stretcher bearers, messengers and relieving troops had sometimes to struggle for four miles through a treacherous morass to reach their destination. Enemy artillery prohibited movement by day. At night men could plough along communication trenches if any existed—this was safer from shells, but a weary business, so slow that men could not usually reach the line and return before daylight. Most Australians travelled across the open, chancing enemy shellfire, blundering often into deep slush or water-filled shell holes and sometimes losing boots, puttees and trousers, and, if they were not lost or stuck fast in the mire, arriving at last cold, wet, filthy, and utterly exhausted. One man took eight hours to walk four miles carrying rations:

Give it best for a moment, and your will power is broken, and despair will lead you to hysteria, and then, death from exposure. Mud from the top of our heads to the bottom of our boots, drenched to the very skin, your thoughts must be alone for the men perishing in the front line . . . No songs are sung & no poetry written about fatigue parties[98]

If they were lost they stumbled into the German trenches, or lurched about until dawn caught them in the open and forced them to crouch motionless, till dusk should permit them to resume their weary task. If they were trapped by the mud, often they remained stuck throughout the day, helpless under the German guns; and if

97. Semple, *L* 11/11/16.
98. Fry, *D* −/12/16.

they survived that ordeal they had to endure the torture of rescue—at least twice rescuers broke the backs of mud trapped men.

All this lay in front of men relieved from the line. It was a terrible prospect, often beyond them. Corporal Thomas wrote,

God, I cannot express the horrors of last night, we were relieved and coming back shelled cruelly and five men knocked. The wounded had a fearful time, God help us in a scrap here, we are four miles from a dressing station. The officer lost us so at 2.30 I asked him to let us bivouac which he did, so we just fell down and slept, rain and all, and shells falling all about us, but we were too exhausted to bother, we didn't mind if we were killed, it was terrible.[99]

Sergeant Brunton described a nightmare march of more than ten hours, then concluded,

we reached the open valley and flung ourselves upon a sloping bank, oblivious of the driving rain and biting wind. This was the lowest depth to which my physical powers had ever sunk. I felt that by a slight effort of the will I could die and end it all. Our officers were in a bad way, too, and vainly strove to rally us, telling us to keep moving lest we die of exposure. Finding us incapable of marching . . . some of them pushed on for the camp five miles away and ordered our cooks to have food and hot tea ready . . . After lying there for twenty minutes I felt so cold that I determined to push on, and with two others I started along the valley for Fish Alley hill. After going a hundred yards one of the two collapsed and we left him on some wet sandbags and went on. After a quarter of a mile I came down on my knees three times, and recognizing the impossibility of going further without rest, the other fellow and I took shelter behind a shattered log, and . . . we fell asleep instantly.

The slowest in Brunton's party took two days to travel that last five miles, and he claimed that afterwards 268 of his battalion, exhausted beyond endurance, reported sick.[100] After all this, troops sometimes reached camp to find it

just a wide muddy ditch about six feet deep. There were no proper 'possies' . . . Finding an entrenching-tool I hollowed out

99. Thomas, *D* 3/11/16.
100. Brunton, *D* 22?/11/16.

*a shelf in the side of the trench, laid my waterproof sheet on it,
and lying down on it I drew my overcoat over me, and praying
it would not rain again, I was soon sound asleep.*

*When I woke it was terribly cold . . . my feet protruded from
the overcoat, and the caked mud on my big legging-boots was
covered with a thin coating of white frost.*[101]

The most agonising journeys awaited the wounded. The stretcher
bearers worked valiantly, but wounded men had sometimes to wait
twelve hours before they were moved, and many died before the
cruel mud released them. An Australian general died during such a
journey, after ten hours travelling; and a 2nd Battalion bearer
recorded that on Christmas Day 1916 he was called up to the line
to ease the pain of a corporal sniped through the abdomen:

*I was to take morphia and Hyperdermic up to where he lay and
give him an injection as they could not keep him on the
stretcher, poor beggar, in his agony . . . Many times [the guide
and I] were waist deep in mud and water and at the best it was
almost up to the knees . . . Found the bearers, 6 of them
struggling along with the stretcher making very slow progress.
Injected the morphia . . . Assisted with stretcher for some
distance and then left to obtain more bearers from Head quarters. Got lost . . . but reached H.Q. eventually but was unable
to get any assistance. Patient . . . unfortunately died and is
buried near Bernafay. No doubt the terrible privations were
responsible to a large extent with his death. He was wounded in
the morning and did not reach Field Ambulance until late in
the afternoon. This is but one instance of many similar cases
. . . The bearers are almost super-human but the odds were too
great.*[102]

Despite every torment and menace, the soldiers were allowed
little rest, and during November Australians several times attacked
German trenches in the Flers-Gueudecourt area. Archie Barwick
took part in an attack by the 1st and 3rd Battalions on Bayonet and
Lard Trenches on 5 November:

*as soon as we [hopped over] . . . the flares were sent up in
batches which lit everything up like day, & showed us men*

101. McInnis, *D* –/11/16.
102. Cpl R. Morgan, 2 Bn, Railway signalman, of Meadowbank, NSW. b.
1894. *D* 25/12/16.

*falling everywhere & the boys struggling through the mud
bogged nearly to the knees . . . I was forcing my way through
as fast as I could & calling for my men to keep up & 'box on'
. . . [In the German wire, I] got badly cut all over & ended up
by getting hung up in the stuff for all the world like a sack of
wool chucked onto a heap of barb wire, but I felt nothing at the
time for my blood was running hot & we only thought of getting
in their trench, the fighting by this time was very fierce, shells,
bombs, mortars, & worse than all liquid fire bombs were falling
amongst us like hail . . . I had one of the most thrilling minutes
of my life for I was rushing . . . down a shallow trench . . . when
. . . a Hun rushed out at me & made a desperate lunge at my
body. I must have parried quick as lightning & . . . his bayonet
slid down my rifle & stuck in the fleshy part of my leg . . . a
sharp stinging pain went through my body . . . but I kept my
block & before he could draw his rifle back for another attempt
I shot him dead.*[103]

This attack was made by weary men, in impossible conditions. It
was repulsed, as were most others made during that futile month,
for mud, cold and exhaustion easily outmatched gallantry, dreams
of glory, and duty.

Early in 1917 the winter delivered one more blow. Snow had
begun to fall in the previous November; by mid-January it had
frozen the ground, ending the worst hardships caused by the mud
and improving conditions overall, but bringing new troubles. Cases
of frostbite increased, and artillery shells, no longer cushioned by
the soft ground, struck with deadly effect at targets brought into
clear relief against a white background. In the billets heated bottles
of ink froze before men could write with them, and boots had to be
warmed before they could be put on. Boiling tea froze within
twenty paces, hands exposed were numbed after five seconds, bread
could not be cut with a knife, and water had to be chopped with an
axe and carried in blocks to the line. In the trenches Australians and
Germans sometimes stamped about on their parapets, ignoring each
other in an effort to warm their aching limbs.

Only a 'blighty' offered honourable escape from these privations,
and despite the fearful ordeals wounded soldiers had often to undergo, men prayed to be wounded. A corporal wrote that his brother

103. Barwick, *D* VI, pp. 131-3 (5/11/16).

was luckily in hospital, added the hope that he would stay there throughout the winter, and explained, 'it is no joke being in the trenches this weather with the rain, snow, and cold weather . . . God knows how I am able to stand it . . . if I get sent to Hospital don't worry about me; it is a rest—the only thing a soldier looks for.'[104] 'All I want now is to get . . . a sickness which will keep me away for the winter',[105] a sergeant told his family, and another reported, 'When I saw . . . [an] explosion . . . I ducked down, but Dingle wouldn't. I mentioned it to him and his reply was—"There is nothing else to get a fellow out of it but one of those shells. It doesn't matter." '[106]

This period was the hardest of the war for Australians. Several shot themselves, more malingered, and one or two deserted to the enemy, an offence usually unheard of in the AIF. Only a fortunate minority were wounded. Most were obliged to soldier on, and their prospects seemed hopeless. Fromelles and Pozières were followed, not by peace, but by Flers and the tortures of a cruel environment. The world seemed a perpetual round of pain, misery, and death, and men seemed condemned to endure ceaseless travail, till their souls were deadened, and they resigned their course on earth to the whims of a malicious fate.

As well, a mental dilemma weighed upon them. Australians had fought the Somme battles with success and distinction, and they knew that in future their reputation would commit them wherever fighting was heaviest, and so more probably to death and more certainly to suffering. They never doubted that they would fight on: they could not deny their manhood, nor by failing in their duty permit the ruin of their world. But they realised that they were assigning themselves to apparently endless agony, and were sacrificing their hopes and probably their lives to defend others. They had chained themselves to an odious necessity. They had come to Armageddon.

1917

After the new year the Australians slowly recovered their spirits. Huts in their back areas and duckboards laid across the mud eased their burdens, they received hot food in the line and hot drinks

104. Elliott, *L* 1/1/17.
105. Moulsdale. *L* 17/11/16.
106. Richards, *L* 26/10/16.

during journeys to and from it, warmer clothes from Australia, and thigh length gumboots from the stores. They were not engaged in heavy fighting until February, when battalions of the Fourth Division attacked Stormy Trench and adjacent areas. Above all they were exhilarated by the discovery, on 26 February, that the Germans had abandoned their trenches.[1] Willingly the Australians broke from their winter lines in pursuit, advancing rapidly, occupying Bapaume on 17 March, pressing the foe, and revelling in the open fighting they encountered now for the first time. A pioneer officer related, 'since the push started everyone has been in wonderful spirits and . . . are all as pleased as punch. The Hun seems to have had all the go knocked out of him',[2] and another, 'This is certainly the most interesting part of the war. We are now on captured territory amongst clean, waving fields instead of that fearful pitted country.'[3] At last the Allies seemed to be winning, and peace beckoned.

Enemy resistance strengthened after 20 March, and early in April the German rearguard several times forced the Australians to fight hard before it gave ground. A New South Wales private, wounded during his first attack, told a friend, 'on April the 8th we done what is known . . . as a hop over . . . we run into plenty of machien guns which fire 46 bullets in two & ½ seconds but it being dark Fritz could not see too well but a swarm of bees around ones head dont sing half as much as those bullets did',[4] and a 3rd Battalion sergeant described an incident during the fighting for Hermies village on 9 April:

There were two machine guns directly in front of us that were making havoc of our second and third waves . . . [a] lance corporal rushed one gun and . . . [a sergeant and a subaltern] made a charge for the other. To rush a machine gun from fifty yards is certain death . . . The Sergeant was hit in the knees at twenty yards and fell. He struggled to his knees and attempted to go forward, but the gun got a direct line on him and he fell with his head riddled with bullets. The officer kept going until

1. The Germans began this on 24 February, and within six weeks had evacuated their 90 mile salient between Arras and the Aisne River. They hoped to shorten their line and to disrupt Allied plans for 1917; they succeeded.
2. Roth, *L* 9/4/17.
3. Carter, *L* 8/4/17.
4. Pte J. A. Ware, 3 Bn, Blacksmith, of Yass, NSW. b. 1896. *L* 8/7/17.

he was within ten yards when he dropped a bomb right into the machine gun emplacement and continued his rush. The bomb killed two of the gunners and wounded a third but the fourth man continued working his gun. and the officer fell right across the machine gun riddled with bullets, and as he fell, he wounded the remaining gunner with his revolver.

The lance-corporal on the left was . . . charging a gun . . . served and defended by eight men. From thirty yards he dropped a bomb amongst them and at twenty yards—just as the bomb burst—he was wounded in the left arm. Undaunted he continued his rush and leapt into the trench and bayoneted in quick succession the remaining three Germans . . . He was L. Cpl. Kenney[5] . . . and he was . . . awarded the V.C.[6]

The fighting in early April checked Australian exuberance, but in any case the buoyancy of even a year earlier was now foreign to them. They hoped for an early victory and were past their worst depression, but they were disenchanted with war, and could not forget the awful year behind them. A lieutenant typified their attitude: 'I read . . . of some recently wounded Australians who . . . said how keen they were to be back in the trenches. They couldn't have been through Pozieres and finished with a winter in the trenches.'[7]

Early 1917 reinforcements caught this sense of disillusion. Usually they were less adventurous than earlier enlistments had been, and at the front they found little to cheer them. As he approached the line for the first time Private Wilfred Gallwey remarked, 'I . . . am having a great time. We will soon have Fritz knocked out and I hope I will be here for the end of it', but this was an echo from the past, and two days later he commented,

Is is very funny when I think of your ideas of war now I have had the experience. Its horrors could not be described on paper neither could the innumerable hardships of an infantry soldier. I suppose you wonder how I stand it all . . . if anyone had told me before I enlisted what I had to go through I would have

5. Cpl T. J. B. Kenny, VC, 2 Bn, Chemist's assistant, of Bondi, NSW. RTA 24/8/18, aged 21.
6. Sgt A. E. Matthews, 3 Bn, Gunsmith, of Croydon, NSW (b. England). b. 1892. *D* –/4/17.
7. Short, *L* 11/3/17 and compare with this chapter, 1916, at n. 7.

*thought I never could have gone through it . . . I only hope I
have the luck to return home and if I don't well my name will be
on the Scroll of Fame and you will be able to hold up your head
proudly with other Mothers who have lost their noble sons.*[8]

In February a late 1916 reinforcement told his brother,

*All my pals . . . I came over with are gone, but 7 out of 150
remain, its simply scientific murder, not war at all. As for seeing Germans its all lies you never get close enough to do that,
unless in a charge. I keep smiling, but I tell you it takes some
doing . . . the premonition I had when leaving Sydney, that I
would never see home again still hangs about me—one would
be unnatural to go through uninjured, if I get out of it with a leg
and arm off I'll be perfectly satisfied, so you will understand
what it is like . . . so don't get married till after the war.*[9]

In January a Queensland officer at the Etaples base informed his
wife,

*Tomorrow morning I leave here to join my Battalion & . . . be
in the thick of it . . . I wouldn't care a rap for my own sake. I'm
not afraid of death because . . . I have always led a good and
clean life. Its you I'm thinking about & if it should not be my
good fortune to return then I'm sure you will be consoled . . .
by knowing that my life has been a happy one & that I have at
least attempted to do my duty.*[10]

He was killed a week after he went into the line. Another new
arrival stated, 'This is an awful war alright. Now I know what it is
really. You people at home are spared a dreadful thing and I'd
fight again . . . to keep it out of our country . . . I hope the war will
soon stop now for it is sapping out the best of men and all that is
beautiful in civilized life.'[11] No comforting light guided these men;
the gay cavaliers who had stormed that first hillside on Gallipoli
were gone.

By 9 April the Germans had successfully withdrawn behind the
Hindenburg Line, a network of trenches protected by barbed wire

8. Cpl W. D. Gallwey, 47 Bn, Bank clerk, of Rockhampton, Qld. b. 1899.
L 1 and 3/3/17.
9. Pte E. O. Neaves, 20 Bn, Cashier, of Glebe Point, NSW. KIA 6/11/17,
aged 25. *L* 15/2/17.
10. Lt R. M. Berry, 25 Bn, Costings clerk, of Sherwood, Qld. KIA 7/2/17,
aged 29. *L* 24/1/17.
11. Lt W. G. Barlow, 58 Bn, School teacher, of Daylesford, Vic. KIA
12/5/17, aged 30. *L* 2/3/17.

up to 100 yards thick, and interspersed with numerous machine gun posts and strongpoints. Almost immediately the Australian Fourth Division was ordered to break this formidable barrier east of the village of Bullecourt, while the British Sixty Second Division attacked the village itself. They were denied artillery assistance, upon which they had come to rely, and to breach the wire they were given tanks, which they mistrusted. Their attempt was to be made on 11 April.[12]

As the tanks rumbled towards the start line before dawn on that day, their noise alerted the enemy, and a fierce fire fell upon the Australians lined out to attack. They were men of the Fourth and Twelfth Brigades, among the best in the AIF. They accepted the bombardment, they saw almost every tank break down, and they watched the bullets spark from the uncut German wire until it 'seemed to swarm with fireflies' under the fusillade.[13] Yet when the time came their dark forms walked across the snow covered ground in perfect formation, manoeuvred carefully through a maze of obstructions while the German bullets scythed them away, and charged into the Hindenburg trenches.

They did what had been thought impossible, and what no Allied soldier had done—broken into the Line without an artillery barrage. They overran two trench lines and began to consolidate their gains, but they had been decimated by the German machine guns, the survivors were scattered and desperately short of bombs, and a brave enemy persistently counter-attacked them. Private Gallwey related of his first great battle, 'I can only describe it as Hell. Every minute I expected to be blown out . . . All round me men were falling . . . I kept cool . . . The awful horrors . . . [were] enough to drive a man mad.'[14] Lance Corporal Mitchell, not long returned from his sickness in England, depicted the fighting at close quarters:

I cannot tell the light and the shade, the things we laughed over, the tragedies, the lifetimes lived in an hour . . . a big German in a steel helmet popped up . . . I fired as he threw his bomb. In my haste I missed. Quickly I worked the bolt. But . . . there were no more cartridges in the magazine. So I shook my fist in

12. Originally 10 April, but the failure of the tanks to come forward led to a 24 hour postponement.
13. Bean, *Official History*, IV, p. 295.
14. Gallwey, *L* 14/4/17.

*sheer rage, and the Fritz grinned amiably back at me . . . for
ten minutes I waited.*

*Up came his head. My bullet crashed into it and his last
bomb was unthrown . . . The muzzle of a rifle peered over
cautiously followed by a head in a pork pie cap. It was he or I
for it. We aimed together. I fired first . . . and the German
pitched back . . . Word came back 'Throw everything away.
Hop over the top and run for it.' But I was not going to abandon my Lewis gun . . . I walked to the barbed wire . . . I heard
the bullets as they hailed all around. I saw the dead, wounded
and dying as they lay huddled everywhere . . . I was in the midst
of our own fierce barrage, and also a German barrage. Machine
guns were playing the devil with us. I unhitched myself casually from the wire . . . I did not even desire to run.*[15]

When the Australian bomb supply was almost exhausted the
British barrage, finally arriving, burst among them, shattering their
ranks and confidence. A German attack drove out the Fourth
Brigade; at this the Twelfth Brigade, ordered to flee, turned, and
walked slowly and deliberately across the shell-swept ground back
to the Australian lines. George Mitchell was among them, and his
brigadier saw him strolling away from the slaughter, his battalion
the last out of the enemy trenches, his Lewis gun slung carelessly
over his shoulder, his example inspiring all about him. He won an
immediate DCM, and, a little later, a commission.

His heroism personified First Bullecourt, but their valour had
won the Australians no material gain, and had broken some of the
finest battalions in the AIF. 1170 men were taken prisoner, a
greater number than in any Australian action until the fall of Singa-
pore in 1942, and in all more than 3000 Australian soldiers, about
80 per cent of those attacking, were lost. The survivors were very
bitter, for again the follies of a British staff had overborne their
courage and endeavours: subsequently the Corps orders for First
Bullecourt were used to demonstrate how not to plan an attack. Yet
the spirit of the Australians remained strong. They had not betrayed
their ideals, and they had combined their old dash and aggressive-
ness with a new competence. The skill of professionals began to
mark their operations, and after First Bullecourt they never
suffered a major defeat in the war.

15. Mitchell, *D* 11/4/17.

To allow the Fourth Division to concentrate for First Bullecourt, the First Division on its right had been assigned a dangerously long front of about 12,000 yards, which it held by the 'defence in depth' system then popular, of successive lines of detached outposts, each sited to protect its neighbours. The Germans, noting the thinness of this defence and hoping to consolidate their recent victory, before daylight on 15 April launched a twenty-three battalion attack against the First Division and the extreme right of the Second Division, which had relieved the Fourth two days before. Four Australian battalions held the threatened front, and although at some points their forward posts by themselves drove back the assault, elsewhere the posts were swept away, and the Germans advanced a mile into the back areas, destroying five guns and capturing the village of Lagnicourt. But then the defence counter-attacked, and by mid-morning had thrust their assailants back behind the Hindenburg defences. The Australians were outnumbered by about six to one in this action, and the result added considerably to their prestige.

On 3 May the Fifth and Sixth Brigades of the Second Division again attacked the line east of Bullecourt, as part of a general British offensive, and under an artillery barrage. Part of the Fifth Brigade was repulsed, but the remaining Australians, alone along the battle front, burst into the German trenches. The enemy counter-attacked bravely, and for two weeks the antagonists fought some of the most savage close quarter fighting of the war. 'I was an absolute mad man', a wounded private remembered, 'I went with my mates don't know, what I did or said Scotty McMillan got it in the ankle, I got a crack in the neck. and had to take Mc to the dressing station', and a day later, 'The re-action set in and a cried for hours. My mates arm was Blown into my chest and Pieces of P----- were splashed over more than a dozen.'[16] He had been wounded early in the battle: his comrades, some equally overwrought, bombed and stabbed and bashed their enemy without remission, until day and night blurred into a timeless whirl. A constant trickle of wounded came from the disputed area, and the dead piled thickly, and the roaring bombs burst ceaselessly, smothering the crackle of rifle fire and lighting the shattered trenches with their flame. Relieving troops quailed as they approached the holocaust: 'I am sure I will be

16. Pte E. J. Flanagan, 57 Bn, Steward. of Bathurst, NSW. b. 1876. *D* 4 and 5/5/17.

either killed or wounded', one stated, 'I will do my duty as a soldier and fight to the bitter end. While I am capable of fighting I will not be taken prisoner and will not take prisoners. Any German that falls into my hands can expect no mercy for I will kill him like a dog.'[17] But gradually the Australians strengthened their hold, until on 16 May the Germans abandoned the 'killing match', and left the area in the hands of their enemies.

After the battle, I Anzac Corps withdrew to rest. Its battalions had manned some part of the line since April 1916, had capped that prodigious stay with one of the British spring offensive's few successes, and had proved themselves among the most effective shock troops available to the Allied command. For that gain 7482 Australians had been struck down at Second Bullecourt, and again a resentful remainder saw a British staff almost uselessly expend their fervour and valour.

By June the Australian infantry lay in Flanders, opposite the Messines-Wytschaete Ridge, a low prominence overlooking the trench lines south of Ypres. This the British planned to capture, and on the southern flank of their attack line they placed the Australian Third Division of II Anzac Corps, which was to attack in the morning, and in support the Fourth Division, temporarily transferred from I Anzac, which was to attack in the afternoon. The Third had been raised in Australia, trained in England for six months, and in December 1916 introduced into the line near Armentières, a far less arduous sector than I Anzac's front on the Somme. Its soldiers had not entirely escaped the rigours of war—

One of our men . . . went suddenly demented. The s.s. [shell shock] had an electrifying effect upon him . . . [He] dropped his rifle and . . . rushed out over the front line trench into No mans land, the Germans blazing away at him: then he turned and ran down between the lines of the two armies: no one seemed able to bring him down. Then he turned again, raced into our system, down overland through the support trenches . . . where men from the Battalion pursued him, overpowered him, and forcibly rolled him in blankets and tied him up with rope . . . He was unwounded but evacuated raving mad[18]

17. Gallwey, L 9/5/17.
18. Capt R. A. Goldrick, MC, 33 Bn, Bank clerk, of Parramatta, NSW. b. 1890. L 13/4/17.

—but Messines was their first 'hopover', and they were eager to prove themselves.

Early on the morning of 7 June nineteen large mines, carefully placed during the preceding months, were exploded, devastating the German positions along the Ridge. The British barrage then descended and pounded the bewildered foe, and the charging infantry swept them easily aside. The Australians advanced two miles, took their objectives, and withstood the German counter-barrage; and most English divisions succeeded equally. Messines was, thus far, the swiftest and greatest British victory of the war.

Victory could not avert tragedy: 6800 Australians were killed or wounded during the battle. Among the dead was George Davies, a Victorian clergyman who prepared a farewell before he went to die:

I am now ready for the 'big push' ready in body, mind and spirit, I was never better in health than I am now, my mind is just as clear, my soul has been purified, and the whole is in God's hands. If I die, do not fear . . . I give my life willingly for my country knowing that it is given in a righteous cause. I can do no more, I give my love to you all and to Jesus Christ my Maker.

. . . [I hate] the curse of military life . . . with my intensest hatred as an unworthy and dispicable means of settling affairs. If I live I shall stand by Red hot socialists and peace cranks to stop any further wars after this one, but while I am at it I will fight like only one facing death can fight.[19]

And victory could not mitigate the barbarity of a great battle's bravery: a soldier wrote, '[I was] . . . in a shell hole & a Hun in another abt 12 feet from one another. one of his Bombs burst at my feet. I imitated an Aeroplane but did not get a scratch, got a shock owing to esplosion. Fritz was not so lucky. I got him with a Grenade',[20] and a corporal manning a forward post remarked,

I've been knocked over by a shell covered by another and dug out disputed the point with four Fritzies and hung on to a position for 32 hours with one man only and four dead stinking Huns. We could not get Food sent up the shelling was damnable

19. Pte G. H. J. Davies, 36 Bn, Clergyman, of Hawthorn, Vic (b. England). KIA 12/7/17, aged 28. L 6?/6/17.
20. Sgt C. C. Serjeant, 14 Bn, Law clerk, of Burnley, Vic. KIA 18/9/18, aged 26. L 26/7/17. (This incident may have occurred in the Messines trenches in late June or early July.)

and eventually the four Napoo Huns were so objectionable that
we had to cut *them up bit by bit and throw them as far away*
from us as possible. I was recommended and the recommenda-
tion said I did the best work in the whole brigade. Not bad for
an old loafer.[21]

He won a Military Medal.

After Messines, the infantry of the First, Second and Fifth
Divisions withdrew to rest. The Third Division and the New Zealanders made a 'feint' attack to assist a general British offensive on
31 July, and then came out of the line, and in mid-August the men
of the war weary Fourth Division followed their comrades into the
back areas. The bulk of the artillery remained in action, and in July
began what proved for them to be the most difficult fighting of
the war. They were still fighting when the infantry returned in September, to spearhead a series of attacks the British generals were
planning.

The word 'Flanders' was already ominous when the Australians
re-entered the line there, for after Messines the British had battled
with mixed success and great loss against mud and the German
Army. Shaken by defeat, they had evolved a tactic of caution and
despair: the 'step by step' method, which in theory used massed
artillery to batter a limited depth of enemy defences, then sent
infantry to occupy it, then called forward the artillery and repeated
the process, and so on.

Eleven divisions, pivoted about the Australian First and Second
Divisions, took the first step on 20 September, against the Menin
Road Ridge. Artillery and infantry co-operated well, and won the
battle in a few hours. 'Stunt started at 5.40 a.m. and we kept on
firing till about 1.15 p.m.', an artilleryman reported, 'Our infantry
gained all their objectives . . . and prisoners have been coming
down. S.O.S. about 2.30 p.m. but Fritz got knocked back. Another
. . . about 5 p.m. and again at 6.30 p.m. Fritz knocked back each
time.'[22] Two similar triumphs followed, at Polygon Wood, on
26 September—

At daybreak our wonderful barrage came down cutting a clean
line just ahead of us . . . The turmoil of even the elements would

21. Lt G. M. Carson, MM, 33 Bn, Entomologist, of Port Moresby, Papua.
KIA 31/8/18, aged 37. *L* 16/6/17.
22. Gnr R. F. Hall, 4 FAB, Student, of North Williamstown, Vic. b. 1894.
D 20/9/17.

THE FIGHTING IN FRANCE 189

be minute when compared with the belching of thousands upon
thousands of big guns supported by a continuous hail from
hundreds of machine guns . . . the 16th (Westralian) lined up
just behind where our shells were churning the ground. It was
grand. Almost every man lighted a cigarette quite coolly . . .
The 14th & 15th who were supposed to be 200 yards behind the
16th were anxious & had come close up. 'We won't wait for the
—— barrage, we'll show it the —— way,' I heard from a 14th.
'What the hell are you in a hurry for?' replied an older soldier;
'we'll get enough before we've finished.' 'Oh, go and get your
face camouflaged,' was the reply courteous. Then the swish
lifted, the [barrage] . . . crept slowly forward never missing a
square foot of ground. 'Come on 16th' some officers exclaimed.
'Here help me over your trench 13' said one after another as
they hurried to . . . their place . . . then the line of 14th &15th
went over. Soon they too were lost to sight. Then the wounded
began to trickle back; first walking cases then stretcher cases.
Then a batch of bewildered but pleased prisoners without a
guard . . . The smoke & dust clearing somewhat we saw the . . .
[attack battalions] in position & consolidating[23]

—and at Broodseinde Ridge, on 4 October.

These were momentous victories, the most resounding the arms
of the Empire had won. Every German counter to the 'step by step'
method—blockhouses, specialist troops, revised organisation, new
tactics—had failed, and for the first time Germany's leaders began
to doubt their power to avert defeat in the war. Broodseinde particularly was disastrous for them. Although they had doubled the number of divisions in the Broodseinde area, their troops had been
driven from one of the most important positions on the Western
Front, and a major counter-attack, long prepared against this
contingency, had regained nothing. 4 October was a black day for
the German command, for it presented their enemies at last with the
possibility of decisive success.

But again the sacrifice was great. 'Mates I have played with last
night & joked with are now lying cold', a sapper wrote after Polygon
Wood, 'My God it was terrible. Just slaughter. The 5th Div. were
almost annihilated. We certainly gained our objectives but what a

23. Capt. T. A. White, 13 Bn, School teacher, of Dulwich Hill, NSW. b.
1886. D 26/9/17.

cost',[24] and an infantry private confided, 'The reaction is still to come and I'm rather frightened of it—I feel about eighty years old now.'[25] The AIF lost almost 17,000 men in the 'step by step' battles, a casualty rate equalling that at Pozières, and it advanced in return about 4200 yards.

Worse followed. On the evening of Broodseinde rain fell in Flanders, swamping the flat ground. Traffic and shellfire made this a clutching bog, almost impassable, but Haig continued his offensive, and British fortunes underwent drastic reversal. Their infantry floundered to exhaustion in the mud or reeled back before the German guns, and over 100,000 were made casualties before that unhappy October ended. The generals reduced their ambitions to capturing the ruined village of Passchendaele; it fell on 6 November, and soon afterwards the British offensive was abandoned.

Australian assaults supported some of the October and November battles, but generally the AIF was out of the attacking line, and by mid-November was manning a quiet sector of the front south of Messines. Since July 38,093 Australian soldiers, almost 60 per cent of the AIF in France, had become casualties, a huge expenditure, which brought not peace but frustration. The old soldiers had almost expected this: since Egypt they had watched their ranks always thinning, till the few surviving seemed marked for an inevitable end. Throughout 1917 they went into battle with dash and determination, but under the shadow of impending doom. 'Tomorrow many men must go to their God . . .', Corporal Mitchell wrote before Messines, 'If I die, I die. We all must die. The best we can do is to die with good grace.'[26] Many of his veteran comrades shared his outlook, for their task had no attraction now. They did an unpleasant duty, and propped their resolve with familiar consolations: 'this . . . is no picnic, but it will be a great experience for a man if he is lucky enough to pull out safely',[27] one veteran thought, and another remarked, 'you know how anxious I am to get back at those stinking 'uns (I don't think) but I suppose a man might as well do his bit now he is here.'[28]

Men thus inclined hoped constantly for a 'blighty'. An artillery

24. McKay, *D* 26/9/17.
25. Lt W. G. Fisher, 42 Bn, Student and law tutor, of Brisbane, Qld. KIA 5/4/18, aged 24. *D* 24/10/17.
26. Mitchell, *D* 6/6/17.
27. Avery, *L* 5/7/17.
28. Gaby, *L* 1/8/17.

officer saw a man walking on top of the trenches 'out of all cover. I had to see him so . . . I hopped up on the parapet and joined him, and we strolled along it . . . Later I heard that D---- was looking for a "blighty", was fed to the teeth with things and wanted to get out.'[29] An officer told Corporal Thomas, ' "you have been given a good job in Blighty for six months, instructing." I nearly fell down the bank I was on and asked him "Did I hear you aright?" and he said "Yes . . ." I was fair stunned . . . I did not touch ground the remainder of the journey.'[30] A wounded man recalled,

what an anxious time I had waiting for a Hospital ship . . . the Port was closed for some reason or other . . . Day after day would come and go and still no Hospital ship. I was afraid my wound would get alright before I got aboard, thus miss my trip (As had already happened to several chaps in the Hospital) . . . At last . . . we were told to be ready . . . what a relief[31]

The few men not disenchanted by war were usually novices to it. They wanted to 'do a hopover', but even theirs was a limited enthusiasm. One recruit remembered of Polygon Wood, 'when I woke up it was near time [to attack] so we got ready we were all jolly and you cannot imagine how one feels so good going over',[32] but more typically a gunner noted before the same battle, 'Have no idea how long we'll be in it but it mightn't be for long. I am as fit as a fiddle and am looking forward to the fray . . . but of course I'm well aware . . . that it will be no joke',[33] and before First Bullecourt Wilfred Gallwey told his parents,

Tonight I am going in to the front line of trenches and you know what that means. I have no fear and will do my duty as a soldier should. I am spiritually prepared for death and should such be my fate remember I shall go straight to Heaven. I made my will in your favour . . . you will . . . never regret your noble sacrifice in contributing a soldier to the Empire.[34]

29. Nicholson, *L* 5/2/17.
30. Thomas, *D* 5/4/17.
31. Pte L. G. Johnson, 20 Bn, Farmer?, of Bridgewater, Tas. b. 1891. *D* -/5/17.
32. Pte J. A. R. Bell, 49 Bn, Bush labourer, of Brisbane, Qld (b. Ireland). DOW 10/4/18, aged 25. *L* 2/10/17.
33. Gnr F. S. Evatt, 1 FAB, Student, of Milson's Point, NSW. DOW 29/9/18, aged 20. *L* 22/9/17.
34. Gallwey, *L* 8/4/17.

While not so entirely disillusioned as the old soldiers, these recruits lacked the adventurous confidence of the first enlistments, and already many of the values which had accompanied them to manhood were broken.

For a time the 1917 victories exhilarated a few men, most of them new soldiers. After Messines a young New South Welshman announced, 'Well I have had a bit of excitement since I wrote . . . I have been *over the top* had a go at old Fritz at last we gave him a very rough trot too. he never put up much of a fight . . . as soon as you get near them they start crying for mercy'.[35] A Queensland officer reported after Broodseinde, 'It was a great experience for me I enjoyed every minute of it . . . It was an absolute walk-over . . . We got all our objectives quite easily & could have gone on except that limits were laid down . . . There are no better soldiers in the world than the Australians and very few as good',[36] and after Polygon Wood a machine gunner commented, 'I realized that we were at a serious game as we . . . lost a few of our pals . . . [but] it was wonderful to see [our boys] . . . walking about the field, not taking any notice of the bursting shells, one would think they were on parade'.[37]

But Passchendaele blighted this optimism, and their triumphs earned the soldiers only a second winter in the trenches. It was less rigorous than the 1916 winter, and more effectively countered, but it taxed Australian wills and strength severely. Rain caused discomfort—

some of our chaps were on outpost for 36 hrs at a stretch during which time it rained incessantly, they never had the slightest covering & were [always] either standing or sitting in water . . . Yet they don't growl a great deal . . . [they are] real roughies but every one of them who plays the game is a real diamond[38]

—and rain softened the ground to mud, 'the pal who sticks', and the troops' worst enemy during winter. Four days after the rains began Sergeant de Vine noted, 'The roads are in a terrible state &

35. Pte F. J. Reynolds, 35 Bn, Grazier, of Moss Vale, NSW. KIA 12/10/17, aged 20. *L* 15/6/17.
36. Lt L. A. C. Boyce, MC, 41 Bn, Clerk, of Toowoomba, Qld. RTA 31/7/18, aged 20. *L* 15/10/17.
37. Cpl G. C. Easton, 2 MG Bn, Commercial traveller, of Camperdown, NSW. DOD 4/11/18, aged 31. *L* 26/9/17.
38. Fischer, *L* 20/1/18.

very muddy, being under constant shell fire . . . [and] are often knee deep in liquid mud', and in November he recorded that men frequently bogged to the hips in mud.[39] A gunner wrote,

Belgian mud is incomprehensible to anyone who has not experienced it . . . If a shell has burst recently it churns the ground up so that it is bottomless and horses, carts, and even men have been known to disappear in it. On several occasions [we] . . . have had to dig people out, one man was up to his shoulders for four hours and another his waist for one, that I personally came across.[40]

The trials of winter concluded a dispiriting year, which had impressed an obvious truth upon Australian minds. They knew their side would win, and they believed Australians could aid the victory. But despite their valour during 1917, victory was as distant as ever. Valour was clearly not enough: the scale of the war was too immense for individuals to affect it, and men knew now that the fighting would butcher many before the great cause they upheld was won. Nothing had shaken their faith or honour, but their former hopes and aspirations were broken. What had appeared probable a year earlier was now certain. Quietly, and in his own way, each man gave up his future and made ready to die, perhaps uselessly, for what he loved. His course was set, and he plodded wearily through a tired world, fighting till an end should come.

1918

At the beginning of 1918 the prospects of the forces of light were very gloomy. Russia had surrendered, the German victories at Caporetto had demoralised the Italians, France had barely recovered from the army mutiny, and Flanders had for the moment destroyed British offensive capability. Germany held the initiative, and was transferring her eastern divisions westwards in preparation for a great and decisive offensive. If she could be resisted, the Entente nations, strengthened immeasurably by United States participation, would win the war. If she could not, they would probably lose it.

39. de Vine, *D* 8/10 and 4/11/17.
40. Gnr A. G. Barrett, 12 FAB, Maltster, of Geelong, Vic. b. 1895. *L* 9/12/17.

Few Australians considered defeat. Many early 1918 reinforcements were encouraged by a relatively innocuous introduction to war: one wrote,

I have become a 'Dinkum' Soldier as I have had 5 days & nights in the very front line . . . we came through alright . . . I was really surprised how I took my baptism of fire & can honestly say that I was not afraid and had no accidents with my breeches . . . After what I have seen of war I am very glad I enlisted as the boys here are simply wonderful[1]

and though few old soldiers deluded themselves about war or gave up hoping for a 'blighty', they were roused by the German ascendancy to fresh enthusiasm, and looked for combat against the enemy. In March 1918 Lieutenant Traill, an original Anzac, recorded,

I found that I was to take 9 men and rush the M.G. post discovered the other night . . . Artillery support was given, and Lewis guns told off to engage neighbouring enemy guns . . . Off we started armed to the teeth with revolvers and bombs at 1.30 a.m. On arrival at our deploying point, the artillery started, and of course one blasted gun was firing short, and right over the ground we intended to crawl over. So we waited a while and shivered on the cold wet ground and then started off, found the possy . . . [three of us] rushed the post and found the birds had flown, evidently scared by our erratic guns. One shell had lobbed right at the foot of his parapet. After that we crawled round and tried to find patrols or runners till nearly daylight. Nothing doing, a blooming fiasco . . . We were well in the mood for sport too, and looked round for a likely pill-box, but [no luck][2]

Another officer declared, 'In spite of all the discomfort, the hard work and the danger there was not a single complaint from the boys, they were only too eager to have a decent go at the Boche.'[3] New and old soldiers alike realised that their efforts in the coming crisis could contribute to victory, and they rallied their spirits and showed a willingness to fight not seen since 1915.

1. Fischer, *L* 1/1/18.
2. Lt S. R. Traill, 1 Bn, Clerk, of Burwood, NSW. b. 1895. *D* 10/3/18.
3. Capt F. E. Fairweather, MC, 38 Bn, Accountant, of Heidelberg, Vic. KIA 29/9/18, aged 27. *L* 4/4/18.

In March 1918 the Australian infantry[4] were in the line near Messines, raiding and patrolling. The fighting was not strenuous, although Corporal Thomas, describing the experiences of a working party he led, wrote:

we were well out in the open . . . suddenly crash & several big musher [high explosive] shells shrieked about our ears, then on they came thick & heavy & what was more disastrous gas two sniffs & I was satisfied . . . I whipped out my helmet & jambed the rubber into my mouth put the nose clip on & then speedily warned my platoon to put on their equipment . . . We have a lot of new men & they completely lost their heads, an easy thing to do when new but it is fatal in these big gassing stunts, a number of them put the hoods on & could not see through the glasses, then they tore them off, so I had to risk everything & yell out orders & help the poor excited humanity about me, of course I got a gut full but I didn't give a damn, my usual faith in things, however I got them moving . . . at a steady walk, it was awful the uncanny feeling of death eating at ones entrails & the gasping of the men trudging behind you, the thunder of the shells, & the fires from the dumps showing ghostly through the gas smoke, a bluish vapour hanging like a pall . . . [For more than an hour, we] just kept on through a veritable hell let loose; it was my job to get my men treated for gas, many of them starting to tumble about as though they were drunk & half a mile away, in a tunnel, was an A.M. Red Cross station; at last . . . we reached the hospital & each man very exhausted & fearfully windy was given a drink of amonia which is supposed to have a benificial effect; however two men died from the gassing, weak hearts you see, poor devils it is terrible & the horror of it; yet we all had to go up again the next night & carry on as usual.[5]

On 21 March the Germans began their offensive, on a 44 mile front south of Arras. Except around Arras where the British Third Army held them, they struck with paralysing effect, breaking 40 miles of the British line, and passing rapidly over the country beyond. Within five days they had recaptured all the ground they had lost about the Somme during the previous two years, had swept

4. Now the Australian Corps, of five divisions, the largest in France.
5. Thomas, *L* 20/3/18.

through Pozières, and seemingly were racing to victory.

The Australians, fretting for battle, watched the German progress with dismay. At last orders arrived, and on 26 March the Fourth Brigade sped southwards through a press of refugees and retreating British soldiery[6] to Hébuterne, to hold the northern flank of the advancing enemy. With the New Zealanders at Colincamps nearby, they stopped the Germans, resisted a series of heavy attacks, then counter-attacked and drove their assailants back. By 31 March their area was secure.

The chief danger lay south of Hébuterne, in the Somme area, where a determined German drive aimed at splitting the French and British armies at their junction, by capturing Amiens. Thus divided the Entente house would swiftly fall; Amiens had to be held. In late March it lay defenceless before the enemy. Haig asked for twenty divisions to defend it, but none was available, and the British general, his back to the wall, threw his last strong reserves, the Australians, to support the valiant remnants of the British rearguard across the approaches to Amiens. The Germans met the northernmost Australians first, then, vainly attempting by strong attacks to break down the thin defence, gradually extended southward, from Dernancourt, to Morlancourt, and at last to Villers-Bretonneux.

Villers-Bretonneux straddled the last open avenue into Amiens, and it stood in the path of the most successful German thrust. After being checked near the village on 30 March, the enemy gathered his strength, and 4 April assailed the Villers-Bretonneux defences. The 35th Battalion, defending the village itself, repulsed the attack, but English divisions holding both flanks gave way, and this forced the 35th to retire. Individual Australians and British cavalry halted the enemy's advance through the broken English line, and soon the 36th Battalion, counter-attacking vigorously, drove their opponent beyond his start line and restored the front. German attacks continued at Villers-Bretonneux and Dernancourt until the evening of 5 April, but nowhere was the Australian line broken. Amiens was safe.

Baulked on the Somme, on 10 April the German leaders attacked

6. During these weeks Australians frequently encountered retreating and dispirited British soldiers, but also many offering to fight if someone would lead them. Almost invariably Australians taking up position found British soldiers still resisting the enemy, while small groups frequently volunteered to stay and fight with the Australian defence.

near the River Lys, in the north. Again they progressed swiftly, and the Australian First Division, which had only just reached the Somme, turned north to meet them. By 14 April the Australians had relieved two British divisions before the town of Hazebrouck, and there for four days they repelled strong attacks by several enemy divisions, halting the offensive, and again forcing their antagonists elsewhere to test their fortunes.

The Somme fighting had left the remainder of the Australian Corps scattered along 17 miles of front, while five British Corps defended an equal length. The Australians therefore regrouped in mid-April, and in so doing gave the defence of Villers-Bretonneux to an English division. The Germans promptly attacked and captured the place on 24 April, and British counter-attacks that day could not dislodge them. But during the night the Australian Thirteenth and Fifteenth Brigades made a brilliant assault, which by the evening of Anzac Day had cleared the village and driven the enemy beyond his start line. The Germans then abandoned their attacks about the Somme.

The failure of their offensive destroyed German ambition, but the British Army lost 316,000 men in the fighting, and was for the time being incapable of protracted effort. By good fortune no Australians had met the initial German blows, and they entered the fight when the Germans were most extended. But, often against great odds, they had won several of the most crucial actions of the war, each for a fraction of the loss suffered during the bloody battles of the previous three years: between 21 March and 7 May, 15,000 Australians were made casualties. For this cost, while many around them reeled in defeat, they averted disaster, and kept open the door to victory. They had fought not, as at the landing, as novices charging to glory for the flag, but as professional soldiers, who knew well the risks of war, but who accepted them eagerly, revelling in the chance to apply their skill with telling effect. 'The fighting was much more to our liking than anything previously',[7] one veteran remarked, and, wearied by years in the trenches, another stated, 'this style of warfare suits us better and the men are keen and in excellent health . . . We fight in open fields, among hedges and farm houses and dig trenches all over the country. We have got right away from fixed trench warfare'.[8]

7. Serjeant, *L* 6/5/18.
8. Lt H. V. Chedgey, 1 Bn, Solicitor, of Arncliffe, NSW. b. 1892. *L* 23/4/18.

Their ebullience now led Australians, while all on their side save the New Zealanders were prostrated, to engage in 'peaceful penetration', or persistent and aggressive patrolling against German positions, killing and wounding men, occupying ground, and shattering morale. For four months, between April and August, 'peaceful penetration' was virtually the only activity on the British front. It suited Australian temperament, for its chief weapons were stealth, individual initiative, patience, and skilled bushcraft. Daily the Australians crept through the long crops in No Man's Land, moving almost at will about the enemy's line, falling upon their victims, capturing entire posts and in time whole battalions, and occupying literally thousands of yards of front and even a town without the knowledge of their own or the German command. Their stealth and aggression terrorised the German divisions placed against them: some were disbanded after heavy loss, a few protested at having to re-enter the line opposite Australians, and most feared to face an Australian sector.

George Mitchell was on the Somme during this period. He had won an MC at Dernancourt, and now led 'penetrating' patrols enthusiastically:

we advanced cautiously through a wheat crop, and then crawled through the long grass. There was a little MG fire. A few flares were coming over. We crawled on and on. At length I found a deep comfortable shell hole . . . Listening we heard coughs, click of rifle bolts and the sound of picks and shovels . . . Sergeant Halliday and I worked forward through the grass . . . [then] squirmed back to the rest of the party. I got them ready. We all stood up together and gave rapid fire on to the party in front . . . silence. No a leaf stirred. We crouched down into our shellhole. Still no answer. So I sent them off in the direction of home.[9]

At Villers-Bretonneux in April an Australian signaller, having sampled the contents of a village cellar, and knowing that prisoners were wanted, fixed his bayonet, 'strolled' over to the German trenches in broad daylight, yelled to bring the Germans forth from their dugouts, selected a prisoner from among the respondents, dismissed the remainder, and shepherded his captive back to his

9. Mitchell, *D* 27/6/18.

battalion.[10] A 4th Battalion corporal noted on 9 July, ' "C Coy" made an advance on "Jerry's" outposts & "salvaged" about 30 prisoners & 6 machine guns', and a day later, 'Our men are going out in daylight to the opposition posts & gathering in "Adolfs" by twos & threes; also their machine guns.'[11]

These men—confident, casual, undisciplined in the parade ground sense, but deadly effective—convey the spirit of 'peaceful penetration'. On the Somme the activity advanced the Australian line three quarters of a mile by 6 May and a further two miles by 8 July,[12] and took more than 1000 prisoners. Patrols of between one and seventy men competed for the highest 'bag' of prisoners: on 5 July, for example, an Australian sergeant[13] captured an officer and twelve men, and on 29 July Australian patrols took 128 prisoners, six machine guns, and two trench mortars. At Haze-brouck the First Division advanced more than two miles and took over 1700 prisoners: on 11 July six Australians captured sixty-eight Germans, seven machine guns, and 300 yards of front, and by 30 July the town of Merris and 180 prisoners had fallen without the knowledge of either command. So it went on, wherever there were Australians, their successes by far overshadowing their 1917 triumphs, their losses only slightly exceeding those of divisions manning quiet sectors of the front, their activity relentlessly regaining the initiative for the Allies.

Not content with this, on 4 July 1918, at Hamel, brigades of the Second, Third, and Fourth Divisions delivered the first major Allied attack in France since November 1917. General Monash, the new Australian Corps commander, planned the attack carefully, training infantry, tanks, aeroplanes, and artillery thoroughly together. Probably his preparation added to the soldiers' pre-battle tension—one admitted on 3 July, 'Put in a poor day, thinking of "hop over" to-morrow morning leaves us all rather "screwed up" . . . No sleep—cold and anxious—but NOT funky'—but in the event the Australians co-operated perfectly. The same soldier related,

Left support trench at 1.40 a.m. loaded up like a mule. Usual

10. Bean, *Official History*, VI, p. 43n. Another remarkable feat is described in ibid., pp. 54-5.
11. Addy, *D* 9 and 10/7/18.
12. In May and June formal Australian attacks on the Somme gained ground not included in calculations here.
13. Sgt W. E. Brown, VC, DCM, 20 Bn, Grocer, of Hobart, Tas. b. 1885.

fighting order . . . 220 rounds: 2 mills bombs: extra water bottle: shovel—down back, and a pannier for Lewis gun—all hellish weighty . . . Knees knocked when barrage opened, but after the start all trepidation vanished. Wonderful barrage put up, ground shrapnel shell on explosion lit up the scene and we caught glimpses of Fritz going for life. No return barrage and no machine gun fire . . . An easy walk over. Slung my gun and stumbled across . . . Experiencing none of the 'blood lust' nor became 'another man'. A most prosaic affair. Met no Fritzes myself until near final objective . . . Spared his life to rat him but found nothing[14]

The battle was won in 93 minutes. For the loss of 775 men,[15] the Australians captured 1472 Germans, two guns, 171 machine guns, twenty-six trench mortars, and much renown: the General Staff praised Hamel's planning and execution, and afterwards used both as models for attacking British troops.

Hamel was the prelude to a greater battle, one in which 'The men were so keen [to take part] . . . that in some cases men detailed to stay out paraded about it and wanted to go in to the fight.'[16] At four-twenty a.m. on 8 August, under the shroud of a river fog, and with tank assistance, the Australian and Canadian Corps moved side by side to destroy the enemy's positions south of the Somme.[17] Despite the usual staunch resistance from German machine gunners, the front line crumpled before them. The Australians advanced seven miles, and took almost 8000 prisoners, 173 guns, and sufficient engineering material to last them the rest of the war. The Canadian success was almost equally stunning: it was the most complete Allied victory of the war, the turning point,[18] the 'black day' of the German Army, which induced its leaders to sue for an armistice.

On 9 August the advance continued. The Australians pushed forward a further five and a half miles, but troops on their flanks

14. Pte F. W. Roberts, 21 Bn, Orchardist, of Upper Hawthorn, Vic. KIA 1/9/18, aged 28. *D* 3 and 4/7/18.
15. United States infantry were attached to Australian companies for this attack, and suffered 134 casualties.
16. Capt W. D. Joynt, VC, 8 Bn, Farmer, of Flinders Island, Vic. b. 1889. *D* 7/8/18.
17. They were flanked by Frenchmen on the south, and by Englishmen north of the river, but these contributed little to the battle.
18. Some, though not the German leaders, consider the French offensive between Soissons and the Marne River, begun on 18 July, to be the turning point of the war.

could not come up, and they were left unsupported. The advance was particularly encumbered on the left flank, where an English division north of the Somme lagged more than two miles behind the Australian front. Observing this, and anxious to discover its cause, six Australians of the 1st Battalion crossed the river and found an English regiment held down by machine gun fire which for two days had impeded its progress. The six immediately advanced, silenced the machine guns, cleared the village of Chipilly and 2000 yards of ground, captured about 300 prisoners, brought the English front into line with their own, and rejoined their battalion.

By 12 August, for the loss of 5991 men, the Australians had advanced between 12 and 14 miles, and taken almost 10,000 prisoners.

Well it was easily the best two days the Australians have ever had in France and it did 'em more good than six weeks in a rest area—I wouldn't have missed it for anything and only hope that they give us another show like it every three months . . . Our chaps are as happy as Larry and simply singing at the top of their voices.[19]

The Corps 'peacefully penetrated' a further mile after 12 August; on 23 August it attacked again, taking 2000 prisoners, and six days later bringing the front to within three miles of Péronne.

This city was guarded by Mont St Quentin, a commanding height believed impregnable to infantry. Known along the Western Front for its thick wire and extensive trench system, the mount was protected by long, open slopes, by a canal near its foot, and at this time by selected volunteers from German Guards divisions. The Australian battalions were worn by ceaseless effort,[20] and some had been reduced by battle to fewer than 100 men. They knew their enemy on the mount outnumbered them, and that British policy was not to attack the place, yet they responded willingly when Monash sent them against it. On 29 and 30 August Second Division infantry cleared the mount's approaches after severe fighting, and on the following day attacked the slopes and the summit. Within a few hours most of the enemy's position and 2600 prisoners, half of them from one of the ablest German divisions in France, had fallen into

19. Duke, *L* 20/8/18.
20. The 38 Bn staff, for example, had by 29 August worked continuously for 89 hours.

their hands. By 2 September a hard fight had won Péronne, and once more the German Army was obliged to seek safety in flight.

Some rated Mont St Quentin as the finest single feat of the war. The achievement surprised Haig, amazed the German officer commanding Péronne, delighted the press, and elated Monash. Yet, save for words, it brought the soldiers no reward. They had hoped for rest; they were sent to pursue the enemy. They reached the Hindenburg Outpost Line on 10 September, breached it eight days later, and on the following day arrived opposite the Hindenburg Line. Monash now planned to rest his troops, but was offered the assistance of two United States divisions if he would assault the Line. The American units were each twice the strength of a full British division and probably ten times that of the battered Australian units; the Line was the last German defence system in the west. Monash accepted, and on 25 September the Americans, in the event the Twenty Seventh and Thirtieth Divisions, filed into the Australian trenches.[21]

The Hindenburg Line comprised three trench systems, the last four miles behind the first, and predictably was well defended, by a canal, by thick wire, and by carefully sited machine guns. The Americans attacked it on 29 September, and at first advanced successfully, but neglected to overpower all the defenders as they progressed, and so shortly found themselves surrounded and brought to a halt in the first trench system. The supporting Australians fought forward and gained ground, but could not make good the deficiency, and the last German line was not breached until 3 October. Two days later, after capturing Montbrehain village, the last Australian infantry division, the Second, withdrew from the Western Front.

Australian infantry never returned there, for as they began to do so Germany signed an armistice. In a swift moment, the war was over.

Almost 27,000 Australians had been killed or wounded since 8 August. Eleven of sixty infantry battalions had been disbanded for want of men, and more must have followed had the war continued, for none could muster more than a quarter of its full complement, many had fewer than 100 men, and all were completely exhausted. By October the men had been fighting for six months

21. This was the first day since 7 April 1916 that no Australian infantry held a sector of the Western Front.

without interruption, whereas three weeks was usual. Ability and success had won them only toil, battle, and the risk of death. Their spirits refused to yield, but their bodies had come close to breaking. Early in May a private reported, 'Most of us are a delapated looking lot, haven't had our clothes off for 60 days . . . I've got the knees and seat out of my pants never went about so ragged before, plenty like me, but for all that we have had a fairly good time'.[22] In June an officer noted, 'There was a mild epidemic of [trench fever] . . . Its like influenza only a bit worse and when a whole battalion starts to get it its a sure sign they are run down and want a rest. As we have been on the go for four months solid we earned one'.[23] By September the men were

battle-worn and weary. Their faces were drawn and pallid, their eyes had the fixed stare common in men who had endured heavy bombardments, and they had the jerky mannerisms of human beings whose nervous systems had been shocked to an alarming degree. So tired, so dead beat were they that many of them, when opportunity offered, slept the heavy drugged sleep of utter exhaustion for twenty-four hours on end. Their faded, earth-stained uniforms hung loosely from bodies which had lost as much as two stone in as many months. Sheer determination and wonderful esprit de corps *had enabled these gallant fellows to work . . . when physically they were done.*[24]

This, and bitter experience, shackled Australian enthusiasm. They were keener to fight than in 1916 or 1917, and spurred by success, but some still preferred peace and rest to achievement and renown, and found their best reward in a 'blighty'. During the eventful April days a lance corporal wrote, 'I got a piece of h.e. [high explosive] shell in my left leg . . . it went through a loose blanket, through a sheet of iron, then my puttee & my leg . . . if [the obstructions] . . . had not been there, I would have got a nice "blighty" however better luck next time'.[25] H. R. Williams, the soldier who had described his debilitated comrades in September, received a 'blighty' soon afterwards, and felt like a little boy unexpectedly

22. Pte R. Mactier, VC, 23 Bn, Farmer, of Tatura, Vic. KIA 1/9/18, aged 28. *L* 3/5/18.
23. Roth, *L* 16/6/18.
24. H. R. Williams, *Comrades of the Great Adventure*, p. 289.
25. L/Cpl H. Morphett, 51 Bn, Farmer, of Bruce Rock, WA. KIA 25/4/18, aged 22. *L* 2/4/18.

given a day off school.[26] 'Albert . . . is back in England to be operated on . . .', another man reported, 'lucky beggar I think he would win Tatts sweep if he went in for it. I have no luck at all that way I always have to carry on . . . I would not be surprised if he did not get home with it he is lucky enough',[27] and in June Lieutenant Chedgey asserted, 'I have been jolly lucky to get such a nice "blighty" and I will be out of the war for a while, only way to get a decent holiday in this stunt.'[28]

The real holiday came in November 1918, and by then the Australians had earned their rest. Since 27 March they had opposed thirty-nine enemy divisions, nineteen more than once. They defeated all, and forced six to disband. They took 29,144 prisoners, 23 per cent of the British total, 338 guns (23½ per cent), and 40 miles of ground (21½ per cent). They made possible much more, and weightily influenced momentous events, yet they made up less than 10 per cent of the British Army. They served King and country well, for few soldiers during that war produced a comparable record.

26. Williams, *Gallant Company*, p. 262.
27. R. A. Muir, *L* 11/6/18.
28. Chedgey, *L* 10/6/18.

FRANCE

7 The Old Days Never Will Come Again

We Diggers were a race apart. Long separation from Australia had seemed to cut us completely away from the land of our birth. The longer a man served, the fewer letters he got, the more he was forgotten. Our only home was our unit, and . . . Pride in ourselves . . . was our sustaining force.

Captain G. D. Mitchell, MC, DCM, 48th Battalion, *Backs to the Wall*, p. 168

The principal haven from the storm and stress of the flame racked years was England. Wounded soldiers were sent to England, troops on leave came there, men marked for home sailed from its ports, veterans and half trained recruits knew it as the last outpost of civilisation. 'Somehow one gets very casual in France and sees men die, without appearing . . . even to notice it', an Australian wrote from Wandsworth hospital, 'but when one gets back to England—to civilisation again—it all seems so horrible—and so unnecessary. I sometimes lie awake at nights, and think things over—and I often on such occasions pray that I shall not suffer from insomnia for a long time after the war . . . it would be too awful.'[1]

England was also head and heart of the Empire, the source of everything great and secure, Australia's shield, and, to many Australians, Home. Some had been born there, others were sons of Englishmen, almost all had learnt of England's glories at school. They were impatient to see the old country, and as they drew near for the first time they crowded their ship rails, eagerly scanning the distant grey coastline that rose slowly from the mists of the morning. 'How often have I heard your glories blazed abroad throughout, Old England,' George Davies enthused, 'and now, and now I view your coasts, thy shore line, your hills and valleys . . . tears

1. Lt C. V. McCulloch, 2 Bn, Student, of Strathfield, NSW. KIA 11/4/18, aged 26. *L* 27/10/17.

205

welled in my eyes at the sight of the Home Land . . . there is no land so sweet, no spot so hallowed as the spot of land we call Britain'.[2]

Australian soldiers, unquenchably curious, toured every part of the British Isles. The length of their leave often limited them to the surrounds of their camps on Salisbury Plain, but a surprising number, perhaps because they respected its soldiers, took the long night train journey to Scotland. Some went to Cornwall and Devon, a few to Kent and Sussex, and a few to Ireland. Every man went to London, where, being well paid, they inspected all the points and scenes conceivably interesting to sons of the Empire. After stopping at AIF Headquarters in Horseferry Road for pay, tourist information, and usually a new uniform, they went to an Anzac Buffet or a 'swank' hotel for a 'good feed', then to Australia House perhaps,[3] then to the Tower, the Palace, Parliament, the Abbey, St Paul's, the Waxworks, the theatre matinees, the museums, the great houses, the law courts, the parks, the docks sometimes, the churches occasionally, and anywhere else that smacked of history or entertainment. At night they had another 'good feed', or saw a live show, or got drunk, or responded as inclination prompted to offers from prostitutes or women made available by the turbulent times.

Perhaps, though a thousand organisations in England hosted soldiers, the Anzacs were particular recipients of English hospitality. They had come further to fight than most, which attracted English sentiment, and they had won a magnificent reputation on Gallipoli, to which the English press paid full tribute. They dressed differently, were easy going, and told tales of a strange land. Their want of discipline weighed against them, but this was more than balanced by the cheerfulness of their wounded, and particularly if they were convalescent and officers they were frequently guests of England's nobility and society, lunching and living in houses open to few Englishmen.

Yet at some point during all this Australians realised a truth. England was cold, wet, and sunless, and mainly a repository for barren camps and bleak hospitals. 'Hurrying crowds of the three sexes surged past,' George Mitchell wrote during an early visit to London, 'They all bore the hall mark of the Cog. Pale faced and undersized, they appeared quite passionless, these people who work year in and year out beyond the reach of sunshine and out of touch

2. G. H. J. Davies, *D* p. 15 (–/7?/16).
3. After it was completed early in 1918.

with nature. They seem to have been moulded to a definite pattern by a machine-like, artifical existence.'[4] 'I will have a better idea of this country after we finish our leave,' a recent reinforcement observed, 'but so far our chaps wonder why the Hell the English did not let [Kaiser] Bill have the blanky place & move out of it.'[5] Most other Australians were less critical, yet, whatever England was, it was not Australia. Many in the AIF never loved their country better than after they had left it, and they longed to return to the sunlit land they had quit so readily. They wrote wistfully of scented gums and golden wattle, and carefully preserved in their wallets and notebooks a leaf or a small sprig to remind them of their distant homeland. George Davies concluded his panegyric by confessing, 'and yet in the midst of it all . . . I still saw the ocean beating upon the shores of far Southern Victoria.'[6] 'We are no more homesick for Australia than an ordinary mortal is homesick for heaven',[7] George Mitchell declared, and a Queenslander decided, 'On the whole life is well worth living. But all the time there is the longing to be back in Australia . . . I hardly realized what a great country Australia is untill I left it.'[8] At Lark Hill camp a man of the Third Division announced before he left for France, 'All I want is to get a good knock soon after I get there and to be invalided back to Australia. They will never get me to leave there again once I get back.'[9] The son of an Englishman told his father, ' "Australia is God's own country" . . . It is absolutely the best place that I know of —the land of plenty. There is practically no poverty there . . . [as] in Blighty.'[10] 'How often do you get leave to Australia?', asked a lady in England. 'Once every war', replied a digger, only half joking, 'At the end of it', and an Australian soldiers' paper wrote,

> *When God knocked off one night said He:*
> *'This world's a rotten failure.'*
> *Lor lumme, though, He'd let 'em see—*
> *Next day He made Australia.*[11]

4. Mitchell, *D* 8/9/16.
5. Pte J. A. Pryke, 21 Bn, Prospector, of Mortlake, NSW and Papua. KIA 4/10/17, aged 43. *L* 14/1/17.
6. G. H. J. Davies, *D* p. 15 (–/7?/16).
7. Mitchell, *D* 8/9/16.
8. Boyce, *L* 14/7/17.
9. Bambrick, *L* 7/1/17.
10. Elliott, *L* 11/7/18.
11. *Aussie* (AIF trench paper), No. 1, p. 3 (18 January 1918); No. 3, p. 9 (8 March 1918).

Their homesickness and their disillusion with England supported a change of sentiment many Australians had already made. Before 1914 martial splendour and the glory of the Empire had intertwined, and England's greatness gave substance to both. But years of blood had destroyed the romance of battle, and also, because they could blame Englishmen for their worst defeats, that high esteem in which Australians had held their Empire. At Lark Hill a recent arrival, the son of an English immigrant, had written,

Paw will be glad to know that my impression of the British Tommy is very favourable. While not so tall as the average Australian he is neat and clean . . . there are more . . . objectionable, ignorant, discordant, half baked and dirty tongued youngsters of about 18 years old among our troops than among the Tommies

but after a year in France he decided,

I suppose you sometimes think that the Australians are overpraised, but . . . the Colonials generally and the Scotch regiments are absolutely the best troops in the British army. We have never yet failed to get our objective and the idea of not getting it never enters our heads. What we do worry about, is whether the Blighters on our flanks will get theirs, a much more uncertain proposition. Most of the Tommies are good, but many of them have no heart.[12]

He expressed exactly the attitude general among Australians. An officer, Garnet Adcock, declared,

Everyone here is 'fed-up' of the war, but not with the Hun. The British staff, British methods, and British bungling have sickened us. We are 'military socialists' and all overseas troops have had enough of the English. How I wish we were with our own people instead of under the English all the time![13]

and some British soldiers aroused contempt by 'playing the Saxon game of "You don't fire, and we won't." The cold footed hounds. The more one learns of the Tommies, the more one despises them. We shake [the Huns] up wherever we go.'[14]

12. Chedgey, *L* 22/7/16 and 15/10/17.
13. Adcock, *L* 20/12/17.
14. Traill, *D* 6/3/18.

Australians doubled criticism of English soldiers after the Germans attacked in 1918. During the First Division's advance to Hazebrouck a man of the 4th Battalion wrote disgustedly, 'The road is a continuous stream of . . . detached parties of "Tommies" who have become "lost, stolen, or strayed" . . . Seems to me that the whole damn lot are more intent on getting back than getting up. They'll make a good advance guard—for the civilian's retreat.'[15] On the Somme a machine gunner included a current AIF joke in his criticism:

There is a lot of feeling among our chaps against the Tommies. They were driven back at Messines as soon as we moved south and lost a village in a sector where they had relieved us a few days previously . . . A Tommy brigadier is reported to have overtaken a hare on the road towards Amiens and said savagely, 'Get out of the road you brute and give a man a chance who can run.'[16]

Whereas formerly Australians had sung of 'dear old Blighty', by 1917, to the same tune, they sang,

> *Blighty is a failure,*
> *Take me to Australia*

'And so with everything',[17] a soldier added. At times AIF parades even received the King in stolid silence, and by 1918 abuse and insulting comparisons floated so freely and frequently about their camps that Australians were reprimanded by the authorities for hampering the war effort.[18] Though they continued to admire much in the Imperial system, during the war Australian soldiers learnt their own worth, which formerly they had doubted, and saw faults and cankers at the heart of their Empire, which once they had imagined great above every imperfection. The war dealt the affections of Empire a mortal blow, and men never returned to the adulation of 1914.

Yet almost every Australian remained prepared to do his duty.

15. Addy, *D* 12/4/18. But see chapter six, 1918, n. 6.
16. Lt J. W. Axtens, 8 MG Coy, Draper, of Mosman, NSW. b. 1894. *L* 2/5/18.
17. Capt C. H. Peters, MC & bar, 38 Bn, Managing bookseller, of Melbourne, Vic. b. 1889. *L* –/–/17.
18. AWM File Nos. 265/3 (Letter from Birdwood to 3 Div, 30 April 1918) and 265/2 (Circular from 1 Div HQ to officers commanding 1 Div units, 23 May 1918); Bean, *Official History*, V, pp. 236-7.

210 THE BROKEN YEARS

AIF reinforcements were trained in England after mid-1916: many knew that a bitter struggle lay before them, but were not daunted, and were ready to try their fortunes. A Third Division NCO at Lark Hill wrote, 'we go to La Belle France [soon] . . . and probably straight into the front line trenches. I can tell you, when the 34th get there the Germans are going to know it . . . They'll make a name for themselves all right',[19] and another, 'Our aim is to fix these Huns as quick as possible—and the quicker the better. I guess Jack could tell some good tales of these savages—he has had a slap at them.'[20] A Second Division reinforcement stated, 'we are ready to go over and Strafe Fritz good and hard. Then it will soon be over',[21] and an artillery reinforcement at Bulford camp reported, 'we are on draft . . . We are all madly delighted and keen to get away as soon as possible.'[22] Many soldiers made impatient by prolonged training adopted this outlook. 'I won't be sorry (for a start at least) to get away,' a gunner decided, 'We have been tin soldiers a little too long',[23] and after four months in England a Victorian private exulted, 'at last there seems a chance of me going to France . . . I need not tell you how pleased I am . . . I have had more than enough of Lark Hill and will be real pleased to get away after my long stay here.'[24]

But most Australian reinforcements after mid-1916 feared the trial ahead. At Codford camp an infantry reinforcement hoped that it would not be long before Germany threw in the towel and gave him a chance to get home again,[25] and at Durrington another wrote,

Its Bad we meet men Here who Have Just come out of Hospital & They vouch for Things being Bad. Fritzs Artillery Is Hell: I am going to work my nut & am Trying all the Time but I can't See my way So Far. There are Plenty of fellows Here at The Same Game . . . But cheero whats The odds. Ive lived & Had

19. Lt V. C. Callen, MM, 34 Bn, Business manager, of Stockton, NSW. KIA 20/8/18, aged 29. *L* –/8/16.
20. Lt A. D. Cameron, 36 Bn, Engineer, of Hillgrove, NSW. KIA 4/4/18, aged 29. *L* 20/8/16.
21. Lt W. D. Baldie, 24 Bn, Farmer, of Thorpdale, Vic. KIA 5/10/18, aged 27. *L* 17/2/18.
22. Evatt, *L* 20/7/17.
23. Spr M. R. Smith, 6 Fld Coy, Student, of Lane Cove, NSW. KIA 1/12/16, aged 23. *L* 7/9/16.
24. L/Cpl C. R. Jack, 35 Bn, Postal assistant, of Alphington, Vic. POW 5/4/18, aged 28. *L* 29/7/17.
25. J. E. Allen, *L* 25/11/16.

a Fair Time as Times go & if I go up well It will be Bad Luck Thats all.[26]

Many at this time had been led by a sense of duty, honour, or shame to enlist, and duty and honour sustained them now, as the inevitable hour approached. An officer stated,

I am still wasting my time here, when I should be up in the firing line assisting my comrades; our poor fellows have had a very bad time of it lately . . . only about 150 men and 2 Officers left out of 1026 so they must send me along now . . . It makes one think a bit sometimes and wish it was all over. I am anxious to go and know the worst.[27]

A private believed that he approached the trenches free from fear, because his God would succour him if he were wounded, and if he were killed a fairer inheritance would be his.[28] A young bombardier thought that the war would end in about six months, and was

glad that at last we . . . are going to have a bit of a hit to help finish it off . . . everyone . . . recognize what we are going into, that its dangerous, but we are trusting in God, and looking forward to, that glorious return to our home folk and loved ones, after a victorious peace for the allied arms, which it will have been our privilege to help to bring about.[29]

At Codford Private Gallwey announced,

We are all in the greatest excitement over our coming departure. At last we realise we are really going to war to do our bit . . . Come what may I am fully prepared for it spiritually as well as physically. I do not expect to get through without a scratch for I know too much about what is going to be done these next few months. I may only get a blighty which would not concern me . . . England expects that every man this day will do his duty[30]

and from Sutton Veny camp a First Division officer told his family, 'I . . . miss you all a great deal, but you could not wish me [in

26. Molesworth, *L* 2/11/17.
27. Lt A. F. Everett, 25 Bn, Storeman, of Brisbane, Qld (b. England). DOD 19/2/17, aged 37. *L* 3/8/16.
28. G. H. J. Davies, *D* pp. 23-4 (–/11/16).
29. Bdr E. O. Collett, 8 FAB, Tramways clerk, of East Malvern, Vic. KIA 28/9/17, aged 20. *L* 30/12/16.
30. Gallwey, *L* 20/2/17.

Australia] . . . in such times as these, I would rightly be termed a
shirker, nearly every family is in the same sad plight, but you must
face it all with a brave heart and . . . look forward to the day when
I come home'.[31]

Veterans in England knew even more clearly the probability of
death and the certainty of travail in France, and many did not wish
to go back. At least two men, fearing imminent transportation,
killed themselves, and a few Australians malingered or deserted
rather than return. Private Bryan was sixteen when wounded at the
landing, but recovered to fight at Lone Pine and Pozières, and
endure the 1916 winter. He bore it all stoically, but in December
1916, just before he was due to return from leave in England, he
noted in his diary, 'I did not Like return to france so I stoped 8
days over leave I gave my self up to the police and was sent to my
Bde training camp.' On 4 January he wrote, 'I was tried at orderly
room and given 32 days pay and 2 days detention I was not striped',
on 13 January, 'we cleared out to London on French leave and had
a good time', and not until 12 March, 'I surrendered to the police
warick square.' He was tried for absence without leave on 17 March,
and convicted, but continued to go absent until classified unfit for
service in July. In February 1918, aged nineteen, he was repat-
riated to Australia. He was not a coward, but he was worn beyond
his youthful endurance, and simply could not face the field of
slaughter again.[32]

Most veterans forced themselves to return. At Le Havre a
Military Medal winner wrote, 'move on to the Bn. at 4 this evening
don't like the idea nor do any of the others . . . [London was]
absolute paradise and . . . [now] the mud again . . . I hope I get a
decent knock that will send me home again to Blighty'.[33] In London
in February 1917 a pioneer private recalled that at Pozières,

*I saw a battallion of 1000 men going up to go in . . . and within
half an hour there was only 300 left . . . every where you would
look you could see pieces of men dead and moaning. it was
terrible I will never forget [it] . . . I expect if I go back I will see
a bit more but I might be lucky enough not to see it I hope I do*

31. Fischer, *L* 11/10/17.
32. Pte E. P. Bryan, 6 Bn, Labourer, of South Melbourne, Vic. RTA
30/1/18, aged 19. *D* –/12/16, 4, 12, 13/1, 12, 15, 17/3, 16/7, 29/8, and
12/9/17, –/2/18.
33. Pte W. V. Wright, MM, 4 Bn, Overseer, of Wagga Wagga, NSW. RTA
10/1/18, aged 23. *D* 21/11/16.

THE OLD DAYS NEVER WILL COME AGAIN **213**

[*not*] *because I have done my share and I dont want to see any more of it*[34]

and after five months duty in England Arthur Thomas decided, 'I may . . . be packed off to France to battle another shocking winter I don't want to kill myself a fair thing is fair, I don't want to see France any more, good sense tells me so.'[35] He was sent to the front in January 1918, and was killed in June.

There were old soldiers willing to go back. Some simply accepted the fortune of war: 'I am off once again to France. I cannot grumble as I have had a fair rest . . . here for ten months, with only four of them in hospital, extremely lucky don't you think. I . . . will endeavour to account for a few more huns.'[36] Others wished to leave England to end the war, to join their friends and units, to appease their honour, or to escape the human parasites that infested Australian camps and English streets. In October 1916 a wounded officer reported,

I'm not going to be in too great a hurry to get back to France, as I reckon I've seen enough for a while; but all the same, I am only stopping my chance of promotion by staying here, and I would like to get back again for the battalion's sake as soon as I can as I would not like anyone to think that I was a 'cold-footer.'[37]

In December another decided,

Although the prospect of spending winter in the trenches is not what one might term appealing, still being back once more among the old familiar faces—or what are left of them—will amply compensate all difficulties. I was looking forward to spending Christmas with the boys again, and it seems as if my ambition will be realized.[38]

'I really don't know why I want so much to get back to the Front', Lieutenant Chapman admitted, 'when I think of the slush and cold over there I shiver, and yet I am a jolly side happier over there than

34. Pte M. Burrows, 4 Pioneer Bn, Tram driver, of Enmore, NSW. POW –/1/18, aged 33. *L* 10/2/17.
35. Thomas, *L* 23/10/17.
36. Sgt W. Rowley, 18 Bn, Clerk, of Paddington, NSW. b. 1893. *L* 6/3/18.
37. Capt F. R. Corney, MC, 25 Bn, Soldier, of Kyneton, Vic. b. 1894. *L* 31/10/16.
38. Worrall, *L* 6/12/16.

here . . . what I really want to carry about with me is a clear conscience—that I have found is better than a cosy billet and a warm fire.'[39] A New South Wales corporal stated, 'No one who has actually gone through this war and . . . witnessed its horrors is anxious to get back to it. I am going back. It is not from choice. It is my duty and that alone makes me go into it again . . . but crave to go back. Never.'[40] And in Fovant camp a Pozières survivor remarked of a new arrival, 'he . . . is itching to get amongst the flying ironmongery that Fritz is so liberal with . . . Guess he'll know all about the game after the first few hours under fire & will realise that all the ancient glory associated with War has disappeared,' and went on to tell his parents,

I have had a long stay in safety on this side of the 'Herring Pond' so it's about time I gave another hand to the boys . . . now hurrying our 'Hun-Kultured' enemy along the Belgian Front . . . Please . . . accept as the Will of our Heavenly Father, the future that is set down for me. Keep up a brave heart & believe in the righteousness of our grand cause—our arms & those of our Allies will win thro' in God's time.[41]

In France by late 1916, most soldiers confessed themselves thoroughly weary of the business. For a time the unexpected length of the war had not discouraged Australian ardour, nor had Gallipoli in the long term, but Fromelles and Pozières had, and thereafter war was only an onerous duty. Even after their senses began to recover from the mid-1916 battles, in about October, men had an awful experience behind them, the winter before them, and peace hidden in the distant future. Their hopes sagged under a succession of afflictions, and a malaise seized their spirits. 'Wish the whole concern was over', an original Anzac declared in October, 'We are all more or less fed up with it. The only real bloodthirsty men are the new hands who have not seen a fight.'[42] 'I can tell you everyone will be glad when it is all over',[43] a 1915 enlistment noted, and

39. Capt P. W. Chapman, MC, 55 Bn, Agricultural student, of Orange, NSW. KIA 12/3/17, aged 30. *D* 7/12/16.
40. Allan, *D* –/2/17.
41. Cave, *L* 6/10/17.
42. Lt W. F. Shirtley, 13 Bn, Salesman, of Orange, NSW. KIA 11/4/17, aged 24. *L* 8/10/16.
43. Cpl B. S. Arnold, 14 Fld Coy, Plumber and gasfitter, of Mosman, NSW. DOW 31/10/17, aged 26. *L* 17/11/16.

THE OLD DAYS NEVER WILL COME AGAIN 215

another told his brother, 'as you love me, KEEP OUT OF THIS, we are not all going to be chopping blocks.'[44]

The 1916 winter brought more casualties and suffering, but not peace. At Flers Lance Corporal Mitchell wrote, 'At times when there is nothing doing I think of all things and feel tired all through. I feel as though I have lived far beyond my span and need a great rest . . . It is better not to have to much thinking time',[45] and during the winter an original in the 4th Battalion complained,

we have to go back [into the line] again thats the crook Part about, once I used to be able to look at dead and shattered men & crook sights, without turning a hair, there were a few thousand at 'Lone Pine' but now I get nervy. been too long at it without a spell I think. Jove I hope my nerves dont give way.

He was wounded three weeks later, by the *tenth* shot a sniper fired at him, and decided, 'it will do me, though he could have hit me harder if he liked. I wont get much of a spell out of this lot but he only missed the heart by 2 inches so I suppose I shouldn't growl.'[46] The war had almost two years to run. In mid-1917 a man asked his family, 'Did you get that group photo I sent you? well all the boys except 4 on the right were either killed or wounded in the last stunt [Messines], I tell you I am full up, and the sooner we wipe Fritz out the better.'[47] 'I am looking forward to coming home again and will not be sorry when that happy time comes I can assure you',[48] a soldier told his wife. Another exclaimed, 'I hope it ends soon. I've got a proper guts full',[49] and a third swore after a mate was killed, 'May this damnable war be over [soon] . . . Tom . . . was as game as they make men . . . But just before the poor fellow got killed he said to me that it was a bit solid and the sooner it finished the better.'[50]

1918 came, still the strife continued, and still men struggled on, praying for an end. 'I wish he would quit and let us all come home. I wish they would take us all to Egypt & do a bit there',[51] a sapper

44. Thomas, L 26/11/16.
45. Mitchell, D 2/1/17.
46. Wright, D 10/1 and 3/2/17.
47. Gration, L 19/6/17.
48. Pte A. Armitage, 11 MG Coy, Storeman, of Muswellbrook, NSW (b. England). KIA 31/7/17, aged 36. L 16/7/17.
49. Serjeant, L 29/10/17.
50. Pte E. Allen, 49 Bn, Farmer, of Gin Gin, Qld. KIA 25/4/18, aged 35. L 6/12/17.
51. R. A. Muir, L 7/1/18.

wrote, and an infantry corporal stated, 'this WAR has knocked the romance out of most of us.'[52] In March the Germans opened their offensive: purpose and success uplifted the Australians, but not their hopes or confidence. 'I am sick and tired of the whole blasted show, it is cruel',[53] one recorded, and another, 'Truly War is not a thing of Romance and wonderful adventure, [as] we imagined it in days gone by.'[54]

These attitudes confirmed another and more fundamental change in outlook, which did much to place the mental framework of soldiers beyond the comprehension of civilians. By about 1917 many in the AIF had abandoned hope of life or happiness: generally they ceased writing of 'after the war', and 'when I get home', and 'I suppose it is summer in Australia now', for these things had sunk into the past, often beyond dreams or memory, almost certainly beyond recovery. Instead, expecting to die, men counted no future save the next battle or the next leave, and no life save their present uncertain existence. George Mitchell remarked, 'I feel that I have lost touch with any life but this one of war. It is hard to recall Australia, and apart from my people nothing stands out vividly. I feel an outsider. We are lost in the magnitude of our task'.[55]

Few soldiers recorded this point—it was hardly the sort of thing to write home about—but perhaps their predictions about victory demonstrated it. In 1914 and 1915 most Australian soldiers expected the Empire to win quickly. More thought a long war possible by 1916, and more still by 1917, while a few by then had decided that Germany would have to be starved to defeat. Yet during much of this time, because their faith was great and because only victory or death could truly release them, men sought desperately to believe in an imminent end. At Pozières a man showed the conviction of despair: 'I don't think that our division will be asked to do anymore advancing for a while . . . [soon] we will have the Huns back well broken. our share of the back-breaking is over I think',[56] and another thought, 'you need not expect us home this year; next year you may but early or late I cannot say.'[57] In 1917 a soldier reported,

52. Thomas, *L* 4/2/18.
53. Thomas, *D* 4/6/18.
54. Stobie, *D* 6/4/18.
55. Mitchell, *D* 18/7/17.
56. Sgt R. H. Adams, MM, 8 Bn, Machine fitter, of Miles, Qld. KIA 4/10/17, aged 25. *L* 27/8/16.
57. Lt J. Bourke, 8 Bn, School teacher, of Wedderburn, Vic. b. 1885. *L* 20/9/16.

'some of the boys say they will be back again in their homes by Xmas next. I hope they are right and I hope I am with them. Peace will come much sooner than we think, and I can see it well in sight.'[58] 'I think we will have to do another winter over here there seems very little signs of it finishing', a young private wrote in July 1917, 'I reckon it will be about this time next year though it may stop as quick as it started. I hope it does it would do me if it finished the day it started. I think I could·hang out till then.'[59] Toil and doubt had sapped the old assumptions, but hope remained, and men could still see victory at the end of a weary road.

But even hope had evaporated by 1918, when Australians had thoroughly learnt the unpredictable sequence of success and disaster, and trusted nothing save reality. One or two veterans, on rare occasions, considered defeat. 'Fritz is making good, unless something happens he will win,'[60] noted Corporal Thomas, and Lieutenant Mitchell asserted, 'I feel disaster in my blood. Curse all the powers that bungled us to defeat . . . My thoughts were bitter as I looked down at my service stripes. What if they were all for nothing.'[61] Few Australian soldiers at any time imagined being beaten, but even as their side advanced to victory most expected a long war. 'Don't expect a Peace worth having, until a least another 18 months. Can't be done!!',[62] an officer assured his parents in January. A month later a corporal confided, 'although at present Germany appears to have the best end of the stick . . . I am very optimistic about us being ultimately victorious, but we'll come to a state of almost hopeless despair first.'[63] In June a gunner declared, 'It is ridiculous for people not to recognise and admit the ability of the Bosche, as a strategist and fighter . . . the Huns will not carry all before them, but it may take many months for the tide to turn.'[64] '[P]eace by a military decision by this time next year',[65] Major Garnet Adcock, a tunnelling officer, predicted in September, and after Australian infantry had marched away from the Western Front for the last time an officer decided, 'Peace is in the air and is cer-

58. G. H. J. Davies, *L* 31/3/17.
59. Reynolds, *L* 8/7/17.
60. Thomas, *D* 1/6/18.
61. Mitchell, *D* 2/6/18.
62. Capt A. W. MacDonald, 34 Bn, Accountant, of Neutral Bay, NSW. KIA 30/8/18, aged 27. *L* 18/1/18.
63. Allan, *L* 27/2/18.
64. Evatt, *L* 16/6/18.
65. Adcock, *L* 30/9/18.

tinaly not more than a year off, perhaps even less.'[66] On the threshold of victory, these were cautious opinions, reflecting a widespread acceptance that war had become the natural mode of existence.

The association between war and sport evident on Gallipoli was broken in France, although the language of games survived. There were 'sides', an action was a 'stunt', men had 'innings' between leave or wounds, men killed were 'knocked' or 'knocked out', men defeated or dead 'took the count', men winning easily 'had a walkover'. Early in 1917 a veteran of Fromelles wrote that he was about to leave England 'to help knock out old "Bill" in the last round of the championship',[67] in 1918 troops chosen for an attack 'got their guernseys',[68] and at Menin Road a brave man dying told his mates that he was still playing and still had a jersey.[69] But usually these words were bereft of their former implications, and now only a procedural similarity connected sport with a detested enemy, and the grim murderous business in which Australians found themselves engaged.

Although ruin and death were perpetually about them, and their hopes were broken, most in the AIF fought obstinately on. A few men, wearied by toil and incessant danger, gave up the struggle, particularly in 1918, when the world seemed so bleak. Packs of deserters marauded the back areas in France:

They live by thieving and gambling. The National pastime of two-up has chiefly given them their living, and when searching B---, we took a double headed penny off him . . . They stole from British and Yankee dumps such things as petrol and clothing, for which they found a ready market among the French[70]

Other men wounded themselves to escape service; an ambulanceman treating one such wound

covered the tell tale [powder] marks with repeated applications of pure iodine and 'wised him up' to keep putting iodine on it

66. Chedgey, *L* 8/10/18. In 1918 both Haig and the French Marshal, Foch, thought the war would end in 1919. Other generals thought 1920.
67. Lt S. J. Topp, 58 Bn, Clerk, of Brighton, Vic. KIA 12/5/17, aged 37. *L* 30/1/17.
68. E. J. Rule, *Jacka's Mob*, p. 319 (26/9/18). (2/Lt, MC, MM, 14 Bn, Railway foreman, of Cobar, NSW. b. 1886.)
69. In Hill, *L* re death, 1/10/17.
70. Nicholson, *L* 18/5/18.

*until it blistered and remove the burnt skin without detection.
Poor beggar had been a good soldier prior to this and was not
really responsible for his nerve collapse. Am glad to say he
escaped detection and subsequently made good. S.I. wounds are
very rare indeed.*[71]

Self inflicted wounds *were* rare in the AIF, desertion was un-
common, and offences in action—cowardice, murder, and desertion to the enemy—were almost unknown.[72] The majority of Australians went into battle whenever it was asked of them, but only
their sense of duty kept them to a task so unrewarding. As on
Gallipoli, duty became equated with necessity, for repeated hardship required some explanation to make it bearable, and Australians
found this in the need to save their world. Early in 1917 a new
arrival reported,

*What really does strike one forcibly . . . is the seeming mad-
ness of two supposedly leading civilised nations hammering
each other with shot and shell in the one great object of killing
as many of the foe as possible. It is only when one gets here . . .
that one really realises what a mad business it is. We have a
great consolation however in the knowledge that we are fighting
for a principle.*[73]

'One thing that makes me happy is to know that I am doing my
duty', another reinforcement stated, 'If I was still in Australia I
would be ashamed to live for I would be a disgrace to my parents
and my country for the rest of my life.'[74] A third man, then untested
in a great battle, remembered of a dead mate, 'He died a glorious
death, and if I should be taken the same way, don't be sad but be
joyous and grateful to know that I obeyed the call and strove to do
my duty as a man.'[75] In 1918 an infantryman recently transferred
from the Army Service Corps wrote,

71. Morgan, *D* 17/6/18.
72. For example, only 701 cases of self inflicted wounds were recorded
against the AIF in France; about half of these were between March and
August 1918. (Butler, *Official Medical History*, II, pp. 864-5, 897.) See also
pp. 236-7; Bean, *Official History*, VI, p. 486.
73. Sgt J. R. Gemmell, MM, 7 FAB, Accountant, of Claremont, WA
(b. Ireland). b. 1887. *L* 31/1/17.
74. Gallwey, *L* –/3/17.
75. Pte W. W. Barber, 36 Bn, Engineer, of Sydney, NSW. DOW 23/10/17,
aged 24. *L* 12/5/17.

Dear Mother and Father,

Am leaving now to go over to the attack. If you receive this, I shall have been knocked out. Do not worry, but only think that I have tried to do my job as your son and an Englishman. I am not afraid.

> *Cheerho!*
>> *Your everloving Son,*
>>> *George.*[76]

He was killed on the Somme a fortnight later.

Most of these were men inexperienced in battle. Other newcomers, and most veterans, tended by 1917 to champion causes commensurate with the extent of their sacrifice: they battled to prevent future wars, or to ensure that their own land remained peaceful and free. Sergeant Elliott decided, 'the more the Germans get of France the closer they are getting to Australia, and this we are determined they will never do',[77] and a reinforcement asserted, 'if only the people of Australia saw what was once happy villages, now simply heaps of bricks and stones they would begin to realise what war means . . . I'm glad I'm here but don't expect to enjoy it.'[78] An engineer told his wife,

if my presence here means that you . . . [and our families] can live their lives in peace and fulfil their destiny, so do I gladly . . . forego for a time that happiness [I] . . . know will be [mine] . . . at some future period . . .

'Twas nothing more than this, not the example of others, not the excitement even that urged me in the face of opposition at first to take the step I did.[79]

An Anzac wrote from hospital,

I'm sure you wouldn't . . . like to have to . . . say that sons or brothers wern't men enough to die for all that Christianity stands for, for the Liberty we've always talked about and for the Country we live in and are proud of, and of the traditions of the English race for centuries back. I've been in the Valley of

76. Lt G. Simpson, 6 Bn, Farmer, of Mildura, Vic (b. England). KIA 23/8/18, aged 26. *L* 9/8/18.
77. Elliott, *L* 11/7/18.
78. Lt T. H. Templeton, 14 Bn, Solicitor, of Yea, Vic. KIA 24/9/17, aged 37. *L* 27/6/17.
79. Capt R. B. Hinder, MC, Mining Corps, Engineer, of Mosman, NSW. b. 1891. *L* 19/9/16.

Death more than once and if I have to stop there next time or any time, I'd feel honoured to join the company of Heroes who have already gone[80]

'[W]hat are we fighting for?', a corporal asked,

Daily hundreds of the cream of our country and thousands of Allies are being killed, or . . . [made] physical wrecks for life. Is the game worth the candle as the boys say. At times I fancy it is not, but as at other times realising that we must win or go under, agree with Lloyd George that we must win for the sake of the generations to come . . . the Germans in Belgium . . . have . . . shot . . . 300 [citizens near Dinant] . . . To pillage, destroy and rape the women of a country is terrible but Good God the act committed above is the work of a devil, no human being could countenance such an atrocity . . . one cannot but preach the doctrine of fight to a finish. God knows what they would do if they became masters of the world. It shakes one's faith in the Almighty to think that such an awful crime against civilisation is permitted.[81]

'[W]hen it is over, I hope we shall have achieved something for future generations. I would go through a lot of this to prevent . . . [my son] from ever having to go through it later',[82] an infantryman wrote, and Garnet Adcock demanded, 'Why should . . . [we] make peace now—so that our children will have to do our work over again? We want to finish our work now'.[83]

The insistence of Australian soldiers upon the worth of their objectives had two main effects. Especially in 1916 and 1917, it gave purpose to their existence, above life and welfare, and even above going home: Sergeant Major Ellsworth remarked, 'Naturally, I am longing to get Home again, & there is never a day or night passes but what my thoughts are of Home, & Home faces, but I hope to be able to see this business thro' before returning'.[84] And it ceaselessly reinforced their determination not merely to win, but to ensure Germany's utter defeat: 'Even if the Germans want peace now, I don't think we should give it before we have got them

80. Mann, *L* 21/8/17.
81. Morgan, *D* 19/5/17.
82. Lt J. G. A. Pockley, 33 Bn, Agriculturalist, of Wahroonga, NSW. KIA 30/3/18, aged 26. *L* 13/1/18.
83. Adcock, *L* 15/9/18.
84. Ellsworth, *L* 24/6/17.

absolutely smashed',[85] Lieutenant W. G. Blaskett considered at Pozières, and in 1917 Lieutenant Alexander exclaimed,

How prominent in practically all the Allied countries of late have responsible persons being emphasising that the autocratic Government (of the Hoenzollerns and their similarly fiendish colaborators) must go. How the unfortunate double-faced arch-fiend must be shaking in his boots now! . . . the World is in agony through the action of one man . . . so I think anyone might say 'God help the poor Kaiser'![86]

Until 1916 Australians had derived their impressions about the Hun almost entirely from propaganda. They therefore knew less than most about him, and throughout the war they hated him with an unusually fierce intensity. In 1917 Australians decorating an English hospital for Christmas discovered pictures of King George printed in Germany, and were perplexed whether to preserve the image of their king, or burn the German paper. A corporal believed:

A nation whose deliberate policy assassinates law, murders human feelings and strangles with brutal hands the very promptings of Mercy . . . had to be punished by Someone with Higher Ideals. A Nation that makes slaves of men women and girls and houses them like cattle without regard to sex had the Devil for their leader . . . Her Kultur as exhibited, which violated women, stuck babies on bayonets and displayed them outside butchers shops, slew priests, purposely destroyed cathedrals etc., is the greatest sham of all[87]

and even George Davies, the gentle clergyman, recorded,

dead Germans can be seen piled thick upon one another. Thus a nation is paying, in priceless souls, for its perfidy and infidelity. These . . . are the lads who were rendered soulless by military government . . . slain by the hand of a devil, who, to suit his own ends, would bring hundreds of souls into slavery and awful death.[88]

'[T]he anniversary of Nurse Cavell's death. we sent gas over and at 7.30 p.m. . . . made a successful raid on the German trench . . .

85. Blaskett, *L* 15/8/16.
86. Alexander, *L* 13/4/17.
87. Allan, *Notes*.
88. G. H. J. Davies, *D* pp. 77-8 (–/5/17).

Many of our men left cards with "Remember Nurse Cavell" on in the Hun trenches. We also sent gas over later',[89] a young New South Wales private related, and Corporal Antill, who had fought for employment and adventure until the landing, asked an aunt in England, 'How close did the air raid come to [you]? . . . it makes my blood boil to think of their dastardly deeds and I am very pleased to be able to say that I counted for a few more huns with my machine gun and . . . it leaves a great feeling of satisfaction behind when one sees them going over like nine pins.'[90] '[W]e read in the paper that the Kaiser had told his troops not to take any more British troops and were to show no more mercy', Private Gallwey recalled, 'We were nettled at this and decided to do the same. We had instructions to kill anything German. Nothing . . . was to be spared. They all had to die.'[91]

Experience taught Australians that Germans sometimes could be humane, generous, and brave,[92] and incidents showed some that travail was universal in war. Lieutenant Chapman recalled of Fromelles,

staggering through the gloom we saw a man—he came about 10 yds towards us, and then fell and started to crawl. I thought it was one of our own men so we went out to him. Poor beggar I have seen worse looking mess-ups but he was bad enough—his left eye was gone— . . . he was a mass of blood and looked as if he had been through a sausage machine. He pleaded something in German . . . it was hardly a plead—it was a moan, or a prayer—so I gave him my hand to hold and said as nicely as I could 'All right old chap'. He kept pushing towards the trench all the time and as it was rather awkward getting along on one hand and two knees while I held his other hand I let it go. Whereupon the poor mangled brute got up on his knee—put his hands together and started to pray! 'Oh cruel—cruel' Gib[93]

---

89. Pte G. Bennett, 8 MG Coy, Warehouseman, of Drummoyne, NSW (b. England). DOW 6/10/17, aged 17. *D* 12/10/16.
90. Antill, *L* 20/6/17.
91. Gallwey, *L* 2/8/17, p. 246.
92. Australians especially admired the 27 (Württemberg) Div, which opposed them at First and Second Bullecourt, and the constant courage of the German Machine Gun Corps.
93. Capt N. Gibbins, 55 Bn. Bank manager, of Ipswich. Qld. KIA 20/7/16, aged 38. Gibbins was killed on the Australian parapet while commanding the 14 Bde's rearguard during the retirement from Fromelles. In happier circumstances the quality of his leadership might easily have won him a VC.

*said when he saw the poor beggar . . . the thought struck me
'How can men be so cruel' . . . and together we helped him
along . . . I think the Germans must have imagined we were
going to eat them when we get in their trench*[94]

and another officer observed, 'It is very funny how one watching the
effect of our guns on the German trenches, remarks "good oh", as
their parapet & dugouts fly up in the air: one does not think till
afterwards that some poor devils may be flying up with it, who are
just as anxious for the war to end as we are.'[95]

Accordingly a few Australians applied rules of fair play to
fighting the Hun:

*At Ypres salient one of C Comp 19th Batt. chaps every morning
used to throw a tin of bully beef to a Hun on post duty 30 yds.
away. One day the tin fell short whereupon relying on Australia's Sports jumped up to get it, when he was shot by another
C's Men who was ignorant of the Bully beef episode. Everybody
was chagrined to learn what had been done and lucky for the
culprit he pleaded ignorance*[96]

and some tried to be generous to a stricken enemy:

*There are a whole lot of Germans buried in a cellar at Messines
we heard them tapping and started to dig for them until they
[the German artillery] started shelling like the devil we then
dropped a message over their line by aeroplane telling him we
were trying to release his men at Messines if he did not shell it
however he must have thought we were pulling his foot for he
continued to shell so that those poor beggars will just have to
die of starvation etc.*[97]

Many treated prisoners kindly, sharing food, water, and tobacco
with those they captured, and several risked their lives for their
opponents. Private Antill was 'dressing a wounded German who had
been out in no man's land for 5 days and had 2 very nasty wounds
. . . just alive with maggots. Well I had just finished leg wound and
was goin to have a go at the back when a shrapnel shell burst over
me and one of the bullets entered the right side of my back'.[98]

94. Chapman, *D* 30/7/16.
95. Fraser, *L* 31/7/16.
96. Allan, *Notes.*
97. Henderson, *L* 13/6/17.
98. Antill, *L* 10/8/16.

But usually Australians defeated the enemy's infantry too easily to respect it, and their own trials were too great and too frequent for most to show compassion to Germans. They remained convinced that Huns were evil, and believed that brave Germans were also misguided sinners. Some of the men cited above detested their foe, and most AIF soldiers hated him vehemently. In 1917 Private Gallwey described a tour of the old Mouquet Farm battlefield:

One dugout had the entrance blown in and a Fritz who was just coming out was pinned down. He could not have been killed but was unable to extricate himself. Circumstances showed that he had lain there and starved to death. He had been there eight months . . . further on there was a shell hole full of white bones . . . a shrapnel shell . . . had got [about a dozen men] . . . There was one boot found full of foot. An arm was found with only a couple of fingers on the hand. As it was a German solider recognisable by the uniform and leggings we had a hearty laugh over it. I do not care how many Huns are lying about . . . We looked in his skull for gold teeth as souvenirs . . . [and] left him lie there.[99]

After Messines he reported,

In one trench I saw three or four Germans pinned in. The side of the trench had closed in pinning them as they stood. The tops of their heads were blown off with machine guns. It was a horrible sight. Blood and brains had trickled down their faces and dried . . . I was filled with delight to see so many Huns killed and could not help laughing.[100]

Their hatred of the enemy and their belief in the necessity of their task were the only important original incentives which survived intact in Australians throughout the war. Yet in 1918 they were still thrusting and successful in battle, partly because they valued the reputation they had won under the sway of the early incentives. Their prestige affirmed their proficiency as soldiers, encouraged their belief that they could contribute to victory, and protected the good name of their units. Perhaps above all, because

99. Gallwey, *L* 2/8/17, p. 85.
100. Gallwey, *L* 2/8/17, p. 263. No doubt this would have repelled many Australians, but 53 (22.7 per cent) of veterans asked in 1967 or 1968 still retained their dislike of Germans.

the world still honoured martial capacity as it had before 1914, the ability of the Australians gave them some common ground with civilians, and earned them the respect of other soldiers. Since the landing the stirring deeds of men from a land so slight and distant had caught the romantic enthusiasm of the English press: 'Anzac' conveyed impressions of almost legendary fighters, dashing and gallant, far from their homes, and almost invariably triumphant in war. Praise came from other sources also, and men from the new nation reacted proudly. After Polygon Wood a British general told troops of the Fifth Division, 'You men have done very well here.' 'Oh', a man replied, 'Only as well as opportunity and ability would allow.' 'Very well put young man very well put indeed,' beamed the general, 'but you have undoubtedly the best troops in the world.'[101] After September 1917 the capacity of Australians as first class storm troops was everywhere recognised: the British staff so employed them,[102] and although it increased their casualties they thought this an honour. Captain Mitchell recalled that at Dernancourt, 'The men we relieved were Ninth Royal Scots, and K.O.S.B.'s.[103] They asked "Who are you?" We told them "Forty Eighth Australians." "Thank God" they said "you will hold him".'[104] Major Adcock stated, 'In the retreat I passed some heavy guns being drawn out by tractors. The Major in command asked "What troops are you?" When I replied "Australians," he said "Thank God! My guns are safe." '[105] In 1918 French refugees stopped their flight from the Hun when they recognised Australians, even in areas in which the AIF had never been billeted, and, turning back with them, joyfully re-entered their homes convinced that these tall, cheerful strangers of formidable reputation would halt the foe. 'Fini retreat mate', the Australians assured them. 'Bons Australiens,' the French tearfully replied, 'Soldats terribles et formidables.'[106]

Even the Germans respected them. Many considered colonials the

101. Lt A. E. Sheppeard, MM, 5 Div Sig Coy, Electrical fitter, of Newnes, NSW. b. 1891. D 26/9/17.
102. Letter from the British Official Historian to Mr. A. W. Bazley (formerly S/Sgt, AIF HQ, Journalist, of Prahran, Vic. b. 1896), 6 December 1955. Copy in my possession.
103. King's Own Scottish Borderers, then of the British 9 Div.
104. Mitchell, D 27/3/18.
105. Adcock, L 14/4/18.
106. From Fischer, L 7/4/18; Barwick, D XIII, p. 5 (25/4/18); Bean, Official History, V, pp. 177, 675; G. D. Mitchell, Backs to the Wall, p. 238; Williams, Gallant Company, p. 243.

best British soldiers, and troops placed against the Australians came to fear the encounter. At Polygon Wood a signaller reported, 'The German prisoners say they do not like being on the front opposite Australians even if not attacking we always manage to make a quiet sector lively.'[107] Germans captured by the 11th Battalion at Merris in June 1918 'were told they were going to a "quiet" sector and only needed "to keep their heads down." One man on realising who we were exclaimed, "Quiet Sector! Mein Gott!" '[108] A German battalion order captured at Mont St Quentin stated,

Forces confronting us consist of Australians who are very war-like, clever and daring. They understand the art of crawling through high crops in order to capture our advanced posts. The enemy is also adept in conceiving and putting into execution important patrolling operations. The enemy infantry has daily proved themselves to be audacious.[109]

General Monash, realising the importance of their reputation to his men, fostered it carefully, and used it to encourage their aggression during 1918. He told C. E. W. Bean in August that 'he was ceasing to appeal to the Australians on the ground of patriotism . . . or public interest. The appeal which he was going to make, and was making, to them was on grounds of prestige.'[110] His message was that his men could attempt anything, and had only to equal their past glories to sweep all before them.

His men agreed. Throughout the war an unshakable confidence, a clear certainty that they would win, marked Australian soldiers in battle. During the 1918 German offensive a Third Division officer wrote,

Some of the English divisions had been badly broken and we passed a number of derelicts all of whom regarded us with a sort of unwilling admiration, as men going up to do the impossible . . . It makes one feel proud to be an Australian to see our boys after all this, pass through a village singing. They are magnificent and wherever they go they inspire confidence, both in the Tommies and the French civilians.[111]

107. Sheppeard, *D* 26/9/17.
108. Lt G. S. Gemmell, 11 Bn, School teacher, of Claremont, WA. KIA 10/8/18, aged 25. *L* 8/6/18.
109. In Pte F. J. Brewer, 20 Bn, Journalist, of Kangaroo Point, Qld. b. 1884. *Notes*.
110. Bean, *Official History*, VI, p. 876.
111. Fairweather, *L* 4/4/18.

'There may be debacles in other armies,' Lieutenant Mitchell decided during those dark days, 'but the A.I.F. will fight till the bitter end',[112] and after three good German divisions had forced the partial withdrawal of two Australian battalions at Dernancourt in April 1918 he recorded, 'The world had fallen. The Australian line had been broken. Not even pride was left. Tears of grief ran down my face.'[113]

Although the prestige of their Corps was always important to them, most Australians were more immediately concerned with the reputation of their units. As the days of their service multiplied they felt, it is true, a widening loyalty, first to their company, then to their battalion, then to their division, and finally to their Corps. But at the same time, as their sense of alienation from civilian allegiances intensified, a considerable part of their loyalty and most of their attachment was to their battalion. In Egypt men had resented their transfer from Gallipoli battalions to 'daughter' formations: years of battle strengthened this affection, until a man's battalion was the centre of his existence. In 1918, after six weeks with his unit, a new arrival exclaimed, 'It is surprising how soon one becomes linked to his Unit & already I have arrived at that stage when I think the 6th is the only Battn.'[114] Veterans felt much stronger attachments: 'Back again with the old Battalion and I can tell you I am just glad to be settled down again with them', Corporal Antill wrote after a sojourn in England, adding, "I hardly know any of them here at all for they are all new to me.'[115] He had come back, not to the company of his friends, for they lay at Pozières, but to the security of home. Late in 1916 Archie Barwick stated that his battalion,

has a fine name & record & we are taught to live up to it . . . many hard & difficult jobs are given to you simply because of your record, & we are then in honour bound to make a success of it or perish in the attempt. this sort of spirit is beginning to make its appearance in the Battalions of the 1st. Division, & they are struggling one against the other to show the finest performances.[116]

112. Mitchell, *D* 2/6/18.
113. Mitchell, *Backs to the Wall*, p. 202. This was the only occasion in France on which an Australian defence gave up ground.
114. Fischer, *L* 8/2/18.
115. Antill, *L* 8/5/17.
116. Barwick, *D* VI, pp. 29-30 (10/10/16).

Annual dinners quickly became a tradition, and by August 1917 H. R. Williams could declare, 'To every Australian soldier, his company, his battalion, was his home. Here lived our truest and most trusted companions, brothers who would share their last franc or crust with each other, bound together till victory or death. Home and civilian associates were only misty memories'.[117] Men made traditions, and when they died their memory survived in the prestige of their units, so that to disgrace one was to shame the other.

For this reason, in September and October 1918, officers and men of eight battalions refused orders to disband. They claimed to prefer any penalty to the sacrifice of their battalion's honour, and requested a difficult battle assignment in which they might win death or glory, in either event thereby averting the detested action. They treated the affair as an industrial dispute rather than as a mutiny, electing leaders, maintaining discipline and propriety, and surviving on the sympathy and support of other units. Seven battalions won brief stays of execution, and none was punished.

The strikes manifested a profound change in the loyalties of Australian soldiers. The early incentives of hatred and duty which Australians still felt in 1918 explained why the war must continue, but, even though Australians never abandoned the objectives of their side, the cause for which they fought had become an onerous obligation. Instead they were inspired by the wish to maintain their own reputations.

In thus seeking the esteem of men, Australian soldiers remained to a degree responsive to their civilian backgrounds. But they knew another world, in which the cause of their fighting was less important than the manner of their daily lives. From long experience in a cruel war they derived a new outlook, which confirmed the worth of their old attitudes towards mateship and discipline, but which included a host of new values. Before the fighting ended they regulated their course by processes alien to civilians, and adopted standards which later set them apart from those who had not fought in the war.

117. Williams, *Gallant Company*, p. 146.

FRANCE

8 The New World of War

[T]he two captains, myself, and the two gravediggers stood bare-
headed in the driving rain and listened to the great words of Saint
Paul concerning immortality . . . Fifty yards away one of our men
was sentry over a dump. He and Hall had been boys together in
Castlemaine and in the same class at school. The gravediggers . . .
filled in the soil and we returned to our duties. The sentry searched
for some timber and made a rude cross, on which he scribbled his
dead mates name and number and stuck it up at the end of the
mound.

CSM A. A. Brunton, 57th Battalion, January 1917

Early in 1919 two Australian lieutenants stood in a line of men at
Buckingham Palace, waiting to meet the King. The King had been
delayed, and the two Australians were restless. 'George is late on
parade,' one finally declared, 'we'll have to "crime" him.' He was
Joe Maxwell,[1] come to receive the Victoria Cross. His mate was
E. W. Mattner,[2] and after the King had given him his third decoration for bravery in the field, the two chatted for a few minutes, while
the King recalled his visit to Australia. In a busy Palace routine a
discussion of that length was unusual, and when Lieutenant Mattner
left the King the Lord Chamberlain, heading a clutch of titled
officials, pressed towards him, asking excitedly, 'What did he say?
What did he say?' 'Well,' the young officer told them, 'he said, "I'm
sick of this turnout. Let's go down to the corner pub and have a
couple of beers."' The Lord Chamberlain, shocked to the marrow,
'dressed him down'.[3]

The divergence between English and Australian attitudes to
discipline and authority survived the war. The Australian veteran in
1918 was not the intractable individualist of 1915: he was less
openly defiant, and he had learnt to tolerate many of the procedures

1. Lt J. Maxwell, VC, MC & bar, DCM, 18 Bn, Boilermaker's apprentice,
of Marrickville, NSW. b. 1896.
2. Lt E. W. Mattner, MC, DCM, MM, 6 FAB, Teacher, of Adelaide, S A.
b. 1894.
3. Statement by Senator Mattner, 14 May 1968.

and formalities important to a military system. But years in the military had strengthened his contempt for army regulation, and at the end of the war he asserted his independence with practised guile and unrelaxed persistence.

Accordingly the AIF was barraged by criticism and burdened by disabilities. 'I hope to see London soon, but the Australians have not a good reputation and our officers do not like giving us much leave',[4] one of the first Australians to reach France noted on arrival, and a year later an old soldier, Sergeant Major Ellsworth, reported,

The Australians have a very bad name in England now, and we get accused of some very terrible things at times . . . recently [an English sergeant] . . . pulled a revolver and shot [an]other, who subsequently died: at the Court Martial . . . the accused . . . asked why he was carrying a revolver . . . , replied 'to protect myself against the Australians.'[5]

General Hobbs,[6] an Englishman then commanding the First Division's artillery, told his unit commanders in May 1916 that he was 'bitterly disappointed' in his efforts to make his men soldiers: their dress was slovenly, their march discipline atrocious, their failure to salute already a byword.[7] Similiar criticism, from Haig, from Army commanders, and from some senior AIF officers continued until the Australians quit the old world. The authorities were usually concerned with slackness in saluting, assaults on police, absence without leave, and untidy dress—they considered, in short, that Australians needed more polish, and less spit.

As on Gallipoli many in the AIF freely admitted this, for their offences arose from convictions they held strongly. They considered themselves unalterably civilian, fighters, not soldiers, volunteers for a job, not subjects to a medley of archaic impositions. Out of the line they held themselves masters of their fortunes, and treated leave restrictions and military police as unjust and degrading impediments to the exercise of natural rights. By late 1915 Corporal Mitchell, sick in England with enteric, was well enough to bait the military police patrolling his hospital. He recorded in mid-October,

4. Lt R. G. Henderson, MC, 18 Bn, Bank clerk, of Hunters Hill, NSW. KIA 9/4/18, aged 26. *L* 28/3/16.
5. Ellsworth, *L* 24/2/17.
6. Lt Gen Sir J. J. Talbot Hobbs, KCB, KCMG, VD. Commanded 1 Div Arty 1914-17, 5 Div 1917-18, Aust Corps 1918-19. b. 1864.
7. Circular to 1 Div Arty unit COs, 13 May 1916, in AWM File No. 265/2.

*Towards evening we strolled out of bounds. A military police-
man arrived and peremtorily ordered us back. We reclined
comfortably and just looked at him. He seemed astonished by
this procedure and climbed down. We then explained that we
had been anxious for his company and so had waited for him.
So we accompanied him back to the building. It is really marvellous the way in which the tommies respect these M.P^s.*

A month later he noted, 'Met several of our boys trailing for the
gore of an uppish M.P. About eleven separate chaps are trying to
pick a fight with him. But he is not having any.'

The police hoped to enforce leave restrictions, which Corporal
Mitchell evaded whenever he could. On 16 November he confided, 'I wrote a letter to myself asking me and Lane out to tea
on Wednesday. Put it into the ward office with a request for a pass.
I will either get the pass or get clink.' Next day he remarked, 'Got
the pass.' He repeated this manoeuvre several times, but came more
and more to ignore both the rules and their enforcers, and between
26 November and 31 December he broke hospital bounds twenty
times. Sometimes he had to bluff police—

*All went well until we saw a military policeman silhoueted
against the light of a lamp. 'Look important' I whispered
'We're officers.' So we stuck our chests out, and cut an attitude
as if we were in love with ourselves . . . [and] marched straight
on. The M.P. clicked his heels together and saluted, we returned it casually, and made our ward without any further
event*

—and occasionally he was caught and sentenced, but nothing
deterred him. In April 1916, at Monte Video camp, he 'Dodged
church parade but the military police made a round up and marched
the absentees up to the orderly room. When no one was looking I
walked off.' He was re-arrested the following day and given seven
days confined to barracks, a sentence, naturally, he took no notice
of. By June he had decided, 'Now I never apply for a pass, but go
out without one. This enables me to return at just whatever time
suits me.' Despite intermittent arrests, this became his practice until
he sailed for France.[8]

8. Mitchell, *D* 19/10, 12/11, 16/11, 17/11, and 31/12/15, 30/4 and
13/6/16, and to 30/7/16.

Many in the AIF shared Mitchell's convictions, and so swelled British crime sheets. Almost every Australian soldier in France must at some time have gone absent from his billet to visit another camp or a farm, or to drink 'vin blong' or 'vin rouge' at a nearby *estaminet*. Many did so habitually, and generally officers cheerfully accepted and even defended their absence. After the Armistice Thomas Cleary took four days off to visit Brussels, and encountered a problem as he made ready to return: 'They wouldn't sell a [train] ticket unless a pass was shown at the Booking office. I went up behind a chap who had a pass and as he was getting his ticket . . . I said make it two he handed them over Saying, pass please. I grabbed mine and flew.'[9]

Australians considered several other military practices objectionable. An officer reported of a court martial, 'A Corporal is charged with striking a Sergeant. No doubt he is technically guilty, but since I have seen the Sgt. I feel that the Corporal would have failed his manhood had he not "donged" him. He will probably get off.' He did,[10] despite the law. Some men dodged compulsory church parades on principle, and avoided other parades that were equally useless: in 1917 Lance Corporal Mitchell dodged the march past that honoured his DCM, and as a lieutenant in 1918 reported that he and fellow officers 'had to attend a lecture on "The law, and why we obey it." Consequently we were bored for an hour. We don't always obey it.'[11] 'We are always getting discipline into us it goes in one ear and out the other,'[12] another soldier remarked, and a singular example of the divergence between English and Australian attitudes to discipline occurred in 1918, when a man of the 2nd Battalion

indicated a Tommy in the lines of the next camp tied to a wooden cross . . . Everybody crowded around and started asking questions, it transpired the poor devil had abused a Lance Corporal and had to do 2 hours morning and afternoon for his trouble. Poor devil, a private in the Imperial Labour Corp Coy., somebody suggested cutting him free, the suggestion was no sooner made than carried out, poor beggar kept saying 'Don't

9. Cleary, *D* 19/2/19.
10. Adcock, *L* c.1/6/16.
11. Mitchell, *D* 12/5/17, 9/3/18.
12. Lt A. P. Earle, 6 MG Coy, Farmer, of Marshall, Vic. DOW 24/7/17, aged 26. *L* 17/9/16.

cut me free chum, I'll only get more,' the raiders assured him he
would not get any more while they were around. Having de-
stroyed the cross, pelted the officers Huts with bricks and jam
tins and named them for a lot of Prussian b---- the raiders
returned to our line. Next morning the Col[onel] read out on
parade 'with a smile and his tongue in his cheek' that he had
received a complaint . . . and that any man . . . who entered
those lines would be crimed. No one was crimed, and the
Tommy next door was not tied up again . . . a couple of days
later, he had not even then recovered from the shock and was
living in fear and trembling that the Iron hand of English Army
discipline would fall on him again.[13]

Because Australians would not surrender cherished prerogatives
to army supervision, like George Mitchell they detested military
police. Near the line this animosity was so great that front line
battalions at rest were obliged to nominate temporary policemen
from their own ranks, because regular military police were totally
unable to maintain order, and invariably provoked brawls, bashings,
or worse. A former architect observed, 'Its a pity the Military
police are not sent . . . to do a bit of fighting instead of loafing
about . . . Low malingerers thats all they are, & a change to the
Infantry would do them good anyway it would get rid of a rotten
lot of fellows.'[14] During the German offensive an Australian
private was scavenging through a deserted village on the Somme
when 'A Tommy M.P. reckoned I was looting and tried to arrest me,
but my mates knocked him out while I departed with the swag.'[15]
Although some Australians could not have defended this conduct,
to others it was reasonable, because the policeman was unnecessarily intervening in what they considered legitimate scavenging.
A similar attitude justified a riot in England:

a redcap . . . saw a Canadian coming out of the rear of a pub
with a bag on his shoulder and concluded that the man had
beer. As a matter of fact he had a pair of boots and this started
a brawl. Finally the man was clinked and also an Ausie was put

13. Morgan, *D* 1/4/18. The punishment was the British Army's Field Punishment No. 1. Although in 1914 it was very occasionally inflicted on members of the AIF, by 1915 Australians in Egypt were releasing English soldiers
from it often enough to bring protests from the British authorities.
14. R. A. Muir, *L* 11/2/17.
15. L/Cpl W. H. Zimmer, 57 Bn, Clerk of Petty Sessions, of Geelong, Vic.
KIA 17/6/18, aged 21. *L* 8/4/18.

in our clink over the same matter. Then to fix matters the village was put out of bounds. In the evening mobs from Canadian NZ & Ausie camps met and decided to get the boys out who had been unfairly put in . . . pretty soon the Ausie was released . . . [and] the Canadian clink cleared. On the way back they passed the Canadian canteen . . . [and] rolled 11 barrels of beer out onto the road and wrecked the dry canteen taking everything in it. They were drinking beer out of fire buckets and anything they could get hold of. They also smashed up the furniture and took the legs of chairs for weapons . . . [and] made for the village where they made a raid on the pub. After that they chased some military police thro' a cafe & then . . . cleared the N.Z. clink . . . and sacked the [N.Z.] canteen rolling out more barrels of beer . . . we were given rifles and marched down as quickly as possible . . . they picked up rocks and anything else handy. We . . . pretty soon scattered them . . . I . . . with most of the others had a feeling of sympathy towards them but when it come to a fight we were obliged to stick up for ourselves.[16]

As this implies, the AIF was noted for one other impropriety. In billets near Armentières Sergeant Barwick recorded, 'our platoon has to do a weeks punishment, on account of the many crimes we have to our credit no less than 22 during the week the boy's have been having a royal time alright nearly all drunks & stopping away from roll-calls,'[17] and at Vignacourt during the 1916 winter Sergeant de Vine wrote,

During the long wait many men wandered into the village where they obtained plenty of rum . . . many returned horribly drunk, about half the Bn must have been affected. When the train was about to leave a strong picquet entered the village to gather up the drunks those not capable of walking were wheeled on to the parade ground in hand carts & tossed out on top of one another like sacks[18]

The reputation of their countrymen or the prospect of fun led many Australians to take part in these diversions—one man, for

16. Sgr N. V. Wallace, 48 Bn, Clerk, of Naracoorte, SA. b. 1897. *L* 15/10/17.
17. Barwick, *D* III, p. 4 (12/5/16).
18. de Vine, *D* 1/12/16.

example, noted proudly that only three places were in bounds to the AIF, the line, the orderly room, and the clink.[19] But as well men very often defended riots, the bashing of military police, drunkenness and the like by arguing that they had enlisted to fight, which they did well, without requiring the mindless supervision of the parade ground.

The critics answered by condemning Australian discipline in the battle area. 182 Fourth Army men were sentenced for absence without leave in December 1916; 130 were Australians. Forty-three prisoners escaped from Fifth Army police in February 1917; thirty were Australians. Of 677 British soldiers convicted of desertion during the first six months of 1917 (an average of 8.87 men per division), 171 were Australians (34.2 per division). Early in 1917 three Australian divisions recorded roughly twelve times the number of absence without leave convictions proved against the twenty-two other divisions in their (Third) Army. In March 1918 nine Australians per thousand were in field prisons, in every other British or colonial force there were fewer than two per thousand.

Although some in the AIF, including several senior officers, would have preferred to subject the force to sterner discipline, most saw that none of the figures described front line offences—desertion to the enemy, cowardice, or dereliction of duty in the face of the enemy—and although every battalion had its shirkers, Australian discipline whilst actually in the front line has never been especially criticised. In the back areas a few Australians went absent to *avoid* duty in the line, and the number of these offenders rose after such severe experiences as at Pozières, at First Bullecourt among the Fourth Division,[20] and in 1918. But in general the indiscipline of Australians is more probably explained by their endemic dislike of the military, and certainly many of the men convicted of desertion had no intention of shirking their duty in the line. It was claimed, for example, that two Australians sentenced in 1917 to ten years' imprisonment for desertion had gone into a nearby town and bought a few towels, and were caught when they knocked over a garbage can as they arrived back at camp; and a sergeant told his

19. Sgt A. N. Roberts, 1 FAB, Inspector, of Glenelg, SA. b. 1886. *D* 6/9/18 and *Notes*.
20. Between January and June 1917, 60 per cent of Australians convicted of desertion were from 4 Div. It had been obliged to accept most of 1 and 2 Divs' rejects in Egypt, and also several large drafts of new men after First Bullecourt.

father that a brother was in 'clink' for 'taking a bit of a holiday without permission'.[21] Besides the fundamental conflict in outlook between British authorities and Australian troops which such incidents demonstrate, other factors affected the rate of Australian indiscipline. Since the AIF, alone among armies, had no death penalty, the most severe punishment it could inflict after Pozières was to return a man convicted of a serious military offence to the line—hardly an effective method of punishing persistent offenders. Subsequent retrials inflated the crime rate, as also did the unusually high proportion of front line troops among the Australians, and their abnormally protracted 'tours' in the line. But none of this necessarily illuminates the motives behind the majority of offences, and while statistically it remains possible that the AIF contained an abnormally high proportion of shirkers, far more probably its indiscipline reflected a forceful Australian assertion of civilian prerogatives.

More than this, Australian success in battle was largely attributable to that same unrelenting independence which so regularly offended law and authority. None could doubt George Mitchell's quality, and by 1918 the best Australian soldier was 'one who can keep himself out of clink by the force of imagination, and the spoken word. He can do his drill well when he wants to; and when the time comes he can fight hard, and if necessary, die hard.'[22] Several observers defended Australians by judging their battle discipline to be well above average, even unequalled, and the chief cause of their success. A British artillery officer greeting Australian infantry during the dangerous days of the German offensive succinctly put the Australian defence: 'We feel quite safe with you fellows on our flanks', he said, 'I suppose we shall lose a few horses but its worth it.'[23] In battle men could depend even on those Australians at other times prone to disorder, for, like George Mitchell, many in the AIF won promotion in the line, and demotion out of it. At the Le Havre base in September 1917 a sergeant was charged with drunkenness and with having called out on parade 'But we are good soldiers though' while the commanding officer was berating Australians for rioting. He was found guilty, reprimanded, and demoted to cor-

21. Serjeant, L 6/5/18.
22. H. Matthews, Saints and Soldiers, p. 22. (Pte, 4 Bn & Pay Corps, Tram conductor, of Sydney, NSW. RTA 29/12/17, aged 28.)
23. White, D 26/4/18.

poral. The riots referred to were probably those at the Etaples base
in mid-September 1917, during which Australians and other soldiers
reportedly threw the commandant and several other officers into
the river in protest against numerous acts of petty tyranny. The ex-
sergeant was John Whittle, a Boer War veteran, who had won a
DCM in February 1917 and a VC two months later, and who was
subsequently again promoted to sergeant for his capacity in action.[24]
'I am well on my way for stripes now,' an infantry private announced in mid-1917,

*I could have had them long ago only for the red lines in my
book for overstaying leave that 21 days and Breaking ship in
Durban and Capetown . . . all the Head[s] think I am just it.
I have been in all their raids and out over the top every night.
any information the want about Fritz's trenches or wire I am
on the job*[25]

A machine gun officer commented,

*Our boys are tricks. They growl like fun when we are in a nice
little town if they have to do a bit of extra work and when they
get to a place like this [the winter trenches] they make a joke of
anything. We never crime men in our company if they play up
a bit when we are out of the trenches and they remember it
when we get into a rough place. They are always there when
they are wanted.*[26]

It was true. The much maligned Fourth Division included some of
the finest battalions in the AIF,[27] and only soldiers highly disciplined
in battle could have persisted at Pozières or Bullecourt, or defended
Villers-Bretonneux, or initiated 'peaceful penetration', or captured
Mont St Quentin.

Discipline implies inequality, and almost every Australian
resented inequality, agreeing with the sergeant in charge of a fatigue

24. Sgt. J. W. Whittle, VC, DCM, 12 Bn, Soldier, of Huon Island, Tas.
RTA 24/8/18, aged 35; 1 Aust Div Base Depot War Diary, 3/10/17;
C. Carrington, *Soldier from the Wars Returning*, p. 245; statement by Mr
A. W. Bazley, 16 September 1971.
25. Sgt H. Barr, MM, 44 Bn, Seaman, of Fremantle, WA (b. Ireland). KIA
13/10/17, aged 30. *L* 11/7/17.
26. Campbell, *L* 8/11/16.
27. 4 Div had more country men in its ranks than did other divs, and there
seems to be much truth in Bean's belief that country men made the best
fighting soldiers.

party who 'didn't *have* to work, but hopped in and dug a good bit. Its jolly fine exercise and . . . Besides, the boys think a lot, if you just stand and look on.'[28] As in Egypt and on Anzac, few ever entirely approved of the system of officers. They realised that officers must exist, but they did not welcome the distinctions accorded their leaders. Officers had batmen and sometimes horses, officially did no physical work, were usually free from military police and restrictions on leave, and on higher pay[29] messed a little better out of the line. Some expected more than these privileges, and demanded the salute, conformity to law, and high standards of dress and drill. Unless they were proven in battle, these were the AIF's least effective leaders, because they tended to substitute formally acquired authority for strength of personality, and often they found life hard. Many had to endure insubordination and non-co-operation, and a few were 'sandbagged' or 'bottle-oed', or worse. Not long after Pozières a party of infantrymen digging a trench were approached by an engineer officer who

growled at us for not doing enough. We felt pretty mad, and I took a handful of clay and hit him in the back with it as he was leaving. Being a bouncing bully he was also a coward and he cleared off without a word, fearing worse treatment, for our rifles were handy, and a shot more or less is never noticed among the incessant firing during darkness[30]

and Corporal Thomas, called as a witness at a court martial, wrote, 'Our man reprieved . . . and is upon another charge. Strange the plaintiffs have been both shot in action.'[31]

This was a practical deterrent to officiousness, but most AIF officers and men scorned authoritarian behaviour anyway, and mocked it in English units. A corporal commented,

Discipline by some persons is believed to consist of breaking a mans natural spirit under continuous and rigorous drill varied with punishment for the slightest failure *to obey*. To get proper discipline *one must first inspire his men with love for the work and pride for the Service; get the right spirit into them as*

28. Blaskett, *L* 8/5/16.
29. After embarkation an AIF private was paid 6 shillings per day, a sergeant 10/6, a lieutenant 17/6, a major 30 shillings. The discrepancies were far less than in the British Army.
30. Brunton, *D* 6/9/16.
31. Thomas, *D* 22/11/16.

humans *and not as automatons.* Give orders *if you will when necessary but give the reason for such orders and your men will carry them out with twice the understanding, 20 times the energy and 100 times the success.*[32]

Early in 1917 a Second Division NCO recalled,

We were listening to . . . [an English Sergeant-Major] drilling a squad one day, and if he were to use the same expressions to our coves as he did to those Tommies, there would be a vacancy for a SM very soon . . . One of the 6th Bde Colonels . . . bought up an orange stall and gave the fruit to his boys, and the Tommies got the shock of their lives. One little cove said 'He's a Colonel too.' . . . Even their corporals do not mix with the privates, and again, sergeants do not walk out with corporals.[33]

After Fromelles an artillery officer complained bitterly of English officers,

They're only a b---- lot of Pommie Jackeroos and just as hopeless. All they think of is their dress and their mess. The heads only see the Front line when its quiet . . . most of them are crawlers or favourites of some toff or other in England. They have to be saved and the common men do the job and suffer and these crawling ----s get the honour and glory.[34]

Such inequality had obvious practical disadvantages. At First Villers-Bretonneux a Victorian officer confided,

All the newspaper talk about heroic British Divisions is mostly rot. All that we saw had 'the wind up' absolutely and were ready to run at sight of the Boche. Its a disgraceful thing to

32. Allan, *Notes.*
33. Lt G. S. Bell, 6 Fld Amb, Clerk, of Melbourne, Vic (b. Scotland). b. 1890. *L* 15/2/17. Two English examples support the point. Firstly, in F. Manning, *Her Privates We,* the central character, an English private, is on unusually informal terms with his officers and NCOs (Introduction, p. 10), yet the degree of formality described did not exist in the AIF. Secondly, Frank Richards, a professional soldier in the Welch Fusiliers, wrote in *Old Soldiers Never Die* that, at Polygon Wood, 'The Brigadier-General of the Australians . . . had arrived before us . . . It was the only time during the whole of the War that I saw a brigadier with the first line of attacking troops. Some brigadiers that I knew never moved from Brigade Headquarters. It was also the first time I had been in action with the Australians and I found them very brave men. There was also an excellent spirit of comradeship between officers and men.' (p. 251.)
34. Nicholson, *L* 20/7/16.

*have to admit but its a fact . . . One crowd [of Tommies] broke
again today and one of our brigades had to restore the line. Its
not the men's fault, its that of the Tommy officer. They seem
to lack the gift of leadership and the quality of inspiring confidence in their men, the whole trouble being probably due to
insufficient care in the selection and training of their officers*[35]

Almost all Australian officers had been promoted on merit from
the ranks, and not many insisted upon strict adherence to rules
about leave, gambling, or saluting. 'The behaviour of our men is
a great surprise,' one noted,

*Only they will not salute and they will talk on parade and move
about when they should be perfectly still. They march splendidly, work well, and are equal to any troops here . . . in such
exercises as presenting arms on ceremonial occasions.*
*We may be a bit to blame on the score of saluting, we
officers, but it goes against our grain to make these fine fellows
salute us when they somehow feel it demeans them*[36]

Unless given to a VC winner, the salute, symbol of authority and
inequality, was particularly repugnant, and the English mania for
saluting and their class bias in selecting officers (a practice also
occasionally evident in the AIF) reinforced the reluctance inherent
among Australian other ranks to salute any officer, of any rank,
from any army. 'It was very amusing to watch the Tommies
saluting their officers', remarked a young New South Welshman in
England,

*The officers appeared to have their hands up and down all the
time. I should think an automatic spring would have served the
purpose thereby saving them a lot of exertion . . . one morning
. . . some Diggers were walking along the street when two
Tommy officers approached and on coming close to the diggers
prepared for a salute . . . The diggers just walked past grinning
from ear to ear . . . a joke the diggers enjoyed immensely as well
as myself.*[37]

One story claimed that Australians not only studiously ignored
officers, but from devilment saluted cinema doormen, railway

35. Fairweather, *L* 4/4/18.
36. Raws, *L* 27/6/16.
37. F. G. Anderson, *D* –/9/17.

Officer: "Why do you not salute?"
Anzac: "Well, to tell you the truth, digger, we've cut it right out."

From *From the Australian Front, 1917*, p. 38

THE NEW WORLD OF WAR 243

guards, hotel porters, and any other civilian under a peaked cap;
and Birdwood reportedly refused to halt Australians in the Strand
for not saluting, because he thought the area inappropriate for
being 'told off'. Monash, who until 1918 had an unfortunate
capacity for offending his men, in mid-1916 was driven to reprimand
some of his division:

*The Div. Commandr. complains that [an NCO] . . . passed
him this morning without saluting. The Div. Commandr. told
him that he ought to salute but he continued to adopt a very
off hand & almost insubordinate manner. He said that he mis-
took the Divisional Commdr. for a Military Policeman & when
spoken to by Gen. Monash he replied in a very offhand [?] way
without addressing the General as Sir.*[38]

Some Australians made merry with greater personages than the
Divisional Commander:

*The King (Mr. Windsor) flew past us in a motorcar the other
day and evoked a few feeble cheers. Thereafter, out of pure
devilment, the men cheered anybody and anything that came
along, and some French officers were immensely pleased . . .
and bowed and smiled with the utmost graciousness, throwing
off salutes at the same time.*[39]

Few AIF leaders would have placed themselves in this predicament, and most saw little value in parade ground conventions.
'[T]he men . . . are probably either drunk or A.W.L. or they would
not salute',[40] one observed cynically. Another believed, 'the way
to get the real good out of the Australian is not by orders, but by
putting him on his honour',[41] and a third asserted, 'to be a leader of
these men with any success one must not fear death.'[42] Men like
these strove to lead by example, often listening with good effect to
suggestions made from the ranks, and in battle pushing forward to
inspire their men. Lieutenant Richards, just commissioned, wrote
after a proposed attack was cancelled,

*I am sorry . . . as I want to show my frame up over that parapet
with the rest of them and let them see that I got the courage.*

38. In Lt J. A. McMichael. 37 Bn. Insurance inspector, of Melbourne, Vic.
KIA 12/10/17, aged 31. D 27/7/16.
39. Chedgey, L 19/7/17.
40. Adcock, L c.17/6/16.
41. Hunter, L 8/4/16.
42. Baldie, L 23/8/18.

Its' remarkable how our Australians stick to their officers when they have proved their gameness. They hold off until they see a man properly tested and then they love him, but if he fails them hes' is right out wide in their estimation.[43]

Although such an attitude improved the AIF's effectiveness in action, it also sent several junior officers to die.

Since personality and courage supplanted convention, an easy informality was possible between the ranks. In France there could not exist that rapport between senior officers and men which the physical proximity of Gallipoli had engendered, so that after Pozières Birdwood, for example, lost some of his earlier popularity, but among the fighting ranks a general amity prevailed. In November 1916 a young sergeant was commissioned in France, and next day another NCO saw the new stars and exclaimed, 'Good God, what will they be doing next?'[44] Bill Harney refused to lead his officer's horse because he did not join the army to lead horses, and because, as he put it, if his officer wanted to ride, he could bloody well lead. Later a superior officer agreed, and gave him 40 francs (30 shillings) for a spree in a nearby village to soothe his ruffled indignation.[45] A (possibly) fictitious AIF officer warned his men as an inspecting brigadier approached, 'Here he comes! Now boys, no coughing, no spitting, and for Christ's sake don't call me Alf!'

'Alf' and most of his fellow officers need never have doubted their men in a test. Their own worth supported them, and many easily became the type of leader that men follow cheerfully to hell. After the war Lieutenant 'Eddie' Edwards, himself decorated and later promoted for bravery to officer rank in the field, recalled of his former company commander:[46]

[He was] . . . the bravest soldier I have ever known . . . [in the Ypres trenches one night] most of us were weary enough to drop. He must have been as tired as any of us but he kept walking up and down the platoon with a cheering word here and there, and when he saw someone breaking under the strain he

43. Richards, *D* 6/12/16.
44. Champion, *D* 22/11/16. This must have occurred a thousand times.
45. Harney, 'Harney's War', p. 5; statement by Mr A. W. Bazley, August 1971.
46. Capt H. H. Moffat, MC, 1 Bn, Grazier, of Longreach, Qld. DOW 21/9/18, aged 33.

would help him along by relieving him of his rifle or other
accoutrement. I saw him at one time carrying three rifles, and
he finished the march with one on either shoulder.
. . . There was no routine with Captain Moffatt, no slope arms,
form fours, right turn, left wheel, quick march—it was gener-
ally 'Right oh'. 'Come on', and he got more out of us than all
the 'guards drill' in the world. He knew the temperament of the
Australian, and we knew that he would never ask for anything
unless it was essential, and consequently when he gave an order
no matter how irksome, it was generally carried out without
a grumble . . . When 'B' Company heard that he had gone the
way of all good men they wept, unashamedly too. I have seen
hardened soldiers with tears in their eyes as they spoke of
Captain Moffatt, M.C.[47]

This was a kind of mateship, and like mateship was a chief cause
for the effectiveness of Australians in battle, for officers and men
judged each other by the test of action, and proficiency there erased
almost any weakness elsewhere. Relations between ranks in the
AIF, contrary to British expectation, succeeded so well that after
the war the British Army's disciplinary system veered towards its
colonial counterpart.

What Australians expected from their officers was 'a fair go'.
This was a principle of openness, equality, and honour, more
generous to Australians than to others because it demanded loyalty
rather than impartiality, but extending to all men, excluding
errant Australians and embracing deserving allies and opponents.
It affected discipline most obviously when it was offended, as
during the several mutinies which occurred in the AIF, those
already discussed,[48] and two which broke out in September 1918.

By late that year many Australians, worn by ceaseless action, only
reluctantly accepted more than their fair measure of battle. Too
often the British lion's share had fallen to them, and too often
British divisions were given the public credit for Australian success.
This was manifestly unfair, and for some weary men it was too
much. On 14 September the 59th Battalion, having been relieved
from the line near Péronne after a week of intense effort, had barely
settled to rest in its bivouac when it was again called forward. To

47. Edwards, *Narrative*, pp. 20-1.
48. See p. 229.

impress their plight upon the authorities, the officers and men of three platoons refused.

A week later, in similar circumstances, men of the 1st Battalion refused duty. The battalion had just emerged after losing a third of its strength in the battle for the Hindenburg Outpost Line when, with the 3rd Battalion, it was ordered to re-enter the line and take positions that had recently repulsed several English attacks. 119 men, most of them from a company made leaderless by loss, refused. The remainder, about eighty men, went forward with the 3rd Battalion and took the objective.[49]

The 59th's refusal was short lived, and authorities took little or no action; 118 of the 1st Battalion were found guilty of desertion, but their sentences were later remitted. Better leadership might have averted their outbreak, but in both battalions the strikers had opposed orders they thought unfair, and this had corrupted the strong senses of duty and prestige usually sustaining them in 1918.

Resistance had been possible only because the strikers were supported by their mates. Many Australian soldiers had grown to manhood believing that distinctions between men were odious, and in the army almost all gladly ignored the divisions of civil life, so that mateship became by far the firmest tenet in their creed. As on Gallipoli men shared everything with their mates, for them they would defy any authority, for them often they would die. Mates were exempt from general custom: they could abuse a man, use his possessions, spend his money, and impose where others could not. 'There is generally a small fire in the billet', a man wrote during the 1917 winter, 'but the only way to get a seat near it is to throw in a clip of cartridges and hop in to a seat before they all explode. It is a bit risky however, on account of the chance of a S.I.W.'[50] This, too, mateship tolerated and made tolerable, for the sense of their distinctive fellowship was valuable to Australians. Together they were the champions of their country in the lists of the world, jointly they possessed a formidable reputation, but more than this, they had shared momentous events, and were bound together by a myriad of mutual debts and services. In the heat of battle mateship gave men their strongest incentive to fight, because

49. It was in this attack that Capt Moffat, who came up from his battalion's nucleus to take part, was mortally wounded.
50. Sgt W. T. Turner, 56 Bn, Public servant, of Roseville, NSW. b. 1887. D 28/1/18.

they prized the lives and respect of their mates, and thought the need 'to succour poor old bloody Bill, beleaguered in a shell hole on the ridge'[51] worth the risk of death. Mates strengthened a man's attachment to his unit, shared and eased the oppressions of battle and hardship, and multiplied the diversions of leave and the back areas. In everything, so far from home, they were all most Australians had, and they became the AIF's greatest cohesive influence, discouraging shirking, and lifting men above and beyond the call of duty.

Often the code operated unconsciously, sometimes it was expressed. 'I know this job is not too sweet', a sergeant confessed, 'But we must carry on. I am not fretting or downhearted. I go in to the trenches prepared to take on any job my mates have to do. that is the spirit we Box on with. If it is good enough for one it is good enough for all.'[52] Another sergeant remembered that at Pozières he was scared, but preferred the front to the rear, because his mates were in the line.[53] Men deserted from base camps to go into the line with their mates:[54] one soldier kept back on medical grounds was found in the front trenches almost too sick to move. 'Why?' asked his officer. 'Well,' he replied, 'I thought my mates would think I had cold feet'.[55] The best Australians were loyal to their mates in every circumstance. One laid down his life by giving his gas mask to a friend; another, shot through the arm, stayed with his wounded mate for seven days in No Man's Land at Fromelles, scavenging food and water from the surrounding dead, and at night dragging him slowly to safety until at last he had rescued him;[56] a third gave up leave in England to search a Flanders battlefield for the body of a mate killed there;[57] a fourth walked 28 miles to tend his dead mate's grave.[58]

These things, and the exclusive experience of having fought a battle, and the numbers killed, forged a firm brotherhood among those who survived. 'My platoon went through the charge 43 strong, and came out with 18', a soldier wrote after his first 'tour' at Pozières, 'But between all of us who had been through the experi-

51. From W. Dyson, *Australia at War*, Frontispiece.
52. Barr, *L* 6/8/17.
53. Campbell, *L* 31/8/16.
54. Ellsworth, *L* 12/9/16; AWM File No. 233/1.
55. Short, *L* 19/11/16.
56. Brunton, *D* 27/7/16.
57. B. A. Harding, *Windows of Fame*, p. 30.
58. Cleary, *D* 21/4/17.

ence together seemed to be a bond quite unknown before . . . we
had all faced the big things together and were comrades rather than
officers and men.'[59] An Englishman in the AIF, formerly critical of
Australian soldiers, reported of them at Pozières, 'they behaved
magnificent. They marched across to the German barbed wire under
machine gun fire and shells of every kind as if they were on the
parade ground . . . I feel proud to belong to them.'[60]

Three statements demonstrate the operation of mateship. A
Scottish born pioneer told his wife that after an attack (possibly at
Pozières),

*we had to follow the Infentry and Cut a communation trench
between our own lines and the German lines we done it but
we had about 40 killed and wounded I dont know what became
of my mate I looked all over the place for him but no one
could tell me anything about him so he is among the missing
Well I come through it thank God without a scratch but very
sore beat up for I took every ounce of strenth out of myself I
worked with all my will for I knew that our men that was
wounded would have a chance as we pusshed through the
communation line and officers and men In fact, the hole company shone splendid.*[61]

Sergeant Callen, a former country accountant and business manager,
noted in 1917,

*Its funny, when they want something dashing or dangerous
accomplished, they always pick on the Australians or New
Zealanders. They do it too, and later one reads . . . that 'the
British did so and so.' . . . Never mind, it will be done, and done
well by these hard-living, hard-swearing, fighting kangaroos,
who don't give a damn for anyone; but who are men . . . good
in every way. I'm just as glad to meet ---- of our Company, who
was a rabbito in Surry Hills, as I am to meet the biggest brass
hat officer alive. They are both good, and war is the leveller.
And any one with a word against any of our fellows who fight
here—the roughest of them—is up against me.*[62]

59. In Cotton, *L* –/7/16.
60. Young, *L* 4/8/16.
61. Pte T. Gormlie, 2 Pioneer Bn, Cabinet maker, of Sydney, NSW (b. Scotland). KIA 11/3/18, aged 37. *L* 15/11/16.
62. Callen, *L* 31/3/17.

The strongest loyalty and affection was that between one man and another: Lieutenant Baldie and his mate fought through France together until September 1918, when his mate was killed near Péronne. The young Victorian farmer wrote an epitaph:

One could not find a whiter man in the whole world. He would never let a pal down . . . and would never allow a word to be said against me, whether I was right or wrong. Whatever he had was at my disposal right to money which we shared not caring whether one had more than his share so long as we had enough for the two. We would have been separated long ago to go to different jobs that may have been better for us no. we both must go or we would not move . . . even now I can hardly believe I'll never see him again.

In the same letter he confessed, 'I've had enough fighting . . . I've lost all my keeness since Sam went west . . . if it should come to the worst I know Jane and the kiddies are in good hands'.[63] He had never before written like this, and it was his last letter home. Early in October he was killed at Montbrehain.

Mateship recognised few inhibiting barriers, and this same free flexibility continually prompted Australians to curiosity about their surroundings. They made it their business to talk with people they met, they explored areas they occupied, and they showed a keener interest in strategy than the average English soldier: 'most of [the Tommies] are very slow tempered. They don't seem to take much interest in the war outside their own part in it . . . whereas our chaps are always speculating on this, arguing on that or giving biscuit tin orations on something else. They are not so good at making themselves comfortable as the Austs'.[64] Any new device of war—a tank, a plane, a flamethrower—attracted them, and groups of Australians could often be seen about a new machine, interrogating its mechanics and prying into its workings. Their own land did not produce such novelties, and they made the most of a rare opportunity. Similarly, particularly at first, they souvenired anything as a relic of the Great Experience. Monash sent his wife 'an actual piece' of a Zeppelin shot down in England, which he thought would be 'renowned in history'.[65] At Flers a French plane which crash

63. Baldie, *L* 15/9/18.
64. Mann, *L* 21/6/16.
65. F. M. Cutlack (ed), *War Letters of General Monash*, p. 137 (10/10/16).

landed and suffered slight damage was swiftly dismantled by Australian souvenir hunters—even the propeller disappeared—[66] and pieces of fabric from Richthofen's plane are still scattered through records in the Australian War Memorial. 3rd Battalion men advancing to attack Pozières village met a batch of German prisoners going to the rear:

our boys from everywhere flocked to see these german prisoners as they were the first some . . . had seen, anyway before long the boys got that thick around the fritz's after souvenirs off their uniforms, that . . . a small shell . . . would have wiped them all out . . . there was a big ring and anybody would have thought they were playing two up or something[67]

Australians in action persisted in 'ratting' prisoners, 'even when the exigencies of the moment require[d] more important activities on their part':[68] by 1918 Germans expecting capture held their personal effects in their hands ready to surrender,[69] and afterwards many shambled to the rear devoid of every possession and distinguishing mark, 'minus all buttons—hats—& anything that could be called a souvenir & are done up with safety pins'[70] and some had not even that wherewithal to hold together the few rags of clothing left them. Shells, bombs, bullets, helmets, pistols, swords, bayonets, badges, medals, uniforms, gun parts, aeroplane pieces, stamps, postcards, coins, notes, letters, *assignats* issued in 1791, and a whole range of curios from shattered chateaux, banks, houses, churches, and farms were lugged patiently about France and England until finally they found rest on Australian mantelpieces. Their owners had been souvenir hunters *par excellence*.

Sometimes, no doubt, men hunting for souvenirs under fire were also demonstrating what Australians considered a particular virtue —readiness to defy hardship or danger. Among bushmen before the war, on Gallipoli, and in France, the man who could resist adversity was admired. During the last minutes before Polygon Wood,

66. Pte E. C. Munro, MM, 5 Fld Amb, Farmer, of Geebung, Qld (b. England). RTA 23/9/18. aged 22. *D* 20/12/16.
67. Pte A. Brown, 3 Bn, Labourer, of Annandale, NSW. RTA 22/7/17, aged 22. *D* 23/7/16.
68. Gemmell. *D* 8/6/18.
69. Bean, *Official History*, VI, pp. 549-50.
70. Pte V. W. Cocks, 9 Fld Amb, Clerk, of Randwick, NSW. b. 1895. *L* 2/3/17.

Our Infantry had a . . . wait . . . in shell holes just behind our forward posts and it would have been fatal for Fritz to guess they were there so absolute silence and no smoking was the order, with a minute to go the order was given men may smoke, and nearly all stopped to light up. While waiting on their first objective for the barrage to lift again they put in time collecting souvenirs. The Welsh and the Scotch on the right were amazed, they had never seen men smoking and collecting souvenirs in an attack before. As the prisoners came down . . . our chaps were laughing and joking, [and] . . . singing out Give us a watch Fritz or Give us a Ring . . . [A British colonel asked] why do they laugh and joke.[71]

In 1918 a veteran wrote philosophically,

The mud well you know the nastiest thing you can get used to and we also look back to some other place and say, Oh well, its not as bad as that joint anyhow and there you are. A joke and a laugh at every poor beggar who goes up to his neck (yourself included) a hand out and there you are. Food . . . I've been hungry at times, but through circumstances that carn't always be helped. So you see altogether we do real well.[72]

Possibly the most effective specific counter to adversity was humour. During the 1916 winter a South Australian platoon was sent from its billets to work under German gun fire. The night was cold, it was raining, several miles of cruel mud lay before the men, and machine guns nightly inflicted casualties upon working parties. But as the grim line set forth a man remarked, 'Good night for a murder.'[73] A popular story was of two Australians who found a man buried to the neck in soupy mud. Carefully they laid duckboards out to him, and pulled. He did not move. His rescuers cleared away as much mud as they could, and tugged and scraped, but the man remained trapped, until at last they decided to find help. Then the man in the mud offered an alternative suggestion. 'Wait a minute mates', he said, 'and I'll take me feet out of the stirrups.' To enliven the monotony of the trenches, 'Our rifles, fully loaded, were placed upside down on top of the sandbags, with

71. Sheppeard, *D* 26/9/17.
72. Mann, *L* 14/4/18.
73. Mitchell, *Backs to the Wall*, p. 62.

a small piece of cheese on the end of the bayonet. When a rat nibbled the cheese, the trigger was pressed . . .'[74] Another joke was the stock reply to civilians who asked what soldiers did in the trenches all day: 'Oh, we just sit around chatting.' 'Chats' were lice.

In battle, humour and defiance were sometimes combined with telling effect. In July 1916 some Fifth Division soldiers sat in a dugout under an artillery bombardment near Fromelles. A shrapnel shell burst against the door of the dugout, and a man inside ordered, 'Open the door and pay the rent; that's the landlord.'[75] 'In captured orders the Germans have called the Australians "The Elite of the British Army" . . .', Lieutenant McInnis reported, 'It is due to the phlegmatic way in which our men as a whole take the worst of privations, and to their humour, which nothing can stamp out.'[76] Private Cleary stated that at Pozières:

Some fellows had to run the Barrage, it was a cool day but when they passed me they were reeking with perspiration and show-ing a lot of the whites of their eyes. But they were game alright. I couldn't help admiring the efforts they made to act normal, making quiet remarks such as 'pretty hot mate' 'He must be annoyed' etc.[77]

Men at Pozières still considered war a test of manhood, but their casual defiance outlived that belief, and created its own tradition. It became a point of honour among stretcher bearers, for example, not to show fear under fire. An officer recalled,

Fritz was making things hot, strafing our line, searching for his old dugouts . . . with heavies . . . in conjunction with . . . H.E. . . . shrapnel and whizbangs. It was a nice spot, I don't think. One of my fellows got his legs smashed by a slab of shell and word was passed for stretcher-bearers. Cassidy came along immediately—walking along the parapet, enquiring who wanted the stretcher. The trench was narrow and half full of mud and by coming along the top he saved a lot of time. The lad was bleeding badly so Cassidy bound him up a bit and got

74. Pte H. G. Hartnett, 2 Bn, Letter carrier, of Batlow, NSW. RTA 27/11/18, aged 26. *Narrative*, p. 49 (1916).
75. 'Tiveychoc', *There and Back*, p. 155 (14/7/16).
76. McInnis, *D* 13/10/18.
77. Cleary, *D* 4/8/16.

three others to help him carry this chap away . . . across . . .
the open. God knows how they escaped.[78]

As on Anzac, the wounded forged a distinctive tradition. 'Hullo,
here is a trip to Australia', a man exclaimed when a shell blew his
hand away, and then turned and strolled to the rear smoking a
cigarette and chatting casually to passers by.[79] A sergeant major
badly wounded at Flers sent a message to his captain, 'Tell the
Capt I couldn't help it! that I am sorry!'[80] Often their courage gave
tragic dignity to the fortitude of such men. 'It is marvellous how the
wounded stand the agony of their wounds, many shot to pieces but
never a murmur, others when forced to cry out apologize for it', an
ambulanceman noted, 'One old chap who was dying kept saying
"stop the bleeding boys and I'll get back to the Mrs and kids" alas
am afraid his wife and children will never see him again in this
world.'[81] Another ambulanceman reported,

Today a man was brought in with a leg amputated . . . a high
explosive shell exploded near him and caught him in the legs
and knocked him into a shell hole Altho' in agony he had sense
enough to realize that if he didn't manage to attract attention
before dawn he stood little chance . . . So he made a rough
tourniquet around the leg . . . and attempted to crawl out . . . ,
but found the leg, which was hanging by only a few sinews
caused too much agony, so he got out his jack knife and cut it
off, and thus managed to drag himself . . . onto the track[82]

Another man performed a similar operation, then waited five hours
to reach a dressing station. He asked for a cigarette on arrival, and
said, 'Now tell me, Doc. Have I a sporting chance?' He died of
gangrene five days later.[83] An artilleryman observed,

I have seen men coming back with legs and arms off smiling
and joking. One man was badly wounded, so badly, that he had
no hope of coming through . . . [he] asked for a cigarett. He
smoked it, then thanked them saying 'Well this is not a very

78. Capt H. S. Davis, 46 Bn, Woolclasser, of Drysdale, Vic. KIA 11/4/17,
aged 28. *L* 3/9/16.
79. Lt C. J. McDonald, MC, 3 Bn, Blacksmith's improver, of Bowral, NSW.
DOW 19/9/18, aged 23. *L* 4/5/16.
80. A. E. Leane, *L* 18/1/17.
81. Morgan, *D* 23/7/16.
82. Munro, *D* 4/12/16.
83. Bean, *Official History*, III, p. 942n.

choice spot to die in.' 'So long boys'! Our Infantry . . . are incomparable.[84]

But the grey dead could rarely inspire such admiration, and their first look at a dead man usually repelled yet occasionally fascinated Australians. Two months after he reached France Arthur Thomas wrote,

> *he is the first dead chap I have dared to look at, but I knew him so well I just had to. I looked at him & felt no horror, for he looked so sereene & the morning was so beautiful & the larks how they sing here, & the stretcher bearers took him away to the graveyard alongside the ruined farm, another life chucked into the gutter soon to be forgotten.*[85]

As no doubt the veterans of Anzac and Pozières could have told him, Private Thomas wasted his words. There was nothing exceptional about the frequent dead. 'I have seen death all round me in its every shape & form, & many of my comrades are dead or wounded', a late 1917 reinforcement explained, 'I don't think of it, & the pressure of new experiences makes for a mere acceptance, without any attempt to appraise their value',[86] and Sapper Muir decided, 'One dares not sit down to think of it all for sickness would soon overcome him & down you also would go . . . Will go and do some work to try not to worry.'[87]

Throughout the war few men dared to sit and think of death, lest its horror overwhelm them, and many hardened themselves against it. A Victorian officer remembered that one night,

> *a Scottie stepped back to let me double past . . . a moment after I heard an explosion behind and looking round I saw that the poor beggar was gone—actually blown to pieces by a shell . . . it struck me as rather funny and I went on down the trench absolutely chortling to myself. Sounds rather callous, I'm afraid.*[88]

Perhaps it was callous; certainly it was an anaesthetic of nature, the same which permitted the living to joke with the dead. A former dental apprentice recorded,

84. Gnr F. L. Byard, 8 FAB, Cellar manager, of Ambleside, SA. b. 1890. *D* 25/11/18.
85. Thomas, *L* 9/6/16.
86. Pte H. Halewood, 35 Bn, Bookseller, of Sydney, NSW (b. England). KIA 6/5/18, aged 43. *L* 9/4/18.
87. R. A. Muir, *L* 21/7/16.
88. Davis, *L* 28/10/16.

During the building of the trench, a Fritz was buried under foot, but with one hand sticking out of the trench wall into the trench, so that each time any one walked over his body, the hand wagged as if shaking hands. Sure enough, every man shook hands with him, and solemnly wished him luck.[89]

A former university tutor wrote, 'For a long time [we] . . . could not get a drain to run; something blocked it . . . [At last a man] remove[d] the obstruction . . . exclaiming "That's the silly --- who blocked it." "That" was the decayed body of an officer of the Sherwood Foresters! I've got one of his buttons', while at Passchendaele the same man recalled, 'One Hun was amusing. He was sitting up against the wall and all his head was gone save the bare skull— it was as clean inside as an egg—just the skull inside and his hair outside—quite neatly done too. He had just written to his mother . . . [saying] he would be home for Xmas. Perhaps so.'[90] Callousness was much harder to feel towards mates killed, but occasionally it was possible. In the Pozières trenches four men were playing cards. One was killed. His body was laid out on the parapet above, a mate took his cards, and the four men continued to play.[91]

Front line soldiers were agents of death as well as its witnesses, and many Australians at some point found themselves placed to watch their enemy die, or to kill him. If he remained merely 'the enemy', dehumanised by distance, the task was not hard. Major Garnet Adcock watched a Hun counter-attack:

They jumped from the trenches shoulder to shoulder. In about 20 secs. our barrage came down and they thinned to a man every ten or twelve yards. After the next burst only two or three were left . . . With wonderful bravery they came on . . . only to be smashed. They were fighters . . . It was the finest day I have had since I was wounded.[92]

Early in 1918 a 1914 enlistment stated,

When daylight came we saw a party of about 25 Huns on the skyline 700 yds. away. So we ups with the Lewis Gun and gave him a magazine or two. They soon flattened themselves and

89. Champion, *D* 29/10/16. This is one version of a well-known anecdote.
90. Fisher, *D* 14/4 and 24/10/17.
91. Shortly afterwards all four were killed. (Bean, *Official History*, III, p. 618n.)
92. Adcock, *L* 4/12/17.

*later started to crawl into the pillbox on their hands and knees.
So whenever they moved we gave 'em a burst, and movement
soon stopped. Later in broad daylight four Huns were seen
calmly walking to a pill-box only 400 yds away. It was the best
shooting I've had for years. We dropped them with rifles and
so to bed for the day, after the best morning's sport I've had.*[93]

Yet for a short time killing even at this distance worried some Australians. A West Australian sniper, recently arrived at the front,
wrote,

*at 6 o'clock this morning I shot a Hun, an observer, at 400
yards . . . he was all alone, looking through a pair of field
glasses, with his head and shoulders above the parapet (foolish
fellow) . . . took careful but quick aim and pulled the trigger
He spread his arms out and fell backwards throwing his glasses
in the air . . . a queer thrill shot through me, it was a different
feeling to that which I had when I shot my first Kangaroo when
I was a boy. For an instant I felt sick and faint; but the feeling
soon passed; and I was my normal self again; and looking for
more shots*[94]

   This was a necessary adjustment, and most Australians made
it. Often they made it abruptly, during the frenzy of a great battle,
when they faced the choice of killing or of dying. Although some
hesitated to kill, few found the choice difficult. Describing a German
counter-attack on the 6th Battalion at Pozières on 23 or 24 July
Private Thomas related,

*they were coming & I felt thankful, really thankful, for so
enraged was I at their infernal bombardment & loss of splendid
young comrades that my blood was up & I was like a fiend &
felt terrible & I worked every man jack of them up to the same
pitch . . . A German officer loomed up & raised his revolver
point blank at me, with a yell I dropped a bomb at him, I held it
two seconds in my hand & it did its infernal job. I suppose we
all went stone mad then for I finished my bombs & then my
bayonet & they ran calling for mercy great big burly hounds,
how they scooted falling over each other, jabbering & shrieking & probably cursing . . . I was lucky damn lucky, & I thank*

93. Traill, *D* 2/3/18.
94. Harford, *D* 14/10/16.

*my God for such wonderful glorious joy to be able to live
through this & see us win our freedom.*[95]

At Pozières a South Australian NCO pronounced himself sickened
by war: 'I can tell you . . . [it] is horrible . . . [none] of us will be . . .
sorry if we never hear another gun fired.' Nonetheless he continued,
'I collected a beautiful German bayonet . . . The original owner and
I had a slight argument about the transfer, but I introduced the
"Savage" into the discussion and won "hands down" . . . he'll
see no more of this war.'[96]

Probably he had been fired by a temporary lust for blood, an
emotion which overcame many soldiers in battle. Archie Barwick
explained,

*I shall never forget the mad intoxication one seems to be in
[during battle] . . . you see absolutely no danger & will do
almost anything, for the roar of the guns are ringing in your
ears, & you can smell the salty fumes from the powder stinging
your nostrils, & . . . the shouts of the boys & the . . . ghostly
lights of the many colored flares . . . these are moments when
I reckon a man lives 10 minutes of this seems to be at the time
worth a year of ordinary life, but the reaction sets in afterwards & nearly all men feel a faintness come over them . . . but
this don't last long either & you are soon itching for another
smack at the rotten Hun.*[97]

Bloodlust, or 'battle madness', facilitated killing, and in every
army men, driven by a fury they afterwards regretted, murdered
helpless or surrendering opponents.[98] Yet Australians, by reputation and probably in fact, were among those most willing to kill.
They had an uncomplicated attitude towards the Hun, conditioned
largely by propaganda and hardly at all by contact, and they hated
him with a loathing paralleled, at least in the British Army, only by
some other colonial troops. Accordingly many killed their opponents
brutally, savagely, and unnecessarily:[99]

95. Thomas, *L* 1/8/16.
96. Blaskett, *L* 10/8/16.
97. Barwick, *D* IV, pp. 122-3 (18/8/16).
98. For Australian examples of this, see Bean, *Official History*, III, pp.
248-9n.; IV, p. 624. Other Australians treated a brave enemy generously
after capture. See pp. 223-4.
99. Equally many prevented such behaviour, and consistently pursued a
course honourable both to them and their country. What follows in no way
refers to them.

Prisoners we are not troubled with now for we kill every bosche at sight.[100]

I accounted for 5 or 6 Germans with bombs and we had orders to bayonet all wounded Germans and they received it hot and strong . . .[101]

In a shell hole further on I saw a wounded man and another one with him. An officer walked up and the German asked him to give his comrade a drink. 'Yes,' our officer said 'I'll give the ---- a drink', 'take this', and he emptied his revolver on the two of them. This is the only way to treat a Hun. What we enlisted for was to kill Huns, those baby killing ----.[102]

one of our chaps the very first German he stuck, his bayonet broke off & he used the butt end of his rifle & smashed 4 of their heads in.[103]

This afternoon we got 15 German Red Cross prisoners, they were marched down & searched & 13 of the dogs were found to be carrying daggers & revolvers they [were] promptly put against the wall & finished.[104]

I always regret not having touched that German prisoner up a bit, I haven't killed one yet, that's my ambition. I reckon I could have licked him into shape a bit. He was a nice little brute . . . There was I marching down behind him praying that he would bolt and let me have a shot at him or fall over something so that I would have some cause for putting daylight through him . . .[105]

at Flers the 27th Battalion had 7 German prisoners . . . [A lieutenant] shot all of them. He tried to shoot one of them with an automatic but the prisoner gripped his hand and the auto missed. He then shot that prisoner and all the rest with his

100. Mulholland, *L* 17/3/17.
101. Cohen, *L* 31/7/16. Bean notes of this what must have been generally true, that such an order could only have come from an NCO or junior officer. Prisoners were valuable sources of information to the higher command.
102. Gallwey, *L* 2/8/17, p. 275.
103. Barwick, *D* IV, p. 2 (23/7/16).
104. Barwick, *D* IV, p. 9 (23/7/16).
105. Lt E. W. Dardel, MM, 24 Bn, Farmer, of Batesford, Vic. b. 1896. *L* 20/10/16.

service Revolver. The Cpl . . . had previously refused to do this.[106]

With the particular bent some of them had for murder, it is perhaps not surprising that, as on Anzac, Australians became known to friend and foe for proficient use of the bayonet:

had some fine stoush in the wood giving the tin openers a chance to make a name for themselves. Hans does not make much noise when he's wounded with the bayonet just throws it in with a sigh.[107]

Strike me pink the square heads are dead mongrels. They will Keep firing until you are two yds. off them & then drop their rifle & ask for mercy. They get it too right where the chicken gets the axe . . . I . . . will fix a few more before I have finished. Its good sport father when the bayonet goes in there eyes bulge out like a prawns.[108]

When I jumped into the trench I saw a man lying there and he moved. I gave him a savage prod with my bayonet and he curled up like a caterpillar drawing his legs up and clenching his fists. His eyes turned upside down showing the white and there was a gurgle in his throat like the water running out of a bath[109]

Even among Australians, killing was random. More killed and died by a shell or a bullet than by a bayonet,[110] more by chance than an aimed stroke, and in time the knowledge of slaughter so frequent and haphazard forced the living to consider their own deaths. Every inclination in men resisted the thought that they might die; every circumstance drove them to accept it. At first most expected to survive, and at odd moments throughout the war many were able to resurrect this expectation, because time healed the worst scars inflicted by fearful experiences. 'Out of the line at last,' Private Wright exclaimed, 'by jove she's been a crook spin this trip . . . [I] fairly didn't care a hang, but we are out now once more so whats it

106. Cleary, *D* 24/1/18.
107. Wright, *D* 22(=23?)/7/16.
108. Hill, *L* 13/8/16.
109. Gallwey, *L* 2/8/17, p. 272.
110. Between April 1916 and March 1919, 52.07 per cent of Australians admitted to Field Ambulances in France had sustained injuries from shells or shell shock, 33.93 per cent from bullets, 11.82 per cent from gas, and only 2.18 per cent from bombs, grenades, and bayonets. (Butler, *Official Medical History*, II, p. 495.)

matter.'[111] Lieutenant Fischer wrote, 'we . . . sang songs and choruses & to have heard us you would never imagine that we were so near such a great war—still it is just this happy go lucky spirit that keeps a man at his job; everyone is the same & . . . the men cheer up as soon as they get out of the line and forget all their hardships'.[112]

Yet more and more died, and horror heaped upon horror, and the war seemed endless, until at some point veteran soldiers, no longer deluding themselves, accepted that they would probably die. A fortnight after Fromelles a Fifth Division soldier decided, 'If I have to pass out, I hope it is by a high explosive . . . If . . . [it] catches you & says *go out*, well, it is out you go, no suffering, no delay; a hurried departure: with the shrapnel & bullets you simply get a 'go out if you please', half hearted sort of order which one does not know whether to obey or not.'[113] Late in 1916 Charles Alexander had felt that a great power was shielding him, and that he was being kept for some purpose in the scheme of things, but early in 1917 he confessed, 'I suppose we can hardly all expect to return again—but after all, that is not a *very* grievous prospect, as we shan't "pass over" unless we are wanted . . . on the other side.'[114]

As time passed the probability of dying approached nearer and nearer to certainty in the minds of Australians. The evidence of their own eyes and the logic of statistics made it clear that ordinarily a man could not long remain a fighting soldier, and hope to survive. Besides, submission to the rule of inevitable death explained the vice of a murderous war, and so comforted men who found themselves its playthings; by about 1917 most old soldiers were fatalists.[115] 'Certain walks in life seem to foster certain beliefs . . .', Lieutenant Chapman noted, 'most soldiers are fatalists . . . when fellows are getting wounded—or dying continually, a belief in these words of Shakespeare, "There is a Destiny that shapes our ends,

---

111. Wright, *D* 10/1/17.
112. Fischer, *L* 10/3/18.
113. Fraser, *L* 31/7/16.
114. Alexander, *L* 28/12/16 and 17/1/17.
115. Asked in 1967 or 1968 whether after they had experienced battle they expected to survive the war, 256 veterans answered:

	per cent		per cent
Yes	36.7	Fatalists	16.4
Hoped so	3.9	No	12.5
Doubtful	21.1	Did not think about it	9.4

rough-hue them how we will" seems to creep in.'[116] After Passchendaele a 1914 enlistment reflected,

*Often one thinks that he is just waiting on and on until he is
killed. We lost some fine chaps in the last stunt, fellows whom
like myself had enlisted at the first only to endure three years
of hell and then be killed . . . We were just in a hole with shell
after shell just missing us, at last the promised one came and
killed five of my best pals and left me, the shock to one's nerves
is beyond belief.*[117]

In 1918 another veteran stated, 'a few years of this & one treats life
very cheaply really . . . lately some of our officers have been killed
who landed on Gallipoli with the Battn. on 25th April so that
apparently it is only a matter of time . . . one must look at this game
from a philosophic stand point.'[118] These and many other Australians believed that 'fatalism is all that counts in France, and if Fritz
has your number, it doesn't matter if you are sweeping the streets in
Paris, he'll get you',[119] and 'You carn't stop a shell from bursting
in your trench, You carn't stop the rain, or prevent a light going up
just as you are half way over the parapet. So what on earth is the
use of worrying? . . . So smile, d--- you, smile.'[120]

Fatalism opened the door to premonitions about dying, and the
frequency with which men were killed, and perhaps the premonition
itself, rendered at least some premonitions accurate. An artillery
officer asserted,

*if a shell or bullet 'has my name on it' I will get it no matter how
I try to dodge it. I have seen scores of our lads walking along
while being shelled without quickening their pace or trying to
get out of the line of fire & yet none of them got hit and again
I have seen others run . . . & run into a shell . . . a lot of our
lads are fatalists now—some . . . say so in . . . letters . . . I
censor. I have heard . . . of lots of cases . . . where men have
been killed who had a premonition of their death. I knew
personally of two in my battery*[121]

116. Chapman, *D* 31/7/16.
117. Lt H. A. Fairweather, 38 Bn, Clerk, of Heidelberg, Vic. b. 1895. *L*
24/10/17.
118. Henderson, *L* 21/4/18.
119. Barrett, *L* 9/12/17.
120. Mann, *L* 13/2/18.
121. Gatliff, *L* 25/5/17.

Another told of a man who

had a premonition that he would be killed, and . . . asked to get off that day, but the sergt. major thought he was trying to get out of going up to the guns and roared him up. He was a quiet decent boy, and . . . He said, 'Alright—I know I'm going to die, even if I stop here.' and he gave all his things away and went up, and just as he was leaving after having delivered his shells, I saw the shell land on him.[122]

In 1918 Archie Barwick was badly wounded by a shell after writing of a premonition: it was only his second wound in over three years of war, and the first premonition to which he had confessed.[123] In March 1918 a Queenslander who had seen a good mate killed at Second Bullecourt and two brothers die at Messines, told his father, 'Well the way things are at present I expect my career to be a very short one in France and will end one way or another very soon now. Probably you are surprised at my speaking in this tone but . . . you will probably understand my meaning. A man cant last forever and it will be short and *sweet* from now on.'[124] He had not previously written like this, and it was his last letter. Within a month he was killed at Villers-Bretonneux.

Many Australians expected in fate's time to die, and most felt ruled by fate. They gave up the future, believing that 'it would be just as well not to build any castles in the air, for fear they would be rudely shattered.'[125] They lived not for a joyous homecoming or a glorious reward, but for their mates and units, and they behaved as befitted a man and would grace the memory of an Australian soldier. They considered only the present, because 'the probability of seeing their own corpses lying in the mud stifled their desire to look into the future',[126] and because they knew too well that 'Good men have answered the last roll call . . . It is to be: so we bow our heads & vow, that if needs be, we will go to death as well.'[127] Their predicament was reflected by a young New South Wales lieutenant who in August 1917 told his family,

122. Nicholson, *L* 29/7/17.
123. Barwick, *D* XIII, p. 28 (25/4/18).
124. E. Allen, *L* 26/3/18.
125. Elliott, *L* 24/8/18.
126. Williams, *Great Adventure*, p. 73.
127. Capt O. A. Jones, 21 Bn, Police constable, of Melbourne, Vic. DOW 3/5/17, aged 25. *L* 9/8/16.

I wonder & wonder when this nightmare is to end? Although I am right in the middle of the struggle I can see no light . . . Men have fallen & died every hour of the day of each year & yet the nations are no nearer their goal . . . tho the awfulness of the toll is realised nobody is prepared to stretch out the hand of peace . . . the armies go on fighting bravely . . . and suffering . . . But . . . every man feels that there is a limit to his endurance and that their [death?] is not so far distant or so indefinite as it was—once . . . Every hour of the day the best men the world can produce are dying. This must go on indefinitely, so imagine if you can the quality of the next generation[128]

Their fatalism, their courage, their manhood, and their sheer dogged determination sustained the Australians, and made so many of their attitudes possible. They fought for their own prestige because that would probably be their last cause, they took greatest comfort from their mates because their mates were all they had, they accepted the sight and spectre of death because they were themselves to die, they adjusted to the daily routine of war because they did not expect to know another. They lived in a world apart, a new world, scarcely remembering their homes and country, and grieving little at the deaths of mates they loved more than anything on this earth, because they knew that only time kept them from the 'great majority' who had already died, and they believed that fate would overtake time, and bring most of them to the last parade. So they continued, grim, mocking, defiant, brave, and careless, free from common toils and woes, into a perpetual present, until they should meet the fate of so many who had marched before them down the great road of peace and sorrow into eternity.

128. Lt J. T. Hampson, MC, 19 Bn, Clerk, of Coraki, NSW. DOW 6/10/18, aged 27. L 15/8/17.

9 The Outbreak of Peace

> Any soul who successfully surmounts the horrors of this war, this
> mad cruel farce, is forever above the run of ordinary men. He may
> be a vulgar brute; he may be a genius; he may [be] just a common
> man of the world; but he is worthy of the intensest admiration &
> respect just because he has suffered so much. The present generation
> is a super-generation. It is the bravest generation since Adam.
> What a terrible pity it is that it should bleed to death!
>
> Lieutenant J. T. Hampson, MC, 19th Battalion, 15 August 1917

The eleventh hour of 11 November 1918 found the Australians
.totally unprepared to receive it. In that sudden instant the world
which had encased their lives and thoughts vanished, and a new
world presented itself, a world bounded not by death and war, but
by life and home. This had been ardently desired but little expected,
so that few soldiers could grasp immediately that the vast business
of slaughter and sacrifice was over.[1]

In England, amid deliriously demonstrative civilians, men
quickly realised the significance of 11 November, and two days
after the Armistice Australians joined a soldiers' celebration in
Trafalgar Square. Around the base of Nelson's Column they
stacked park seats, sign boards, wood blocks from the road, and
anything else combustible and accessible, and then set fire to the
pile, so that soon a huge blaze was throwing its cheery glow over the
revellers. Later a barrel of tar and several German field guns from
the Mall were added to the flames, while some London firemen
bent on dampening proceedings were playfully sprayed with their
own hoses. So some Australians celebrated the end of the fighting
much as others had celebrated its beginning, in the Wasser in Cairo
almost four years before.

The Australian infantry in France had begun its return to the
front before 11 November, but on that day only a few AIF
specialist troops were in or near the line. Hardly a man anywhere
reacted to the momentous news. Of forty-six men writing from

1. From a statement by Mr J. H. Sturgiss (formerly Sgt, 12 LH Regt,
Farmer, of Lower Boro, NSW. b. 1890), 23 October 1967.

France during this period, nine did not mention the Armistice, twenty-one noted 'Armistice signed today' or an equivalent, and five described the exultant excitement of English or French civilians.

Three men were joyful. One, a late 1917 artillery reinforcement, was writing home when the news caught him. 'By JOVE!!!', he burst out, '*Crikey*!!! what shall I say? . . . glorious news . . . *What a Godsent Xmas box for the world!* . . . Funny how calmly they all take it though, considering the tremendous thing it is'.[2] The only relatively enthusiastic infantryman was Wilfred Gallwey. He had written 350 page letters during the war, yet now commented in his diary simply, 'Peace and end of war. Mad with joy', and in a letter two days later, 'I am intoxicated with joy.'[3]

The remaining eight soldiers noted the silent apathy of their comrades, or confessed their own sense of anticlimax. '*The day of days*,' Private Cleary exclaimed, 'We had two victory's today. we won the War and defeated the 5th Field Coy @ Soccer. The news of the Armistice was taken very coolly . . . nobody seemed to be able to realise it.'[4] 'After such a long term of this life,' an officer explained, 'the War has become so much a habit that it has become impossible to realise what peace would really mean. Consequently this news was received very quietly and with little demonstration by all ranks.'[5] Six days after peace broke out, another officer supposed that his family 'all heaved a sigh of relief on hearing that an armistice had been signed . . . The end came suddenly . . . and we could hardly believe the news at first.'[6] What happened to the men of the AIF on that quiet November morning was, for the moment, beyond their comprehension.

Of course they looked forward to going home. An Anzac reported, 'a car of shrieking brass hats [passed], waving their caps and yelling the war was over. "Garn, yer silly bastards," was the diggers comment . . . there was no great elation or hysterical outburst among the fighting troops . . . for the Aussies—the war was over, and the question was "How soon can we get home to be civvies again?" ',[7] and a Queensland lieutenant predicted, 'its na poo war

2. Gnr K. S. Dowling, 107 Howitzer Bty, Clerk, of Chatswood, NSW. b. 1889. *L* 11/11/18.
3. Gallwey, *D* 11/11/18 and *L* 13/11/18.
4. Cleary, *D* 11/11/18.
5. Stobie, *D* 11/11/18.
6. Chedgey, *L* 17/11/18.
7. Nicholson, *L* 11/11/18.

now barring a few minor little affairs that are always liable to crop up . . . but I don't fancy us 6/- a day tourists will be required to do any of it . . . hang the war we have a sporting chance of seeing Aussy now and that's the main thing.'[8]

Not every Australian would see his country. Corporal Thomas was dead, shot near Merris in June 1918. Lieutenant Alexander was dead, killed at Messines. Private Harford was mortally wounded near Bapaume, and Sergeant Major Ellsworth died under artillery fire in Flanders. Lieutenant Aitken was killed at Lihons, Corporal Antill at Ploegsteert, Captain Armitage at Noreuil. They were put to rest under the green grasses of France, and more than 60,000 of their comrades, marking the tide of war on three continents, shared their exile. Perhaps 7000 remained of those gay legions— about 32,000 men—which had set forth in 1914, and in some battalions over 1000 soldiers had been killed in battle.

The lucky survived. Lieutenant Richards was invalided home in June 1918. George Mitchell served in the Pacific during a second war, and died in 1961. Archie Barwick went back to farming in New South Wales, and Garnet Adcock to engineering in Victoria. Wilfred Gallwey, Les de Vine, and Thomas Cleary all returned to Australia.

The living would never forget the dead, for war and youth had bound men closely, till their united brotherhood contained everything worthwhile. During the war soldiers had mourned when a mate was killed, but they had restrained their grief because they too expected in time to die. Now the living would sail away, breaking cherished associations and bearing only sorrowing memories. For the first time, or perhaps for the first time since the evacuation of Gallipoli, they felt the pangs of parting, and for the first time many wrote farewell to their dead friends, rebelling as they wrote against the waste and horror of war, and confessing at last that sense of irreplaceable loss which would stalk them throughout the long years ahead. During the war a man himself to die explained their attitude:

Many chaps who were so good & unselfish that I loved them more than a brother have died . . . some of them in my arms & such things sadden a man, not so much at the time as the Angel of Death is hovering over us all then one goes in daily & hourly

8. Mann, L 14/11/18.

*expectation of a violent and terrible death, but afterwards when
one is . . . relieved of the mental strain of actual warfare, the
memory of such scenes is ineffaceable[9]*

'One is jolly glad to be out of it', a private in an English hospital
wrote,

*yet . . . men you have been friendly with and stood side by side
for months or perhaps into years . . . have been killed—ones
heart fills with sadness—and one has a hankering to be back
over there with 'the boys' once more. Whatever one may be in
private life when you are in the line facing the same enemies
fear, death & other horrors you are absolutely one, and one
gets momentary glimpses of that truer and greater democracy
which is gradually opening out to solve all human problems[10]*

and on the day of the Armistice a 2nd Battalion corporal recorded,

*At about noon . . . was told an Armistice had been declared . . .
it was hardly creditable . . . so to all intents and purposes the
war is finished or seems so. And as one sits and ponders sadly of
those many pals who are 'gone to that home from which no
wanderer returns.' It seems so strange that it should be, that
one's dearest pals should fall and that I even I should still be
here. The very flower of our manhood have paid the greatest
price, not willingly for not one of them but longed to live,
return home and forget, yes just forget the horrors of the past.
Most of us enlisted for . . . Patriotism or Love of Adventure but
not one . . . had the slightest conception of the terrible price
required . . . Please God . . . the sacrifices have not been in vain.
Brude old pal of mine, would to God that you were here with
me this day, but no, God willed it otherwise and so 'farewell'.[11]*

He was turning, as many would turn, to the great bonds of the
past, remembering the well loved mates who in the end had been the
chief solace of existence.

The living were united by ties almost equally strong, for war had
forged among them attachments firmer than anything possible in
peacetime. Now mates who for years had meant life, purpose, and

9. Jackson, *L* 10/3/16.
10. Pte J. P. Scott, 45 Bn & AIF HQ, Accountant, of Sydney, NSW (b. England). b. 1886. *L* 5/11/18.
11. Morgan, *D* 11/11/18.

home were to disperse, and units which had symbolised so much love and loyalty were to disband. It would be a melancholy dissolution. 'I am disappointed in a way at not going back to the battery,' one man admitted, '. . . I don't think it possible to strike such a fine lot of fellows in civil life',[12] and in Australia many returned men nostalgically remembered the brotherhood of war. 'It was hard to break away from the boys and each time I went into the City we met and still talked shop',[13] a demobilised Sydney man recorded late in 1918. In 1932 Joe Maxwell began *Hell's Bells and Mademoiselles* in a similar vein, in 1933 E. J. Rule dedicated his *Jacka's Mob* 'To that grand companionship of great-hearted men, which, for most of us, is the one splendid memory of the war', and in 1937 George Mitchell recalled of his last days of service, 'The battalion, our father and our mother of unforgettable years, was drifting to pieces. The links that connected us with the unforgotten dead seemed to be snapping one by one. As each draft left, mateships were sundered [usually forever]'.[14]

The men disbanding had profoundly affected their nation. Australia stood firm upon the world's stage, a member at the peace discussions, and in its own eyes proven to men. 'Up to the time of this war we were merely an offshoot of the British race . . . Now we are a Nation',[15] General White declared in 1919, and in the same year Bean told a Sydney audience,

Australia rides safely in harbor to-day, a new nation. Five years ago the world barely knew her. To-day, the men who went to fight for her have placed her high in the world's regard. During four long years, in good fortune and ill, they so bore themselves that when the tide changed, the great and free nations . . . counted Australia amongst them . . . She has been given a place in the conference of nations; the great world has recognised her right to mould her future as she pleases[16]

In 1919, few Australians would have contradicted this assessment.

12. Maj J. Doherty, MC & bar, 7 FAB, Company manager, of Balmain, NSW. DOD 26/2/19, aged 30. *L* 3/1/19.
13. F. G. Anderson, *D* Conclusion, –/12?/18.
14. Mitchell, *Backs to the Wall*, p. 281.
15. In K. T. Henderson, *Khaki and Cassock*, Introduction, p. 4. Lt Gen Sir C. B. B. White, KCB, KCMG, KCVO, DSO, Soldier, of Melbourne, Vic. b. 1876. Chief of Staff, 1 Div 1914-15, Anzac and Aust Corps 1915-18, Fifth Army 1918-19.
16. From a speech for Peace Day, in the Grace Stafford Collection, AWM.

At the same time, a bloody war and bitter experience weakened the affections of Empire. Australians met the English during the struggle, and the acquaintance lifted the veils of distance and ignorance, and qualified their old enthusiasms. 'Before the war the Australian had almost believed his grandfather's statement that everything truly good was found in the Old Country', a New South Welshman declared, 'But [now] . . . his soldier grandson will only smile and say "Australia will do me." '[17] Despite its attractions men found England cold, crowded, and corrupted by class division, but more important, they saw flaws in Britain's martial capacity. Englishmen could err, and err badly, and Australians thought them less able in war and less reasonable about discipline. England's image suffered, so that the men of the AIF could not only discharge the debt of tradition, but go on to evolve a separate heritage for their country. Andrew Fisher, who four years before had spoken of 'the last man and the last shilling', told Lloyd George in 1918, 'the question is, If the D[ominion]s have not won a man's place during this war:—What are they expected to do to earn it at some future day?'[18] Britain would still be much respected after 1918, but she would also be more nearly an equal.

But in 1919 what they had achieved for their country did not immediately concern most soldiers. They confronted their return to civil life, and the war and their own expectations had ill equipped them for this. 'Its a pretty strange feeling to know that the war is practically over', a man confided three days after the Armistice, 'and it makes one realize how difficult it is going to be to settle down again to civilian life. One has . . . settled so much down to this life that one will feel more or less like a duck out of water'.[19] Some soldiers, at a disadvantage beside those who had never sailed to defend their country, feared to become civilians again. They felt lost in a community that could not use the skilled trades of war, and they dreaded a new fight for a livelihood. In 1916 a Queensland private spoke for such men when he protested,

when it is all at an end we will . . . have to fight again in the struggle for existence, to compete against women & against men

17. L/Cpl J. S. Bartley, 30 Bn, Hospital wardsman, of Armidale, NSW. b. 1889. *D* —/4/16.
18. Fisher to Lloyd George, 10? November 1918, File No. F/94/3/71, Lloyd George Papers, Beaverbrook Library, London.
19. Duke, *L* 14/11/18.

*who have remained at home. There is nothing in the world more
short lived & fleeting than a nations remembrance of her fighting men after peace is declared, the Public has no gratitude &
being a discharged soldier will act as a deterrent when seeking
a billet. I am thinking that Australia will be a pretty deadly
place for a returned soldier after the war, until he can live down
the fact of his having served his country.*[20]

To a degree, this fear was justified. To many civilians in Australia, it seemed that the soldiers were well rewarded for their suffering and service. They came home to the cheers and thanks of a
grateful nation, and to better payments and benefits than fell to the
lot of returned men in other lands. They had given their country
a tradition, and for that, for the rest of their lives, they would be
especially honoured. Yet before the last veterans reached home the
cheers were already dying away, and it soon became clear that the
soldiers' rewards would be less than had been promised during
the war. Worse, 'when I got home in 1919 Ex Diggers were singing
for a living in the streets. Men without arms or legs, some in wheel
chairs.'[21] Probably that was not common in 1919, but it became
more so with time, as stay-at-home Australians, weary of war,
recoiling from its horror, and sickened by the number of its victims,
tried to forget those tragic years as quickly as possible. They could
continue in ways and occupations they had not quit, and they easily
resumed pleasures and relaxations the war had caused them to
abandon. They were unable or unwilling to comprehend either the
magnitude of the soldiers' ordeal, or the force of the memories, good
and bad, which separated returned men from others. They wanted
a return to normalcy, and they expected returned men to show a
similar desire.

Some veterans did so readily, and easily took up the old or new
conventions of peace. Others blended past and present: they
resumed civil life, but always remembered the security, purpose,
and companionship of war. Many of this outlook considered the
years of blood the happiest of their lives. 'Those days, months and
years will ever remain memorable to us, there being many bright
and happy days as well as the bad ones',[22] a man predicted,

20. Jackson, *L* 8/11/16.
21. Statement by Mr H. Brewer (formerly Lt, 54 Bn, Groom, of Newtown,
NSW. b. 1895), 8 October 1967.
22. F. G. Anderson, *D* Introduction, –/1?/19.

THE OUTBREAK OF PEACE **271**

probably early in 1919, and a disabled veteran wrote down a song popular among his old comrades:

> *Now the bleedin' war is over,*
> *Oh, how happy was I there;*
> *Now old Fritz and I have parted,*
> *Life's one everlasting care.*
> *No more estaminets to sing in,*
> *No ma'moiselles to make me gay;*
> *Civvie life's a bleedin' failure,*
> *I was happy yesterday.*[23]

This was in part the spirit of the RSL, which many joined to show a united front to their detractors, to keep in touch with old companions, and to pass over and over the momentous events which had first brought them together.[24]

There were less happy adjustments. In 1914 H. G. Bennett had quit his peacetime job and sailed as a twenty-seven year old major in the 6th Battalion. He returned in 1919 a brigadier, having seen all his brother officers killed or wounded within a fortnight of the landing, having survived Pozières, and having won several decorations. He was offered his old job at the old terms, a fair offer by his employer's standards, but one which by his own set an impossibly low value on his war service.[25] In such situations the war had opened a gap which even the most tolerant will found difficult to

---

23. 'Tiveychoc', *There and Back*, pp. 261-2.

24. In 1967 or 1968 139 returned men gave the following reasons for joining the RSL:

	per cent	
Fight for concessions or rights	31.87	Many gave both
See old mates	31.87	these reasons
Help less fortunate or crippled mates, help dependants	17.58	
Continue AIF spirit	8.24	
Assist Australia's progress	7.14	
Other (usually personal)	3.30	

Forty-five returned men asked did not join the RSL, usually because they disliked a class or political bias they saw in RSL leadership. Less common reasons were, in order: object to presence of non-combatants; not interested; wish to forget war; dislike RSL clubs. Note that while 83 per cent of those asked were or had been for a considerable period RSL members, only between 40 and 50 per cent of all returned men joined. (G. L. Kristianson, *The Politics of Patriotism*, pp. 116-17, 210-11.)

25. Brig H. G. Bennett, CB, CMG, DSO, VD, Actuarial clerk, of Melbourne, Vic. b. 1887. Commanded 6 Bn 1916-17, 3 Bde 1917-18, 1 Div (temp) 1919. (In F. Legg, *The Gordon Bennett Story*, p. 142.)

bridge, and in relation to employment particularly, where preference for returned men was legally supported, misunderstandings
and felt injustices for decades after 1918 continued to rankle with
old soldier and civilian alike.

For some men the hardest adjustments were those of the mind.
In the cities there was an upsurge of violence and drunkenness in
1919, while in Queensland Bill Harney rode 800 miles into the bush
after he was demobilised, and never applied for his service medals,
and refused for almost forty years to admit that he had fought in the
war.[26] Men like him were trying to forget, to blot out the gruesome
sights and the waste of a horrible past. A mid-1915 enlistment felt in
August 1919,

*I would be a nervous wreck before ever I got within miles of
the front and I am certain that I am not an exceptional case.
Already many of the horrors of war are fading and one calls to
mind more clearly the good times and the funny incidents,
never-the-less warfare will always remain in my mind now as
something most cruel and merciless, and a future war to me is
something too awful to contemplate.*[27]

For some the mental wounds of war never healed. 'When I go to
bed at night,' Dudley Jackson stated in 1967, 'if I allow myself to
think of the war I'll get no sleep for the rest of the night, thinking
of the things "I should have done" and what "I should not have
done".'[28]

And more and more as the dull years passed, peace, inert and
implacable, set its own problems. In 1931 Garnet Adcock described
the peacetime senses of disruption, despair, pettiness and monotony
which still afflicted many returned men:

26. Harney, 'Harney's War', p. 12.
27. Sheppeard, *D* 10/8/19.
28. Statement by Mr D. Jackson, 4 July 1967. In 1967 or 1968, 237 returned
men offered 249 general comments about their active service, which were
proportioned as follows:

	per cent
Quality of mateship incomparable	32.93
War or AIF service an invaluable experience	28.51
Miracle respondent survived	9.64
On average, a good war	8.43
On average, a bad war	6.83
War bad or futile	5.22
Respondent satisfied with own performance	4.82
Generals bungled conduct of war	3.62

It is said that the war has been over twelve years. For we of the generation who went out as young men, to learn the trade of soldiering at our most impressionable age, and to lead a life which would ever after make any other existence drab and colourless, demobilisation meant the commencement of an era harder than the war.

. . . we came back to our careers as clumsy beginners, yet lacking the humility of beginners, demanding of ourselves the same skill and . . . success as we had achieved in the business of soldiering.

We came back to a changed world. Old values had been lost and new standards were changing overnight. The world was going through the upheaval from war to peace . . . a greater upheaval than from peace to war . . .

We were welcomed back with promises of a rosy future . . . and perhaps a little more than our share of the common load to carry . . . Some were installed in 'steady' jobs and people wondered, and many condemned, when they did not 'settle down'.

Others did 'adapt themselves' at a cost, bearing the burden of the lost years . . . and their share of the legacy of madness. To these the struggle was greater, more constant and more disheartening than any in the war . . . Peace could crush with care, or dull with monotony. There was no medal ribbon for success, and no hero-worship. The greatest prize was escape from failure.

. . . the comradeship of war, was lost in peace. Men who lived together as brothers, sharing every danger and privation, drifted apart in peace. Those two factors, 'women' and 'possessions', which only occupy the background in war, came in between friends. Men took wives . . . [or] accumulated possessions, and in the end, though they would have shared their last crust in war, they mentally ranged themselves, like all others with some prize, against the rest of the world, lest someone should rob them of it.

The Peace following a War is worse than the War.[29]

29. Adcock, *L* Conclusion.

When they returned to peace, as when they had gone to war, the soldiers were asked to adapt to unaccustomed ways. But the war had taught them a new system of values—mateship, the worth of the individual, courage, humour, straightforward action, generosity, determination, integrity, and patriotism—which they could not easily apply to peace. Bean had hoped they would,[30] but in every mind the war was a sphere removed from ordinary life, so that the sheer immensity of the experience which brought so many Australian attitudes to full flower also divorced them from what went before and came after. The values themselves were linked with a unique and tragic event, but as well the men who had upheld them in war had become an exclusive association. They considered their wartime ideals part of their common experience, and tended to keep them to themselves rather than corrupt them among the petty frictions of peace. So they stood apart, and the lengthening years, stealing freshness from their own opinions and pity from the opinions of others, set the seal on their difference until, whereas before 1914 a basic social unity had prevailed, it seemed to some that the war in Europe had created 'a nation within a nation' in the far antipodes. For in the same land a veteran could write in 1922,

I am a soldier teacher who spent four years on active service, and now suffer from an eye injury, received 'over there.' I receive a pension, which is gradually being cut down . . . Must I compete with slackers, &c., who are sound in body and limb? If so, then there is little hope for me, as my injury prevents me from studying for further scholarship which is necessary for promotion. I have a wife and two children to support, and hope that our country will not forget the promises made to the diggers, whose motto was at all times—'Country first, self last'[31]

and a young civilian in 1931,

I was born in 1913 and some of my boy and girl friends are thoroughly sick of war pictures, and especially sick of anything relating to Australian soldiers.

We see nothing to interest us in these plays and talkies. What we actually see every day till they have got on our nerves are crippled, blind and battered wrecks, with brass badges on,

30. In *In Your Hands, Australians*, and in an address in the Grace Stafford Collection, AWM.
31. *Argus*, 7 February 1922.

THE OUTBREAK OF PEACE 275

begging in the streets, howling about pension reductions, while
their women and children are in dire straits, so if there was ever
any honor and glory in the wretched business, it vanished before
I grew up.
   . . . the general opinion among fellows like myself is that
Australians were very foolish to let themselves be lured into
going . . . none of my friends like returned soldiers.[32]

That they could not be understood seemed especially unjust to
many returned men. They found it difficult to become civilians in
spirit, for the war was etched into their souls, purging them of the
trivial and unnecessary, binding them with associations and
memories, and circling them with contradictions when they took up
the ways of peace. In religion and in politics, at work and at play,
they found dull what others thrilled to. They had killed men, and
their bloodied hands turned awkwardly to gentler tasks and
pleasures. They had watched the bravest and best of their generation die, so that they feared for their country's future, and shrank
back from a world which wanted to change and forget. Once a
year they were honoured for their part in the war, but they found
it hard to accept an attitude which others easily adopted, that what
was part of Australian life was also part of Australia's past. They
could not forget or ignore or make peripheral, and the consequent
division in society was the last of several they were obliged to bear.

Yet, probably, in the end, that mattered little to most of them.
The whole world had lost the firm attachments of 1914, but the
fighting also destroyed the hopes many soldiers had held for their
own lives. They had accepted this, and become devoted to war.
Again they were broken, and after 1918 each began again to adjust
to unfamiliar ways. Yet always the war stayed with them, in the
gapped ranks of their comrades, in the monuments to their friends
raised in every Australian community, and in the images which
flashed from the dark shadows of their memories. They had become
men apart; but this was their pride as well as their burden,
because usually they recalled the good times and the mates who had
served with them in the struggle. Throughout their quiet after-
journey most caught the old echoes eagerly, for they had learnt to
prize what lies in the souls of men above all the agonies thrust
upon them during the broken years.

32. *Labor Daily* (NSW), 25 November 1931.

Epilogue

Not one of those emotions described in the prologue as bearing deeply upon Australian thought before 1914 remained unaffected by the Great War. Assumptions about race, nation and Empire, and war and its attendant enthusiasms were all amended, not so that the thinking of every Australian was at once transformed, but sufficiently for the passage of time to show that the way in which Australians looked at themselves and their world had been radically adjusted.

At first it did not seem that this would be so, for while it continued the war strengthened pre-war values. The martial virtues—duty, honour, courage, and self sacrifice—became paramount, and the men who most clearly possessed them were the heroes of the hour. Nation and Empire demanded and were given unswerving allegiance, and race was made pre-eminent in explaining the bestiality of the enemy and the need for victory.

But in time the extremes to which they were carried contributed to the decline of the old ideals. Most obviously, the conviction that war was manly and glorious almost entirely disappeared, while notions at the time connected with war—duty, honour, manhood and the like—all suffered from their martial association. Less obviously, the war affected Australian assumptions about race. Before 1914 Australians had assumed a hierarchy of races, in which 'the white race' was supreme, and the various entities within the white race, the Anglo-Saxons, Teutons, Slavs, and Gauls, were ranked roughly according to their presumed Britishness. Wartime propaganda took up these assumptions, but also attempted to force them into conformity with wartime alliances—with results that sometimes verged on the ludicrous. The Germans, for example, were 'bad' but white, while the Japanese were 'good' but not white, and the Russians were white and 'good' until December 1917, but white and 'bad' thereafter. Further, during the war Australians learnt that 'bad' Germans yet possessed at least some British virtues, and that 'bad' and non-white Turks displayed qualities regrettably lacking in many an Anglo-Saxon. Whiteness and virtue and to a lesser extent whiteness and superiority could no longer be considered inevitably synonymous, and although nothing was sufficient to shake a general Australian conviction of white supremacy, the war did make more difficult the drawing of racial distinctions within 'the white race'. The consequent long term damage to Australian notions of a racial hierarchy was fundamental, and perhaps a necessary precursor to any enlargement of racial tolerance in Australia.

In some respects the war induced Australians to express more fulsomely than ever the strong Imperial affections they had felt before 1914. Even without the passion generated by the strain and sacrifice of those years, Australians felt a deep attachment to their Empire, and for many of those who outlived the Great War this was to remain essential to their emotional lives. But with the withering of the notion that war was glorious there died much of the fervour which had given strength to Imperial adulation, and as time passed the spirit of eager self sacrifice which had marked Imperial sentiment before 1914 became less and less noticeable. The conviction remained that the Empire and its Navy were necessary to Australia's security, but when events during the Second World War challenged even this opinion, the days of Empire in Australia were numbered.

Even during the war the affections of Empire had yielded a little before an upsurge of Australian nationalism. Before 1914 most Australians had hoped at best to see their country attain partnership status within the Empire. On Gallipoli these hopes had been more than fulfilled, and from the moment of the landing a long felt Imperial need was fully satisfied by the story of Anzac. But Anzac also provided a glorious focus for specifically nationalist sentiment: it was that peculiarly Australian achievement which until then had been lacking, and in the eyes of its contemporaries it made Australia a nation at last, with international recognition, national heroes, a national day, and a worthy tradition. It established an ethos which seemed to express the best of both nation and Empire, and this inevitably reduced the Imperial attachment of Australians.

But the Anzac tradition also introduced a deep division into Australian life. Australians before 1914 had wanted a paradise for the majority, and by and large only certain minorities had been disadvantaged by that desire. Yet roughly half those eligible had joined the AIF during the war, so that by 1918, willingly or not, a considerable proportion of Australians stood apart from the remainder. A great rift had opened, a rift between those who had fought in the war, and those who had not.

In significant ways, this was disastrous. Before the war radical nationalists had led the drive for a social paradise in Australia, but ultimately they were least at ease with the Imperial and martial implications of the Anzac tradition, and during the war they divided over the proper conduct of Australia's war effort. By the 1916 referendum on conscription the confidence and cohesion which had given impetus to their pre-war social welfare ideals was gone, and they found themselves caught between the increasingly discordant claims of the nation as they conceived it, and the Empire. In 1916 their political representatives, the Labor Party, split, and so surrendered political power and social control into the hands of the conservatives. For their part the conservatives, who before 1914 had exerted a tenuous influence on Australian politics and society, were united and given purpose by the war, because the Empire and victory were causes to which they could dedicate themselves without reservation. Naturally enough, that dedication and the motives behind it appealed to the men in the trenches, so that for thousands of soldiers and their relatives the conservatives came best to represent the new nationalism of Anzac. The aptly named Nationalist Party, formed in January 1917, thus expressed the ideals not only of the conservatives, but also of many of those who in 1914 had supported the radical nationalists, but who had been converted by their enlistment into champions of an unreserved prosecution of the war. In short, that general majority which in 1914 had sought to create a social paradise in Australia was both split and made leaderless by the war, and by 1918 no longer existed, while the conservatives had joined with those who had fought in the war to take firm possession of the spirit of Anzac, and to maintain an influence in Australian life which is only now diminishing.

So the Great War brought change to the outlook of Australians. In September 1917 an Australian soldier wrote into his diary the following memorable lines:

> *Adieu, the years are a broken song,*
> *And the right grows weak in the strife with wrong,*
> *The lilies of love have a crimson stain,*
> *And the old days never will come again.*

The words suggest how great was the impact of the war on Australia—on the lives and hopes of individuals, on the direction and cohesion of society, and on the assumptions and opinions of the nation. For while the boundless eagerness of August 1914 is a world removed from our present time, what began to happen on Gallipoli nine months later is with us yet.

Appendix 1

Social comparisons between Australian adult males, the AIF embarked, and the writers of the diaries and letters consulted for this book

OCCUPATION

	per cent	
	Males 15-64 in Australia at Census 3 April 1911	Diary & letter writers
Professional	4.87	29.1
Domestic	2.56	.8
Commercial	14.86	17.4
Transport & Communication	8.84	8.9
Industrial	28.90	16.3
Primary Producers	35.00	24.5
Independent	.13	.1
Dependents	4.84	2.5
Unknown	Allocated proportionately	.4
Numerical total	1,497,456	1000

	per cent	
	AIF embarked	Diary & letter writers
Tradesmen	34.00	19.7
Labourers	30.00	Urban—13.2 ⎱ Rural—13.5 ⎰ 26.7
Country callings	17.36	11.0
Clerical	7.36	20.2
Professional	4.75	15.8
Miscellaneous	3.89	4.1
Seafaring	1.98	1.9
Nurses	.64	.2
Unknown	—	.4
Numerical total	330,770	1000

Note: The 1911 Census classified each occupation according to the *industry or calling* with which it was associated, and took no account of the status of an individual within his category. Thus a judge and a policeman are both found under 'Professional', a businessman and a grocer's assistant under 'Commercial'. But apparently the 'AIF embarked' figures were based on the social status of individuals. A valid correlation between the two tables is therefore not possible, and I have compared my own sources first with one, then with the other.

Sources: Census of the Commonwealth of Australia, 3 April 1911, Vol. 1, Statistician's Report, p. 374; Butler, *Official Medical History*, III, p. 890. Criteria for classifying occupations in the 1911 Census are in the Statistician's Report, pp. 347-56.

RELIGION

per cent

	Males 15 and over in Australia at Census 3 April 1911	AIF embarked	Diary & letter writers
Church of England	39.40	49.22[a]	55.8[a]
Roman Catholic	22.30[b]	19.26	10.7
Presbyterian	13.29	15.01	17.0
Methodist	11.36	10.19	9.7
Other Christian	10.92[c]	—	2.9
Non-Christian	1.64[d]	6.33[e]	.5
Indefinite and No religion	1.09	—	.3
Unknown	65,227[f]	—	3.1
Numerical total	1,597,042	330,770	1000

Notes: [a] Includes some who gave 'Protestant' or 'No religion'
[b] Includes those who gave 'Catholic'
[c] Includes those who gave 'Protestant'
[d] Includes 7047 Hebrew
[e] Comprises 5.96 per cent 'Others' and 0.37 per cent Hebrew
[f] This number not considered in reaching above percentages.

Sources: Census of the Commonwealth of Australia, 3 April 1911, Vol. 2, Detailed Tables, p. 772; Butler, *Official Medical History*, III, p. 890.

PLACE OF BIRTH

per cent

	Males 15-64 in Australia at Census 3 April 1911	AIF embarked	Diary & letter writers
NSW	30.33	26.56	40.2
Vic	28.65	27.90	24.8
Qld	9.98	8.52	7.0
SA[a]	9.42	8.40	5.7
WA	1.44	2.42	3.7
Tas	4.31	3.95	2.5
			unknown .1
Total Australia	84.13	77.75	84.0
Overseas[b]	15.87	22.25	16.0[c]
Numerical total	1,497,456	331,781	1000

Notes: [a] Includes Northern Territory
[b] Mainly British Isles
[c] Figure probably incomplete.

Sources: Census of the Commonwealth of Australia, 3 April 1911, Vol. 1, Statistician's Report, pp. 120, 135, 143, 148; AIF Records Section: *Statistics of Casualties etc.*, p. 20.

AGE

For the age distribution of the AIF embarked, see Butler, *Official Medical History*, III, p. 890; the average age of the diary and letter writers was approximately twenty-five years.

Appendix 2

The price: Outline of AIF enlistments,
embarkations and casualties

Note: Great War statistics are notoriously variable, and the following
are indications only. Alternatives in brackets follow some figures.

416,809 Australians, 13.43 per cent of the white male population and
probably about half those eligible, enlisted in the AIF, and 330,770
(331,781; 331,814) embarked for service abroad. The majority, about
295,000, served in France.

63,163 (59,330; 58,132), or a little fewer than one man in five, died
on active service. 152,422 (156,128) were otherwise made casualties,
including some later killed. Casualties therefore totalled 215,585
(214,360), which was 64.98 per cent of those who embarked with the
AIF. 27,594 of these casualties were suffered on Gallipoli, 4851 in
Sinai or Palestine, 179,537 in France or Belgium, and the remainder in
England, Egypt, Malta, or at sea. There were more occasions on which
Australians reported sick (332,901) than there were Australians em-
barked, but only 4084 were taken prisoner, including 3848 captured in
France.

About 2000 returned men were permanently hospitalised as a result
of the war; 22,742 veterans were in hospital in 1926, and 49,157 in
1939; in 1920 90,389 and in 1940 70,462 disabled men were receiving
pensions.

Sources: See *Official History*, Vols I-VII, XI, especially XI, pp. 871-4, 888;
  Butler, *Official Medical History*, II, p. 492; III, pp. 823, 880, 895-6, 965;
  the honour rolls at the Australian War Memorial; AIF Records Section:
  Statistics of Casualties, etc., passim; The War Office: *Statistics of the
  Military Effort of the British Empire*, pp. 237-9, 252-4. These have various
  and conflicting statistics.

Selected Bibliography

A. CONTEMPORARY MATERIAL

1. Diaries and letters

The chief and essential sources for this book were the diaries and letters of over 1000 soldiers of the First AIF. Most of these records are in the Library of the Australian War Memorial in Canberra, many are in the Mitchell Library in Sydney, and a few are in the State Library of South Australia, the National Library of Australia in Canberra, the LaTrobe Library in Melbourne, or in private hands. The bibliography attached to my thesis, copies of which are in both the Menzies Library at the Australian National University and the Australian War Memorial Library, specifically locates all but three of the records cited here. The exceptions are:

Pte J. A. Kidd, 15 Bn *Narrative*   Australian War Memorial Library

Tpr A. C. Lumley, 5 LH Regt *Letters*   Pryke Papers, National Library of Australia

Pte J. A. Pryke, 21 Bn *Letters*   Pryke Papers, National Library of Australia.

2. Newspapers and periodicals

Most contemporary general news material was useful, and in addition the Australian War Memorial Library holds a good collection of AIF, unit, and troopship newspapers. Again, these are listed in the thesis.

3. Books, articles and pamphlets

Ashmead-Bartlett, E., *Despatches from the Dardanelles*, London 1915.
AIF, *From the Australian Front, 1917*, London 1917.
AIF Records Section, *Statistics of Casualties etc., to 30th June 1919*, London 1919.
AWM Library Files, particularly Nos. 233/1-3, 265/1-3; recruiting posters, pamphlets, etc.
Back from the War: what it feels like, Melbourne 1919.

Baker, E. K., 'Some Impressions of the Gallipoli Campaign', *Australian Army Journal*, No. 203, April 1966, pp. 31-5.

Bean, C. E. W., *In Your Hands, Australians*, London 1919.

——— *Letters from France*, London 1917.

——— *On the Wool Track*, Sydney 1968 (1st ed. 1910).

——— (ed.) *The Anzac Book*, London 1916.

Blake, R. (ed.), *The Private Papers of Sir Douglas Haig*, London 1952.

Buley, E. C., *Glorious Deeds of the Australasians in the Great War*, London 1915.

Cavill, H. W., *Imperishable Anzacs*, Sydney 1916.

Cutlack, F. M. (ed.), *War Letters of General Monash*, Sydney 1934.

'de Loghe, S.' [F. S. Loch], *The Straits Impregnable*, Melbourne 1916.

Dyson, W., *Australia at War*, London 1918.

Fitchett, W. H., *Deeds that Won the Empire*, London 1899.

——— *How England Saved Europe*, Vol. 3, London 1900.

——— *The New World of the South: Australia in the Making*, London 1913.

Foiled! The Enemy in Our Own Land, Sydney 1915.

Gellert, L., *Songs of a Campaign*, Sydney 1917.

General Staff of the British Army, *Staff Sheet 218: Operations by the Australian Corps at Hamel . . . 4th July, 1918*, 1918, copy in the Australian War Memorial Library.

Hogue, O., *Trooper Bluegum at the Dardanelles*, London 1916?

Idriess, I. L., *The Desert Column*, Sydney 1965 (1st ed. 1932).

Jebb, R., *Studies in Colonial Nationalism*, London 1905.

Masefield, J., *Gallipoli*, London 1916.

Recruits Companion, Melbourne 1918.

Report of Proceedings of Royal Commission appointed to Inquire into the Administration of Liverpool Camp, July, 1915, 1915.

Returned Soldiers Association (NSW), *Anzac Memorial, 1917*, Sydney 1917.

Schuler, P. F. E., *Australia in Arms*, London 1917.

4. Private papers

Ashmead-Bartlett, E., Diary, File No. 1583, Mitchell Library, Sydney.

Lloyd George Papers, Beaverbrook Library, London.

Novar Papers, National Library of Australia.

Pryke Papers, National Library of Australia.

B. POST-WAR MATERIAL

1. Histories of the war or the AIF

Aspinall-Oglander, C. F., *Military Operations, Gallipoli* (Official British History), London, Vol. I, 1929; Vol. II, 1932.

Barnett, C., *The Swordbearers*, London 1966.

Bean, C. E. W., *Anzac to Amiens*, Canberra 1961.

———— *Official History of Australia in the War of 1914-18*, Sydney, Vol. I (13th ed.), 1942; Vol. II (1st ed.), 1924; Vol. III (1st ed.), 1929; Vol. IV (4th ed.), 1936; Vol. V (1st ed.), 1937; Vol. VI (1st ed.), 1942; Vol. XII (Photographs, 13th ed.), 1940.

Butler, A. G., *Official History of the Australian Army Medical Services, 1914-18*, Vol. I (2nd ed.), Melbourne 1938; Vol. II (1st ed.), Canberra 1940; Vol. III (1st ed.), Canberra 1943.

Cutlack, F. M. (ed.), *The Australians: Their Final Campaign, 1918*, London 1918?

Edmonds, J. E. (ed.), *Military Operations, France and Belgium* (Official British History), London, 1916, Vol. II, 1938; 1917, Vol. I, 1940; 1917, Vol. II, 1948; 1918, Vol. I, 1935; 1918, Vol. II, 1937; 1918, Vol. III, 1939; 1918, Vol. IV, 1947; 1918, Vol. V, 1947.

Gullet, H. S., *Official History of Australia in the War of 1914-18*, Vol. VII (1st ed.), Sydney 1923.

———— and Barrett, C. (eds.), *Australia in Palestine*, Sydney 1919.

James, R. R., *Gallipoli*, Sydney 1965.

Jose, A. W., *Official History of Australia in the War of 1914-18*, Vol. IX (11th ed.), Sydney 1943.

Marder, A. J., *From the Dreadnought to Scapa Flow*, Vol. I, London 1961.

Moorehead, A., *Gallipoli*, London 1963.

North, J., *Gallipoli: The Fading Vision*, London 1966.

Scott, E., *Official History of Australia in the War of 1914-18*, Vol. XI (14th ed.), Sydney 1938.

Wolff, L., *In Flanders Fields*, London 1961.

Waite, F., *The New Zealanders at Gallipoli*, Auckland 1921.

2. Unit histories

Belford, W. C., *Legs-Eleven* (11 Bn), Perth 1940.

Chatto, R. H., *The Seventh Company* (7 Fld Coy), Sydney 1936.

Collett, H. B., *The 28th*, Vol. I, Perth 1922.

Colliver, E. J. and Richardson, B. H., *The Forty-Third*, Adelaide 1920.

Dean, A. and Gutteridge, E. W., *The Seventh Battalion*, Melbourne 1933.

Devine, W., *The Story of a Battalion* (48 Bn), Melbourne 1919.

Dollman, W. and Skinner, H. M., *The Blue and Brown Diamond* (27 Bn), Adelaide 1921.

Fairey, E., *The 38th Battalion*, Bendigo 1920.

Gorman, E., *With the Twenty-Second*, Melbourne 1919.

Green, F. C., *The Fortieth*, Hobart 1922.

Harvey, N. K., *From Anzac to the Hindenburg Line* (9 Bn), Brisbane 1941.

Harvey, W. J., *The Red and White Diamond* (24 Bn), Melbourne 1920?

Kennedy, J. J., *The Whale Oil Guards* (53 Bn), Dublin 1919.

Keown, A. W., *Forward with the Fifth*, Melbourne 1921.

Lock, C. B. L., *The Fighting 10th*, Adelaide 1936.

Longmore, C., *Eggs-a-Cook!* (44 Bn), Perth 1921.

—— *The Old Sixteenth*, Perth 1929.

Mackenzie, K. W., *The Story of the Seventeenth Battalion, A.I.F.*, Sydney 1946.

McNicol, N. G., *The Thirty-Seventh*, Melbourne 1936.

Newton, L. M., *The Story of the Twelfth*, Hobart 1925.

Paterson, A. T. et al., *The Thirty-Ninth*, Melbourne 1934.

Reid, F., *The Fighting Cameliers*, Sydney 1934.

Richardson, J., *The History of the 7th Light Horse Regiment, A.I.F.*, Sydney 1923?

Sloan, H., *The Purple and Gold* (30 Bn), Sydney 1938.

Stacy, B. V. et al., *The History of the First Battalion, A.I.F.*, Sydney 1931.

Taylor, F. W. and Cusack, T. A., *Nulli Secundus* (2 Bn), Sydney 1942.

Wanliss, N., *The History of the Fourteenth Battalion A.I.F.*, Melbourne 1929.

White, T. A., *The Fighting Thirteenth*, Sydney 1924.

Wilson, L. C. and Wetherell, H., *History of the Fifth Light Horse Regiment*, Sydney 1926.

Wren, E., *Randwick to Hargicourt* (3 Bn), Sydney 1935.

3. Personal reminiscences

Bradby, W. J., 'Polygon Wood and Broodseinde', *Stand-To* (ACT RSL journal) Sept.-Oct. 1963, pp. 19-20.

Bean, C. E. W., *Two Men I Knew*, Sydney 1957.

Frewen, H. M., 'The Somme Winter and Arras', *Stand-To*, July-Sept. 1966, pp. 18-21.

Graham, W. A., 'Lone Pine', *Stand-To*, Oct.-Dec. 1967, pp. 26-9.

Green, F. C., 'After the Battalion Reunion', *Stand-To*, Jan.-Feb. 1955, pp. 23-5.

—— 'German Offensive 1918', *Stand-To*, April-June 1967, pp. 5-7.

Harney, W., 'Harney's War', *Overland*, No. 13, Oct. 1958, pp. 3-12.

Henderson, K. T., *Khaki and Cassock*, Melbourne 1919.

Hogue, O., *The Cameliers*, London 1919.

Jackson, D., 'Diary of a Footslogger', *Stand-To*, Nov.-Dec. 1964, pp. 1-8.

—— 'Flanders 1917', *Stand-To*, July-Sept. 1967, pp. 6-13.

—— 'In the Back Areas 1919', *Stand-To*, April-June 1969, pp. 38-40.

—— 'Winter on the Somme 1916-1917', *Stand-To*, Oct.-Dec. 1966, pp. 17-25.

Mackenzie, C., *Gallipoli Memories*, London 1965.

Manning, F., *Her Privates We*, London 1967.

Malthus, C., *Anzac—A Retrospect*, Christchurch 1965.

Matthews, H., *Saints and Soldiers*, Sydney 1918.

Maxwell, J., *Hell's Bells and Mademoiselles*, Sydney 1932.

McKinlay, J. L., 'A Sapper goes to War', *Stand-To*, July-Sept. 1966, pp. 16-17.

———— 'Lone Pine and German Officers Trench', *Stand-To*, July-Sept. 1969, pp. 31-2.

Mitchell, G. D., *Backs to the Wall*, Sydney 1937.

Monash, J., *The Australian Victories in France in 1918*, Sydney 1923.

Richards, F., *Old Soldiers Never Die*, London 1964.

Rule, E. J., *Jacka's Mob*, Sydney 1933.

'Tiveychoc, A.' [Lording, R. E.], *There and Back*, Sydney 1935.

Williams, H. R., *Comrades of the Great Adventure*, Sydney 1935.

———— *The Gallant Company*, Sydney 1933.

4. Books, theses and articles

Bean, C. E. W., *Gallipoli Mission*, Canberra 1948.

———— 'Sidelights of the War on Australian Character', *R.A.H.S. Journal and Proceedings*, Vol. XIII, Part IV, 1927, pp. 209-23.

Firth, S. G., 'Schooling in New South Wales, 1880-1914' (M.A. thesis, Australian National University 1968).

Gollan, R., *Radical and Working Class Politics . . . 1850-1910*, Melbourne 1966.

Gordon, D. C., *The Dominion Partnership in Imperial Defense, 1870-1914*, Maryland 1965.

Harding, B. A., *Windows of Fame*, Melbourne 1963.

Howe, H. V., 'The Anzac Landing—A Belated Query', *Stand-To*, Sept.-Oct. 1962, pp. 1-3.

Inglis, K. S., 'The Anzac Tradition', *Meanjin Quarterly*, No. 1, 1965, pp. 25-44.

Kristianson, G. L., *The Politics of Patriotism*, Canberra 1966.

Legg, F., *The Gordon Bennett Story*, Sydney 1965.

O'Connor, P. S., 'Venus and the Lonely Kiwi', *New Zealand Journal of History*, Vol. 1, No. 1, 1967, pp. 11-32.

Serle, G., 'The Digger Tradition and Australian Nationalism', *Meanjin Quarterly*, No. 2, 1965, pp. 149-58.

Thirkell, A., *Trooper to the Southern Cross*, Melbourne 1966.

Turner, I., *Industrial Labour and Politics . . . 1900-21*, Canberra 1965.

Terraine, J., *Douglas Haig*, London 1963.

Ward, R., *The Australian Legend*, Melbourne 1965.

Wigmore, L., *They Dared Mightily*, Canberra 1963.

Name Index

The fullest biographical information about any member of the AIF is on the first page cited after his name.

General Index

Note: Since emotions and attitudes have myriad subtlety and variety, it would not be useful to index their entire range here. Instead they may be found under one of the following general headings: Adventure; Anzac tradition; Arabs; Australian Imperial Force; Battle; 'Battle madness'; Boredom; British Army; British Empire; Courage; Death; Defiance; Discipline; Duty; Egyptians; Embarkation; England; Enlistment; Fatalism; Germans; Glory; Homesickness; Humour; Manhood; Mateship; Nationalism; Officers; Politics; Prestige; Race; Religion; Self-respect; Sex; Turkish Army; Units; Victory; War; Wounded; Wounds. Unless otherwise evident or stated, any entry or sub-entry refers to the AIF.